Capoeira and Candomblé

Capoeira and Candomblé

Conformity and Resistance through Afro-Brazilian Experience

floyd merrell

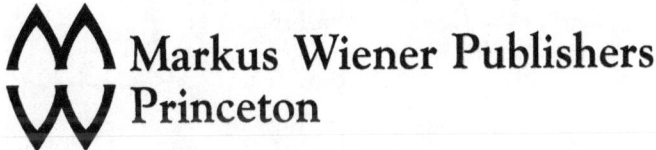
Markus Wiener Publishers
Princeton

Third printing, 2018.
Copyright © Vervuert/Iberoamericana, 2005
First Markus Wiener Publishers edition, 2005

All rights reserved. No part of this book may be reproduced or transmitted in any form or by any means, whether electronic or mechanical—including photocopying or recording—or through any information storage or retrieval system, without permission of the copyright owners.

Book design: 'Damola Ifaturoti
Cover design: Maria Madonna Davidoff

For information write to: Markus Wiener Publishers
231 Nassau Street, Princeton, NJ 08542
www.markuswiener.com

Library of Congress Cataloging-in-Publication Data

Merrell, Floyd, 1937–
　　Capoeira and Candomblé : conformity and resistance through Afro-Brazilian experience / by Floyd Merrell.
　　p. cm.
　　Includes bibliographical references.
　　ISBN-13: 978-1-55876-350-0 (pb : alk. paper)
　　ISBN-13: 978-1-55876-349-4 (hc : alk. paper)
　　1. Candomblé (Religion)—Brazil.　2. Afro-Brazilian cults—Brazil.
3. Brazil—Religion.　4. Capoeira (Dance)—Brazil.　I. Title.
　　BL2592.C35M47 2005
　　299.6'73'0981—dc22
　　　　　　　　　　　　　　　　　　　　　　　　　　　2004022891

Markus Wiener Publishers books are
　　　　　　on acid-free paper, and meet the guidelines for permanence and durability of the Committee on Production Guidelines for Book Longevity of the Council on Library Resources.

Contents

Preface . . . . *vii*
Acknowledgments . . . . *xi*

Part I: Capoeira: Playfully Practicing Philosophy 1
Chapter One
    A Brief History of the Art 3
Chapter Two
    Capoeira Becoming 23
Chapter Three
    How the Art is Becoming 43
Chapter Four
    How the Becoming Is Processual 59
Chapter Five
    Nonlinear and Sinuous is the Road 79
    Postscript to Chapter Five 93

Part II: Candomblé: Living Philosophy, Philosophical Living . . 101
Chapter Six
    Rhythms and Rituals of Resistance 103
Chapter Seven
    Hegemonic Pressure 121
Chapter Eight
    Does Syncretism Give an Adequate Account? 135
Chapter Nine
    More Complex than Meets the Eye 159
Chapter Ten
    Process: Perpetual Change within Stability 169
Chapter Eleven
    The Dichotomies Become More Pliable 193

Part III: Those Other Logics within Cultural Processes 205
Chapter Twelve
    Qualifying the Process: An Impossible Task? 207
Chapter Thirteen
    Attempting to Refine the Figure Further 225
Chapter Fourteen
    Still in Search of Process 239

Part IV: Capoeira and Candomblé as Cultural Logics 257
Chapter Fifteen
    Brazilian Haziness 259
Chapter Sixteen
    Capoeira, Again 269
Chapter Seventeen
    Candomblé, One More Time 277

Afterthoughts 289
Appendix A 293
Appendix B 295
References 299

Preface

At the outset, allow me a few disclaimers. This book is neither anthropology nor sociology. Nor is it a historical treatise or literary analysis. I offer no meticulous recapitulation of a tradition; I engage in no close reading of texts with the assumption that I can reveal their inner secrets; I do not enter into current debates over fine details regarding postcolonialism, poststructuralism, postmodernism, subaltern studies, or cultural studies.

I only wish to offer reflections. Reflections, after having dedicated time and thought to what is *Capoeira* and *Candomblé*. I would like to think that a form of other logic, an alternative cultural logic—or better, an "a-logic"—about which Walter Mignolo (2000) eloquently writes—will gradually emerge from these reflections. Then could the pages that follow be labeled philosophy? Perhaps, to a limited extent. But my reflections are not philosophy in the common sense. Rather they emerge from readings on Capoeira and Candomblé life in Salvador, Brazil, as well as readings on current philosophical, sociological, anthropological, and cultural issues. They are also more than that. They emerge from actual participation—however clumsy and naïve that participation might have been—with my friends in Capoeira and Candomblé communities. This book thus could be seen as philosophical in the sense of Richard Shusterman's (1992, 1997) concept of "practicing philosophy." The idea of "practicing philosophy" aids and abets my firm belief that there should be no separation of meaning, understanding, and practice, or of body and mind for that matter (Comaroff and Comaroff 1991; Levin 1997; also merrell 2002, 2003a, 2004).

Indeed, I would like to illustrate how Capoeira and Candomblé are in the most concrete way practicing philosophy. To know them one must not only read about them but also practice them to the best of one's ability. It is to feel them, to sense them corporeally. Take Capoeira. Mestre (Master) Bira Almeida writes that the genuine *capoeirista* lives a philosophy: Capoeira philosophy. Learning this philosophy is no bookish matter. It requires sweat, mental discipline, sometimes pain, and always the magical experience of reverently kneeling under the *Berimbau* (a one string bow-shaped instrument that governs the Capoeira rhythm). "The philosophy must be felt from inside out because only personal participation will make it real. Eventually, an organized body of philosophical concepts must be developed to guide the students in the discovery of the Capoeira path and to help them in opening themselves to it" (Almeida, 1986:7).

In a different sense this book is also philosophical. It merges with much of my previous work with philosopher and polymath Charles Sanders Peirce. However, the Peirce you will find here is not the Peirce I used to write about during those days when I was obsessed with semiotic theory. My current interpretation of Peirce's complex philosophy is due in large part to my experience of everyday life in Brazil, especially that of Salvador in the northeastern section of the country. While there, during May, June, and July of each year, I doggedly pushed myself through some of my recent work on Peirce's concept of the sign (merrell 2000a, 2000b, 2000c, 2000d, 2002, 2003a). The problem is that I found myself theorizing about Peirce while at the same time trying to bring him down to earth, to concretize him in view of his suggestion that we should try to be as concretely reasonable as we know how. But I knew I was failing. I was failing, because I remained inextricably caught up in abstractions.

While I continued struggling with my texts on Peirce, I became interested in Capoeira and Candomblé. I soon found myself striving, now euphorically, now painfully, now depressed, now smug and confident, now caught up in anxiety and doubt, to weave my way through some of the most enigmatically profound and inordinately complex cultural phenomena the world has to offer. Yet I continued tapping out Peircean abstractions on my notebook computer. Finally, I decided to try combining Peirce with Capoeira and Candomblé life. What you have between the covers of this volume is the outcome. It offers both theory and concrete living and yet it is neither one nor the other, strictly speaking, for it represents an effort to get beyond the two horns of the dichotomy. If the following abstract writings coupled with meditations emerging from gut-wrenching, concrete experiences are not what "living philosophy" is about, I have no idea what I've been doing over the past years.

The journey leading to this book's creation, you might have guessed, has been taxing. There were many expansive highways, intricate crossroads, hairpin curves, chuck-holed streets, and blind alleys. The topography was labyrinthine, like that bewildering confusion you will confront if you try to decipher a map of Salvador, a city of over two and a half million people. You must have lived there virtually your entire life to know it. Otherwise, you trust your luck to friends and people on the street to give you directions toward your destination.

Scanning the table of contents might give the idea that the organization of this book is linear. But it is not. The surface pretense of linearity is a structured veneer that hides nonlinearity. Basically, the story I have to tell is cumulative. But its development is along a tangle of lines. My story should not be set out in any other way, I would suggest, because its pattern reflects Capoeira and Candomblé practices. Given this interweaving pattern, I would like to avoid a chapter-by-chapter preview. Nevertheless, a few brief words are necessary. Parts I and II contain five chapters on Capoeira and six on Candomblé. The three chapters of part III usher in theoretical abstraction. It is an attempt to confront the problem of what we are missing in our obsessive quest for ultimate knowledge and how we might be able to get back to renewed feeling and sensing and thinking within our situated forms of life. I temporarily take leave of my Capoeira and Candomblé stories and enter into a meditation on some heated contemporary topics: hegemony, subalternity, homogeneity, heterogeneity, multiculturalism, pluralism, dialogism. However, I approach these topics from an angle that avoids all postmodern, postcolonial, poststructuralist, and cultural studies forms of debate and discourse. What are my motives for so doing? The search for an other logic, an alternative cultural logic, as mentioned above. My tangential turn, then, is not a departure from, but an intensification of, parts I and II, for I am guided by the focal idea that few cultural phenomena reveal this other logic as effectively as Capoeira and Candomblé. Thus the method to my madness, I trust, will eventually become clear.

The final three chapters in part IV return to Capoeira and Candomblé living in a somewhat new light, hopefully suggesting how we can retrieve what we've been missing at least to some extent. It can by and large be found, I believe, in the "practices of concrete, embodied living" (Stoller 1997; Varela et al. 1993). In contrast to this sense of embodied living, we textual-oriented scholars usually prefer to continue our relentless push onward and upward within the realm of written signs. We often become lost in the ciphers, assuming they are all there is, taking them for the genuine article. We often forget that textuality is never enough (Hall 1992:284). As James Clifford (1986:25) puts it, "No one can write about others any longer as if they were discrete objects or texts" (see also Abram 1996; Hastrup 1995; Leder 1990; Spretnak 1999). Indeed, there is more to this than textuality and discrete objects with regard to others; much more. For, others are, like us, concrete, embodied individuals within their respective culture; all cultures are unceasing, situated practice, practice is continuous process, and process is ongoing change within space and through time. My own entry into, and participation in, the flow of concrete cultural processes eventually left me in the role of a swivel-chair warrior on the battlefield of textualism. The experience was rewarding and refreshing. But then, I found myself once again having to take up my textualist role and do with it whatever I could, in whichever way I knew how, by trying to write a book. Needless to say, I met bewilderment at every turn in the road.

Acknowledgments

Before I get on with my Capoeira and Candomblé stories, I must state that all translations from Portuguese texts are mine. Moreover, I have chosen to use fictitious names for some of the capoeiristas and candomblistas I discuss in order to protect their role in the profession and their anonymity; I trust that in so doing I have acted prudently; if not, I apologize for any discomfort I might have caused. Second, I must express a debt to all my friends from certain Capoeira and Candomblé communities—whose names remain anonymous—in the Salvadoran neighborhoods of Barra, Ondina, Pelourinho, Castelo Branco, Periperi, Itapuã, and Fazenda Grande do Retiro, and in the village of Areia Branca outside the city. In one way or another they are behind every page of this book. I also extend my appreciation to anthropologists Jeferson Bacelar and Carlos Caroso of the Centro de Estudos Afro-Orientais (Center for Afro-Oriental Studies), as well as to anthropologist Ordep Serra, philosopher Waldomiro José da Silva Filho, and educator Virginia Dazzani, who are affiliated with the Universidade Federal da Bahia (Federal University of Bahia). Of course, without Araceli's companionship on my yearly trek to Bahia, motivation for this project would have remained severely limited. I thank all of you.

Part I

CAPOEIRA: PLAYFULLY PRACTICING PHILOSOPHY

Chapter One

A Brief History of the Art

The spirit of Capoeira is growing in the United States, Europe, and other areas outside Brazil. I write "spirit," for Capoeira not only unifies body and mind, but also spirit. This is not to say that Capoeira involves some religious attitude; at the same time in a certain manner of speaking it *is* to say that Capoeira involves some religious attitude. I am, of course, contradicting myself. But that's no problem with regard to Capoeira, which is a labyrinth of contradictions. Better said, from the broadest possible perspective, it is a perplexing paradox replete with many incongruities. That's the way we should conceive of Capoeira. For it is one of the most complex mixtures made up of old and new, popular culture and dominant culture, of races and ethnicities, religions and customs, to be found in the world today.

Capoeira plays havoc with our need for a clear-cut world conveniently classified and labeled. Say what Capoeira is, and you say what it is not. Say it is slam-bang, in-your-face rumbling, much as in martial arts, and it is not; it is good-natured play. Say it is dancing, and you're wrong; it is struggle, a ludic form of struggle. Say it involves instruments and singing, and it is not only that; it is much more. Say it is frivolous play, and you're off the mark again. From another perspective, it is serious business. Say it is fine-tuned acrobatics, and it is also something else; it is on the spot creativity. Say it is a matter of brute strength, and, you guessed it, it is more than that. It is finesse. Say it is strictly rule-governed, and it is; but that's not the whole story, for it involves constant spontaneity. Well, then, you say it is nothing but improvisation, and you're both right and wrong, for there are rules that must be followed within the improvisation. Capoeira is never either one thing or the other. It is always both, and neither.

So, you decide to embrace the contradictions within Capoeira. Then, against your better judgment, you try once again to conceptualize it. You try packing Capoeira's particular characteristics into one pigeonhole or another, and it gives you a subtle twist and squirms away into neither that pigeonhole nor any other, but evinces something else, always something else, something different, something new. Frustrated, you decide to throw in the towel and forget about Capoeira's enigmatic attraction. But you can't. The haunting sounds of its instruments, the attraction of its songs, the rhythmic, dancelike quality of its moves, continue to entice you. You try to resist, but you eventually give in. You're hooked, suspended in a world of either -or. You want to articulate Capoeira, and you stutter and stammer. You wish to rationalize it, and you end in a mental knot. You continue your effort to comprehend it, and you teeter toward the black hole of bewilderment. Your ears try to get the rhythm, and they lose it. Your eyes try to follow the moves, and they lag behind. Your body tries to emulate the twists and turns, and it flounders about. Yet, you can't forget it. So, you try to try again, and then again.

What is this poetry in motion called Capoeira? It is a scrappy, ritualized ballet, an embattling challenge of physical ability and mental agility practiced to the rhythm of instruments and chants. Slaves from Africa created this complex conjunction of ritualized techniques and physical confrontation in Brazil. Everybody who has been a capoeirista for years and has reached the venerable status of *Mestre(a)* is ready to tell the tale of its history at the drop of a hat. It's in blood, a constant reliving of Capoeira's history by entering the *Roda*, the ring where Capoeira is played. But every capoeirista's history of Capoeira is different. In fact, every time the history is narrated, it is narrated in a slightly different way. Who is to be believed? This Mestre or that one? This or that author of the many books on the topic? The more experienced students in class? It's difficult to know, if not well nigh hopeless. The tradition is complex, with many side streets and blind alleys. Scholars are unanimous in telling us that the history of the art is problematic.

Yet, if I expect to discuss the subtle art of Capoeira, I must at least make an attempt to come to terms with its enigmatic origins.

Uncertain Sources

The earliest records suggest Capoeira was probably created somewhere between 1624 and 1654, when the Dutch occupied northeastern Brazil. According to a somewhat romanticized account, Capoeira emerged as a means of defense without sophisticated tools of war. It consisted of evasive measures taken against the dangers of the enemy's weaponry, and an attack whenever the possibility would arise. Capoeira became a means for survival. If indeed it started out as an expression of defiance against the Dutch in favor of Portuguese colonial rule that had enslaved the Africans in the first place, at a deeper level, it was something else. It was a pure expression of denial: denial of bondage, denial of the colonial system that subjected them to a subhuman existence.

Recent debates over the origin of Capoeira have invariably evoked two basic sources, Africa and Brazil. J. Lowell Lewis suggests a third source: Portugal. The songs are in Portuguese, sprinkled with local colloquialisms and words from African dialects. Moreover, Catholic saints and various Christian symbols are present in songs, gestures, and forms painted in and around the typical Roda and found on the walls of the halls where Capoeira play takes place (Lewis 1992:118). Yet neither Lewis nor any other Capoeira scholar would go so far as to claim Portugal as the art's origin. Whatever Portuguese elements exist in the art, they are no more than embellishment.

Even the origin of the word "Capoeira" is uncertain. Some claim it comes from the Amerindian language Tupí-Guaraní. The sound in Tupí-Guaraní comparable to the Portuguese Capoeira means "bush," or in other words, what was once "forest" (*caá*) but is now "extinct" (*puêra*)—perhaps from the very beginning the Amerindians were aware of the calamitous effects of deforestation. In another interpretation, the suffix "capo" of Capoeira might have the same origin as the English words "capon" or "rooster." This would seem quite natural, since the observation is often made that two partners in a Capoeira match create moves that look like a cockfight. Capoeira itself could be in reference to the African slaves who in colonial times carried fowl to market in small cages on their heads, and while in the plaza engaged in a little Capoeira play (Vieira 1995). Other scholars place their bet on Capoeira's Angola origins (Kubik 1979). It is seen to resemble the Angolan ritual in which stalwart young men engaged in kicking action reminiscent of a zebra's defending itself against predators. According to this story, the winner's prize was the maiden of his choice. Other scholars, like Edison Carneiro (1977) and Waldeloir Rego (1968), hold that Capoeira is exclusively a Brazilian creation by Africans. Of course, some African rituals and other activities, chiefly in Angola, have body moves similar to Capoeira, but Capoeira, in its various Brazilian forms, doesn't exist in Africa. Nevertheless, most scholars still consider Capoeira chiefly of African origin, developed for defense and identity (Moura 1980; however, see Dossar 1992 and Araújo 1997, who contest this view). After all is said and done, precise origins of the term and the practice remain elusive (Matias da Silva 1994:102–104).

The etymological obscurity of the term "Capoeira" is quite appropriate, since Capoeira breeds elusiveness by its very nature. The adept capoeirista is also an adept dissembler, an adroit ironist saying one thing when meaning another, a clever magician creating visual illusions for the purpose of catching an opponent off guard. In this respect, Capoeira is an alternative form of living, the slaves' skillful attempt to outmaneuver their masters' brutality—subservients trying to survive the harsh existence the dominants dole out. It is subalterns subtly and extralinguistically negotiating with those in power over possible ways and means of diminishing the cruelty of their lot. For these reasons, narrating the history of Capoeira is in the capoeiristas' blood. The Mestre may offer a brief story to disciples at the beginning of a training session, as the students crouch at the perimeter of the Roda in rapt silence, heads bowed in respect. During class, he may allude to slavery, persecution, discrimination, and the painful beginnings of Capoeira. Then, after class, he may give an account to sweating bodies, instruments still in their hands, cocked, as if ready to launch a series of defiant musical renditions, or as if ready to use the *Berimbau* bow as an instrument of attack against adversaries. (Incidentally, the first time I tried to board a plane for the United States with a recently purchased made-for-tourists berimbau, I was stopped and told it would have to go with the checked luggage. Why? Because, since it appears much like the bow of a bow-and-arrow set, it is considered a lethal weapon!—and that was a couple of years prior to the terrorist attack of September 11, 2001.)

The Mestre might tell his students of seemingly superhuman feats slaves accomplished during the colonial period, of capoeiristas who, after the days of slavery, were adept in eluding persecution by police and soldiers, and of old Mestres who always managed to get the better of brash young challengers. These narratives have passed from Mestre to Mestre. Each Mestre likely omits a little while adding a few of his own touches here and there. Most accounts have become distorted, and some of them exaggerated to the extreme. But the spirit of the narratives is there. It is strong, healthy, and vibrant. It has survived, and it will live on.

OUT OF SLAVERY
As mentioned, according to a popular interpretation, Capoeira developed as a means of self-defense for slaves attempting to escape captivity—though this interpretation is likely, in part at least constructed . Especially during the seventeenth century after the Dutch invaded the northeastern hump of Brazil, slaves took advantage of the confusion to find their way to freedom. Many of them formed communities called "Quilombos," the most notorious of which was Palmares, established soon after the Dutch invasion in the state of Alagoas (Freitas 1982).

Palmares became a tight-knit confederation of villages that virtually constituted a nation-state, dubbed the Republic of Palmares. It flourished. It became a state within a state, reviving African traditions and recreating a complex social order. The warriors from Palmares carried out frequent raids on nearby plantations to liberate slaves and take them to the Quilombo. Portuguese authorities saw Palmares as a threat and launched a campaign of extermination against it. After a series of futile attempts, the Quilombos were finally wiped out in 1695 after some forty years of existence and ten years of military resistance. One account has it that the inhabitants of Palmares disciplined themselves through Capoeira in preparation for the day when they might have to enter into combat with the Portuguese forces (Kent 1965). This story has likely been inflated over the years. The effectiveness of Capoeira vis-à-vis canon, muskets, and swords is questionable at best. (The 1984 film *Quilombo*, directed by Carlos Diegues, shows romanticized scenes of boys turning cartwheels and other Capoeira moves in training for the defense of their people.)

Capoeiristas from Rio de Janeiro and northeastern Brazil gained some respect during the War of the Triple Alliance, Argentina, Brazil, and Uruguay, against Paraguay from 1865 to 1870. Capoeirista recruits, volunteers and conscripts, were used chiefly as canon fodder on the battlefront. They fought valiantly and returned to Brazil with a share of the notoriety—a few Capoeira songs have lyrical allusions to the war. According to one report, by the 1880s even though free Afro-Brazilians outnumbered slaves by about four to one, the number of capoeiristas who landed in jail consisted of 60 percent free and 40 percent slaves. It seems that Capoeira was still an act of hope and aspirations against forced servitude. At the same time, given the reputation of the capoeiristas during the War of the Triple Alliance, white professionals gradually began taking notice, and on occasion they even found themselves playing Capoeira. In fact, by 1885 up to 20 percent of the capoeiristas in Rio were considered to be white (Bruhns 2000:25–26).

Marginality
After the War of the Triple Alliance, Brazil returned to life as usual and capoeiristas were all the worse off for it. Once again, they had to go underground. Slavery was finally abolished in 1888, and an independent Brazilian republic was formed the following year. Two years later, all archives containing records of African slavery were burned under the presumably noble pretext of erasing the institution from the country's past. Everybody would just forget the atrocities and go on their merry way. Of course, the record burning also conveniently destroyed evidence that might have revealed slavery in Brazil for what it really was. This turn of events also set the stage for renewed prohibition of Capoeira and other Afro-Brazilian practices.

According to the common conception among white Brazilians of the time, capoeiristas were vagabonds, ruffians, thieves, and drunks, given to knifings and other forms of violence. They gained a reputation as *malandros*—loafers, vagabonds, idlers, and rascals out to get something for nothing at the expense of others—perpetually engaged in *malandragem* (the *malandro's* stock-in-trade practice). Before long, malandragem became closely related to *malícia*—roughly comparable to the English "malice" or 'treachery," but carried out with an ingratiating demeanor—a common term among capoeiristas. Calling someone a "capoeirista" became about the same as calling him a "malandro." Actually, malandros knew Capoeira, but certainly not all capoeiristas were malandros. Nevertheless, labeling capoeiristas malandros and attaching malandragem to the subtle art obviously furthered prejudice against Capoeira and its persecution. Word of mouth reports had it that capoeiristas traveled in *maltas* (gangs) who attacked and robbed respectable citizens and raped their women (Rego 1968).

However, among common folks, the malandro was often seen as a heroic figure rooted in Brazilian folktales. His misfortune was that he began with two strikes against him. He was born a slave or in poverty, and he was not of European racial and ethnic origin. Consequently, he had no recourse and had to learn to live by his wits. Through use of subtle, ambiguous language and deceptive behavioral strategies, he converted his weaknesses into strength. He turned cultural traditions upside down and stood them on their head. As a member of the have-nots, he created unorthodox social situations, to the utter bewilderment of his presumed superiors, the haves. He lived on the thin line between legality and illegality. Neither conventions nor laws were capable of holding him back because of his astute maneuvers and his ability to improvise within every situation and find subtle paths around customary ways of doing things. He refused to accept the injustices built within society, and as an outsider, his every act breathed a bit of fresh hope for the have-nots throughout society. Thus he was not usually considered a criminal by the have-nots, though he may have been by the haves.

As a consequence of the malandro's reputation, in large part fabricated, a penal code was passed in 1890 calling for fifteen to thirty days in jail for vagabonds practicing their Capoeira craft, two to six months in prison if they are members of a malta engaged in any illicit activity, and three years for repeat offenses. Some testimonials have it that a method of punishment consisted of tying one wrist of a capoeirista to the tail of one horse and the other wrist to the tail of another horse and sending the animals galloping toward the police station. Needless to say, the victim often died before reaching the destination. While this and other forms of brutality undoubtedly occurred from time to time, they were most likely exceptions rather than the rule (Almeida 1982:13–14).

In spite of persecution, a first attempt was made in 1907 to form an institute of Capoeira gymnastics and a tract, *O Guia da Capoeira* (*A Guide to Capoeira*), was published by an army officer who kept his name anonymous, for obvious reasons. The movement came to naught and Capoeira soon returned to its underground status (Matias da Silva 1994:103–104). But memory is a persistent fellow. Capoeira held on to its slavery past and the injustices heaped on it during the early national period. In fact, racial memory within Capoeira culture became intensively aware of contemporary prejudice and discrimination, and a sense of racial pride emerged, as evidenced in many of the song lyrics that have endured, such as:

Dizem que o capoeira	They say the capoeirista
É aquele negrinho sujo	Is that dirty black guy
Negrinho que não trabalha	Black guy who doesn't work
Negrinho que é vagabundo	Black guy who's a bum

And:

Dizen que o preto é feio	They say the black guy is ugly
O preto não é feio não	But the black guy is not ugly
O preto joga capoeira	The black guy plays capoeira
Seu defeito é ser ladrão	Any defect he has lies in his being a thief [hence not a genuine capoeirista]

(Vieira 1995:46–47)

Academies Emerge

In 1929 Aníbal Burlamaque organized a small group of Capoeira enthusiasts and published a small tract, *Ginástica Nacional* (National Gymnastics). The publication caught the eye of a few middle-class kids"" who would show up for some of the practice sessions. Encouraged by this modest success, other Mestres began organizing small academies.

In 1932, Manoel dos Reis Machado (1900–1974), or *Mestre Bimba*, set up the first legitimate "official academy" in Salvador. In 1937 he offered a course registered as "physical education" with the secretary of education. He gained a reputation for accepting only students who could prove that they had a job or were studying (Almeida 1982, 1994; Vieira 1995:145). By this time another Salvadoran, Vicente Ferreira Pastinha (1889–1982), or Mestre Pastinha, was gaining public attention. While Bimba adapted moves to the Capoeira play that reminded many of Jiu Jitsu and other martial arts, in addition to a massive dose of acrobatics that added a spectacular note, Pastinha became increasingly obsessed with conservation of the Capoeira tradition. From that time onward, Capoeira branched off into the two directions, *Capoeira Re-*

gional led by Mestre Bimba, and *Capoeira Angola*, promoted by Mestre Pastinha (Matias da Silva 1994:103–105; Pastinha 1969). Largely as a result of the efforts of Bimba and Pastinha, Capoeira eventually came in off the streets and alleys. No longer regarded as the pastime of vagabonds and scoundrels, it gravitated from the margins of society toward the center, ever-so-slowly.

Thick, powerful Mestre Bimba brought about a transformation through his Capoeira Regional (the "region" was presumably the state of Bahia). He took special interest in making the art respectable, in contrast to the malandro image with which it had been shackled. He eventually attracted many light-skinned students from the middle and upper socioeconomic strata of Bahia. He demanded strict discipline, set codes of conduct for his students, and made his classes more intensive than anything previously known to the art. His students received diplomas and a *cordão* (literally, a "cord" to be tied around the waist, comparable to a "belt" in the martial arts) after completing a *curso*. In time, he surrounded himself with many university students and professionals. By the 1950s his academies were organized in Rio de Janeiro and São Paulo, and by the 1970s they were appearing in Europe and the United States.

Small, wiry, Mestre Pastinha, in contrast, held onto the Capoeira tradition—at least according to what was known of it at the time. Pastinha set for himself the goal of keeping the art in its original form. However, the most certain certainty we have is that the only thing that doesn't change is change itself. Capoeira, even Capoeira Angola, simply couldn't stand still. It changed. Nevertheless, since Pastinha insisted on conserving the Capoeira tradition, Capoeira Angola's changing face took on an increasingly conservative look. The irony, as we shall see in greater detail, is that since tradition is always fabricated as much as it is found, a culture can hardly hope to revive its past in pure form and maintain it intact. Tradition can be no more than an idealized version of an irretrievable past (Butler 1998; Serra 1995;Sousa Reis 1997.)

Over the years, Capoeira Angola in Salvador became even less overtly combative, as it distanced itself from Capoeira Regional. That is the downside, though many *angoleiros* (those who are faithful to Capoeira Angola) would balk at the idea. The upside is that Capoeira Angola allowed for increased individual expression and a greater range of moves. The degree of freedom of improvisation varied widely, however, according to the group and whoever was in charge. Even though Capoeira Angola moves became increasingly slow and deliberate in comparison to whip-lash Capoeira Regional action, it was actually part of the disguise: when quickness became necessary, it was always there, like a bolt of lightning. So the angoleiro was certainly no slouch. He was not in the ring merely to frolic and have a jolly good time. Amongst the smiles, playful gestures, and feigned taunts, there were moments of tight-lipped determination that suddenly set the play into a twirling cyclone of action. In short, both forms of Capoeira embodied game and play; both were creative and efficient, deceptive and aggressive, and flexible and rigid (Capoeira 1992:378).

CAPOEIRA ANGOLA	CAPOEIRA REGIONAL
Traditional	Modern
Change from within Capoeira Living	Transformation from within the Larger Culture
Slow Play *(Jogo Lento)*	Rapid Play *(Jogo Rápido)*
Low Movements *(Jogo Baixo)*	High Movements *(Jogo Alto)*
Relatively Flexible Rules, Improvisation	Relatively Rigid Rules, Application
Personal Strategies and Techniques	Codified Strategies and Techniques
Deceptive, and with Much *Malicia*	Aggressive, but with Little *Malicia*
Creativity, Individualized	Efficiency, Regimented
Play, Recreational	Game, Sport

TABLE 1
COMPARISON OF AND CONTRAST BETWEEN CAPOEIRA ANGOLA AND CAPOEIRA REGIONAL

Thus Table 1 should by no means be construed as just another set of oppositions. Granted, Capoeira Angola evinces an implied attitude of resistance to white society since the time of slavery; consequently it more specifically embodies affirmation of Afro-Brazilian identity and a sense of black consciousness than Capoeira Regional. In this respect, it entails a reinvention of a tradition, in the sense of Eric Hobsbawm and (Hobsbawm and Ranger 1983; also Sansone 2003). Capoeira Regional, in contrast, does not affirm Afro-Brazilian exclusion from white society; it affirms its becoming present within that society. Its eclecticism is not accompanied by an overt search for lost black identity, but identification with the larger society in the sense of inclusion, not exclusion. Nevertheless, the two forms of Capoeira converge on important points. Capoeira Regional to a degree manifests all the Angola characteristics, and vice versa. They both emerge and submerge, according to the rhythm that is set up by the battery of instruments, the chants, and the okay nods from the head berimbau player, who is usually the Mestre.

In a manner of speaking, Capoeira Angola and Capoeira Regional are both sacred and profane. Capoeira Angola includes allusions to Candomblé *Orixás* (Afro-Brazilian deities—about which more later) as well as to Catholic saints. These sacred origins are usually either hidden or entirely absent in Capoeira Regional. Capoeira Regional began a process of desacralization from the very beginning, given its adoption of influences from outside. Yet at its roots, one still finds in Capoeira Regional a sense of mystery and the mystical, a feeling for the African spiritual, life-giving energy, called *Axé*. This sense of the mystical is apparent in both Capoeira Regional and Capoeira Angola, from the forlorn twang of the Berimbau to terms with religious connotation, to colors on the Berimbau and elsewhere that, like Capoeira rhythms, songs and verses, depict a lingering reverence for the Afro-Brazilian religion, Candomblé (Bruhns 2000:133–135, Capoeira 1999:141–144). Moreover, during a Roda, the sign of the cross is an important gesture, especially in Capoeira Angola. It is usually made before the action begins, and when one calls for a break in the action, one stands at the edge of the circle with outstretched arms in the form of the crucifix, and then, after a series of ritualistic moves, the action commences. One could go so far as to suggest that the cartwheel (*Aú*) is an inverted cross, whether we are speaking of the Capoeira Regional cartwheel with legs extended or the Capoeira Angola cartwheel with legs closed in "gorgeously ugly, elegantly awkward" fashion (Browning 1995:118).

Subtly Coping with the Horrors of Bondage

Well into the twentieth century, many angoleiros continued to play in the streets, in parks, and in other informal settings, though the practice is now generally discouraged. Above all, Capoeira Angola continued to stress malícia over raw power, subtle unexpected moves over a fixed repertoire of moves in invariant sequences, and deception over seriousness. It was a matter of having a good time, singing a little, dancing a little, now engaging in some "trash talk," now getting low and dirty, now seriously confronting the opponent, now just having fun with the best of friends. It remained more of a family affair than the clublike affair Capoeira Regional was becoming.

Consequently, angoleiros were on the average darker and less affluent, folksier and less professional, than regionalistas. This is not to say that they were not as dedicated as regionalistas. On the contrary, ethnic memory of their slavery past was part and parcel of their art. It was the very spirit of their art. When dancing and singing and gesturing and mock fighting, they played the role of their ancestors, who were even less fortunate than they. And in incessantly evoking the memory of their ancestors, angoleiros relived their own personal past, replete with hardships, prejudice, repression, and brutality. During this process, the body enacted what the mouth couldn't say. In this respect it is significant that Capoeira music was replete with syncopation: a beat is suspended, which leaves the body in "silence," a silence that must be filled with motion, so the body twists and turns, elusively, slyly, cunningly, with a wry, wordless smile.

While it is a common assumption that Capoeira Regional has incorporated Asian martial arts into its moves—though Mestre Bimba on occasion denied this—Capoeira Angola has continued to resist such influences. However, as I will suggest below, in Mestre Pastinha's refusal to separate matter from spirit (body from mind) in the Western sense, at its deepest levels, Capoeira Angola in terms of its world vision approximates certain aspects of Asian philosophy. To some extent, the same might be said of Capoeira Regional. This spiritual or bodymind nature of Capoeira is also most emphatically highlighted in its syncopation. The subtle moment of hesitation, vacillation, apparent uncertainty: it is a moment of emptiness, when time for a fleet moment seems to stand still. Syncopation emerges from the instruments, the songs, and the moves within the Roda. It is everywhere. It contributes a note of mystery, an eerie feeling, perhaps even mysticism, to the art (for the notion of "bodymindness" within Capoeira, see Sodré 1983:203–215, 1991:13–19).

This characteristic of Capoeira Angola, and to an extent of Capoeira Regional, is a far remove from the idea of Capoeira as nothing more than a pastime for ruffians with nothing to do. Indeed, Capoeira Regional most particularly attempted to rid the art once and for all of its image as the subversive activity of malandros and vagabonds. At the same time, it divorced itself from the idea that Capoeira is just *brincadeira* (from *brincar*, gratuitous play as in a child's fortuitous activity). In other words, there was an attempt to modernize Capoeira and give it a progressive, industrious work ethic. One might be prone to say that the idea was to whiten and westernize the art. In this guise, the most appropriate use of Capoeira, given the nature of the art, was for personal defense. In presenting this image to the public, Renato Ortiz writes, courses must be offered, with a fixed code of rules and in the best of all worlds a text outlying the advantages of preparing oneself for confrontation with all those undesirable elements out there that might waylay one (Ortiz 1985:105, also Vieira 1995:158–171). After all is said and done, Bira Almeida concludes, 'the capoeirista should be a good fighter in the mode of the *capoeira regional* but without losing the spirit, rituals, and playful characteristics of the *capoeira Angola*" (Almeida 1986:43).

This combination of features effectively brings Capoeira Angola and Capoeira Regional together into a whole. Both diverge, each in its own way, from social norms through conformity and resistance. Conformity and resistance, because from the time of its inception Capoeira was a potential defense technique. In order that the defense technique might not be snuffed out entirely, it had to take on airs of conformity (dancing, music, singing, playing). Yet, there was underlying resistance (in the lyrics, the offensive-defensive moves, the mock fighting). Combining conformity and resistance, from the big picture, both Capoeira Angola and Capoeira Regional are incongruously, contradictorily complementary. They are incongruous, because, taking on a confusing, ambiguous countenance, they tend to diverge from rather than converge with the dominant social norms; they are contradictory because they resist encapsulation within normal social categories; and they are complementary, because, as we shall note in greater detail below, on the surface there is appearance of conformity but underneath lies seething resistance.

What many white newcomers don't realize is that, at its roots, Capoeira is black, through and through. It is black in the union of body, mind, and spirit. It is black as a defense technique of slaves in a struggle that gushed forth from the depths of their soul. This struggle reveals itself not merely in militant action, but in rhythm, song, dance, and furious play, while slipping through the syncopated lapses. Capoeira is black, and it can be none other than black. I would venture to suggest that many whites who embrace Capoeira as their own—captivated by its charm, how can they resist?—nonetheless often remain out of tune with the deeper gut feeling for the art, as well as the religious and, ... yes, ... even the mystical sense of participation. This black Capoeira spirit is always there, lurking within the shadows of each and every Capoeira move. For the Capoeira process can never be entirely removed from its black origins.

At the same time, Capoeira as process keeps the art open to change. Every Roda is testimony that Capoeira is process. As such, it is always continuously becoming something other than what it was becoming, within space and through time. In this sense Capoeira, like all vibrant cultural phenomena, is a living organism. It evolves. Although angoleiros make a concerted effort to preserve Capoeira's authenticity, the same is true, albeit to a lesser degree, of the regionalistas. Thus the underlying, intrinsic characteristics of the art endure. Yet the two forms of Capoeira allow for a spontaneity that always emerges when the lead berimbau evokes the spirit of the capoeirista. This spontaneity cannot but lead to emergent processes that render Capoeira practices something other than what they were. Capoeira is always becoming something other than what it was becoming.

Still, the Question Remains

So, in the final analysis, is Capoeira in both of its incarnations resistance in motion, rhythmic resistance, or an outward show of conformity concealing a seething cauldron of rebellion? Barbara Browning has this to say:

> If capoeira is regarded as historical evidence of black resistance, they want to show that African forms are in themselves valid, durable and effective weapons. This is doubtless true. But if part of the genius of African religion in Brazil is syncretism, its ability to absorb or account for Catholic or other systems, part of capoeira's genius has also been its ability to absorb rather than be displaced by other forms. It is a survival tactic consistent with the premise of the game.... Locating what is "really" African in Brazilian culture is,... not a simple project of mapping surface continuities. But more interesting is the continuity of strategies for cultural survival. Of course, this argument itself is a tricky maneuver. It's what allows Bimba—and his students—to give two accounts of the sources of capoeira regional. Bimba "laughed at" the charges of foreign influences. He also "admitted" drawing on U.S. and Asian techniques. His student tells us not to take the statements (which ones?) literally, because they were strategic—and the strategy is recognizable to anyone who is familiar with the strategy of the game. In other words, the apparent contradiction is resolved by the fact that the very strategy of appropriating extrinsic movements is intrinsic to capoeira. The larger argument is that the very strategy of appropriating extrinsic culture is intrinsic to African culture. (Browning 1995:102–103)

In this light, one might wish to label Capoeira Regional "modernization at the margin." It is a hybrid form in the sense of García Canclini (1995), for sure. But it is not really that, not quite. There is also conformity and resistance, rather than mere cooptation of subalterns by the dominant culture. Edison Carneiro (1977:14) tells us, Capoeira Angola, has hardly anything in common with Bimba's school. And Waldeloir Rego (1968:362) puts forth the claim that Bimba's capoeira is "completely prostituted," a nostalgic view of Brazil as a "racial democracy" through the process of *embranquecimento* (whitening) by successive dilution of Afro-Brazilians as a consequence of intermarriage—more about this later. Yet, there is the counterclaim that by way of Bimba's academies, Capoeira Regional became legitimized in the eyes of the dominant society to complement Capoeira Angola as legitimate for the subservient society (Vieira 1995:16). All told, both Capoeira forms manifest both conformity and resistance. They are both to an extent modern; yet, they remain laden with slave-society undertones.

So, is Capoeira blackest when most distinctly Angolan and whitened in its Regionalist form? If it was legitimized chiefly through Bimba's efforts, does this not imply that Capoeira Regional brought black respectability to the art instead of depicting merely a whitening process? Where, finally, is the answer to the question regarding the genuine spirit of Capoeira? The answer is that there is no spirit of Capoeira if we are searching for a unifying thread that weaves the subtle art into a homogeneous fabric. This is because there is no single fabric, but many fabrics and virtually uncountable weaves. In this light we might wish to say that, on the one hand, Capoeira Angola remains to a certain sense enchanted with the world, with culture, and with life. Capoeira Regional, on the other hand, is disenchantment and consequently a rationalization of the art so that it might conform to modern culture. We might go on to conclude that recently, and parallel with the becoming of a spirit of negritude and pride in the race, there has been renewed interest in Capoeira Angola, which we could consider a move toward a deepened form of enchantment or, we might say, toward re-enchantment (Carneiro 1977:14). (The terms "enchantment" and "disenchantment" of the world are originally from sociologist Max Weber; my interpretation of the terms draw inspiration chiefly from Morris Berman [1981] and his notion of "re-enchantment.")

What, then, might be the motivating force behind the somewhat disenchanted Capoeira Regional? As mentioned, some observers have attributed an Asian martial arts influence to Bimba and his disciples. Whether this is the case or not, Vieira believes that military rigor and regimentation found in Bimba's methods corresponds to the militarism of the *Estado Novo* (New State) during Getúlio Vargas's dictatorship (1937–1945). This interpretation places Capoeira Regional in a negative light. A more benign counterargument might be that Bimba's style exacted obedience, discipline, organization, and order to produce good and noble citizens (Vieira 1995:158); for, it is true that Bimba created Capoeira Regional in reaction to what he considered the 'sloppy" street Capoeira of the twenties (Almeida 1986:2). At any rate, Capoeira Regional's disenchantment would seem to involve a more conscious and conscientious effort to put the subtle art to use for the purpose of improving individual and community well being. Yet, an element of enchantment often seems to linger, even in Capoeira Regional.

If one were asked to provide the strongest link between Capoeira Angola and Capoeira Regional, one might come up with the African concept of *Axé*. The word, tinged with mystery and even mysticism, is at once more and less than a concept. It is more, because, as mystical space, words and concepts simply cannot account for it. It is less, for it is pre- or extra-linguistic; it is prior to language; it is raw feeling; it is in the heart and guts rather than in the head; it is spirit rather than reason. *Axé* "is the magic force that moves all things in the universe according to the African religions of Brazil. It exists in all realms of nature and can be transmitted through specific rituals" (Almeida 1986:6). Although Capoeira has no direct connection with religion, capoeiristas, like the majority of Brazilians, are related in one way or another with Afro-Brazilian rituals. Axé in Capoeira signifies a connection with its roots, a special energy to be developed by any capoeirista. Among capoeiristas, daily greetings and farewells can come in the form of a tenderly enunciated yet implicitly defiant: Axé. To wish Axé to someone means to wish for harmony within the Capoeira community, to wish that each individual's mind and body and spirit may enter into concert with one another. Capoeirista Axé embodies a desire for proper Capoeira living. As far as true-blue capoeiristas are concerned, their Mestre transmits Axé through her/his daily conduct. Nevertheless, even in the meaning of Axé there seems to be a basic difference between Capoeira Angola and Capoeira Regional. The difference basically lies in *spirit*. Mestre Bola Sete once remarked: "Mestre Bimba foi o *tal*, Mestre Pastinha foi *Tao*" (Mestre Bimba was a rough and tumble guy, Mestre Pastinha was *Tao*—had *Tao* spirit; see Bola Sete 1997:88).

I leave Bola Sete's subtle idea to your contemplation; meanwhile, back to the historical account of Capoeira.

Toward Institutionalizing the Art

Surprising as it may seem, the greatest boost to Capoeira came from Brazilian populist dictator Getúlio Vargas. Although Getúlio Vargas's *Estado Novo* persecuted Capoeira, in 1953 during his second term as president, he witnessed an exhibition by Mestre Bimba and his students in the government palace at the invitation of Bahia Governor Juracy Magalhães. He was so taken by the demonstration that he immediately proclaimed Capoeira the only purely and legitimately Brazilian sport. Soon thereafter, Capoeira took a place in the spotlight, and as a consequence it found its way into clubs, schools, theaters, and tourist resorts. Afro-Brazilian capoeiristas hardly enjoyed any preferential treatment, however. Their status remained the same as that of any other Afro-Brazilian. The only difference is that their art was now valued to some an extent, and they were given some respect insofar as their talents could be tapped (Souza Reis 1997:106–107).

Partly as a result of Capoeira's newfound popularity, by 1972 it was officially accepted as a sport by Ministry of Education and Culture of the military dictatorship that began in 1964 and lasted until 1985. In 1986 the National Secretariat of Physical Education went so far as to establish a national program of Capoeira in public education. While some proponents of Capoeira Regional looked upon this move to institutionalize the art with favor, others, especially from among the Angolan Capoeiristas, criticized it as an attempt to systematize Capoeira, homogenize it, whiten it, and co-opt capoeiristas by bureaucratizing the academies and using them for propaganda purposes. What is worse, they feared the institutionalization campaign would put Capoeira academies on the level of folk art (Lopes 1996). They were also afraid that genuine capoeiristas, with little formal education, would be barred from the schools, while physical education teachers, after no more than a crash course in Capoeira, would give their students a vulgarized form of the art. At worst, they envisioned capoeiristas performing in a circus atmosphere before gawking camera-laden foreigners who had no appreciation for Capoeira culture. This, they thought, would be nothing more than an extension of a romanticized folklorist, and even racist, image of Capoeira as an exotic practice that lies on the margins of modern Brazilian society. To make a long story short, Capoeira was never effectively institutionalized, though the debates over the consequences of institutionalizing the art still rage on (Santos 1998b). I have often witnessed the Angola Mestre I have worked with—let us call him Mestre Rapôsa—wage battle against those who take the art into the markets and the streets. He tells of how they spectacularize and thus falsify their moves in order to render them more attractive for tourists. He invariably goes on to criticize public educators who want to include Capoeira in the physical education curriculum and have it taught by teachers and professors who know little of the art save for a couple of dozen classes they once took.

For sure, institutionalizing the art has to an extent commercialized it, rendering it a tourist commodity. Capoeira for tourists stems from the art as black folk culture, while genuine Capoeira culture lies deep in the heart of Afro-Brazilian culture. There is the other side of the coin: whitened Capoeira, primarily found in the Capoeira Regional academies, where lighter and often professional Afro-Brazilians pair off with their middle- and upperclass counterparts from the dominant culture. Alejandro Frigério (1989) dubs the two forms of Capoeira as they are often practiced in the cities to the south of Brazil not Angola and Regional, but Capoeira-Culture (from black folk culture) and Capoeira-Sport (from white dominant culture). A quick look at a typical Capoeira-Sport class in Bahia might have a group of nine capoeiristas, three black angoleiros born and raised in Bahia, five white students from São Paulo in the south of Brazil and their more white than black professor. The black students might be showing the white guys some angoleiro moves that never found their way into the literature on Capoeira-Sport. The professor, product of literate culture, would thus have much to learn from chiefly oral black Capoeira-Culture. In a São Paulo Capoeira-Culture scene, by contrast, we might find eight white students and their white professor in a physical education program going through a few Angola moves and many others besides that are reminiscent of the martial arts. These moves would leave any

Bahia angoleiro from Capoeira-Culture in northeastern Brazil who might happen to be present with a puzzled brow; the moves would hardly be reminiscent of what he had learned to love as Capoeira Angola.

Frigério (1989) observes that Capoeira-Culture is primarily black culture: most of the moves have come down through the tradition, many of them by word of mouth and by example. Capoeira-Sport is chiefly a matter of mainstream white culture that has more liberally cannibalized elements from elsewhere, and most of the tactics are codified in a set of rules and strategies. Capoeira-Culture retains more vestiges of its early malícia, by its ludic, deceptive qualities, marked by ambiguity and irony. Capoeira-Sport is a more serious, competitive affair; hence most every move is for the purpose of gaining the advantage over the adversary. Capoeira-Culture is more attuned to play: one plays at it for the sheer love of it, as a manner of deepening the bonds between all members of Capoeira-Culture. Capoeira-Sport is more gamelike; it is driven by rules and hard and fast strategies. It is definitely more of a game than play: the object is to win, usually at all cost and in whichever way possible, by means of force, domination, and knowing how to apply the rules of the game with utmost precision. One might wish to conclude, albeit tentatively, that Capoeira-Culture is chiefly for the sake of devilish fun, while Capoeira-Sport is more in the spirit of war. It bears mentioning also that to the chagrin of Capoeira purists, in recent years there have been efforts to commercialize Capoeira by introducing it into other areas, such as aesthetics (Capo-ballet), water aerobics (hydro-Capoeira), medicine (Capo-therapy), and pugilism (Capo-box). Some presumably well-meaning folks have even proposed getting a place in the Olympic Games for the art.

My Own Bias Revealed

It has likely become apparent that my own sentiments lie with Capoeira-Culture, or better put, Capoeira Angola. This is for a practical reason: I can't kick up my heels like the young Capoeira-Sport guys can. It is also for a personal reason: Brazilian traditions when at their best fascinate me, and Capoeira Angola is closer to its traditional past than Capoeira Regional. Capoeira Angola also more concretely patterns life. As the obsessive angoleiro Mestre Rapôsa once explained:

> I love Capoeira because it is life in miniature. It is living. It is a philosophy for living. I love to *vadiar* [literally, to goof of, dawdle, piddle around], because it gives me a look at life, in the home, on the streets, in the world of business and politics. We are all capoeiristas at heart. The problem is that most people don't know it, so they go around trying to act according to the rules of proper politics, busi-

ness, and everyday conduct tell them. That is the way "regionalistas" do Capoeira. They think a lot of rapid, acrobatic exercises, with much contact,... zass, zass, zass, and feverish berimbau strumming and atabaque drumming,... bum, de de bum bum, de bum, is Capoeira. Nonsense! Capoeira is life. Where do you see all that in life? Nowhere, except in the violent movies and on TV and when people are trying to ape scenes they see there. Life is too sophisticated for Capoeira Regional. Capoeira should be life. Those who think Capoeira is a lot of brawling don't know Capoeira, and they really don't know life. Capoeira can't be rationalized; it can't be reduced to a lot of rules and sequences of moves like a robot. Hell, a bunch of capoeiristas drinking beer and telling jokes in a bar can be at the same time practicing Capoeira. (private conversation, my translation, July 6, 2002)

How in the world can Capoeira enter the bar room? It can enter, because it is life itself; it is life at its best when in the form of nonverbal dialogue. Capoeira is not just talk about reasoned, codified moves and how to make them. It is playful interaction between two bodies; it is "body rhetoric" (Lewis 1992:106). This corporeal dialogic can take place in a bar or anywhere else during everyday living, as long as a Capoeira spirit is in play. The Capoeira spirit supersedes alcoholic beverages, lewd talk, and another other sort of bar room activity, because it is radically extralinguistic. It is felt and sensed more than it is analyzed and conceptualized; it is in the gut, not in the mind. I believe Mestre Rapôsa would agree.

Capoeira, wherever and whenever, inside the Roda as microcosm of the world or within the world itself, is dynamic interaction between two interdependent, interrelated individuals whose lines of interconnection are never lines of opposition. They are criss-cross, divergent and convergent lines; they are incongruously, contradictorily complementary lines. When these interconnected lines come into play, each capoeirista has her own style, her own personal, idiosyncratic ways that complement the ways of her partners, whether in the Roda or outside. These ways are not out of some recipe book of rules for performing Capoeira or for getting on with life. The capoeirista follows a few informal conventions, for sure, but she makes up her strategies as she goes along during a match or in life's situations. Attuned to the particular context within which she finds herself, and attuned to her body—its position with respect to her partner, its location in the Roda, its movement with respect to the people around her within concrete living—she improvises. She makes do with what she has for the moment. Since each moment presents some situation that is never exactly the same as any previous moment, she must improvise, as a means of coping. And all the while, she dialogues, corporeally.

> Capoeira is not a costume to be worn and taken off according to the situation.... It is our own skin. We carry it all the time. We are cats, rats, and monkeys, ferocious and gentle beasts in cavalcade through the many Rodas of life. We are clowns, masters, and slaves of the art who regain the freedom of ourselves only when cooked in the cauldron of Medea which is the *jôgo* in the Roda. (Almeida 1986:55)

Incidentally, I might add, Mestre Rapôsa is illiterate—though in my estimation he is a very intelligent, homespun philosopher. He abhors the idea of videos, books, and written lyrics used for instructional purposes. He believes that since Capoeira is life, it must be lived in the most concrete sense, corporeally. You shouldn't waste time reading about it, watching it, and talking about it. You should do it. If you just do it, memory of your doing it won't exist solely in the mind. It will be in the body. If it's in your body, it is you; if it's in your body, and if you are alive, and since you *are* alive, Capoeira is life itself. Rapôsa doesn't want to let the most special songs he has created for use in his academy out on paper. They're only for the group. If he lets them out of the group, he's afraid that someone will copy them and print them as their own.

The same goes for particular lines that are repeated during group gatherings in the form of litanies. They are almost like a rosary. They must be learned word for word, orally, and they cannot leave the circle. I could reveal many of Rapôsa's more personal songs and especially his philosophical-religious discussions in this text. But I choose not to do so, in honor of the Mestre—indeed, I've even suppressed his actual name. I must say that as somebody who happens to be a professor who earns his living by reading and talking and writing ad nauseam, I find Mestre Rapôsa's philosophy of Capoeira at once perplexing, intriguing, and refreshing. Personally, I would have it no other way. Mestre Rapôsa's philosophy has helped me to develop what I consider alternative pedagogical methods for classroom use that include visual, musical, and somatic-kinesthetic exercises in addition to fixed textual methods.

In this respect, my experience has been somewhat comparable to that of Heloisa Bruhns (2000:24), who became "sentimental" when she knew Mestres João Grande e João Pequeno —both of them are, like Rapôsa, students of Mestre Pastinha—who "don't know how to articulate themselves [in proper academic fashion], yet they know everything about Capoeira and its history." In this vein, I also heartily embrace Barbara Browning's (1995:167) assessment of her own experience with Capoeira: "Many things I learned in Brazil I learned with my body."

Before continuing my story about Capoeira practice, a few words on Capoeira practicing philosophy are in order.

Chapter Two

Capoeira Becoming

IT'S NOT REALLY WHAT IT SEEMS

To recap, throughout the colonial period, Capoeira developed into a subtle strategy of resistance through the appearance of conformity, a struggle against conditions of slavery in part by means of deception (Rego 1968; Sousa Reis 1997). For instance, the one-hundred-two-year-old capoeirista and father of Mestre Rapôsa tells that since Capoeira was outlawed in the early years of the twentieth-century, on Sunday after Mass, Afro-Brazilians often practiced their art in the streets while dressed in white suits. Who could possibly suspect wrongdoing?

Conformity is appearance, while resistance is what is actually going on. Apparent conformity and actual resistance or subterfuge is of the nature of deception. Deception through conformity and resistance became a matter of survival. The slave created the image of conformity while scheming subtle forms of resistance by producing ways to slow down, construct glitches in, and even sabotage, progress on the plantation or in the mansion. In order to bring this about, the slave fashioned deceptive strategies. He pretended to be doing one thing while doing something else. He put on a good-natured face while cursing between his teeth. He put on a show of obedience while subverting the rules. He obeyed, and at the same time he practiced clandestine noncompliance. He played the game of masters and slaves; yet he secretly planned clever patterns of rebellion (Butler 1998; Souza 1999).

These techniques of pretense and deception became rooted in Capoeira. For this reason alone, Capoeira is difficult to explain. But that's only in part why it is Capoeira. And that's why it must be much more than simply a matter of pretense and deception. So once again, how do you talk about this poetry in motion? What can you say about apparent fighting that isn't really fighting? Dancing that is at the same time both more and less than dancing? Songs appropriate only when they are accompanied by two people in a friendly struggle subtly and delicately trying to outdo one another while making it a matter of rollicking fun? Musical instruments that set the rhythm of an apparent struggle? What can you say, when you realize that in Capoeira culture, artichokes and pineapples and cabbages and bananas mix with apparently no problem at all?

A Few Enigmatic Words from the Masters
When once asked about Capoeira, Mestre Pastinha replied: "Capoeira is what the mouth eats" (Almeida 1986:14). "Outlandish!" one might wish to retort. "Where's the connection?" Mestre Pastinha's response has a Zen quality to it. He answered the question with an evasion that circled around and eventually hit the mark. If Capoeira philosophy is practicing philosophy, if it is life itself, then whatever sustains life sustains Capoeira. The wily Mestre might have responded: "Capoeira is what the hands don't rhythm (on the instruments)." He might even have blurted out: "Capoeira is how the body doesn't move," "What the eyes don't see," "What the mind doesn't know," "What the throat doesn't sing," or "What the feet and hands don't do." But he didn't. He was much more evasive when encapsulating Capoeira as "what the mouth eats."

What is the meaning of such self-denying sayings? The message is that there is no explicit message, and no explicit meaning. There is nothing that meets the eye, the ear, the feeling and sensing body and the thinking mind that simply is as it seems. In Capoeira, everything is something other than we would ordinarily expect it to be. No,... wait. Did I write "to be"? No!... that's not right at all. There is no to be; there is no being insofar as there being something that is what it is, yesterday, today and tomorrow. There is only Capoeira becoming, process. There is no more than a becoming of being and a being of becoming, if I may be allowed to put it that way. Whatever we sense or think about Capoeira when we experience it, it is already becoming something other than what it was becoming. It is always in a process of becoming; it is never something fixed and static.

Mestre Bimba put it this way: "Capoeira is treachery, a way of coping with the dangers of life" (Almeida 1986:1). "Now," we think to ourselves, "this makes more sense, does it not?" Well, not really; not if Capoeira is indeed a matter of process. That is to say, in order to comprehend Mestre Bimba's notion of Capoeira in the fullest possible sense, we must learn about treachery, about coping with the dangers of life within the Brazilian context. And how do we do that? We don't, because we can't, not really. If we could, we would go back to the nineteenth century, or perhaps before that, and begin our becoming as an African slave. We would experience prohibition and repression of Capoeira after slavery was abolished in 1888. We would suffer from racial prejudice when Capoeira academies were created in the 1930s and thereafter. We would witness whitening of the subtle Afro-Brazilian art when it became popular among lighter skinned youth throughout Brazil, while we people of African heritage and evincing many shades of skin color, would still have to put up with discriminatory practices. So, I should confess: Am I, a white guy, really qualified to write about Capoeira? I have asked myself the question dozens of times. My initial responses were negative. Eventually, I arrived at the premonition that if I made a sincere effort to become a participant within a Capoeira family, if I could experience Capoeira as a practicing philosophy, if I could somehow slip into the flow of Capoeira becoming, perhaps I might be able to say a few words of worth. That, eventually, became my desire, even my obsession.

As a way of beginning Capoeira becoming, "treachery" in the English language gives a somewhat distorted image of what Mestre Bimba said of Capoeira. As mentioned above, one of the key words for Capoeira in Portuguese is malícia, in part roughly comparable to treachery. But there are differences between malícia and treachery that must be highlighted. Malícia comes with the same roots as the English "malice" and "malicious." The Portuguese word, however, is subtler than its English counterparts. It is a little bit of malice, but with a sly, clever, roguish twist and an ingratiating gesture. It involves awareness of what's going on under the surface appearances of some form of social interaction between two people; then suddenly, at the propitious moment, the person with subtlest malícia cunningly puts something over on the other person before he knows what's going on. It might include a dose of double-dealing, but with a wily, jocular quality. It might suggest deception, but a big smile accompanies it. It might imply duplicity, but there's an appearance of honesty; cheating without taking it seriously; guile with a little ironic humor; pretense for the purpose of playfully catching you off guard; trickery that is ingratiatingly revealed to you when you are taken in by it; a show of trust and then you are raucously yet jocularly slammed when you accept it.

Malícia is one person's creation of expectations in the mind of the other person and then acting contrary to those expectations. The intent is a good-natured way to make the other person out to be a fool, a clown. The act is brought about by deception, or as they sometimes put it in Brazil, by an *indireta* (indirection, a deceptive maneuver). The person putting himself up for the deception is led along a tangent. Then, at an unexpected moment, the table is turned, and he falls into the trap. The slaves in Brazil developed malícia into a carefully honed instrument by means of which to generate subversive acts against their masters. Malícia became their way of coping with life, a way of life that became the heart and soul of Capoeira. It helped make up for their subservient position in society; it allowed them when at their best to subtly slip a figurative knife between the ribs of their masters. Malícia, above all, was commensurate with the slaves' outward conformity to the role fate had handed down to them coupled with an indomitable inward sense of resistance through clever, subtle fakes and maneuvers through word and action (Carvalho 1977:12–18). In comparable fashion, Capoeira malícia today can make up for lack of strength, quickness, and knowledge of difficult Capoeira moves. Malícia is, in short, an equalizer.

All this is to say that malícia always appears to be what it is not. In order to practice Capoeira malícia, you must take on the appearance that you are one thing and then suddenly reveal yourself in a different mask. The accomplished capoeirista must become a master of deception. He must pretend he is angry when he is not; he must act as if he is injured when he is fine; he must feign fear when he is as confident as could be. He creates an indireta that sets your senses and your mind off in a circuitous route. The Capoeira master of the indireta leads you to expect he will do one thing and then he does something else. He tricks you, subtly; he slays you, softly. He plays you for a fool; then he laughs with you when you take the bait. He brings you to an awareness that the world is never as it appears. You become aware that surprises are always just around the corner. Capoeira malícia always has yet another surprise in store.

As Mestre Pastinha once counseled: never give it all you've got; always hold something back, just in case; then, at the strategic moment, draw from your reserve and deliver an unexpected move. This involves subtle tactics of malícia. As we shall see in the pages that follow, malícia lies at the heart of Capoeira culture. It is dancing within ruthless combat, poetry within discourse of dominance and subservience, music within the roaring din of conflict (Capoeira 1992:128). Mestre Pastinha also remarks, in this regard:

> They [the apprentices] leave the Academy knowing it all. They know the struggle [of life] is very *maliciosa*, and full of trickery, that, they must take things calmly, subtly. That it is not simply a matter of attacking, but of waiting for the opportune moment. The Capoeirista never tells anyone he is a fighter. He is wily and astute, like the game of Capoeira that pretends it is dance in order to survive after it was introduced from Angola. The Capoeirista is a supreme dissembler. Against all odds he always presents himself as something other than what he is. That's what he is. (cited in Bola Sete 1997:71)

My other Capoeira mentor, Mestra Jararaca—Mestre Rapôsa's student—once told me a capoeirista practicing malícia is the uncomfortable combination of the actions of a malandro (vagabond, idler, rascal) and a *mandingo* or *mandingueiro* (literally, a sorcerer; in Capoeira contexts a marginalized black or mulatto who lives by his wits and exercises deception—and according to the popular image even magic—in order to survive). The malandro-mandingueiro engages in his deception playfully as if he had no serious bone in his body. At the same time he remains earnest in his every move as if there were no tomorrow.

Jararaca's explanation did no more than add perplexity to my furrowed brow. In search of an answer, I contemplated the meanings of the three Portuguese terms, malícia, malandragem (what the malandro practices), and mandinga (the feminine noun form for mandingo, denoting witchcraft, sorcery), asked questions here and there among weathered capoeirstas, and still never found any satisfying solution. I don't yet have the answer, intellectually speaking, though with time I would like to think I've acquired a certain feel for malícia. That, Mestra Jararaca would likely tell me, is all I need. Throughout Brazilian history the malandro (who practiced malandragem) and the mandingueiro (skilled in mandinga) were forced to make do with what they had, which was virtually nothing regarding social standing and material possessions. Thus they had to live by their wits through guile, cunning, and subterfuge, often with a subtle ironic twist. It entailed a capacity for taking advantage of certain precise moments while avoiding direct confrontation, and without taking these deceptive practices to their brutal extreme. Quite significantly, these same practices are today found in Brazil's notoriously unique form of soccer, and in samba, around which the very idea of Brazilian national identity revolves (Bruhns 2000; Soares 1994). In fact, Roberto DaMatta (1991b) elevates malandragem to the status of a general Brazilian trait, as does Lívia Barbosa (1992) with the concept of *jeito*, which bears certain similarity with malícia—to be discussed below.

TRYING TO GET A BETTER HANDLE ON THE ART

In keeping with the spirit of the Capoeira, I'll continue with an aside that will likely appear as a strange tale that is not about Capoeira. But I present it in order hopefully that it might give you a feel for what Capoeira is about.

The clinical neurologist Oliver Sacks writes that he once heard a roar of laughter coming from the aphasia ward in his hospital. What was going on? It was time for one of then President Reagan's speeches the patients had eagerly been awaiting. Ronald Reagan, the Hollywood Actor, President of the United States, known as the Great Communicator, must be up to his homey quips again. Dr. Sacks entered the room where he saw the patients beside themselves with belly laughs. Well, not all of them. Some appeared bewildered; others were outraged; but most of them were amused. The president was giving one of his usual moving speeches. And he was certainly moving his small audience in the hospital ward, to laughter, for the most part. But obviously, that was not the sort of reaction the president had intended to provoke. What could they possibly be thinking? Did they understand his words? Were they really getting the message?

Sacks's patients suffered from global aphasia: large portions of their brains functioned improperly or didn't function at all. Consequently, they could hardly understand the meanings of most words addressed to them. However, they were experts at understanding extraverbal cues—tone of voice, intonation, and all visual cues such as gestures, posture, body language, the speaker's interaction with the entire environment while speaking. They didn't hear language in the form of a series of sounds. They saw language in action. They saw language's evasion, language in its deceptive act of showing with the body something other than what the words said. In other words, speech does not consist of words alone. Understanding the spoken word involves much more than word recognition. Although a string of spoken words may be virtually meaningless, the tone with which they are spoken can be full of meaning. The aphasiacs might not understand the spoken word very well, but language in action was a piece of cake for them (Sacks 1990:80–84).

Animals are quite adept at this sort of understanding. If I fear a dog, in spite of my apparently stern verbal commands, my wily canine friend can see right through me: it is of the intuitive nature of animals of higher intelligence. Such intuition among animals can also get them in trouble. For example, there's the infamous Clever-Hans hoax. Clever Hans was a horse that, according to his owner, could solve problems of arithmetic. When told to add 4 and 6, for example, Hans would tap his hoof on the ground ten times. One day Hans's owner was invited to place himself outside the horse's line of sight when giving him a problem to solve. Hans thereafter failed to produce the right answer to all the problems given him. What was going on here? Hans had learned to read his master's subtle facial cues, and he eventually picked up the habit of ceasing his hoof tapping at the opportune moment so he could receive his reward consisting of a small serving of hay. In the absence of his master, he had no idea what was expected of him (Sebeok 1991:112–115). Understanding subtle nonverbal signs was, for Doctor Sacks, a clue to the aphasiacs' understanding of President Reagan's message. They understood him virtually without the need of words. They had no use for our obsessive academic textualism. They could tell an authentic from an inauthentic message by the speaker's facial expressions and other nonverbal signs. Thus it was the grimaces, the histrionisms, the false gestures and, above all, the false tones and cadences of the voice which rang false for these wordless but immensely sensitive patients. It was to these (for them) most glaring, even grotesque, incongruities and improprieties that my aphasiac patients responded, undeceived and undeceivable by words. This is why they laughed at the President's speech.... Here, then was the paradox of the President's speech. We normals—aided doubtless, by our wish to be fooled, were indeed well and truly fooled.... And so cunningly was deceptive word-use combined with deceptive tone, that only the brain-damaged remained intact, undeceived. (Sacks 1990:82–84)

How can we effectively explain these aphasiacs' behavior? Sacks gives few details in this regard. He doesn't even reveal the nature of the president's presumed untruth. He does, however, write that the aphasiacs somehow might have known the president's words could possibly appear authentic if taken in the context of his words alone. But with respect to certain of his words in concert with his gestures, they might have sensed—or perhaps they thought they knew—that he was lying through his teeth. We can suppose that most normal viewers of Reagan's speech heard what they wanted to hear. They saw their president doing his act and they saw what they wanted to see. Unlike the aphasiacs, most of them might also have been taken in by the act. The moral of the story? I suppose it might be this: don't try to lie to an aphasiac—or a dog or a horse for that matter.

What is the relevance of this strange tale to Brazilian Capoeira? Once again, deception. According to one interpretation at least, Sacks's aphasiacs sensed a particular form of deception, whereas we ordinary humans ordinarily could not. Whether Reagan was intentionally creating deception is beside the point. The aphasiacs sensed it. How did they sense it? Basically by means of extralinguistic cues. They didn't simply listen to so many words; they experienced the president's entire performance involving nonverbal cues. Sacks's aphasiacs apparently felt what they felt and knew what they knew in the gut, through corporeal feeling and knowing. Words can deceive with the greatest of ease. The entire body, along with words, can also deceive, and if we are attuned solely to the words, we might risk falling into the deceptive trap. But not the aphasiacs, it would seem. In this sense at least, they are more perceptive than we are. We might even say that, in this sense at least, they are more human than we are. For, deception—self-deception and deception of others—intentionally and perhaps unintentionally, in jest or in all seriousness, in fun and play and at work and in politics and business, is with us in all walks of life (for more along these lines, see Fingarette 1969; Mele 2001).

Capoeira, as we will see time and time again, is primarily nonverbal—aside from the song lyrics, of course. Moreover, as suggested above, deception, and discernment of deception is the beginning toward an understanding of Brazilian Capoeira. The weathered capoeirista is adept in the act of deception and keen to perceive deceptive acts. But actually, the ability to dissemble with remarkable facility, whether out of innocence or with ulterior motives in mind, is at the heart of what makes us all human. In this manner, I would submit, the heart and soul of Capoeira is within the heart and soul of our very humanity. Lest my Oliver Sacks example be misconstrued, I would suggest that deception is part of our ordinary forms of life. Politicians practice it. Business executives practice it. The rich and the famous practice it. Performing artists and athletes practice it. Competitors in contests of all sorts practice it. Children and adults alike practice it. In my opinion, based on my observations of Capoeira life in Bahia over the years, the chief difference between ordinary deceptive maneuvering and Capoeira deception is that the former can be ludic, for sure, but it is often serious business—to get ahead and reap rewards, gain power and prestige, win friends and influence people—while the latter is a matter of deception for deception's sake while paying homage to the Capoeira tradition.

DECEPTION FOR LACK OF AN ALTERNATIVE?

Deception became part and parcel of the Brazilian slaves' practices vis-à-vis their masters during the longest period of slavery in the Americas, from around 1538 to 1888. In the course of three and a half centuries about 3.5 to 5 million Africans (six to eight times the number taken in captivity to the United States) survived the brutal ordeal of the Atlantic crossing to Recife, Salvador, Rio de Janeiro, and other ports. Pierre Verger (1964, 1981, 1987) outlines four waves of slaves arriving in Brazil: (1) the Guinea cycle (today's Senegal to Sierra Leone) during the sixteenth century, (2) the Angola cycle (Angola and Congo) during the seventeenth century, (3) the Mina Coast cycle (Ghana and Togo) during the first three-quarters of the eighteenth century, and (4) the Gulf of Benin cycle (Benin and Nigeria), from 1775 to 1850, which brought great numbers of Yoruba speaking people.

Brazilian slavery manifested all the cruelty inherent in an institution charged with the duty of completely subjugating people from another race. African men were considered hardly more than beasts of burden—they were called *peças* (pieces)—and they were brutally tortured when they deviated from the strict rules meted out to them. Slave women were often forced to give in to the carnal appetites of their masters. Mutilations, scars, and sores became part of life for all slaves. The psychological damage was no less devastating. Families and communities suffered disintegration. Life expectancy was dismal. In fact, there was hardly any expectancy at all to speak of. There was only uncertainty. Some slaves found their condition so wretched that they chose to take their own lives as a desperate affirmation of their humanity (Schwarcz 1999). Freedom for the slaves in Brazil actually came in slow, painful steps. In 1850 slave traffic from Africa to Brazil was abolished. In 1871 slaves who served in the War of Triple Alliance (1865–1870) between Brazil, Argentina, and Uruguay, against Paraguay were declared free. In 1885 the Law of the Free Womb was passed. In 1885 also, slaves that managed to reach sixty-five years of age were declared free—big deal, now that they were most often too old to work on the plantation, or to support themselves elsewhere. And finally, in 1888, slavery was abolished Fernandes (1971).

Yet, somehow many slaves survived, by their wits, by deception and evasion, and perhaps in small part through Capoeira as an outlet and an act of solidarity. According to the story among most Afro-Brazilian capoeiristas, Capoeira played an important role in the game of survival, which was not really just any game, mind you: it was a way to stay alive, a way to assert one's humanity with some form of dignity. When the slaves practiced Capoeira, the masters from their mansions might have seen what they wanted to see regarding the slaves' activities outside their shanties. What they saw in Capoeira was the folks having a good time. There was obviously no harm in that. The attitude on the part of the masters might have been: "Let them enjoy themselves in whichever way they can, for tomorrow will be another rough day." The capoeirista slaves, however, were likely busy practicing deception. They were enacting one thing that was actually another thing. They were engaging in an activity that deviated sharply from its appearances. There were instruments making music, and there was singing and dancing and gaiety. That's usually what the masters saw and heard. The slaves, however, might have been singing something like this:

A liberdade	Freedom
tantas vezes sonhada	dreamt so many times
era agora realidade	was now reality
chegou a meta final, camarada!	the final goal was reached, my companion!
liberdade... liberdade	freedom... freedom
(Bola Sete 1997:84)	

The Capoeira Roda as a space for engaging in deception was for the slaves and is today for the capoeirista a protective circle. It was and is a microcosm of the world, and Capoeira within the Roda is an allegory for life out there. What the masters didn't see in the Roda was the slaves engaged in their acts of deception, as they played out their role in the bigger world, practicing deception at every step of the way insofar as it might be possible.

What goes on in the Roda in terms of deception is frequently a world upside-down. Every Roda begins with the most basic step, the swinging, swaying, rocking *Ginga*—about this more later. Besides the *Ginga*, one of the most notable characteristics of Capoeira action is body inversion, the amount of time spent on the hands, with feet in the air while either making a cartwheel (*Aú*) move, or in a head-down position, with feet cocked and ready to lash out like a zebra warding off a predator. Or, the capoeirista might perch on the top of his head and twirl like a spinning top (*Apião*) (an act that has led to speculation that break dancing in the United States might have had some influence from Capoeira). These aspects of Capoeira play give it an acrobatic look. Another inverted position is the *Queda de Rins* (literally "a fall on the kidneys"). It finds the capoeirista on his head and one hand with his elbow against the kidney area for support, or he might support his entire body with one hand and the elbow against his kidney section. The object is for the capoeirista somehow to become comfortable in the most bizarre and unaccustomed positions imaginable. For the slaves, caught in the most humanly degrading and unaccustomed of situations, found in Capoeira a world turned topsy-turvy as a means of practice for survival value.

In fact, in Capoeira action the hands are rarely used as an offensive measure. This is quite natural for slaves. After all, they were in chains. So if they entered into combat with their oppressors they would be forced to use their forearms, head butts, and sweeps (*rasteiras*) with their feet to trip up their opponent. This is important. For, since the slaves were in chains, which in most circumstances restricted wide sweeps with arms and legs, the objective was not to block blows from the adversary but to avoid them altogether. Defensive moves include a quick fall into the *Cocorinha* (squat), with hands up in protective fashion, the *Resistência* (a fall back with feet and one hand on the ground with the other hand up for defense), the *Queda de Quatro*, a fall back on both hands in readiness to kick upward with the feet and thus take on a slightly inverted position, and the *Esquiva*, a fall to the left or right with one hand down for support and the other one up for defense.

Following these defensive tactics there are various kick moves that are either offensive, or at least deceptively offensive, for the purpose of setting up further defensive moves. These kicks include, for example, the *Meia Lua de Frente*, an outstretched leg moving as far as possible in the form of an arc and a return to the original position, the *Queixada*, brought about with a twist of the torso while swinging one leg in an arc in the direction of the twist, the

Chapa de Costa, a kick backward toward the adversary with one leg, with hands and the other leg supporting one's weight while one keeps an eye on one's adversary through the crotch area from a near-inverted position, and the *Benção*, a kick forward while thrusting the torso backward for defense. Other offensive moves include the *Martelo*, hammer blow from an upright position with the leg cocked, and the *Meia Lua de Compasso* or *Rabo-de-Arraia*, which begins like the *Chapa de Costa* but the kick is in the form of a wide arching sweep backward. All these moves are enacted while the capoeirista keeps her eyes glued to the other person, at every moment in anticipation of his own deceptive act (for graphic illustrations, see Capoeira 1995, 2002).

Indeed, Capoeira frequently helped capoeirista slaves carry on with life regarding whatever circumstances might happen to pop up. For, like Capoeira, life doesn't correspond to its appearances. The world of the slaves' imagination penetrated their world of blood, sweat, tears, and death. Their imagined world could come alive in the Roda, where all humans stand on the same ground, and they will rise or fall according to ways of their *malícia*, their ability to improvise, and their skills.

MERELY SUPREME DISSEMBLERS?

But a dissenting voice might be heard. "Come now, Capoeira as deception? Really! If so, is the capoeirista no more than a con artist? If deception is Capoeira art's chief characteristic, should it not be despicable rather than laudable?"

Well, no, not really. For survival purposes during the slavery period, deception was often the only available option when open rebellion was not feasible. Granted, dissembling is an act of deceit, a special form of deceit. The capoeirista slave dissembles, and he appears to be someone he is not. He gives the appearance of happiness when in fact he is sad. In so doing, he is not exactly lying or deceiving those around him. He is presenting himself in a manner other than who he, himself, is becoming at the moment he presents himself as someone he is not. He is misrepresenting himself by his gestures and body language. He might be in a bad mood; nevertheless he takes on a positive appearance by use of subtle nonverbal cues without necessarily having to say "Yassa masta, we're all in high spirits!" If he lies in this manner, he does so with his mouth. But he doesn't only lie; he also dissembles with his body, often without the need of saying anything at all. The danger is that if he dissembles long enough, his dissembling act might eventually fall into forgetfulness. And he then dissembles, unaware of the fact. Survival through dissembling thus becomes part of his very nature; his dissembling is dissembling out of ignorance. There is no longer any resistance through conformity. There is no more than the appearance of zombie-like obedience.

Today's capoeirista, like the wise capoeirista slave in times past, must always be aware that his dissembling act is like a performance on a stage as if it were conformity concealing resistance. He must never play out his role in ignorance. In this manner he is not really dishonest, nor is he simply innocent. He is painfully aware of his present condition: he knows he must dissemble in order to survive, and he must maintain constant vigilance over his dissembling act. In other words, his dissembling, unlike lying and dishonesty emerging out of ignorance or innocence, must be a conscious act of prevarication. As a dissembler, he can pretend a role he does not feel, while he is aware of the distance between his dissembling performance and his true self. He is presenting another self, not necessarily a false or fake self, but another self, a self he knows he must present, for he hardly has any alternative. He consciously and conscientiously performs the role of someone he knows he is not. He is dissembling, willfully disregarding that self that might otherwise have been presented. He is creating, improvising a self other than that which he would otherwise present and other than what would otherwise be expected of him in a given situation.

Then one might wish to query is this not indicative of complete lack of morality? Does it not imply a total absence of scruples? Not necessarily. Traditionally speaking, the capoeirista as slave and the post-abolition capoeirista as dissembler is not by his very nature morally bankrupt. It might be the case that the dissembling individual does what he does as a matter of survival in the big wide world where he must confront the dominant society. For if not, he may pay the consequences of contempt, exploitation, repression, discrimination, and violence, and on occasion even death. However, he presents another face entirely within his own community; this face is his genuine self, for he is now among his people and no longer has to resist through conformity.

The capoeirista, in short, must be a supreme dissembler. He gives his partner a smile when in pain. He puts on a face of pain when readying himself for an attack. He makes a fake attack to the left and gets his partner to draw back so that he becomes vulnerable. He extends his hands, pleading for mercy, when he knows he can get the better of his partner whenever he wishes. He is also adept at reading his partner's deception. At the same time the capoeirista must be engaging in his own dissembling practices for the purpose of duping somebody else. Jeremy Campbell's fascinating book *The Liar's Tale: A History of Falsehood* (2001) may lead one to assume that Capoeira pretense and deception are just other ways of saying lying. However, the original capoeiristas practiced deception for what could be considered a worthy cause. So now one might wish to argue that deceiving for a worthy cause could easily be converted into deceiving for any cause, whether worthy or not. However, Capoeira deception brings high stakes with it: survival. In this case, I would suggest that deception or false conformity coupled with covert resistance for the purpose of survival is justifiable: it is the only way open to the powerless when confronting the powerful.

Even after the interpretative license I've allowed myself in this brief section, I feel I'm still not doing the topic justice. Though the capoeirista is a dissembler, there is much more.

WOMEN RESISTING THE "WOMAN'S PLACE": CAPOEIRA-LIKE TACTICS?

If you will indulge me, then, I will strike out on another digression. Consider the woman's place, traditionally speaking. When women knew their place was in the kitchen keeping things spic and span—or perhaps I should say, they thought they knew because they were supposed to think they knew—most carried out their role honestly and forthrightly. But did they really? What if we consider their carrying out their role of conformity dishonesty, for their role didn't reveal who they really were but the mold within which society had placed them? If this is the case, then if and when they deviated from that role as a matter of resistance, then, they were actually being honest with themselves, for their deviation defined who they really were.

With this problem in mind, philosopher and feminist Judith Butler in *Gender Trouble* (1990) tries to come to terms with Simone de Beauvoir's (1952) puzzling idea that a woman is not born a woman; rather, she becomes one, because of social coercion. Butler writes at length that the term "woman" in any language is not a biological given, but something human cultures have constructed. When a woman has become properly "programmed," she performs in such a way as to reinforce the meaning of woman in her particular culture. This, de Beauvoir tells us, is dishonesty. The body learns to behave (conform) like a woman, and this body learning becomes entrenched to the extent that women act and react in accord with tradition (and devoid of resistance). Eventually the individual can become ignorant of her dishonesty; she comes to believe that this is the way life must be, that there is no other conceivable way. But what if she takes on a different strategy by dissembling that she is someone other than who she ordinarily would be? She goes against the current of her accustomed role. In doing so she becomes less ignorant of her prior dishonesty, for sure. She is now smarter, and to boot, she is honest. But is she now not simply dissembling in another guise? At first that might seem to be the strategy. She dissembles in order to become more genuine and less dishonest—she becomes more genuine by resisting within her role of conformity. In so doing, she subverts the system. She willfully chooses a tactic that deviates from the norm, and her new performance evinces an honesty she previously didn't have. So she is dissembling. Yet her dissembling act emerges from her genuine self, and she is now more genuinely herself. But in order to become herself, she must put on a dissembling act. Strange, all this. It's much like Capoeira's strangeness.

I've often heard it said by male capoeiristas that women are by nature superior in the fine art of Capoeira than men, since for survival value in a male dominated society they have been forced to become adroit dissemblers. They had to learn deception in order to become competitive (Bruhns 2000:39–46). Whether this is the case or not—who am I to say?—I would prefer to follow the tactic picked up by Mestra Jararaca. Actually, Jararaca is her *Nome de Guerra* (warrior name, the name she goes by in capoeirista circles). A jararaca is a lethally venomous snake found in Brazil. That should give you an idea. Figuratively speaking the word "jararaca" is also attached to an annoying and sometimes ugly woman; this, I must hasten to add, is not the case with Mestra Jararaca, who is quite attractive.

Jararaca tells the women in her class, usually teenagers and young adults, that the days are over when a woman can whimper and claim incompetence for the purpose of winning the sentiments of a male companion and endowing him with a sense of manliness in his lending her his protection. Now, Jararaca counsels, women must either stand on their own two feet or they wilt. The female capoeirista must be a warrior, who is determined to attain skillful Capoeira moves and manifest creative improvisation equal to the best men on the block. If not, she might as well give it up here and now and be done with it, for she will get no pity in the Capoeira ring. When young ladies in Jararaca's class complain that they can't make a move according to the model she presented to them, I've known her to run over—not walk mind you—and give the student a swift kick in the *bunda* (butt). Capoeira moves are neither a man nor a woman thing. They are simply a Capoeira thing; they know no gender; they know no age—and yes, I've received a few unexpected blows to my *bunda* too, when I wasn't putting out the effort she demanded. Back to de Beauvoir and Butler and women on deception.

Perhaps we would like to say that a woman's dissembling is to honesty as her ignorance is to dishonesty. But how dishonest is her dishonesty if that is how she was brought up in her culture? How can we say that her performance is out of ignorance if that is how she has learned to perform? And if she performs well, is she is not doing so in accord with and by giving a nod to the customs of her times? Consider the problem this way. She has learned to perform according to the norm. When she obediently performs, she does so for others. In so doing she is honest with respect to those others; yet she is ignorant and dishonest in regard to herself. In contrast, if she conscientiously dissembles in order to give the others the idea she is conforming to the norm when actually she is resisting, she is honest with and more aware of herself. But she is violating the norm; hence she is not true to her customs.

How did she learn to become honest with herself while violating the norms of her culture? Was she really and truly practicing deception? Or was it simply as if, for example, she were simulating pain when she was actually not in pain? According to her role, if she is in pain but must attend to her duties anyway, she simulates nonpain in order to give the appearance she can effectively play out her role. She is dishonest in addition to ignorant with herself. Then, when not in pain, if she simulates pain in order to avoid her responsibilities, responsibilities that are unjust and morally wrong since she knows she shouldn't really have to sacrifice herself in this way for the well being of husband, family, friends, and associates, she is in a sense more honest with herself. She is honest with herself through her dissembling that she is experiencing something she is not experiencing. In a sense, so to speak, it is as if she were lying.

Lying. That word again. Now I seem to have jumped from the frying pan into the fire. If after everything is said and done, dissembling women and capoeiristas are no more than liars, then where, pray tell, can we find anything laudable in the clever art of Capoeira?

Ludwig Wittgenstein, philosopher and creator of language games, such as buying and selling, courting, teaching and learning, praying, commanding and obeying, tells us that lying is a language game we must learn along with all other language games. He then writes about his canine friend's natural born honesty: "Why cant a dog simulate pain? Is he too honest? Could one teach a dog to simulate pain? Perhaps it is impossible to teach him to howl on particular occasions as if he were in pain, even when he is not. But the surroundings that are necessary for his behaviour to be real simulation are missing" (1953:§250).

Humans can learn to lie with the greatest of ease, but even more intelligent animals cannot. That is a commonly held assumption by most humans, it would appear. There is a problem here. If Judith Butler is correct when she writes that we are deceiving ourselves when we play out the roles an unjust society hands down to us, then from the very beginning we did so as a matter of course, without necessarily having previously learned how to lie. The only way we can strike out on the winding road toward honesty is by becoming aware we are living in self-deceit and then dissembling we are someone other than who we would ordinarily be according to the norm. Thus we become honest. That is to say, we were deceiving ourselves all along, but didn't know it, and now that we know it we can knowingly practice a new form of deceit in order to cease practicing our unknowing deceit. In this manner of speaking, complete absence or emptiness of lying preceded the original lie (or self-deceit), which preceded awareness of that lie that could then lead to honesty.

But do we really reach honesty only by piling deceit upon deceit. Are we, when all is said no more than natural born liars? Wittgenstein himself asks how it is that we could learn how to lie if we had never before done so. If we had no idea how we could become someone other than who we were, how could we learn to do so? The task seems as hopeless as our teaching a dog to lie.

The concept of negation, of *not*, is crucial here. Why? Because it is more than the product of mere opposition or contradiction. It is the relationship between what something *is* and what it is not, the not which, like emptiness, in reality includes everything, absolutely everything, that is *not* that which *is*. Significantly enough, Wittgenstein immediately following the above quote, writes: "What does it mean when we say: "I can't imagine the opposite of this" or "What would it be like if it were otherwise?"—For example, when someone has said that my images are private or that only I myself can know whether I am feeling pain, and similar things" (1953:§251). My pain is *not* some other person's pain. My pain is also *not* a dog, a tree, a chair, a stone, or anything else in the world. What my pain is *not* is absolutely everything other than what it *is*. If our above lady friend is *not* in pain and she simulates pain, the world of her simulation is *not* what it *would be* if she were performing a non-pain role. When she begins dissembling, everything in her world changes to a greater or lesser degree. In other words, when we pretend, we are living in an entirely different world. Let's listen to Wittgenstein again:

> Pretending is, of course only a special case of someone's producing (say) expressions of pain when he is not in pain. For if this is possible at all, why should it always be pretending that is taking place—this very special pattern in the weave of our lives? A child has much to learn before it can pretend. (A dog cannot be a hypocrite, but neither can he be sincere.) There might actually be a case where we should say 'this man *believes* he is pretending." (1953: §228–229)

Perhaps a dog can be neither a hypocrite nor sincere. But we can safely assume that he at least knows when and where to plant himself in front of the door so as to meet his master when she appears at the doorway at the same time each day after work. However, is it possible for the dog to create an imaginary scenario in which his master does not appear at the otherwise expected time? Or, can he imagine that the familiar person will not come through the door at the usual time and believe his imaginary construct? It's quite doubtful. To create such an imaginary situation and believe in it is to create another world, an alternative world, a parallel world. Creation of imaginary worlds, it would seem, lies at the heart of distinctly human communication.

And yet, the roots of this capacity for communication also exist in animal forms of behavior. Anthropologist, psychiatrist, ecologist, and general systems philosopher Gregory Bateson writes an essay about play. He begins with a couple of dogs scampering about the lawn and nipping at each other. I'm sure you've seen the act. The canine friends nip rather than bite each other; they are play fighting. Bateson writes that the nip constitutes a sign that is less than, yet it is a part of, the complete sign denoting bite. The bite denotes something like 'this is war," while the nip denotes "this is play." This situation is unlike that of the two dogs engaged in a fight. In nipping activity the one dog creates a sign representing the opposite of what would ordinarily be created in fight activity. Consequently, the sign denoting "this is war" is negated. Now, however, the message denoting "this is play" is part of the message denoting "this is war." Hence part of a sign (nip) does not denote what the whole sign (bite) would ordinarily denote. Moreover, war activity is similar to play activity (Bateson 1972:177–193). So a nip is not only part of the bite; it is also a metaphor of the bite. What is the gist of this?

Let nip and bite be a basic set of signs, and let "this is play" and "this is war" be messages engendered by the signs. Since the nip is part of the bite, call the nip-bite interrelation "metonymy" (a figure of speech using a word to signify something else it would ordinarily not signify; a nip is less than and part of a bite, thus the metonymic relationship is part to whole). And since play activity is similar to war activity, call this interrelation "metaphor," a figure of speech using a word whose meaning is comparable to that of another word; play activity is like war activity, thus play is a metaphor for war. To use a nip is to convey a message that means something other than but yet something similar to what it would ordinarily mean. In this sense a message conveyed by nip is fictitious. The receiver of the message must be aware that it is meant to be interpreted figuratively rather than literally. But confusion can ensue. One dog might nip another dog—part for whole—which denotes the equivalent of play activity that is analogous to war activity. But the nip seemed rather aggressive, so the second dog interprets the message as if it were the real item, taking it for war. A fight breaks out, perhaps until one animal marks off a sign that denotes the opposite of those signs denoting war activity. If this occurs, the two dogs may subsequently resume their play activity.

Our dissembling canine gladiators, we must suppose, are incapable of communicating explicitly *about* nips and bites: they either nip or they bite, or they go from one activity to the other one with the proper nonlinguistic cues. They engage in a rudimentary form of communication *about* their communication insofar as the distinction between play activity and war activity is made by a more-or-less variation of the same message, and insofar as the context surrounding the activity in which the two animals are engaged to a major degree determines how the message will be interpreted. Since one sign can constitute part of another sign within the same context, and when using that sign it must refer to itself but on distinct levels, the nip-bite context entails essentially a paradoxical situation. War activity and play activity, although similar in a metaphorical sense, depict two incompatible wholes at distinct levels. In contrast, nips and bites that create messages within these two activities exist at the same level of organization.

Now what bearing does all this have on the problem of Capoeira deception and dissembling? First, as we shall see below, Capoeira is play. It is in this respect like nipping activity. In the form of play, like nipping, it is also metaphorical of the game of war, struggle, fighting. Capoeira may be play (as if it were conformity), but figuratively speaking, it is of the nature of war (resistance). In a manner of speaking, it is what it is (play, conformity), and it is not what it is (it is war, resistance). At the same time, it is neither what it is nor is it not what it is, because it is something else: it is Capoeira. And, as Capoeira, in view of the above comments on Sacks's patients and the extralinguistic nature of deception, play-war, dance-struggle, song-challenge, frivolous-serious, and so on, is caught up in ambiguous, self-contradictory, paradoxical interdependent, interrelated, interactive processes at the deepermost levels of communication. These are the levels of communication humans share with other organisms, as in the Bateson and Wittgenstein examples. They are also the levels where, to evoke Judith Butler's concept, humans become honest with themselves by breaking the rules and practicing what would otherwise be deemed dishonesty.

As far as my aging body permits, I've participated chiefly with a Capoeira Angola group under Mestres Rapôsa and Jararaca. Angola capoeiristas, and most specifically those of Rapôsa's group, shun the idea of Capoeira as war, struggle, and fight. Rapôsa once explained that the concept of Capoeira entails struggle and battle. But playing Capoeira in a Roda should not be construed as a competitive war between two antagonists (although this is Capoeira according to its definition among some Capoeira Regional schools). Rather, while in the Roda, Capoeiristas engage in a highly ritualized form of playacting. They are actors on stage: the Roda. On the other hand, Capoeira *is* a struggle in the sense that today's capoeiristas, like capoeiristas during their slave past, engage in Capoeira play as a metaphorical battle against the dominant society in their effort to salvage a modicum of human dignity. That, I would submit, is Capoeira struggle in its most profound sense.

All this is to say that Capoeira in general, like Sacks's, Bateson's, Butler's, and Wittgenstein's examples, defies explicit classification. It's not something you can slap a word onto and be done with it. I repeat: it's something you must get a feel for. Get a feel for, since you must always be ready for the unexpected. In other words, the tacit, metaphorical advice is: "Olha a cobra que morde" (Watch out for the snake that bites) from a popular Capoeira song. Get a feel for Capoeira by becoming actively engaged with it, while cautiously observing what goes on within the Roda, and if you're lucky you may become more effectively aware of, and you may more successfully be able to cope with, your everyday world out there. Then, and only then, you can become a genuine dissembler.

"Get a feel for? Really? That's an inordinately vague way to put the matter. Is it not?" Yes, I see I'll have to try again in my effort to account for that form of life called Capoeira.

Chapter Three

How the Art Is Becoming

QUALIFYING CAPOEIRA

Capoeira has been qualified as fortuitous play, serious struggle, game, sport, malícia, dance, ritual, musical performance, theater, drama, philosophy, and life. Indeed, if we take the whole of all Capoeira schools and philosophies into consideration, we will ultimately be forced to conclude that it is all of the above. At the same time, it is none of the above, that is, if we take each one of the qualifying terms for Capoeira living within the whole of Capoeira individually. We might at the deepest level resort to saying something like:

Capoeira não tem raça	Capoeira knows no race
Capoeira não tem cor	Capoeira knows no color
Capoeira está no sangue	Capoeira is in one's blood
Capoeira é só amor	Capoeira is simply love
(Vieira 1995:x)	

One might observe, then, that if Capoeira is all the qualifications I have attached to the term, and if it is at the same time none of them, then I am in big trouble. However, not really. That is, if we take things one at a time, while maintaining mindfulness that things can't effectively be taken one at a time. And why not? Because, with respect to the trio of terms I have adopted for this essay, Capoeira participation is interdependent, interrelated, and interactive.

What do I really mean by these words? Perhaps the most effective answer is: they mean what they do as words. The qualifying terms for Capoeira are "interdependent," "interrelated," "interconnected," and "interactive." You can't have one word without its counterpart, and indeed, without all the other qualifying words in the whole range of Capoeira stories and Capoeira action. The terms are interrelated, because, since you can't have the one without all the others, within the one there is something of the others such that they are interconnected, like the crossings of a finely knitted sweater. Take the sweater and separate one knotted overlap from another one by severing the yarn, then pull the loose end, and the entire piece of clothing unravels. The qualifying terms for Capoeira are also interactive, because they are always engaging with one another and they are always in the process of change, as the Capoeira process itself unfolds. In sum, the meanings of the qualifying terms for Capoeira are a matter of process: ongoing change within space and through time. Likewise for all the extralinguistic signs we might be able to draw from Capoeira living. Capoeira bodies in seemingly perpetual motion bring about now an image of play, now combat, now malícia, now dance, now musical rhythm, now ritual, now theater and drama, now sport, all of which compose an elaborate philosophy, a practicing philosophy of living. In short, every aspect of Capoeira living can be said to be complementary, in fact, incongruously complementary, with all other Capoeira aspects.

In order possible to render all this a bit more intelligible, let me resort to yet another tactic.

Capoeira as Game versus Play

Perhaps the nature of Capoeira exists in the interstices between game and play (Carse 1986; Caillois 1961). There is a problem, however. The difference between these words doesn't exist in Portuguese, for there is only one word: *Jogo*. Jogo can apply to basketball and football games as well as to children frolicking on the beach or engaging in a make-believe world of Mommy and Daddy and the kids in the form of dolls and toys. But the verb, *jogar*, cannot be used in the same way we use play in English as in playing an instrument. The word in Portuguese for playing an instrument is *tocar* (literally in English, to touch).

Capoeiristas customarily use the term *jogo* in the sense of joyful play (not game)—other words often used in connection with Capoeira are *vadiar* (to fool around, wander about, dawdle, go bumming), and *brincar* (to engage in gratuitous play, like children). The word *luta* (fight) rarely comes up—in fact, Mestres Rapôsa and Jararaca prohibit its use. This helps keep Capoeira activity closer to dancing and playing an instrument and singing. Capoeiristas don't fight a match. They play it, ideally with the pure joy of a wide-eyed child exploring the world through her freedom of movement. And it isn't a competitive game, for ideally there are no winners and losers—except for some proponents of Capoeira Regional who want to make it a competitive sport. Yes, tough guys, tough capoeirista guys, do dance, and they sing and play the Berimbau, and all the other instruments as well.

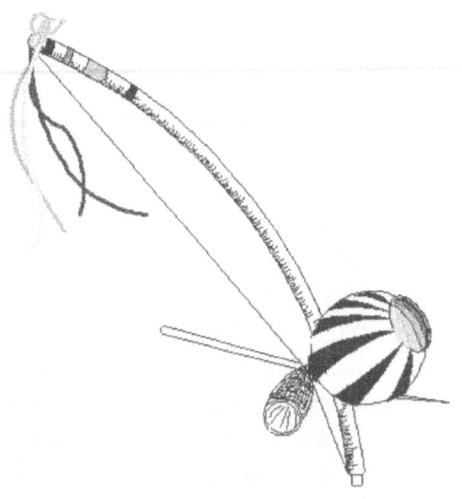

THE 'BERIMBAU' IMAGE—THE BOW A GOURD INSTRUMENT

Now, let games be defined as finite. They are usually guided by a rigid set of rules. In one form or another, they can include, in addition to sports, commerce, war, politics, mathematics, science, law, marriage, the arts and the humanities, and even religion. The goal is to win. Winners take all; losers hang their head in shame. There's no middle ground. You either triumph or you are defeated, by hook or by crook, honestly or by cheating. Of course you want to triumph, so you use whatever means you have in order to accomplish your goal. The end justifies the means. Let play be defined as "infinite." It is infinite, because there is no rigid code containing rules that ideally you must follow to the letter. In some play—make-believe scenes, friendly banter in the streets, barroom joke-telling marathons, free verse poetry, jazz, dance improvisation, and so on—you occasionally alter the rules as you go along and according to your strategy within the context of your play. In other forms of play—acting, movie making, painting, metrically oriented poetry, music played from a score, and so on—there are rules you must follow, but you're always allowed some degree of freedom. Play, then, is infinite, because there is in principle no end to the possibilities that might emerge in the future. Since there is no end, the means are in part or wholly created on the spot.

Games are structured by rigid boundaries: here/there, now/then, we/them, permitted/prohibited, legitimate/nonlegitimate, and so on. If you don't fit one side of the opposing categories, you must fit the other side. It's like a life-and-death matter. You win, and, surrounded by adulators, you live to enter the contest on another day. You lose, and you lose alone; you are out of the tournament; you might as well be dead. If you continue winning, you are given virtual immortality status. You have been able to do a slam-dunk on death. Since play, in contrast, knows of no ultimate winners or losers, all boundaries become vague, fuzzy. There is no all-or-nothing demarcation between life and death as far as play is concerned. You don't play in order to acquire some sort of sham immortality. You play simply because you are alive. Life is most fundamentally play, with little or no concern over death, since it hardly enters into the equation. Games are serious business. The play of life, in contrast, is joyous. It resounds with a kind of laughter. It is not laughter at the expense of others, but laughter with others.

Play, disrespectful of any and all boundaries, thus becomes inherently paradoxical. Games are predicated on oppositions, on antagonists engaged in a struggle. The overriding desire is to bring the action to a victorious conclusion. Since play knows of no ultimate winning or losing, players only desire is to continue playing, and when some other form of play catches their interest, the play takes a turn toward another form of play activity. There is no end, because play is life itself. The joyfulness found in play comes with a sense of knowing you somehow began something you can't finish.

Some of the labels one would ordinarily attach to games can under other circumstances be applied to play. Commercial art and art for material gain are games, for sure. But genuine art is play. Cubist artist Pablo Picasso played, and when fame and fortune happened to come his way, he continued to play much as before. If Picasso had donned a suit and tie and rubbed elbows with the rich and famous while commercializing his art, his play would have become more like a game. Physicist Albert Einstein also played. He dabbled with images, ideas, and formal abstractions like a child. He was always uncomfortable with success. For him, play was in the quest. He was always looking for the ultimate answer, the Grand Unified Theory of the universe. But he never found it. Had he found it, his play likely would have ended, for he would have had nowhere else to go. His play would have become like a game: closed. He would have won: the end, and that's all folks.

If science at its best is indeed genuine play, then the ultimate theory will not be found. If somebody were to find it, then there could be no more surprises. Science as quest would come to an abrupt halt. It would have all been a game after all, and the scientists finally conquered nature. Scientists who push their army of graduate students in the laboratory to the limit in their obsession with their reputation and with finding ultimate answers that will stand for all time are gamers. Scientists engaged in genuine play, by contrast, know there is no final answer to any problem, for there is no victory in the absolute sense.

Games look to the future. The goal entails triumph of the future over the past. Games are therefore purposeful: the future holds a reward, and he who gets there first gets the gold. For this reason, games are relatively easy to define. They specify what must happen in the future when the gamers are in combat. Play, in contrast, is excruciatingly difficult to define. Since each moment presents some new context and different circumstances, improvisation becomes the name of the play. In other words, play lives for the moment. Whatever the future brings, it will bring, and it will be negotiated whenever it enters into the present. Living for the moment, the player improvises according to the particular context and whatever the situation presents. If we live to play during each moment, the future will somehow take care of itself. Of course improvisation within play is not limited to Capoeira. Play is one of the most pervasive processes characterizing Brazilian culture. For example, popular musician Carlinhos Brown says of his feverish *timbalada* (drum rhythms during a vocal performance), "in Bahia it is customarily a disorderly ordered form, and orderly disorder. We organize the notes as we go along, and the drums lead the way.... With drums there's dialogue in the sound.... Everything's all mixed up" (in Guerreiro 2000:170, 184). Such also is life in Bahia: improvisation.

So much for play and games. Why do I bring this topic up? Because genuine Capoeira is play, play in the most profound sense. It is no game according to the definition I have given above.

Capoeira Music and Play

Aphasiacs, liars, dissemblers, play? So after such beating about the bush, how—one might wish to ask—can we get on with our professed topic in a forthright manner? Actually, it's not so difficult, since these preliminary topics are quite germane to the very idea of Capoeira. Let's begin by experiencing some action in an imaginary Capoeira Angola Roda.

A man and a woman are squatting, their faces turned toward a seated, elderly man, the Mestre, playing a Berimbau and voicing a song to initiate the Roda. The song is a solo (*Ladainha*), of the sort customarily sung by the Mestre and the Mestre alone. The Ladainha is the chant that creates the spirit of the art. It sets the mood, the mood the Mestre feels at the moment. If it is voiced effectively, even an initiate can intuit the spirit of this particular moment. I write 'this particular moment," because every moment is unique. Since Capoeira is play, every act is to an extent improvised and hence is one of a kind (Capoeira 1992:123). I might also add that the Mestre plays the lead Berimbau, called the *Gunga*. A second, smaller Berimbau, is usually called a *Médio*, and a third one, smaller still, is the *Viola*. Each Berimbau has its own rhythm and function. There is something deeply sad and spiritual about Berimbau music. Mestre Rapôsa, a natural born folk philosopher, once told me it is the appropriate instrument for communicating with natural forces and with the dead. This is because the pitch of each Berimbau is always at variance with that of the other berimbaus; each berimbau is always very carefully slipping off into another world.

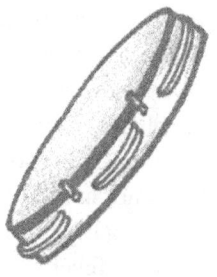

THE PANDEIRO (TAMBOURINE)

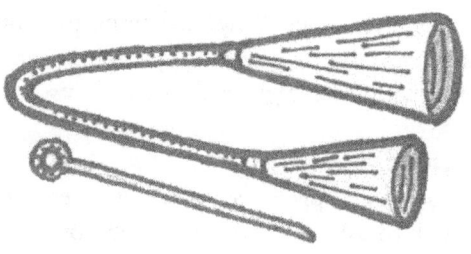

THE AGOGO (GONGS)

To the Mestre's right are two younger individuals, male and female, playing the smaller berimbaus. To their right, two people are playing tambourines (*Pandeiros*). Then there is somebody holding a gong with two bells (*Agôgô*), and following him is a woman with a bamboo scraper (*Reco-Reco*). They are not playing at this moment; yet they are ready for action on cue. Finally, a man is sitting behind a tall drum (*Atabaque*), also awaiting the moment to initiate his rhythm. The solo chant (*Ladainha*) ends. The *Agôgô*, *Reco-Reco*, and *Atabaque* begin creating their own variations of the beginning rhythm. All eight people, along with the players around the Roda, enter into another song (the *Entrada* or *Chula*). This song consists of a call by the leader playing the large Berimbau followed by a chorused response. After the *Entrada*, the Mestre, or perhaps one of the students, belts out the third type of chant, the *Corrido*:

O meu Senhor, que é dono da terra	Oh my Lord, who is Master of the land
Protege este povo	Protect these people
Que já está na guerra	Who are now at war
O meu Senhor, que é dono da lua	Oh my Master, who is Lord of the moon
Protege ás crianças	Protect the children
Que moram na rua	Who live in the streets

The two people squatting have now received an okay sign from the Mestre. They cross themselves and, facing each other for a second or so, stretch their bodies horizontally less than a foot from the floor, balanced in a seemingly impossible way on one hand and supported by an elbow at the lower portion of the rib cage (a *Queda de Rins*).

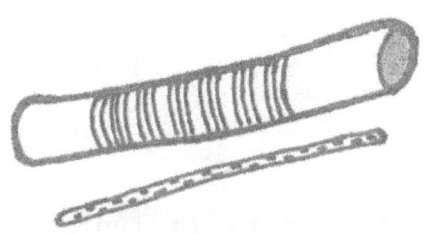

THE RECO-RECO (SCRAPER)

Then they slowly, cautiously, begin moving toward the center of the Roda of about four yards in diameter, around which there are about fifteen people seated on the floor with legs crossed and clapping their hands and chanting. Movement toward the center of the Roda may go like this. With her body in the lowest possible position, the person to the right slowly arcs her leg over the back or her partner, while he is at the same time gyrating his body away from her and bringing his left leg around and over her. They continue, apparently entangling their bodies together, but not quite, since at the point where they could lock their partner's torso in a leg or arm hold they slither out. At the same time they are gradually directing their movements to the midpoint of the Roda. When they are at the center, with rhythmic, undulating movements, they slowly rise and begin what appears to be a dance step (*Ginga*). This step consists of alternating shifts of body weight from the right to the left leg, backward and forward and to the right and the left, in a rocking motion. It is all done to the rhythm of the instruments and songs. The rocking and swaying motion reminds one of a fisherman in his small boat, trying to maintain his balance while the boat is bounced to and fro by the waves—in this sense, the Ginga is comparable to the dance activity within *Candomblé* and *Samba*—about which more below. At the same time the person's arms are moving back and forth and forward as if in a sculling or rowing motion. Indeed, the word "Ginga" can mean to sway or waddle as well as to scull, as in rowing.

THE ATABAQUE (DRUM)

The *Ginga* is the most basic of Capoeira moves. If the lead berimbau, the *Gunga*, sets the mood, the Ginga initiates the action. It is neither an attack nor a defensive move, yet it contains the possibility for both. Any experienced capoeirista will tell you that, above all else, you must always engage in the Ginga. It is always present, in the Roda, and outside the Roda. When you walk you are *Gingando* (walking with a Ginga rhythm), when you talk your body is Gingando, when you listen you are Gingando, when you eat you are Gingando, when you sleep and dream, you are Gingando, when you make love you are Gingando, when you defecate you are Gingando—in fact, there is a Capoeira position called the *Cocorinha*, the word to indicate the squatting position. Life is Ginga. Ginga provides the flow of Capoeira play; it is the flow of life; it is life itself. A Mestre might even tell you he has experienced trance-states during play as a result of his incessantly Gingando (Chnaiderman 1989). Indeed, Gingando, one is incessantly improvising: now, going with the flow, now conforming, now resisting, now negotiating, now, eluding any and all attempts to hog-tie one into submission (Sodré 1999:226). It is significant, in this light, that Brazilian soccer and Carnival Samba are variants of Ginga moves. In sum, Ginga, along with its complementary, *malandragem* (carrying on like a sly bad-ass), entail a certain knack for Brazilian becoming, for the becoming of being Brazilian, as Heloisa Bruhns (2000:147) puts it.

Activity within the Roda now picks up, as the chant takes a new form of calls and responses:

Marinhheiro, marinheiro	Sailor, sailor
Marinheiro só	Lonely sailor
Quem te ensinou a navigar?	Who taught you to navigate?
Marinheiro só	Lonely sailor
Foi o tombo do navio?	Was it the wake of a ship?
Marinheiro só	Lonely sailor
Ou foi o balanço do mar?	Or was it the rolling of the sea?
Marinheiro só	Lonely sailor

The Capoeira partners in the ring are now in a prone position, Gingando, always Gingando, and, crouched low, they make swinging motions with their legs, to the right, to the left, a fake kick here, a head butt there, while the opponent is busy setting up a defense in order to prepare himself for a bit of counteroffensive.

And,... what's this? The female capoeirista is singing along with the instruments, with a big smile on her face as she rhythms around the Roda, while looking directly into the eyes of her partner. Now we begin to understand why this is not merely a game. It can also take on the countenance of carefree, joyous play! They are not really fighting at all, but going through the motions. They are dissembling while engaged in mock fighting. In its contemporary dress Capoeira is a ritual, an age-old ritual they are playing out in commemoration of the injustices suffered by slaves during bygone times. They, along with the instrument players and the capoeiristas sitting round the Roda, are in a theater, and the action is a play; it is an enaction of the human condition as it should be, a community of people in communion with one another. So this is what Capoeira is all about! The Roda is a microcosm where the grand human drama is played out.

Now the female partner abruptly turns and places both hands on the floor, still eyeing the other person from between her legs. Then she does a quick hand-stand with legs cocked as if ready to unleash them in the direction of her partner's belly. He nimbly cartwheels away from her, landing on one foot, and then arches the other foot in her direction, but with his leg retracted just enough so as to make no actual contact. She lithely drops to the floor, balancing herself with one hand and then a leg. Then she turns, with back to the floor, and, supported with both hands behind her and one leg in front of her, she does a feigned jab with her other foot. He rapidly draws back and prepares to retaliate, as she rises to a prone position. Poised on one foot, he arcs his back and brings about his own jab with his right foot (*benção*), careful not to extend his foot too far so as to come in contact with her.

All the while, they maintain close vigil on one another. Their eyes never take leave of each other. As the song comes to a close, the Mestre breaks into another one and picks up the tempo. All instruments follow suit. The *Viola* sings, da—da—da—do—da—do, and the Berimbau *Médio* does its thing, da—da—da—do—do, both of them following the Gunga's cadence, do—da –da—da—do—da—da—da—do—do—do—do—do—da—da—do—da. *Pandeiros* shiver and shake, Agôgô dings and dongs, Reco-Reco scrapes, Atabaque dum-dum-de-dum-dums. The rhythm is now lively.

The male capoeirista breaks into a wide grin and gestures to the right, and then quickly does a pirouette to the left with his left let arched high. She once again falls to the floor, does one more quick handstand, and momentarily holds her inverted position, eyeballing him, with a sly smile. He circles around her. She gyrates on her hands, then falls on her feet toward him and slips to the floor with her torso twisted and her legs extended in the form of a pair of scissor. Then she rapidly locks his legs at the knees between her legs and tightens her grip. He extends both hands as if to say "I give up," and theatrically looks at the sky, crossing himself in the form of a petition to the gods for divine guidance. The audience roars with approval. Both partners approach the head songster, the Mestre. They squat, pensively, then they slowly cross themselves, and begin anew. That's a possible scene from among the virtual infinity of scenes when playing (*jogando*) Capoeira. I should point out in passing that the Berimbaus, accompanied by the other instruments, can produce a wide number of rhythms or *toques*. These rhythms vary according to the Capoeira play. The number and types of rhythms depends on whether the group follows Capoeira Angola, Capoeira Regional, or perhaps some combination of the two. Most Mestres are known to have developed a repertoire of rhythms for their group, some of the rhythms of their own making. Some of the most common rhythms go by the names of São Bento Grande, São Bento Pequeno, Benguela, Cavalaria, and Luna. (for further, see Almeida 1986:67–86).

FIGURE 1
THE CAPOEIRA RING

Figure 1 gives us an image of the Roda. Section I consists of the instruments. From right to left, we have the Mestre with the lead berimbau, the gunga, the middle berimbau, the médio, and the small berimbau, the viola. Then come two Pandeiros, an Agôgô, a Reco-Reco, and an Atabaque. Sections W represent capoeiristas who are hopefully in wait along the periphery of the Roda to enter Capoeira play with their partner on the other side of the Mestre and the instrument players. Section A is the audience. All are seated in the circle, clapping hands and singing. The small circles, P, are two partners in a squatting position before the Mestre awaiting the cue to begin their Capoeira moves within the Roda, depicted by the squiggly lines showing that after an indefinite number of moves they return to their original position to cross themselves, pay homage to their Mestre, and give each other a hand shake or a hug.

The Roda is a world within a world, metaphor of a larger society, yet it is both like and unlike that society. It is the circle where the Ginga begins. Circle where rhythm begins. After Capoeira play comes to a close within the Roda, it never really ends, for the capoeirista walks more lightly. He returns to his day-to-day reality, with the same problems he left aside during his brief time in the Roda. But, as he nurtures and fortifies his outlook on life as a result of his times in the Roda while *gingando*, things gradually begin to change. His problems are the same, but they no longer oppress him. It is not the problems that have changed, but the capoeirista himself, when in the Roda. Capoeira has changed his outlook on life" (Capoeira 1999:124–125).

Just Dialoguing

As suggested above, Capoeira is dialogue, with words and with body. But the idea of Capoeira dialoguing I have alluded to isn't simply a matter of words and nothing but words. There are words, of course, in the lyrics, and in perhaps a minimum of talk between partners. But the dialogue is primarily extralinguistic. It has to do with signs that resist precise linguistic windowdressing. This is where kinesthetics and somatics put on their best act.

Kinesthetics the sensing of body position, presence, or movement, principally from stimulation of sensory nerve endings and in muscles, tendons, and joints. Kinesthetics involves that feeling in the gut with respect to what you are doing, your entire body and mind, and with respect to the harmony—or lack thereof—between yourself and your environment. And somatics: that which pertains to the whole body as distinguished from everything other than the body. Together, kinesthetics and somatics involve sensations and effects of sight and sound and touch and smell and even taste. Hereafter in this inquiry I will combine the two words into one: kinesomatics. Kinesomatics pervades Capoeira action. In academic circles languages and texts are customarily prioritized, and the kinesthetic signs of the body are often ignored. In contrast psychologist Howard Gardner (1983), for one, puts bodily-kinesthetic knowing in his seven classes of "multiple intelligences"—though he virtually ignores smells and tastes (for a study of the senses that includes all the senses, see Classen 1993; Howes 1991; Stoller 1989; Synnott 1993; merrell 2000b, 2003a). The combined term "kinesomatics" complements "proprioception," a sense of the body's position and movement within its environment—used prevalently by Oliver Sacks (1990)—and "motility," a combination of mental imagery and body motion in the creation of spontaneous physical activity—in the sense of Maurice Merleau-Ponty (1962; also Cataldi 1993).

A brief discussion of kinesomatic knowing may help us get a better handle on the extralinguistic nature of Capoeira. A mime performance by Marcel Marceau draws on a form of knowing we all know but ordinarily do not notice. We can recognize it but cannot adequately describe it, for it is virtually indescribable. Kinesomatic knowing is by and large tacit knowing, knowing that exists in the body, where knowing *how* to do things resides. This knowing *how* comes into play when you ride your bicycle, drive your car, play tennis, play a musical instrument, or draw a cartoon figure. You know how to do what you do but you run into problems when someone asks you to explain precisely and concisely what it is that you know and how you do what you do. This knowing *how* in many instances can be taught by example, but hardly by explicit instruction. It is learned not exclusively by explicit means but by following examples, mimicking the master, imagining and feeling the body going through certain motions and then actually bringing about those motions—like the athlete imagining her performance before actually stepping onto the track to do it.

Think, for example, of a disparate collection of comedians—Charlie Chaplin, Cantinflas (Mario Moreno, the Mexican comic), Carol Burnett, Bill Cosby, Robin Williams—and their extralinguistic, kinesomatic capacity for sending signs to their audience. Think of athletes—Michael Jordan, Sammy Sosa, Joe Montana, Venus and Selena Williams—as they do what they do in such rapid succession that they couldn't possibly reason out all of their moves. Think of actors—Robert de Niro, Meryl Streep, Sidney Poitier, Andy Garcia, Denzel Washington, Jodie Foster—who can give voice inflections to their words and make facial gestures and body language in apparently the most natural way. These examples can hopefully give you a feel for the kinesomatics about which I am trying to write, but regarding which my words are inadequate to the task. So I inevitably fail when I attempt to articulate kinesomatics. Nevertheless, I would suggest that your own feeling for kinesomatics can complement what I am trying to put in words. In this manner, my words and your feelings and sensations can perhaps somehow get close to the mark.

With respect to kinesomatic knowing, there is no clear-cut distinction between the physical and the mental, the active and the reflective, or between feeling and intellection. However, our preconceptions, deeply embedded in our very psyche as a result of our proper upbringing, dictate that thought or mind-stuff is the universal imperative, and everything else trails along behind as best it can. But we do not and cannot live by the force of mind alone. The body has its own form of knowing and thinking about which the mind knows little. This form of knowing and thinking is paramount in skilled activities—like those of the above-mentioned performers when they are at their best. Take the artist with brush in hand and carefully placing paint on the canvas before her, the machinist at her workbench, or the surgeon conducting an operation. They are intensively focused on the task at hand and the signs it involves—a drive toward the basket, the diameter of a piece on the lathe, the brain tumor now revealed to the eye.

At the same time, they are nonfocally or peripherally (kinesomatically) attuned to a myriad array of signs in the near vicinity. The skilled performance submits to the performer's central control tower, and in near simultaneity signs are picked up from the environment, with awareness that the unexpected always stands a chance of occurring. Although after the fact the performer may be able, with a greater or lesser degree of verbal aplomb, to describe and explain her actions, during the performance the body did what it does best, in many instances with hardly a nod to the mind, which was simply not nimble enough to keep up with the action. Along these lines, anthropologist Ruth Benedict (1946:269) reports on teaching children calligraphy in Japan. The instructor takes the child's hand and guides it through an ideograph, thus giving a feel for the activity. This exercise is carried out before words of encouragement and explicit instruction enter the picture. In this manner body learning to a degree precedes mind learning, implicitness precedes explicitness.

Playing a musical instrument, dancing before an audience, acting out a part in a play or a movie, going through a gymnastics sequence, all these activities are more kinesomatic than cognitive and mental, more a matter of feeling than form, more the product of action than reason or reflection. And they are, during the course of their enactment, chiefly wordless. In this vein, Norman Mailer in one of his novels writes of pugilism as follows:

> There are languages other than words, language of symbol and languages of nature. There are languages of the body. And prizefighting is one of them. A prizefighter ... speaks with a command of the body which is as detached, subtle, and comprehensive in its intelligence as any exercise of the mind. [He expresses] himself with wit, style, and an aesthetic flair for surprise when he boxes with his body. Boxing is a dialogue between bodies, [it] is a rapid debate between two sets of intelligences. (in Lowe 1977:255)

The body? Intelligent? Yes. A kinesomatic intelligence the nature of which, when body is doing what it does, it leaves mind in large part unaware. Dialogue, extralinguistic dialogue? Yes also. Silent dialogue. Dialogic give-and-take without the need of words, like two squirrels playing hide-and-seek around a maple tree, like two pigeons doing their courtship thing, like the above example of two dogs nipping in a mock fight. There is a show of signs and a response, which elicits a counter response, and the action goes on.

Detached, subtle, and comprehensive? Of course. The conscious mind is too slow to become actively involved. The movements are of attenuation, a refinement that defies language; they are more subtle than the most carefully honed rhetorical figure, which, however fine spun, still depends upon language. And comprehensive, for the body can take in, and react to, a barrage of signs with hardly a moment's notice, faster than the eye can see, quicker than the most powerful computer. I could also write here of an inner sense of movement: the visualizer who imagines pole-vaulting at 20 feet and then does it. This entails a kinesomatic feel for things, the body in harmony with the mind: bodymind.

When Thought Becomes Tacit

Bodymind-kinesomatic activity is of numbing complexity. Howard Gardner (1983:210) writes that it calls upon 'the coordination of a dizzying variety of neural and muscular components in a highly differentiated and integrated fashion." For example, quickly toss a ball against a wall and retrieve it. There is intricate interaction between the eye and the hand. They work in coordination with one another, from feedback to response and anticipation of more feedback.

Such voluntary movements demand almost instantaneous comparisons and contrasts and action regarding similarities and differences. The eye and hand codependently rise to the occasion in order to do their thing in rapid-fire fashion. If you're a little rusty at a physical skill you once knew well, practice it a little, and your game will once again improve. It will improve, because in this case, after each try, your relatively sluggish mind can have time to appraise the situation and formulate instructions to the body so that next time it will hopefully perform with more style:

> Much voluntary motor activity thus features the subtle interaction between perceptual and motor systems. At least some activity, however, proceeds at so rapid a clip that feedback from perceptual or kinesthetic systems cannot be used. Particularly in the case of overlearned, automatic, highly skilled, or involuntary activities, the whole sequence may be "preprogrammed" so that it can unfold as a seamless unit with only the slightest modifications possible in light of information from the sensory systems. Only such highly programmed sequences will allow activities of the pianist, the typist, or the athlete, each of whom depends upon lengthy sequences of movement that unfold at great speed. (Gardner 1983:211)

"Idiot savants" or autistic children, for example, can be totally cut off from their community in terms of language—somewhat like Oliver Sacks's aphasiacs. But with respect to nonverbal communication, they may have remarkable powers, especially in the area of kinesomatic activity and spatial knowledge. Their paintings may be worthy of the greatest surrealists. Their ability to take in a scene in all its details is extraordinary. Their capacity for numbers is astounding. Their musical sensitivity leaves us dumbfounded. Other feats by such individuals are equally impressive, such as designing electrical wiring for a house, making a windmill out of a clock, creating musical compositions, reading a map to perfection with one perceptual grasp, giving the tally of a few dozen marbles strewn on the floor after a second or so. There is need of little to no language here. Hardly any talking is necessary. There is just sensing, knowing with *bodymind*, feeling what there is to feel in the bones, knowing with the certainty of the so-called lower organisms who have not learned those human virtues of disbelief, skepticism, cynicism, or nihilism.

In other words, to evoke the Capoeira spirit, in bodymind tacit knowing there is Axé, Axé that enables one simply and very subtly to know what must be done in the Roda, and one does it—that is, bodymind does it. Kinesomatics and Axé are of the most profound nature of Capoeira. Two bodyminds in silent dialogue negotiate. Negotiation begins with the Ginga; then a complex repertoire of moves develops, each move emerging according to the context and the personal style of the capoeiristas, the capoeiristas' personal styles complementing each other such that they set up a rhythm that spontaneously enacts a subtle wavering and weaving concert. Play proceeds; it must proceed, for the kinesomatic action must be ongoing; the action swings out along an indefinite number of possible lines, and where it will end nobody knows. But,... no,... that's not really the way to say it. For there can be no ending. After a rhythming session of Capoeira play, the partners shake hands, perhaps enter into an embrace or make a sign of the cross, and leave the Roda. The singing has stopped; people are releasing the taut strings of the Berimbaus and putting other instruments away. Others head for the rest room to change clothes, maybe take a shower. There are a lot of voices, perhaps some laughter, a little playful banter.

The match is over. But Capoeira isn't over, because the Roda is now the world, and Capoeira is life. Capoeira there will always be, for the capoeirista. In Bira Almeida's (1986:7) words, Capoeira "should always be present in our minds." Yet knowledge of Capoeira can never be "absolute because no one can explore the infinite possibilities of Capoeira regardless of methods, quality, or intensity of training." Methods, quality, and intensity of training are concrete, finite matters. Capoeira itself implies infinite possibilities. As such, Capoeira's playing out finite bits and pieces of this continuum of possibilities suggests that it is *process*. Process, but never finished product. Perpetual change in space and time, never a fixed repertoire of rules and moves. This notion cries out for further elucidation.

Chapter Four

How the Becoming Is Processual

Eu nasci pra capoeira	I was born for capoeira
capoeirista eu hei de ser	a capoeirista I must be
só deixarei a capoeira	I'll take my leave of capoeira,
quando eu morrer.	only when I die.
(Mestre Bola Sete 1997:78)	

FIVE FEATURES OF THE ELUSIVE NATURE OF CAPOEIRA
Honing in on the Word

A problem with the word "Capoeira" is that it is not a concrete something that gives us the illusion we can know it if we properly label it. Our problem isn't hopeless, however. We might get a feel for Capoeira through a form of nonverbalizable knowing—somewhat akin to kinesomatic knowing as briefly described in the previous chapter.

Suppose we have a musician and a guy who couldn't carry a tune if his life depended on it. The tone-deaf guy says, "I hear a bunch of notes, but I can't make out any melody." The musician assures him that what he hears is not just individual notes; they all combine to make up a beautiful whole, an unorthodox melody composed of twelve chromatic tones. Both musician and nonmusician hear the same individual notes as sound waves in the air, since they are endowed with common sensory equipment. But what about the melody? One person hears it, and the other person does not. Do the notes exist out there as so many sound waves while the melody is something totally distinct that only exists in the musician's imaginative mind? That would be a strange way of putting it. The musician hears the melody, or says so. But it is not a simple imagining, like a child imagining there is a goblin in the closet. For the musician, the melody exists. It is very real indeed. But it isn't a thing that exists out there like the notes, nor is it simply the product of the musician's imagination. On a more concrete level, the melody is real in much the same way other comparable activities are real. It is real because it is constructed in the musician's imaginative mind from the concretely real notes out there. But it is also nonreal, according to the nature of the beholder. It is "nonreal", because if there were nobody present capable of imagining and constructing the melody, it would remain nonreal, or the possibility of what might at some future moment become realized as a melody.

Here's another example. I've seen tourists gawking at sculptured male and female bodies in impeccable white garb going through the motions of sham Capoeira tailor-made for foreigners outside Modelo Market in Salvador, Bahia. These tourists from all parts of the world see legs flailing and arms flying and bodies gyrating. They are quite impressed with the acrobatics, and many of them take photographs of the action and appreciatively dig into their pockets for some money to place in the outstretched hand making its way from table to table. Do they see Capoeira? They see a lot of impressive moves, for sure. But they don't really see Capoeira. In fact, a Capoeira purist would tell us that Capoeira isn't there at all. What the tourists see is a fake: non-Capoeira posing as the genuine thing. It is concocted and dished out to gullible visitors. Were they to see the genuine article, they would not find it so attractive. Why? Because it is considerably less spectacular, especially relatively slow moving Capoeira Angola, but also Capoeira Regional. Real Capoeira is a matter of kinesomatic feeling, sensing, and thinking with respect to strategies improvised at each moment. There simply is no place for a lot of repetitive, rather robotic karate-like kicks and fancy cartwheels.

One day when Mestres Rapôsa and Jararaca were passing by Modelo Market on their way to the bus stop, they ran into my wife and me sitting at a table sipping a soda during a performance of this pseudo-Capoeira. I was embarrassed. What would they think of me, there, witnessing the goings on as if I was just another tourist? But to my surprise, after a few customary salutations, they paid our presence in the tourist trap hardly any mind. In fact, they became as engrossed with the performance as were the most attentive tourists. What did they see? In a manner of speaking they saw non-Capoeira, in contrast to the tourists, who thought they were watching Capoeira. With a knowing smirk on their face they were giving a cynical eye to this vulgarization of their venerated art.

Questions arise. What exactly do I mean by non-Capoeira? Is it simply the absence of Capoeira? If so, is it in any form or fashion real? If non-

Capoeira at the Model Market that goes as Capoeira isn't real, then how is it that there can be non-Capoeira? It would seem that first there must be something that goes by the name of Capoeira, and only then can there be an absence of Capoeira, or non-Capoeira. But actually, I should go a giant step backward and ask: If genuine Capoeira is real, then could it have become real if non-Capoeira (as the absolute absence of Capoeira) were not equally real? If that is the case, then should non-Capoeira, implying the possibility of Capoeira, precede the concept of Capoeira? If so, then non-Capoeira must precede Capoeira as the possibility for Capoeira before Capoeira can begin its becoming, its realization.

Now, perhaps, we're getting at the meat of the issue. There must first be non-Capoeira. It is the emptiness of, yet the possibility for the emergence of Capoeira—recall my earlier use of the term "emptiness." In this sense everything we conceive as real, before it was becoming real, made up the range of possibilities for the emergence of Capoeira, and everything else. We might say that non-Capoeira is empty of Capoeira and at the same time it is the possibility from which Capoeira can emerge, there, in some originally created Roda, prior to the first twang of a *Gunga* and the first shout, "*Iê!*" by a Mestre. Then, after Capoeira was created, a virtually unfathomable number of possibilities from within Capoeira could emerge during any and all instances of Capoeira play. In other words, first there was non-Capoeira, the emptiness of anything that could be called Capoeira; next there is an imaginary ring or Roda that separates the world inside from the world outside; then Capoeira began to emerge; it began its becoming. Now that Capoeira has been realized, whether there is a Roda going on or not, Capoeira is always ready to re-emerge at a moment's notice. This is because it is always becoming; it is living process. (I have vaguely alluded to emptiness much in the Buddhist sense, and below, I make additional reference to Buddhist philosophy. This is not out of any religious conviction. Simply put, I sense an affinity between emptiness and a sense of strangeness surrounding any and all attempts objectively to define Capoeira [for more on emptiness, see especially Glass 1995; Huntington 1989; Kalupahana 1986, 1987].)

Capoeira is in this sense like the melody for our musician who heard it, imagined it, and for whom it was real, at least at that particular moment. It was as real for the musician as anything else, though it did not exist, properly and physically speaking, and though it was not a thing. Had the musician heard a mere garble of notes, the concoction would have been real, but it would have been non-music? In comparable fashion, Rapôsa and Jararaca saw non Capocira at the Modelo Market. But when in the proper environment during a Roda, they customarily see Capoeira. What is this Capoeira they see? In the right context and in the right spirit, it is a collection of humans and instruments playing and mouths singing and bodies dancing and swaying and a lot of jostling moves to a rhythm. The entire context makes Capoeira what it is becoming every moment it has emerged as real. Capoeira is neither in the head, in the bodies moving about in the Roda, in the word Capoeira, nor in any connection between the word and the action. It's in the entire cultural context.

The first of five Capoeira qualifying features, then, is: there is no fixed thing or essence that can be called real capoeira, though capoeira itself as a contextual process emerging from non-capoeira is real.

Focusing on the Capoeirista

> The East has Zen
> Psychoanalysis was developed in the West
> In Brazil we have Capoeira.
> (Capoeira 1992:106)

Among dedicated students of Capoeira I've heard the suggestion that by losing yourself in Capoeira, you find yourself. In a manner of speaking, you must become egoless. This includes surrendering your will to Capoeira through your Mestre, whom you fear yet respect, whom you love yet occasionally resent because of his frequent authoritarian tactics. It entails something like the aspiring monk who must somehow give himself to the Buddha.

The idea of surrendering one's will to Capoeira does not seem to be in synch with what one would like to think of as Capoeira. However, one's will and ego are but a part of Capoeira living. The great Mahayana Buddhist philosopher Nagarjuna propagated the idea that if we try to go against nature—including human nature—we must do so from within nature, so we cannot really go against nature. In a somewhat similar vein, Western philosopher Ludwig Wittgenstein (1953) believed that if we think we can step outside language we can only do so from within language, so we can't really step outside language. This is in a sense like saying that, whatever the capoeirista does, willfully or not, is within Capoeira. The genuine capoeirista cannot go against Capoeira because she is within it, and if she steps outside it she is no longer a genuine capoeirista:

Vou levando a vida	I get on in life
De qualquer maneira	In whatever form or fashion
Tocando berimbau	Twanging the berimbau
E jogando a capoeira	And playing capoeira.
	(Vieira 1995:105)

In other words, if for the capoeirista Capoeira is life, like life, every move the capoeirista makes, whether in the Roda or in the larger world, is Capoeira. Capoeira, life, nature, and the whole of language: the genuine capoeirista loses herself in them.

Allow me to offer a Buddhist parable as illustration. Before a monk experienced enlightenment, mountains were mountains and rivers were rivers. Eventually he became filled with unknowing and mountains were no longer mountains and rivers ceased to be rivers. Finally, after a moment of enlightenment, once again, mountains were mountains and rivers were rivers. What are we to make of this? That according to our cultural conventions, when we consider mountains as mountains and rivers as rivers, we are placing undue priority on language. Mountains are mountains because we have a word, "mountains," that presumably corresponds to those majestic objects out there. The same can be said of rivers. When the Buddhist novice apparently loses touch with the world, objects are no longer what he thought they were, for they are process rather than things: he has lost the presumed connection between words and their fixed correspondences. Then he becomes enlightened, and mountains and rivers are just what they are, no more, no less. They are neither mountain-objects nor are they mountain words; they are just what they are, whether we wish to call them "mountains" or "sqwezzicks" or "kupstids" or whatever. They just are. The same can be said of rivers and everything else, ourselves included. My allusion once again to Buddhism stems from the conviction that there are certain commonalities between Asian thought and basic patterns of general human comportment within everyday life, including Capoeira life, and certain aspect of Western thought. (Since this is not the time and place to elaborate on this topic, I would suggest a look at Abe 1985; Grigg 1994; Nishitani 1982, 1990; Odin 1996; also merrell 2002.)

The first stage of the Buddhist parable saw an ego- and language-bound individual who thought he could put everything in its proper place. Then he lost his ego. He lost his will over the world, and the very idea of a right place for something became undecidable. Finally, he retrieved his will, but without having imperiously to impose himself on words, things, or the world. In his enlightened state, he became aware that there are no right places, that everything just is what it is becoming. So it is not a matter of his having been ego-bound before but now he has given up his ego. His ego is still there. But it is not differentiated from anything else, except when out of necessity he must use language to communicate with others, or when he must actively interact with other people and other things in his world. In another way of putting it, he now realizes that his will was always part of the world, part of everything. He is now aware that his world was at one with the Buddha from the very beginning. Even his loss of self when nothing had its place was part of what *is becoming*. So in his state of undecidability, he was just what he was, like everything else. The only difference was that he didn't know it. Now, he knows.

In this light, the second feature is: Regarding the Capoeira self, or non-self, there can be no *is*, for there is only becoming, process.

So Is Capoeira Merely Purposeless?

No Céu entra quem merece,	One enters heaven on one's merits;
Na Terra vale é quem tem.	Here on Earth what one worth is what counts.
Passar bem ou passar mal,	Fare you well or fare you poorly
Tudo na vida é passar, Câmara.	Everything on this Earth is but farewell, comrade.

(Traditional Capoeira song)

Is Capoeira's purpose simply to dominate and therefore vanquish the enemy? Of course, not. In the true spirit of Capoeira, there is neither dominance nor subservience, strictly speaking. Just as for the genuine capoeirista there is nothing we would appropriately call the ego in the sense of that ego existing apart from the environment for the purpose of dominating it, so also Capoeira neither dominates nor vanquishes. It is there neither to rule nor to obey, neither to use nor to be used or abused. Once again, Capoeira is what it is becoming. It has no predetermined purpose, at least no purpose that can be put in cause-and-effect language.

I use the word "purpose" in the hard-driven, ego-oriented, individualistic, hell-bent-for-leather Western sense, usually with some goal in mind that is oriented around control, power, and domination. In this use of the word, Capoeira has no predetermined purpose. Consequently, it fulfills its purpose admirably: it is for practical purposes purposeless. Does a tree have a purpose in growing? Does a river have a purpose in flowing? Does a mountain have a purpose in just sitting there and slowly changing? No. Yet, they all somehow serve some purpose. The tree flows into the same water that feeds the river. The mountain flows into the tree's flow into and with the water. The river flows into the mountain that provides the downward slope for it to follow, in the process passing by the tree along its bank. They need each other to become what they are becoming; they complement each other. They serve some roughly definable purpose. Their purpose is becoming what they are becoming; hence they have no specifically definable purposeful purpose. And what is the purposeless purpose of Capoeira? Just that, Capoeira becoming (for further along these lines, see Sodré 1983:203–215, 1991:13–19, 1997).

One might wish to protest: "All this is fine and dandy for mountains and trees and rivers, and perhaps in some strange way of putting it even for Capoeira; but not for thinking humans. We are rational beings. We must have reasons for our actions. And there must be purpose in our reasons. That is what sets us apart from the dumb beasts." But the questions are: Do we rationally develop a hypothetical purpose for doing what we do before we do it? When Michael Jordan was at his best did he think out, rationally and logically, all of his moves before he made them in order to do a slam-dunk in the face of his opponent? No. He had become so adept at what he did that he did it—that is, bodymind did it—as if he were doing it spontaneously.

I am by no means against anybody having a purpose, or against anybody creating a rational argument for that purpose. In fact, there is very definitely some good reasons and purposes for the moves the Capoeira Mestre teaches you and me when we are trying to become comfortable with the art. There is obviously some purpose in the Capoeira art when we practice it. However, in its most supreme moments, Capoeira is supremely purposeless. The beauty and the bestiality of Capoeira is that when it is at its best, its practitioner is completely spontaneous in such a way that her every move seems to have a reason and a certain logic to it: it appears purposeful. Yet at the moment when she does what she does, she does not do it with a purpose: her doing is purposeless. Ultimately Capoeira does have a grand purpose, though that purpose is spontaneous and hence purposeless—in the linear cause-and-effect sense, that is. In other words, since Capoeira moves in their purest form are made spontaneously, they are simply becoming what they are becoming, purposelessly. Only when we become aware of the interdependent, interrelated interaction between one Capoeira move and all others, and of the Roda and the people surrounding it and the Capoeira hall and everything else, only when we become aware that Capoeira is living process can we conceive some purpose.

Thus the third feature: Capoeira process is purposeless; that is its purpose.

A capoeira, por eles inventada	Capoeira, invented by the slaves
Era um grito de liberdade	Was a cry of freedom
De um povo de raça e capacidade.	From capable people of African heritage.

(Vieira 1995:48)

Does the Capoeirista Have No Freedom of Choice?

Capoeira has rules, and it requires great concentration and rigorous training. If one's purposeless purpose is to reach a point where some level of gratuitous spontaneity seems to apply, it might appear that one has the freedom to do what one wishes. Not so, however. Like Michael Jordan creating his magical basketball moves, when one acts as if out of spontaneity, one is doing precisely what one has to do to get the job done. One is anything but free to do as one pleases; yet one freely creates one's moves according to some spontaneously engendered strategy. A person who spontaneously moves without any apparent preconceived purpose is enacting the purpose of Capoeira's purposelessness.

One would likely still wish to retort: "What you say is too contrived. Either there is purpose or there is not". Well, yes,... there is,... and no,... there isn't. This creates a paradox that might appeal to some people, but is too vague and ambiguous for most. How so? People of poetic bent have a warm feeling for ambiguity and vagueness. Logicians, by contrast, abhor ambiguity and vagueness. But logicians are in love with paradox; they like their job of fighting with paradoxes, for paradoxes are puzzles, they must try to solve. Poets, by and large, simply do what they like; for that reason they crave ambiguity and vagueness, and they generally accept paradoxes for what they are. Genuine capoeiristas like what they do, and hence do what they like, for that is the way of Capoeira. Ambiguity, vagueness, and paradoxes give them no headaches. For they are in tune with Capoeira; they accept it and themselves for always becoming somebody other than who they are becoming. However, if they decide to assert her freedom of choice and try changing their becoming, it must be because they didn't accept themselves according to the way they were becoming. In this case they are not genuinely following the way of Capoeira, because they are not going with the flow. So apparently they are damned if they go with the flow because they thereby lose their freedom of choice, and they are damned if they exercise their freedom and don't go with the flow because then they seem to step outside the way of Capoeira. How can they be at one with Capoeira becoming and, at the same time, exercise a modicum of freedom?

This question seems to put the capoeirista in a dilemma. If I presented the dilemma to my Mestre in the form of a question, he might respond by slapping me over the head with a *Pandeiro*. And I would deserve it. The fact that I'm asking the question shows that I'm still caught up in my dualistic thinking. It is as if I were still calling mountains "mountains" while sensing that mountains aren't mountains. I shouldn't ask such questions. I should just follow my Mestre; that is, I should follow the way of Capoeira, silently, unthinkingly, and somehow let my bodymind learn the answers. I should have no choice on the matter. Yet, someday, if I could somehow manage to find the way of Capoeira, I would like what I am becoming, and I would be free, though what I am becoming at each moment is exactly what I must be doing if I expect to do it properly, so I wouldn't be free. In another equally clumsy way of putting this, if my body, or better, bodymind, is just doing what it is doing, spontaneously, and without purpose or expression of purpose at each particular moment, it is following the way of Capoeira, and it is free, paradoxically.

One might now complain: "You are advocating a comedy of satire, irony, nonsense, and semantic inversions that can lead us nowhere. What you need is a serious articulation of Capoeira." However, a serious articulation of Capoeira would not be of the nature of the art. Since the art is born of slavery and the most brutal ethnocidal practices imaginable, it might seem that capoeiristas have just cause to take their art seriously. But since they are masters of deception, their seriousness is rather paradoxically manifested with an ironic grin, a cynical wink, and an extended foot tripping you up when you least expect it. So their art is what it should be: as magically unimaginable and as sordidly brutal as their slave ancestors' inhuman condition.

According to our traditional linear thinking, sensible ways of life, philosophies, and practices should be sober, proper, rational, and admirably analytic. For example, appropriately logical, rational and serious people—often called philosophers—take the infamous Cretan paradox, 'this sentence is false," to heart. They dissect it and ponder over it, trying their best to understand it for what it is and then rationalize it out of existence. Is the Cretan sentence true? If so, then it is false. But if it is false, then it is true. Those who are sober of mind beat their heads against the wall trying to place the anomaly under their control. But they can't. The Capoeira way is something else entirely. Capoeira, like other seemingly illogical ways of life, philosophies, and practices, is characterized by what might appear as madness: spontaneity, playfulness, humor, uninhibited freedom—or its lack, depending on the perspective—and total abandon to paradoxes. Consequently, the capoeirista, with a wry, knowing grin, gives all paradoxes an appreciative nod and a chuckle, and then gets on with life. For she knows life itself, and Capoeira, which is another way of saying life, are paradoxical through and through.

Indeed, not only poets but also children and creative scientists seem to be in love with paradoxes, though they might not always recognize them as paradoxes. In fact, some of the people we would expect to be most serious were actually off the wall, so to speak. The physicist Niels Bohr (1961:19) once quipped that if a new scientific theory wasn't crazy enough, then it most likely couldn't possibly be correct. Bohr's fellow physicist, Louis de Broglie

(1939:280), wrote that if a theory is a paragon of clear and distinct ideas, then it can't be very close to reality, and if it is as close to reality as can be, then it can't be absolutely clear and distinct but vague and ambiguous (for physical science as a vague, ambiguous, and paradoxical way and thus comparable to the Asian way, see Capra 1975; Goswami 1993; Hagen 1998; Smith 1995)

The fourth feature, in this vein, is: If you follow the way of Capoeira and like what you do, individual freedom, or the lack thereof, becomes of relatively little importance.

Is There No Truth of the Matter?

Ô sim, sim, sim	Oh yes, yes, yes
Ô não, não, não.	Oh no, no, no.
(Mestre Bola Sete 1997:163)	

The truth of the matter is that there is an apple on some tree out there, somewhere, that is ripe, and it will soon fall. But some apples are riper than others; hence the truthfulness of their ripeness is greater than that of the truthfulness of less ripe apples.

This more-or-less nature of many truths is the project of what is now called "fuzzy logic". I cannot enter into the details of this logic here. Yet, the idea of "fuzzy truth" is germane to Capoeira. So I'll have to entertain the spirit of fuzziness, if not the nitty-gritty details. Fuzziness has to do with the question: Does the apple know it's ripe? In a certain manner of speaking, yes. The apple's purposeless purpose in life is fulfilled when it is ripe, and when it is time to fall, it falls. There is no all-or-nothing truth to the matter. There just is what is becoming, the ripe apple; and it will fall when it falls. What it is becoming, is what it is becoming, and what it does, it does, when its time comes. The accomplished capoeirista is able somehow to operate in this manner as well. For this reason, Capoeira is like the fuzzy truth of the apple's ripeness. For this reason also, the truth about Capoeira is that it is exceedingly vague and imprecise.

Actually, Capoeira is no more vague and imprecise than many of other ideas we have about ourselves, the world, and life, such as beauty, goodness, happiness, mind, self, democracy, knowledge, and intelligence. These terms' vagueness is notorious, and for a good reason. Their definition in large part depends on the heart and mind of their beholder. The happy person and the unhappy person, she who sees beauty in a sunset and she who sees it as the end of just another day, she who is of penetrating mind and she who merely takes things at face value, they all live in different worlds. Wittgenstein often said and wrote this much. Capoeira's vagueness, like the vagueness of these terms, has a curious feature: if by its very nature it is vague, should not our idea of it be correspondingly vague? If so, then with respect to vagueness, should not our idea of Capoeira be at its best a mirror-image, in all its vagueness, reflecting their nature. We would most likely respond to this question with a resounding "No!"

However, just for kicks let's entertain the idea that the proper answer is "Yes". What are the consequences of this response? If our vague account of Capoeira mirrors Capoeira's vagueness, then our account must be precise. If this is the case, then with respect to Western demands for preciseness our account should be inadequate, due to its very preciseness. An adequate account of Capoeira must be as vague as is Capoeira itself, paradoxically.

But hold on! If in accord with out first characteristic, prior to Capoeira there is no-thing, nothingness, emptiness, and if Capoeira does not exist as a fixed essence or entity, though it is real, then there is nothing against which to hold up the mirror. If we have nothing to mirror, then no vagueness will be seen in the mirror. Or perhaps the mirror will suggest infinite vagueness, that is, no-thing, nothingness, or emptiness. Our very problem is that we are striving to hold a mirror up to Capoeira; we are trying to put it into language, say it, and give it a definition, a meaning. Once again it was Wittgenstein who untiringly counseled us to stop looking for definitions and meanings and look at what words and things *do*. We should pay little mind to discourse about things; we should contemplate their use within the context of human affairs. The same could be said of Capoeira. Let the body sense it, feel it, internalize it, incorporate it, assimilate it, accommodate itself to it, and eventually, body, body and mind, bodymind, will be Capoeira, and Capoeira will be bodymind, the particular bodymind that has begun to rhythm to Capoeira's rhythms.

Finally, then, the fifth and last feature is: Capoeira offers no truth of the matter; it is always in the process of becoming what it was, is, and will have been becoming.

The next move calls for a mind shift. It entails consideration of Capoeira as process in light of an important aspect of Charles Sanders Peirce's philosophy—the full importance of which will become more evident in part III.

Capoeira as Sign Processing

Peirce developed a notoriously elaborate theory of signs. His general idea is that all forms of communication are a matter of our now familiar terms, *interrelations* of *interdependency* and *interaction*. (The italicized terms are not exactly Peirce's, but as I have argued elsewhere, they effectively encapsulate his processual philosophy [merrell 2000b, 2002, 2003a].)

These three words are themselves interrelated with what Peirce calls the categories of the universe's proce*ss*: *Firstness*, *Secondness*, and *Thirdness*. While I do not wish to enter into a full discussion of Peirce's complex theory of communication through sign processes, commonly going by the name semiotics, I sense the need to explain some key aspects of his view on signs in order that we may better understand the processual nature of Capoeira. Peirce's signs, like Capoeira according to its first feature discussed above, are not a matter of fixed things or essences. And like the second feature, there is no invariant "isness" to signs, for they are process, not product. (J. Lowell Lewis [1992] evokes Peirce's philosophy of signs and communication in his penetrating and knowledgeable study of Capoeira. While his background and expertise in Capoeira exceed mine, I'm afraid I must write that his use of Peirce's semiotics falls slightly off the mark. What I wish to suggest in this inquiry, in addition to Lewis's semiotic interpretation of Capoeira, is that there is a striking parallel between Peirce's fusion of his categories in sign processes and the notion of Capoeira as process [for a more detailed look at Peirce's philosophy, see Peirce 1931–135: 2.227–434; Hookway 1985; Rosenthal 1994; Stearn 1952].)

Rather cryptically put, Firstness is what it *is*, and nothing more. In other words, some possible process at the stage of Firstness simply is what it *is*, without its (yet) having entered into interaction or interrelationship with anything else. It stands alone; it recently emerged from emptiness as a self-contained, self-sufficient possible process. I write "possible process" for if there is no more than Firstness, there is as yet no genuine process; there is no interdependent interrelatedness between something and something else. In other words, Firstness has no Other, no-thing that is Other than itself. The notion of some Other ushers in Secondness, which is what there *is*, or better, what is now becoming, insofar as it has come into interaction with some Other. But it has not (yet) come into interrelationship with that Other by means of the mediation of something else. Thirdness, is that something else. It is a mediator and moderator. It brings whatever was Firstness together and into interaction with the Secondness of the Firstness in the same way that it enters into its own interrelationship with that Firstness and that Secondness.

For a more concrete sense of Peirce's categories, consider this example. The Capoeira Roda is an image that has emerged from emptiness. Now it is there, painted on the floor of a Capoeira hall, and surrounded by fifteen or so sitting bodies with legs crossed (figure 2).

As an image, and outside any and all considerations of anybody or anything else in the immediate environs, the Roda is just that: a Roda, a simple ring, before it has entered into any form or fashion of interrelated interaction with anything or anybody else. It is just what it is, no more, no less. It is Firstness, pure and simple. It is the simulation of a ring. It is a ring, for sure.

But in order that it may be seen *as* a ring, its contemplator must bring it into interaction with rings she has experienced in the past, with her general concept of rings, of which this image is an example.

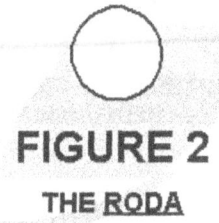

FIGURE 2
THE RODA

But I'm getting ahead of myself. If I write that the image is brought "into interactions with rings she has experienced in the past," then I am interrelating the ring with some Other (figure 3).

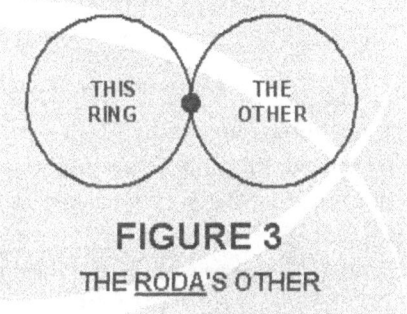

FIGURE 3
THE RODA'S OTHER

This Other is a matter of Secondness. The initial image of unrelated Firstness has entered into interaction with something else, a ring. The ring's similarities and differences with respect to Other rings, can now become part of the its contemplator's attention. And a sign can be attached to it, in this case the word "ring." The image and the concrete ring have been seen *as* a ring. They have been named a "ring" with awareness that they have certain attributes that endow them with ringness, with ringlike qualities. This is Thirdness, which endows the image and ring with meaning. It brings the particular image (sign) and the physical entity corresponding to the image (object of the sign) into interplay such that they become interrelated with a general class of things called "rings." The image (Firstness), the concrete physical entity (Secondness), and the general class of things to which they belong (rings or Thirdness), have entered into genuine interdependent, interactive, interrelationship with themselves and at the same time with some interpreter, who is instrumental in bringing about the Firstness, Secondness, and Thirdness of the image, *ring*, and the concept or meaning of a ring.

It's within the Process

But actually, the Roda is a microcosm of the world. In this sense, as Firstness it is an image in synecdochic or part-to-whole interrelationship with the macrocosm, the world—or the Secondness of the Firstness. Thus further to complete the function of the Roda we have Figure 3a.

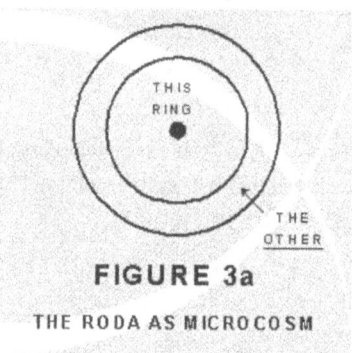

FIGURE 3a

THE RODA AS MICROCOSM

In this regard the ring interrelates with its Other and at the same time it is within its Other. It is set apart from its Other and at the same time it is one with it. It is and it is not its Other. This is the enigma of the Roda that renders it so intriguing. What happens there is part of the world, but it is the world; what happens in the world is properly worldly, but for the true blue capoeirista it is Capoeira, for it is living process.

Moreover, this act of seeing the Roda as a ring that has certain attributes, requires the contemplator's awareness of the image here and now and the range of comparable images the contemplator has experienced in the past. Now, the ring's contemplator can give an acknowledging nod that this is a ring, that like all rings the distance from its center to its circumference is the same no matter at what angle you draw the line of measurement, that the circumference serves to distinguish what is inside from what is outside, and above all, that this ring is a Capoeira Roda. This puts the ring's contemplator squarely in the arena of Thirdness.

Notice that in figure 3, a point links the initial image to past recollections of comparable images in order to identify the original image for what it is, a ring or Roda in this case. In figure 3a the point has taken its rightful place at the center, the center of the Roda, of the world. And now, in figure 4, with inclusion of a third image, the point lies suspended within, yet it brings about a fusion of, three rings. The first ring—take your pick, for topologically they're all the same, including the point—is Firstness, the image of a ring. The second ring, Secondness, enables identification of the initial image as a ring in interdependency and interaction with its Other. The third ring, Thirdness, interrelatedly brings the image and the ring together in order that the concept "ring" might take on meaning. Notice that the rings are the same, yet they are different. For, first there was the initial image, then there was identification, and then there was mediation by the engenderer of the sign's meaning. Or, if you will, and as I discuss further in chapter 12, whichever of the three circles is considered Firstness can be occupied by a sign; Secondness, the Other of Firstness, is the sign's respective object with which it interacts; and Thirdness ushers in the sign's meaning.

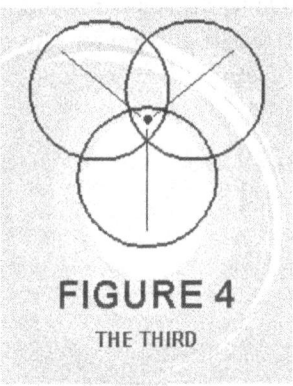

FIGURE 4
THE THIRD

In the Peircean sense, Thirdness mediates between Firstness and Secondness. It renders them mutually interpenetrating through their interdependent, interrelated, interactivity, and it brings about the same mutual interpenetration between itself and its two others, Firstness and Secondness. Thirdness brings on full-fledged time in the sense that there is now something and something else and now the something and something else are becoming something other than what they were becoming. In other words, Thirdness introduces *process*, the flowing becoming of all that is in the universe. Thirdness never allows anybody or anything to flop down on the nearest park bench and watch the world go by. Thirdness brings about the flow of Firstness into Secondness and it brings about its own flow into them and them into it. In short, Thirdness is author of Capoeira flow; for that matter, it is author of all flows.

In sum, there is no fixed, static somebody or something apart from the world that is going by: everything is perpetually becoming. The watchword is *semiosis*. It is the process of signs becoming signs. Everything in the *semiosic* process has some level of Firstness, Secondness, and Thirdness the mutual interpenetration of which brings about the flow of something and everything else. Process gives way to and flows into some other process and that other process and the first process become one with themselves and with some third process that perpetuates the flow as it flows into them in the same way they flow into it. So once again, what is the purpose of semiosis? *Semiosis* is process and process is *semiosis*, and process just *is* what it *is*. In a manner of speaking, as goes Capoeira's qualifying feature as purposeless purpose, so also semiosis.

How the Process Comes about

Let me relate what I am trying to say about signs in communication to an above topic. The Ginga consists basically of a three-way set of movements as illustrated in figure 5. Ginga moves are at the heart of Capoeira; they are also somewhat comparable to the steps in Candomblé and Samba. The action begins with Firstness, the image within the Roda. Right there, in the gyrating movements about the center, is where and how rhythm begins, where music and dance gush forth.

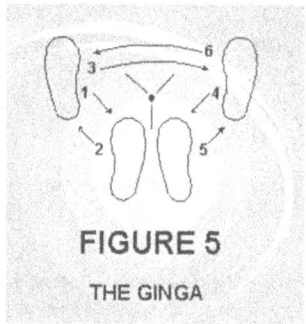

FIGURE 5

THE GINGA

Contemplate figure 5. Let your eyes flow with the arrows and imagine your feet doing the same. Imagine the moves in the form of a three-way, syncopated, slightly offbeat rhythm with the central point of emptiness and the three lines making up a tripod. Imagine that the tripod is wobbling back and forth and up and down, liquidly, wavingly, undulatingly, like a combination of figures 4 and 5, as your feet flow through the steps. Now, get up off your seat and let your feet do what they do while slowly and syncopatedly counting: one-two—three—four-five—six ... one-two—three—four-five—six .... Slowly, at first. Let your feet flow. Then very gradually pick up the tempo. Above all, never resort to jerks and jumps.... Got it?

Your initial move (Firstness) emerges out of the inner space, within the Roda, the Roda, that itself emerged from the emptiness preceding it. Your second move is the Other of the first move. It is Secondness. It marks emergence of the Other. There is also, of course, the Other of the Other, Thirdness,

Capoeiristas at the portal of the Cathedral in front of the plaza, Terreiro de Jesus, Pelourinho, Salvador

potentially your partner in Capoeira play. Your third move acknowledges the presence of this Other person. You are now set up for spontaneous attack or defense, whichever the situation calls for.

In other words, first there is Ginga. Then Capoeira play begins. You flow along with the current, and you also have to roll with the feigned blows, give a little and take a little, give a few in-your-face moves and expect others to do the same to you, dish out a little malícia, in the form of roguish, deceptive give-and-take, with a sly grin on your face. All the while, keep the Ginga going, rhythming, dancing, wobbling and weaving, moving, always moving, to the berimbau's mournful weeping.

That way, you'll never be surprised that you aren't surprised when an unexpected turn of events occurs. For you expected the unexpected anyway. That way, you'll be able to enjoy the logical inversions, the brutal contradictions, the subtle ironies, the vagueness and ambiguity, and the allegories acted out in Capoeira and in life. That way, you'll become a philosopher, philosopher of deceptive conformity and clever resistance. It is all play, of course, but dead serious play, ludic gamery, tight-lipped irony, grim humor, painful laughter, friendly trickery.

Capoeira moves: they make up a world that is upside-down and turned inside-out. When your partner is upright, you are upside down. When he kicks high, you go low. When he moves in, you twirl away. When he thinks he's got your goat, you feign anger and look for your chance. When he thinks he's humiliated you, you deceptively put your tail between your legs as if you were cowed and you prepare to launch an attack. When he has you on the run, you act scared. When he thinks you won't give ground, you give it to instill false confidence in him. Put on airs of superiority, but place yourself in a state of expectancy. Give him a few torpid moves, then dance in and out with a flurry of activity. Pretend you are dizzy or inebriated, and cautiously keep an eye on his eyes to catch some sign of a change of heart on his part. Allow him to think he has you at bay, then lash out viciously. Act like you're tired when you have energy to spare. Ask him to give you mercy when you know you can get the upper hand. Act surprised when you know exactly what is taking place. Give him the appearance of weakness when you feel your greatest strength. When you are dog-tired, never show it. When he shows you cruelty, give him a big smile and prepare to retaliate. When he lands a lucky blow, act like you're in pain when you aren't. Float like a butterfly, sting like a bee, slither like a fish in the sea, and show him the persistence of an army ant.

You become passively aggressive, dominantly submissive, defiantly humble, meekly antagonistic, inertly nimble, clumsily dexterous, more limber than you appear, more enduring than your dancing Capoeira partner could imagine, more cunning than he thinks, more malicious than he would expect, more resilient than your looks would suggest. Try to be more than you thought you could be, and you are not surprised that you are surprised that you did what you didn't think you could do. Do all this, and you are on the long road toward becoming a genuine capoeirista. So, in light of Capoeira's last two qualifying features, what about freedom within sign processing and the truth of the matter about signs? Freedom is exercised when following the way of all signs, the *semiosic* processes, which is to say there is freedom in just doing what you do when you are properly prepared to do it. And the only truth of the matter of signs is that they are becoming something other than what they were becoming (for more on the ways of semiosic processes, see merrell 2002).

That is what practicing Capoeira philosophy is all about.

Ié, maior é Deus.	Oh, God is greater than I am.
Ié, maior é Deus, pequeno sou eu.	Oh, God is great; I am so small.
Tudo que tenho, foi Deus quem me deu.	Everything that I have, God gave to me.
Na Roda da Capoeira,	Within the Capoeira Roda,
Grande pequeno sou eu!	I discover my own greatness.

Mestre Pastinha (Almeida 1986:94)

We must take a further look at this living philosophy.

Chapter Five

Nonlinear and Sinuous is the Road

> Capoeira!
> *Chorus*: Ô lêlê
> Capoeira!
> *Chorus*: Ô lalá
> (Mestre Bola Sete 1997:165)

ON THE WAY TO BECOMING A CAPOEIRISTA

From beginner to *batisado* (baptized one, or initiate, after eight months), to *profissional* (after twelve years), to *Contramestre* (an associate Mestre, after about seventeen years) to genuine *Mestre* (after about twenty-three years or more), the way of Capoeira is long. The journey is continuous, with no abrupt promotions. The student must follow a natural process that requires dedication, discipline, training, and cultivation of a profound feeling for the art. There should be no haste, nor is one expected to lunge into week after week of furious activity. There is meditation and contemplation just as much as there is strenuous practice. Capoeira is not merely strength, acrobatics, or a striving for mechanical perfection. It is subtlety embodied.

Throughout the journey, the capoeirista must always strive to go beyond her limits. And the Mestre must aid her in reaching this stage. When an earnest twelve-year-old student is playing against the Mestre, it gives him great pleasure to guide the young pupil through the moves, but he never forgets to add a few subtle malícia strategies to keep things honest and let her know who's boss. Older beginners, who may lack knowledge of the art, experience, or physical ability, or be past their prime, need not give up or cease striving. These are not seen as disadvantages in the same way as in a competitive, ego-driven sport. Students are expected to create their own expression of the art to the best of her capacity. Nothing more is asked of them. Who they are, where they came from, education, social standing, sex, race, age, are of no consequence. The capoeirista who bullies less experienced partners, the young lad who sets out to embarrass an older partner, or the *macho* male who wants to kick some female ass: they are all setting themselves up for rebuke and perhaps even expulsion from the Capoeira family.

And family it is. The Capoeira group may be found in the local school or academy, a tight-knit cadre of enthusiasts, a group of fervent apprentices in class with a Mestre from Rio, or just some neighborhood buddies practicing their skills. In whichever case, if they are genuine capoeiristas in body, mind, and spirit, they will make up a caring, protecting, compassionate, loving family. Quite often, many capoeiristas in a given family are raw beginners, and some of them might be batisados. There may be one or two *Contramestres*, who have entered into the spiritual depths of the art and are now willing to dedicate their time, whether receiving remuneration or not, toward helping others discover the subtleties and develop a spiritual understanding of the art.

For example, in the spring of 2001, I was a wide-eyed sixty-three -year-old Capoeira beginner who also happened to be a college professor. I soon realized that when in class, I deserved neither more nor less consideration than a ten-year old, a bemused teenager who will obviously not last more than a couple of weeks, an athletic but struggling young woman, or a dedicated student reaching near-Contramestre level. The only difference was that I was given some allowance, due to my age, when the back-bending, leg-twisting, and upside-down maneuvers come up on the agenda. I was expected to show my Mestre the same respect as everybody else. And she gave me the same respect I gave her. I would never insult her by questioning her methods or motives, and she would never treat me with anything but compassion and consideration.

I am, of course, writing of an ideal family. In real Capoeira living, tensions can develop out of envy and resentment; egos become bruised; emotions rise to a shrill pitch; and aggression occasionally breaks out. Yet, everybody is aware of how the family should function in the best of all worlds, and most Capoeira citizens aspire to that ideal.

How does one go about becoming a member of a Capoeira family? Above all, the road is by no means a linear step-by-step maneuver. It is sinuous and at times treacherous. Let me try to illustrate my point with the following set of examples.

Steps along the Nonlinear Way

Bira Almeida (Mestre Acordeon) (1986:144–150) outlines five levels through which a capoeirista moves in her road to becoming a genuine Mestre within the Capoeira family. The first he calls "playing in the dark," when students begin to learn clear and defined movements of attack and defense, developing discipline and self-control. They jump into the *jôgo* without knowing exactly what is happening. They are lost in space; they see nothing. Not only do the movements of the opponents seem to materialize by magic, but their own movements are beyond control" (Almeida 1986:144). I must emphasize Almeida's jumping into the *Jogo* "without knowing exactly what is happening." This entails a leap of faith. The Mestre or Contramestre tells you to do something you've never dared attempt before, and you do it, without question. Or at least you try to do it. And you should register neither regret nor repentance when you bungle it. You throw your body around apparently with reckless abandon, and with neither inhibitions nor fear. It is as if there were nothing but you and your partner and the Roda. In a manner of speaking, both of you are suspended within the Roda, outside normal time and space. It is as if there were no mind reminding the body that caution must be exercised, as if body were exploring its limits, as if somebody else, some other ego or alter ego, had occupied the space and time of your ordinary body and mind in their customary Western separation. It is as if you were somebody else in another reality. You, your conscious mind, doesn't understand this somebody else, this Other. Nor can you follow it. The most you can do is trail along behind.

No, ... that's not exactly right. You, your ego-centered conscious mind and your ordinary body obedient to the mind's commands, don't really trail along behind, for you are not even an outside spectator. There is no outside. It is just you, that vague Other you, and the Roda. That's all. At least that's all, I would like to believe, when you are truly playing in the dark.

At this level, there is feeling, for sure, and plenty of it, especially when you land on your butt due to your own lack of flexibility or coordination or because your Mestre tripped you up to keep you on guard or to teach you a lesson. But this is great! And you know it. You have left your usual world out there. That other world is the world of your selfish whims and wishes, the world of your inhibitions, your fear of trying out something new out of fear that your friends and associates won't approve of you. Here, in the Roda, all that is of no consequence, for you are part of the family, in here, where everybody does things some of which they wouldn't dream of doing under ordinary circumstances out there.

Whether you know it or not, you are somehow getting a feel for the art. But at this stage there is hardly any conscious awareness of what you are doing, why you are doing it, or where or when you should do what you do during the furious activity of a Jogo. You just do it because your Mestre said over and over again during the practice sessions "Do it!" You always tried to do it in the form of that Other you of whom you are not (yet) genuinely aware and who you do not (yet) know. Now, in the Roda, you just try to do it, because you somehow feel the art, though you're in the dark as to what it is you feel.

Following Peirce, I'll call this level "tone." It is like a musical tone that you feel and perhaps sense in some nonaware way that it is a tone with which you are familiar, but you can't quite put your finger on it. You can't identify it, though you feel some remote, perhaps long-lost, familiarity with it. It is who you have always been but didn't know it. It is as if your genuine self, your Other self, were giving you a gentle nudge, very softly, tenderly, easing its way into your awareness. But still, you can't (yet) put your finger on it. Feeling, in the dark, is, like figure 6, uniform darkness.

FIGURE 6

PLAYING IN THE DARK

There is not (yet) any distinction. There is no division, no something here and something else there. There is just an obscure continuum of sameness. This is tantamount to the solitary circle in figure 2, as if it were in the dark. There is nothing but deep, dark Oneness. Or to put it another way, at this level of feeling there is nothing but Peirce's Firstness.

The Grand Division

Almeida calls the next level "playing in the water." At this level capoeiristas

> progressively gain a clear perception of their own movements as they begin to apply different variations for kicking and body positioning according to their personalities and the needs of the *jôgo*. They be-

> come aware of the blows that could have taken their heads off, and can feel the defense against their most effective attacks. Although seeing the game, students at this level do not yet have sufficient experience and physical skill to use the Capoeira movements properly. I call this stage "playing in the water" because the lack of knowledge and skill at this level constructs the possibility of constant flow and consistent effective action. (Almeida 1986:144)

What happened when you were throwing your body around at the order of your Mestre and he tripped you up? Surprise! Something you didn't expect. What was that something? It was some Other (your Mestre in this case) that was other than your own inner Other of which I have been writing. This is the brute physical Other of action and reaction.

At this level, when during a Roda you are playing in the water, there's you and the physical world out there: the floor, the Roda, physical entities in the form of human beings, instruments throbbing, vocal chords chanting. When you become in tune with your environment within the Roda during a Jogo, in Almeida's words, you begin to "gain a clear perception" of your self, as you "apply different variations for kicking and body positioning" according to your personality and the flow of the Jogo. You also begin becoming genuinely aware of the physical Other of the Roda, the dangers it can present, how you can prepare yourself to confront these dangers, and how you can set up your defense and create counterattacks. Yet, since the Jogo is flow, process, perpetual movement, you are still lagging behind. Your mind still thinks it can properly appraise each and every situation, formulate the proper strategy, and act, all in eternal separation from your body. You are still drowning in your body/mind separation. Consequently, you appear vacillating, uncertain, indecisive. And you are. You are, because you have not reached the level when body plus mind, or better *bodymind*, acts as a whole in concert, moving the way it moves because it is now one with the flow. Nevertheless, you have at least reached a new level of performance.

However, to your utter disappointment, your Mestre gives you an emotionless scowl, and then, slowly, an almost imperceptible nod. Why isn't he profusely congratulating you during each practice session and especially after you perform in the Roda? Doesn't he realize you're making miles of progress? Why does the road seem so lonely in spite of all your efforts and your apparent success? The problem is not his. It's yours. You are thinking of success as opposed to failure, loneliness as opposed to immersion within a community, progress as opposed to digression, effort *as opposed to* lethargy, and so on. That's ego-driven thinking. You're not supposed to think, not in your accustomed way at least. You're supposed to allow bodymind to do its thing.

When it does, it is doing what it should have been doing all along. So why should you expect applause? Actually, your superiors are elated over what you would call "progress." They just don't look at it in the same way as you do.

FIGURE 7

PLAYING IN THE WATER

In figure 7 the waters have been divided. There is now you, your Other (bodymind), and the Other of the your Other—the roda and everything in it. But the line of demarcation, like all lines of demarcation at this stage within that world called the Capoeira Roda, is jagged. In terms of your performance in the Roda, there is no genuine flow, because you're still doggedly holding onto your customary and cherished patterns of thought and behavior. After the jolt of surprise, you came into confrontation with the physical Other of the Roda. And you tried to cope as best you could with a few of the moves you learned and according to the way you had practiced them. But that's the problem. You tried to commit the moves to mental memory, like the multiplication table in your arithmetic class when you were a child. You tried to maintain supremacy of mind over body. However, Capoeira flow is not a matter of mind over body. There is no mind against body in the first place in order for there to be mind over body. There is just bodymind, period. Yet, you persist in your effort to maintain the distinction, and all distinctions between you and the Other, in terms of oppositions, dichotomies, and dualisms, in an eternal horn-lock. For that reason you can't see the Capoeira flow for all the particular moves in the ring the Other throws at you.

I would like to call this level of the capoeiristas way to knowing the "sphere of tokens," following Charles Peirce once again. There are tokens, in the sense of particular actions without their having (yet) entered into the process. A particular token is only this, here, now. It is no more than Secondness. There is no authentic flow. Rather, there is a myriad collection of particulars, like atoms colliding with one another within an inflated balloon. Or like capoeirista apprentices in the Roda bumping into each other because they don't know naturally and spontaneously how to carry through with their offensive maneuvers and make their defensive escapes. This stage of Capoeira, "playing in the water," is comparable to the Buddhist stage, mentioned above, where mountains are just mountains and rivers are just rivers. It is comparable to "naïve realism" according to which what a word names is what the thing is, with no further ado.

Somehow into the Flow
Almeida's third level is "playing in the light". At this level, students

> work to perfect their movements, the timing and rhythm of their fighting. As the sharpness of their games improves and their bodies learn to respond correctly to the tactics of the *jôgo*, they become able to defend and attack with precision, power, and grace. They are now mature fighters who demonstrate impeccable skill in using proper Capoeira techniques, and who know how to transform the *jôgo* with completely new and unexpected movements in the heat of the battle. At this point, the emphasis in training must change from physical achievements to controlling of emotions and comprehension of philosophy. This is the level one must reach in order to become a *contra-mestre*. (Almeida 1986:144–145)

To reach this level the capoeirista dedicates years to intensive training, challenging personal limits and becoming quite proficient at the art. Bodymind begins responding in the ring in concert with the flow. It is all music to bodymind, bodymind that now shows off its precision, power, and grace, demonstrating impeccable skill in using proper Capoeira techniques, creating new and unexpected moves within the flow. Bodymind is now in control of its emotions. This is not to say that it is emotionless or passive with respect to what is happening. The capoeirista is by no means passive, as passive (concealing emotions) in opposition to active (openly displaying emotions)—being passively active, actively passive. The capoeirista is capable of aggressive sham attacks when the opportunity, arises and lightning defensive maneuvers when necessary. This requires a remarkable intensity of emotion. But technique takes precedence over outward shows of emotion.

Such outward shows might have surfaced when she was practicing the art at the second level. But no more. No more, because the jagged distinctions in figure 7 have been smoothed as in figure 8. You have noticed that this icon is the Asian Yin-Yang sign, minus the small black circle in the white area and the white circle in the black area. This is for a reason. At this level of the Capoeira way, there is distinction. It has progressed from jagged two-way binary differentiation to undulating, flowing, rhythmic distinction. Yet it is still fundamentally a two-way distinction. At this level it becomes easy to settle down into the flow and become complacent, giving a little here and taking a little there, always with a wry smile, a dose of malícia, a few subtle moves, properly singing the songs, playing the instruments, and giving newer capoeiristas a helping hand. The way becomes blocked. There is flow within the Roda, and there is a line distinguishing the Roda from what lies beyond. Inside, flow; outside, the cold and cruel world. That intransigent opposition continues to exercise its force.

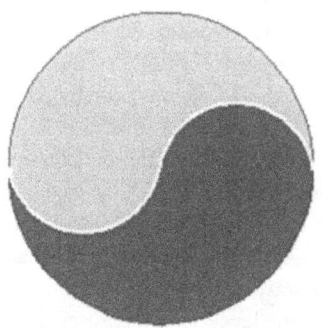

FIGURE 8

PLAYING IN THE LIGHT

Playing in the light is like Peirce's Thirdness, or what he calls type, the nature of a general sign depicting a class of signs to which it belongs (the word "tree" used to evoke the idea of the class of all trees, for example). There is Yin, there is Yang, and there is mediation between them bringing about their undulating, rhythming flow. But this is incomplete Thirdness, for there is no tinge of Yin within Yang and Yang within Yin. Firstness, Secondness, and Thirdness have not (yet) genuinely merged into one another to create an interdependent, interrelated, interactive, mutually interpenetrating whole. Something is missing, still.

I must point out that I bring in Yin-Yang and the Tao for metaphorical purposes, and intend no confusing mix of Taoism with Buddhism philosophy to which I have alluded above and will briefly discuss below. However, by no means do I engage in a comparative analysis of Capoeira and Asian thought in this inquiry. As I pointed out above, I sense a commonality among key aspects of certain non-Western ways—including Capoeira—that call out for our attention. I feel, quite deeply, that in Bira Almeida's words one can find such a commonality.

As If Back to the Future

Almeida writes how his progress had passed through "playing in the dark" and "playing in the water" to "playing in the light." Later, after pushing Capoeira to the margin of his life for some years and then coming back to it, he found he was beating his head against the wall—or metaphorically speaking, he was pushing against the line separating the ring from the outside world. He somehow felt there was a higher level but he couldn't reach it. He tried, and he tried to try, and he tried to try again. It seemed useless. Then, without knowing how it happened, another horizon opened up to him, and he began learning once more like a beginner playing in the dark. He realized, now, that there was indeed another level of knowing that was a spiritual level, in addition to bodymind knowing.

A weathered Mestre can usually get the best of younger capoeiristas even if they are stronger, more flexible, quicker, and have greater stamina. How does he do it? By availing himself of his experience. He knows how to pace himself, to hold back when necessary, and to strike at the propitious moment. He is also remarkably adept at the subtle art of deception. He can still fake the younger guys out of their jocks because he doesn't buy their acts of deception and they aren't able to distinguish between his deliberate moves and his fake moves, his sincere gestures and his mock gestures. But above all, the Mestre's advantage over the younger capoeiristas lies in spirit, in addition to bodymind. Spirit endows him with exceptional qualities that compensate for his decreased physical abilities.

Almeida labels this level of the art "playing with the crystal ball." When playing at this level, he writes he is "attempting to read" the opponent's mind, conducting the *jogo* by setting myself in the right place at the right time. My journey along this path has been a very difficult and painful process of growth, involving self-control, patience, and the capacity of exercising a positive resistance against the odds, not only in the Roda but in my personal life. Sometimes it seems to me that it has taken too many years of physical training, too much emotional struggle in confronting my feelings and values, and an apparently irrational and unnerving effort to open myself to spiritual insights beyond my understanding" (Almeida 1986:148–149). In order to reach this stage, the capoeirista must in Almeida's words once again take on the role of the beginner, become innocent like a child, see the Roda and the entire world in a new light.

This is comparable to the Buddhist apprentice upon entering the stage of awareness when mountains are no longer mountains and rivers are no longer rivers. Language is no longer of any consequence. The word "mountain" has lost its link with mountains, "river" is no longer tied to rivers. There is no longer any word here and the thing there, word here and thing there and a meaning somewhere else. In fact, there are no longer any dichotomies at all. Most significantly, there is no absolute demarcation between the Roda and what previously was assumed to exist outside. The Roda has become the world and the world has become the Roda. Each thing is everything and everything is each thing. In another way of putting it, "playing with the crystal ball" is like collapsing the Peircean sign containing the three categories as depicted in Figure 4 into the solitary point, into the infinitesimal nothing. From this nothingness, or emptiness, the point can then engender a line, and the line can engender the three-dimensional depiction of Firstness, Secondness, and Thirdness.

But, ... actually, I shouldn't say "thing" or "everything" or "point." It's not a matter of things at all. There are no things. Nor are there such things as those things called "points" in the ideal mathematical sense. Nor is there everything. There's just "nothing"—I put nothing in scare quotes since I am obviously limited to and by words. There's nothing but pure emptiness, Almeida's "crystal ball." There is neither lightness nor darkness, neither Yin nor Yang. There's just emptiness. This word "emptiness" is what most translators of Buddhist thought use in place of the Buddhist *Sunyata*. It is the word I have chosen to use here, for I believe it best describes this level of Capoeira, and of any other comparable art form. It is awareness of the gaping jaws of what there is not, pure emptiness. Emptiness, depicted by the infinitesimal point in figures 3, 3a, and 4, is nothing, a no-thing, from whence the three lines of the tripod emerge and begin twirling, gyrating, scintillating, vibrating, undulating. The beginning of the three-way means of communication through the one, the Other, and the mediating Other of the Other. Or it the beginning of the Ginga, which is to say the same thing.

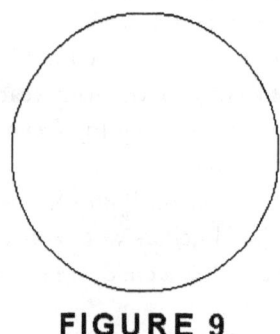

FIGURE 9

PLAYING WITH THE CRYSTAL BALL

Of course, the crystal ball in figure 9 has an outline. This is necessary in order to demarcate it as a crystal ball. We also have in the crystal ball once again the problem of language. The problem is in the idea of "signifying" since to signify there must presumably be something that signifies and something else that is signified. Actually, there shouldn't be any line of demarcation between something and something else, for the crystal ball, that is, emptiness, is all there is. There is nothing other than, and nothing outside of, emptiness. It is the emptiness before "playing in the dark" begins. One must become aware of this total absence of anything and everything before one can begin playing in the dark anew. This is the pointless point where one becomes aware in an awareless way that mountains are not mountains and rivers are not rivers, that nothing is anything without its interdependent, interrelated, interaction with everything else. And what lies nowhere and nowhen behind what is taken to be everything? Emptiness, that which contains, within itself, the possibility of everything but which, it, itself, is merely emptiness. This, I sense—and I hope without doing violence to Almeida's subtle thoughts—is Capoeira spirit. It is the fourth level.

And Suddenly...

What, then, could the fifth level possibly consist of? Almeida calls it "playing with the mind". He writes that there are stories about Capoeira and notorious capoeiristas of the past that

> Allude to skills, knowledge, and power beyond normal comprehension. There were *capoeiras* with *corpo fechado* (closed bodies), invulnerable to bullets; *capoeiras* who transformed themselves into animals or trees to escape persecution; *capoeiras* who disappeared at will in a moment of necessity, fighters undefeated in impossible situations; and healers of extraordinary success. There are no rational explanations for the fests of many in the lore of the art.
> Sometimes, during rare *Jogos*, situations arise that cannot be explained through physical and technical resources, such as when a *capoeirista* seems to have absolute control of the opponent's will. In the level of "playing with the mind," I envision that the opponents do what you are almost silently ordering them to do. It is not only the advantage of experience or technical knowledge, but a special force, an *ache* [*axé*], which undoubtedly must have no purpose other than to help one's opponent evolve and reach a universal harmony through the Capoeira way. (Almeida 1986:150)

This level, Almeida believes, is of the nature of those Mestres whose sole concern is the development of their students. They no longer care about themselves, not really. They have attained a selfless sense of Capoeira living. Only after a Mestre explores virtually all possibilities, after she spends years pushing at the limits of her physical abilities, after she found the courage and modesty to becomes once again like a beginner, then, like a child, taking in the Roda of Capoeira and that larger Roda we call the "world" with wide, innocent eyes, it can begin to "play with the mind."

Well and good. While I have unconditional admiration for Almeida's Capoeira story, and while in my wildest dreams I could never hope to reach any possible level even remotely approaching his Capoeira maturity, I would very respectfully make a modest amendment to his idea of "playing with the mind." I venture to do so in view of my premises in this inquiry—Capoeira and Candomblé cultures as complementary manifolds of interdependent, interrelated, interactive processes—that will hopefully become more evident as these pages unfold.

My amendment is this: before entering Almeida's fifth Capoeira level, body and mind have become one, *bodymind*. Almeida, I believe, implies so much. It is at the fifth level that, finally, spirit makes its entry to give us the genuine fusion: bodymindspirit. Or perhaps, since body and mind and spirit are felt and sensed and conceptualized in terms of signs if we wish to follow Peirce's philosophy, we have: *bodymindspirit* = Capoeira living. Now, as in the Buddhist tale, mountains are mountains and rivers are rivers once again, in the egoless, selfless sense, which is to say that *bodymindspirit* is at one and tantamount to *Capoeira living*. This is, I would humbly suggest, Almeida's "quality of mestres touched by the blessing of the *Orixás*" (spirits of Candomblé practice, to be discussed in part II) (Almeida 1986:150). I might point out that the polarity of Yin and Yang, or female and male, "is an ever-present theme in Candomblé, as prominent in its mythology as it is in its social structure and ritual practice. [Mythology, social structure, and ritual practice] work as analogies to one another,... mirroring each other enough to create an extremely coherent lived world" (Johnson 2002:41).

CAPOEIRA AND ITS NEXT OF KIN

In fact, we find the makings of a Roda in three Brazilian interrelated activities: *Capoeira, Candomblé*, and a particular type of Samba called *Samba de Roda* (Guimarães 1978). The dance steps within each of these Rodas are comparable.

Regarding Capoeira, the Afro-Brazilian religion-philosophy, Candomblé, and Samba de Roda, Barbara Browning writes: "The circle of candomblé dance is the space where human bodies incorporate divine energy. The roda de samba rather lifts humanity, secular energy, to a higher level. In capoeira, the roda contains bodies all too aware of their earthly nature" (Browning 1995:108). This is not to say that Capoeira is contrary to Candomblé's spiritual dancing, or that it doesn't lift humanity within the cultural realm as does Samba. Capoeira is culturally uplifting by its very nature, and many capoeiristas feel a profound sense of Africa's spirituality and cultural past. All three cultural activities provide a link to Africa to the memory of diaspora, of a sense of slavery and all its abuses. Capoeira emerged as a way of coping in a concrete, immediate, material way. In this manner it complements Candomblé's spirituality and Samba's culturality.

FIGURE 10

PLAYING WITH BODYMINDSPIRIT

The final level of Capoeira, which I prefer to call "playing with bodymindspirit," offers us more than a rough distinction in figure 7 and more than the flowing distinction in figure 8. It offers the *Yin-Yang* black circle within the white and the white circle within the black (figure 10). Emptiness, or the crystal ball, are at the deepermost level the same. At this level, no matter from whence the spirit enters, from whatever philosophy or religion, the capoeirista enjoys a genuine feeling for Capoeira, that is, for the Roda, for the Capoeira community, for the human community, and for the entire world. Moreover, it is in this final level that the five qualifying features of Capoeira as outlined in the previous chapter come through with full force: nonessence and nonfixity, process, purposeless purpose, freedom within nonfreedom, and truth through truthlessness.

At this final level, we might say that we should never mind mind and matter is of no matter, at least in the customary sense; as far as genuine Capoeira is concerned, there is only bodymindspirit. Within Capoeira living, there is no such thing as races but only race, the human race; so also, there are neither masters nor slaves, neither dominant nor subservient, neither strong nor weak, neither aggressive nor passive, neither rich nor poor, neither haughty nor humble. There is only Capoeira.

Adeus… adeu	Good bye… good bye
Eu vou m'bora	I'm takin' my leave
E vou com Deus	And I'm goin' with God
E Nossa Senhora	And our Blessed Mother (Mary)
Adeus…	So long…

Mestre Bola Sete (1997:167)

Postscript to Chapter Five

Capoeira, Close to the Earth

Playing with bodymindspirit is, above all, playing close to the earth, with limbs contracted and body compacted (*fechado*, closed) in Borromean knot (pretzel) fashion—something like figure 4. Bodymind is one and in the flow. Spirit is contrite yet full of malícia. All is close to the earth. This is especially the case of Capoeira Angola, traditional Capoeira. Playing close to the earth is *Jogo de Dentro* (inside play, down low, low and close to the other partner, ready to dish out a dose of malícia). Capoeira Regional, in contrast, is chiefly *Jogo de Fora* (standing up and at a distance, maneuvering arms and legs up and out).

    I would suggest that *Jogo de Dentro*, Jogo close to the earth where Capoeira's roots lie, is the most faithful expression of "playing with bodymindspirit." With every move, you remain as close to the earth as possible. That is where life began and that is where it will end. You give your partner a *Benção* and you begin doing so in a hunched, seemingly contrite position. You do a *Meia Lua de Frente* (half-moon sweep forward with one leg), a *Martelo* (hammer blow), a *Rabo de Arraia* (a backward sweep), a *Meia Lua de Compasso* (a sweep backward down low, with hands on the floor), a *Cabeçada* (head butt), or a *Rasteira* (sweep with a leg), and you do so from the lowest possible position. Your partner thrusts a *Tesoura* (scissors lock) in your direction and you twirl away like a pinwheel with an *Aú* (cartwheel), except with legs doubled up and body curved in that elegantly grotesque way. All, close to the earth, where your (that is, the Afro-Brazilians') ancestors flopped down after fifteen or so hours of bone wracking physical labor, where they fell in their own blood after a flogging, or where they came to permanent rest after their last gasp of life giving air. (Please do not misunderstand my motives here. My conjunction of the non-Afro-Brazilian apprentice and the experienced Afro-Brazilian playing Capoeira and acting out her ancestors' wretched condition is not to say that I, a white Anglo male, am in some form or fashion capable genuinely of empathizing or feeling and sensing the Capoeira world as it has been felt and sensed over the generations. I do wish to suggest that when the non-Afro-Brazilian practitioner is engaged in the art, she is beginning the sometimes painful, sometimes playful, but always rewarding, process toward a profoundly universal human experience.)

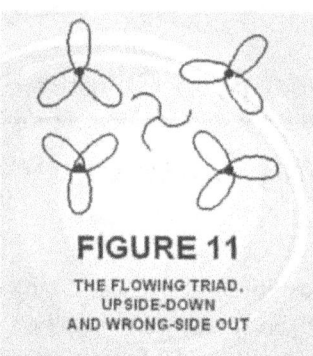

FIGURE 11

THE FLOWING TRIAD,
UPSIDE-DOWN
AND WRONG-SIDE OUT

Your compacted bodymindspirit also affords you protection, and readiness for launching an attack. It makes you less vulnerable. You remain more enigmatic, mysterious, undecipherable, close to the earth. This low and apparently (though not actually) dirty play of malícia is, in part, the reason Capoeira fell into ill repute. In Mestre Pastinha's words:

> The blacks used Capoeira to defend their freedom. Nevertheless, bad asses (*malandros*) and wretched souls discovered a way to assault respectable folks, reap vengeance on their enemies, and confront the police, by use of these Capoeira moves. It was a sad time for Capoeira. I know; I saw. In the gangs along the docks ... violent rumbles, nobody could contain them. I know that all this throws dirt on the history of Capoeira, but is a pistol to blame for the crimes it is used to commit? Or a knife? Or cannons? Or bombs? Capoeira Angola looks like dancing, but it isn't, not really. It can kill; it has killed. Beautiful! Violence hides behind its beauty. (Bola Sete 1989:190)

While in the Roda you are often in an inverted, upside-down position, viewing the world in mirror-image form. The world is seen as if through a looking-glass, for sure. From your top-down vantage point you try to see another world, a world less painful, a world other than what it is, as did your (the

Mestre Pastinha

Afro-Brazilians') ancestors. But even the looking-glass is twisted at a ninety-degree angle, over to the side, such that everything becomes topsy-turvsy.

You don't believe me? Look in your bathroom mirror. How do you see yourself? Your mirror-image is enantiomorphic. Your right hand is your left hand; your right ear is your left ear, and so on. It's as if your body had turned itself inside-out. Now imagine you are looking at your mirror-image in the same way except that the image is given a one-hundred and eighty degree rotation. Not only will your right hand be your left hand but your feet will be where your head was and vice versa. Everything is awry. It is inverted visual irony. It is vagueness, ambiguity, contradiction, paradox. You see the world in an involuted, convoluted, inside-out way, but you must imagine it as it would normally appear, because that is the world within which survival is at stake. Yet you can see it as it might otherwise be. You are entering the world of that subtle trickster, that master of *malícia*, the wily Candomblé *Orixá*, *Exu*—about which more below. You (the Afro-Brazilians' ancestors) have become a Black Alice through a cloudy Looking-Glass; you have metaphorically entered a world of horror, suffering, and death. Yet it is at the same time the most humanly human world possible

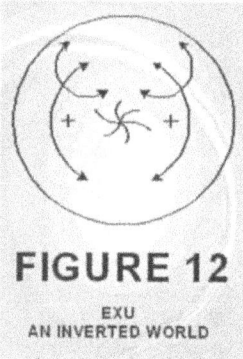

FIGURE 12
EXU
AN INVERTED WORLD

But now,... what's happening? You're now imagining you're in the Roda, the Roda that is the world, that is life itself. A sly grin spontaneously appears on the surface of your otherwise tortured countenance. Why, it's a grin evincing its own form of malícia. So that's it. Your inside-out world actually gives you (the Afro-Brazilians' ancestors) an advantage. It is an escape; it allows you a break from the pain; it gives you a different angle on things by means of which, through deception, you can somehow get the better of those who hold you in respite, contempt, and derision. They—the powerful, hegemonic haves—might not know you actually have the advantage, because their conveniently comfortable world is an either/or affair. They know only dominance and subservience, good and evil, beautiful and ugly, playing and fighting. You, in contrast, close to the earth, know that reality is too subtle to allow for such simplistic distinctions. You, with your *malícia*, take irony, ambiguity, vagueness, contradiction, and paradox, into your heart and mind and spirit. You know that whatever appears, will disappear in the next moment and then appear as something other than the way it was appearing. This is because you, bodymindspirit, have *Exu* quality. *Exu*, the roguish *Orixá*, "lord of *rasteiras*," as Lewis puts it, is always both who he is and who he is not and he is *neither*, who he is *nor* who he is not. *Exu* is always becoming, always on the go, always twirling as if in a perpetual *Aú* (an inverted world, a world with feet high, and a grinning, taunting, mischievous face down low) (Lewis 1992:xii, Thompson 1984:114).

Yes. You've got 'em coming and going, you, bodymindspirit, close to the earth. They, the haves, are trying to interpret you; you, in contrast, are trying to interpret your (the Afro-Brazilians') ancestors; but those ancestors are interpreting the haves as well as you at the same time. Past is present and present is past; your (the Afro-Brazilians') ancestors are you and you are them; the haves when in the Roda are havenots, and the havenots are haves. The poor have inherited the earth, within the Roda.

Where There are No Certainties

When you're at your best during a series of Capoeira flurries, you have the upper hand, because, given your ironic inversions, your deceptive moves, your ambiguous countenance, in short, your malícia, you are aware of the uncertainties of the cosmos

They, those other people, the haves, are not so aware. Limited by institutional rules and regulations, bureaucratic labyrinths, and stultifying social procedures, prohibitions, and prejudices, they torpidly plod along, with tunnel vision. They are blind to alternative paths, like a hedgehog. You, in contrast, are a wily fox. Those who claim powerful credentials try to dominate you, and you allow them to think they are doing so by giving the appearance of subservience while going your own way, by obediently responding in subtle ambiguities whose ulterior meaning gives you a tinge of freedom of which they remain ignorant. They try to hold you in their grasp, and you slither free. They try to trap you and cage you, and you are wise to their unwavering ways. They try to get more productivity out of you, and you create devious glitches in the works. They try to demolish human bonds between yourself and others, and you become more united, you become as one, close to the earth (the Afro-Brazilians' origins).

You have fused with your companions and with your world. In the process you have become everything, and you have become nothing, mere emptiness. After all, what is black and what is white? Figure 6, "playing in the dark," is only gray. It is neither black nor white. In figure 7 and especially figure 8, "playing in the light," the grand separation makes itself known. There is black, and there is white. Within the Roda, you can have either the one or the other. Taking the ring in its entirety, however, you have both black and white. "Playing in the light" depicts the beginning of rhythmic coexistence between the *either* and the *or*. But you have no ambiguity, no complementarity, not yet at least. Figure 9, "playing with the crystal ball," leads you to the brink and you confront that absolute absence of everything and anything, emptiness. There is neither black nor white, nor is there anything, any-thing, that can be subdivided, as in figure 7. There is just emptiness, period. Figure 10, "playing with bodymindspirit," finally, hints at the ambiguity, the incongruous, contradictory complementarity, the cosmic uncertainty, within which you are suspended. The notion of complementarity I evoke here is akin to Yin-Yang complementarity. It is also vintage Niels Bohr, the physicist-philosopher and author of the quantum complementarity principle. It is no coincidence that he was inspired by the implications of Yin-Yang (Plotnitsky 1994).

Becoming aware of Capoeira irony, ambiguity, deception, malícia, philosophy, and life, is becoming aware of the ecology of edges. Looking through mammoth telescopes at vast distances, looking through electron microscopes at minuscule distances, or looking closely at digital scans, what seemed gray turns out to be minute points of alternating black and white. If we take all that is becoming other than what it was becoming into consideration, we realize we are caught in the vast field of emptiness. We become aware, finally, that all that is, all that has emerged from emptiness, is not simply either black or white, for it can be both black and white, or it can be neither black nor white, as we see it or as we so choose.

Our obsession with certainty is what demands either blacks or whites. Capoeira is more subtle, however. With a hearty guffaw that is at once taunting, haunting, and defiant, Capoeira gives us the illusion of certainty and then takes it away. It never ceases chipping away at whatever certainty we might have thought we had in our grasp. It never ceases revealing the elusive nature of all edges, all borders, and all lines of demarcation. Thus, playing with bodymindspirit is never complete. In fact, completeness is not even an issue, for all is process, with neither discernible beginning nor ending nor center. Indeed, deep down, I would suggest, we all have Capoeira nature, whether we know it or not. For, to repeat myself once again, the effervescent, scintillating, swirling vortex that is Capoeira, is life, and life is Capoeira.

Now for a look at Capoeira's cultural cousin, Candomblé.

Part II

CANDOMBLÉ: LIVING PHILOSOPHY, PHILOSOPHICAL LIVING

Chapter Six

Rhythms and Rituals of Resistance

My Candomblé story is more academically oriented than my Capoeira story. This is for a practical reason: my contact with Candomblé life is not as extensive as my concrete experience with a Capoeira family. Be that as it may, since according to the premises of this inquiry Capoeira complements Candomblé, I would like to believe the two stories effectively dovetail with each other.

THE SETTING
Candomblé is chiefly concentrated in the city of Salvador (often called Bahia). Located at the mouth of the magnificent Bay of All Saints, Salvador became the commercial center of sugar plantations and mills in the rich agricultural stretch of land along the coast. During the early colonial period, it sported opulent merchant families dealing in sugar exports and the import of African slaves. The best of times for the merchants came to an end, however. Intensive sugar production in the Caribbean began depressing the Bahia area economy. Yet, Salvador continued as capital of the Portuguese colony until 1763. By mid-nineteenth century it still managed to maintain its status as the second largest city of the country, after Rio de Janeiro.

Candomblé is often dubbed by Westerners a fetishist cult, an irrational, "primitive" belief, and at best a religion. Rarely is it considered a rich philosophy of life. Actually Candomblé is more than a one-day-a-week religion in much the contemporary Western sense: it is a twenty-four hour a day affair. It is also more than the sort of intellectual Western philosophy that remains divorced from concrete living: it involves bodymindspirit as a whole. Candomblé incorporates a coherent world vision; it is a holistic way of life; it is practicing philosophy in the broadest sense (Luz 1995). How did this practicing philosophy come about? It began, when the first Africans arrived in the Americas.

The Portuguese colonial economy rested on the broad but weary, lash-marked backs of African and mulatto slaves and so-called free—but still brutally exploited—workers. This climate eventually gave rise to Candomblé practices involving a mixture of diverse African religions and Catholicism, with a sprinkling of Native American (*Caboclo*) religious elements. Through Candomblé philosophy-religion, the Afro-Brazilians eventually developed a sense of community. This community spirit gave them the wherewithal for coping with, and eventually resisting, the awful lot destiny seemed to have held in store for them. It became a means of survival. In order to survive, however, first and foremost the slaves had to present a show of *conformity* toward their masters. Conformity suggested peaceful coexistence. The aura of peaceful coexistence put the masters into a soporific state, blissfully confident that all was well on the *fazenda* (plantation). But all was definitely not well. The outward show of conformity concealed seething *resistance*. Conformity and resistance became the name of the game. And it still is, for Brazil's downtrodden people, as Marilena Chaui (1986) effectively argues.

In light of the above chapters, conformity and resistance can be construed as other names for Capoeira deception and malícia. They entail the process of creating a world that goes against appearances, a topsy-turvy world. In this manner, Candomblé as practicing philosophy-religion complements Capoeira as practicing philosophy-art. These practices create appearances of conventionality that conceal brooding conflict. It is like a rephrasing of Caliban's words to Prospero in Shakespeare's *The Tempest*: "You taught me to speak your language, master, and I patiently learned it; and now, I can more effectively engage in 'deception'." This is also comparable to the rule of thumb João Ubaldo Ribeiro suggests throughout his novel *Viva o povo brasileiro* (1984; *Long Live the Brazilian People*). Violence against others usually breeds reluctant conformity, and at the same time an obstinate will to resist.

For sure, the Portuguese tried their best to impede development of Afro-Brazilian community spirit. One of their methods was to force the diverse African "nations" together into a wretched concoction of human souls. By mixing Africans of different linguistic and ethnic origins, they attempted to keep their assortment of slaves in a state of confusion—divide and rule, as the adage has it. The idea was to limit communication. Without being able effectively to communicate, the slaves could hardly organize a rebellion. What the slave owners didn't take into account was the Africans' ability to cope. They coped by bringing their ethnic differences together and organizing them into a vibrant, dynamic, perpetually changing cultural whole capable of making do with whatever resources might be at hand. They made do through intensive, often clandestine, and always cunning, imagination, invention, and improvisation.

The slave owners underestimated the Africans' ability to bring their differences into an amorphous whole. They simply didn't understand the African communities' organization and function. They assumed the so-called African nations were just that—nations in the European sense constantly at odds with one another. African "nations" were actually not European-style nations at all. There were no strictly defined territorial boundaries and features of national identity. Communities existed according to language. The boundaries were ethnic rather than national. They were cultural rather than economic. Consequently, interrelationships between communities were more complementary than competitive in the Western precapitalist and capitalist sense. This allowed each community to maintain certain autonomy with respect to the other communities. At the same time, the communities were woven into a whole punctuated by conflict and wars over ethnic rather than territorial, economic, or political issues. The Portuguese mixed African slaves from different nations together in order to prevent them from organizing into a rebellious force. But their project backfired. Their reasoning was no match for the slaves' ability to improvise with the sparse resources at hand.

The Portuguese overlords didn't know they were creating the possibility of a wholesale heterogenizing cultural process: ethnic differences among the slaves came together in an effervescent contradictory yet complementary cultural flow. As differences proliferated, they eventually gave rise to apparent homogeneity that concealed myriad heterogeneous variations so slight as to remain imperceptible to untrained eyes and ears. An important facet of this *heterogenization* was the emergence of Afro-Brazilian Candomblé. As mentioned in passing, Candomblé sports a combination of religious-philosophical practices from a diversity of African nations: Ketu-Nagô (Yoruba), Ijexá (Yoruba), Jêjê, (Fon), Angola (Bantu), Congo (Bantu), and Caboclo of the Amerindian tradition (Santos 1995). This heterogenization grew throughout the colonial period. It became self-perpetuating in the nineteenth century, and it eventually contributed to today's Brazilian culture as a grand reunion of cultural elements of diverse forms and fashions (I discuss what I call "heterogeny" with respect to its kindred terms homogeny and hegemony more fully in part III).

Thus the slave owners' effort to create a bewildering Babel of nations and languages in order to keep the slaves in a state of confusion was one thing. Dynamic, perpetually changing, vibrant human interaction on the *fazenda* proved to be another thing entirely. João José Reis and Eduardo Silva (1989) demonstrate in their case studies that intricate ties across nations and cultures provided powerful mobilizing forces. As the generations went by, these forces eventually served to break down ethnic distinctions between slaves. Distinctions were also partly erased between enslaved Africans and those relatively few Afro-Brazilian Blacks, Mulattoes, and *Criolhos* or Creoles (Africans born in Brazil) who might have enjoyed the good fortune of having gained their freedom. The Europeans presumed Creole slaves and free Creoles would hold the African slaves in disdain, since the slaves brought an alien culture with them while the Creoles surely must have become comfortable with the dominant culture. Creole and slave distinctions dissolved, however, for the social issues became a matter of white Europeans, on the one hand, and everybody else, on the other. Consequently, the planters' efforts to foment Creole/African rivalry and hence hamper slave resistance failed to pan out. After all, Creoles were children of Africans, and family ties crossed this fault line in Afro-Bahia in the same way they bridged the divide between slaves and free Afro-Brazilian laborers.

The Africans' tactic of conformity yet resistance was enhanced by the fact that the Church was weaker in Brazil than in Spanish America (Gibson 1966). The slaves were baptized Catholics, for sure. But in Brazil—and to an extent in the Caribbean and the Gulf Coast—they introduced strange, suspicious practices into the Catholic ceremonies. Since the Inquisition in Brazil was less powerful than it was in the Spanish colonies, control of what were considered the slaves' unwarranted doings became difficult. The slaves, as would be natural, took advantage of the situation. As a result, from the very outset a sense of insecurity played on the Portuguese Catholic mind. Given this insecurity, the Portuguese attitude became more conducive to laxity and tolerance regarding the slaves' so-called syncretistic tendencies—disguised Catholicism for the purpose of engaging in African rituals. This laxity and tolerance gradually led to a Catholicism tinged with a diversity of African religious customs. Over the decades, these practices managed to wound Catholic sensibilities and blemish the white Europeans' coveted image of their civilized society in the tropics. Consequently, shortly after Independence in 1822 there was a concerted effort to snuff out so-called heretical and pagan African religious activity (Mattoso 1986).

Nevertheless, I must repeat, the Europeans' efforts were largely in vain. In vain, for if we peruse the chief characteristics of Candomblé life, its survival value becomes evident. Candomblé life, in a nutshell, entails: (1) internalizing traditional knowledge, including awareness of one's strengths and limitations; (2) maximizing individual potential in complementarity with the community's potential; (3) cultivating self-reflection regarding oneself within one's community; (4) taking on a humble demeanor with respect to one's relationship with the universe; (5) developing a sense of personal dignity and self-worth while remaining in community with all others; and (6) coming into conformity with one's surroundings while at the same time creating means for resisting any and all forms of adversity. For the sincere Candomblé practitioner, the individual self existed, but its existence was chiefly for the purpose of backing the whole, the community (Braga 1988). This is a far cry from the idea of Candomblé considered by the Portuguese colonizers as a mere cult, fetishism, or primitive, irrational belief system. It involves the slaves' pride in tradition, their resilience, and their resistance toward any and all attempts to emasculate their sacred practices. Candomblé, I must emphasize, is a living, practicing religion-philosophy; it is a holistic form of life, even more so than medieval Catholicism (Aflalo 1996).

Indeed, Candomblé pervades everyday living. Its purpose is to live life to the utmost, through outward conformity to the norms set down by those who were in control, coupled with clandestine and on occasion open resistance; it is conformity, for the very purpose of survival. Resistance, for there was no breaking of the African will. And resistance, afforded by the social cohesion that emerged during the colonial period. These characteristics become strikingly evident from the earliest anthropological works (Bastide 1945, 1971, 1973 1978; Nina Rodrigues 1935, 1977; Ramos 1937; Verger 1964, 1981, 1983).

Possible Origins

When the Africans became the adopted children of the Catholic Church, they had to come up with some means of holding onto and perpetuating their traditions. There are various stories telling how they accomplished this. According to the most prevalent of them, the slaves took to hiding their *Orixá* deities behind Catholic saints, thus deceiving their masters. How did this practice come about?

The combination of African languages and ethnicities shared an extensive pantheon of deities consisting of some four hundred to six hundred *Orixás*—*Ori* (head, mind) plus *Axé* (dynamic, vital energy or force). About fifty of them survived the transatlantic nightmarish passage to Brazil. Similarities among these Orixás found in the diversity of religions practices by the Afro-Brazilians were unified. Most of them were gradually phased out, but a few dozen remained by the nineteenth century. During the first half of that century, a mixed Candomblé form emerged in the state of Bahia, chiefly from the Nagô and Jêjê, though varying degrees of admixture remained. As a result, today's Candomblé focuses on a couple of dozen or so of the original Orixás. Each Orixá has its particular attributes and functions. Much the same can be said of Christ, the Virgin, and Catholic saints. Given the commonalities between these attributes and functions, the Africans found sympathetic analogies between their Orixás and certain Catholic personages. Thus they linked saints with Orixás. In so doing they initiated the practice that eventually came to be known by that now familiar term "syncretism."

Volney Berkenbrock (1995:103–104) places the origin of syncretism in anthropologist Roger Bastide's early studies. Berkenbrock qualifies the term, however. The vast diversity of African cults brought to Brazil created a heterogeneous setting of the first order. This mixture was rendered less heterogeneous by syncretizing many elements from the diverse African religions. This gave rise to Afro-Brazilian practices that were in certain ways unlike anything found in any particular region of Africa. Then, these syncretized African elements were further syncretized with elements from Catholicism. The yield was complex to the maximum. Berkenbrock synthesizes this complexity along four syncretic mixes: (1) between African cults; (2) between African cults and Catholicism; (3) between African and Amerindian (Caboclo) cults; and (4) between African cults and French spiritism (Kardecism) in the form of a religion that goes by the name of *Umbanda*—more about which later. During these processes, some Orixás took on more importance in Brazil than in Africa, while others fell by the wayside. In the terms of the present inquiry, all this made up a rich *heterogenizing* process. At the same time, each Candomblé group became a family. In a certain fashion it replaced the lost family, the vanished sense of community (Berkenbrock 1995:116–117). The religious family is one of the reasons African roots penetrated more deeply into the earth of Salvador's culture than into that of Rio de Janeiro to the south, and why relationships with the Orixás were more profound. The excruciating misery of slavery transformed a combination of African religions into basically one, resulting in a profoundly religious black community within the racial hierarchy that prevails in Salvador to this day (Bacelar 1989, 2001).

The first permanent Candomblé religious center, *Ilê Axé Iyenasso Oka*, or "Casa Branca" (White House), is believed to have been founded in 1830. Rivalries soon erupted among families associated with the Casa Branca. Numerous groups of Candomblé practitioners—I'll henceforth call them *candomblistas* to complement the term *capoeiristas*—split off and took up practice in various parts of Salvador. Nevertheless, Candomblé eventually became quite widely disseminated among many of the slaves and free blacks alike, although their activities had to remain under cover for the most part. By keeping their traditional practices in hiding, they presented the outward appearance of obedience to white rules and regulations and customary cultural practices, while beneath the surface an entirely different culture of struggle manifested itself. Indeed, this struggle was so extraordinary that virtually every attempt on the part of the Europeans to erase the Afro-Brazilian religious practices out of existence was in vain. Prolonged repression on the part of masters and administrators alike, often vicious and inhuman, was nevertheless no less violent than brutal treatment by the police. There were incessant complaints by proper folks of the upper classes, and demands that the black "evil" be snuffed out once and for all. The slaves' struggle persisted in the guise of conformity, however, and Candomblé as a way of life continued, spreading out and engulfing other cities in the state of Bahia. The Candomblé place of worship, the *Terreiro*, is where this resistance emerged as a unique Afro-Brazilian practice.

The *Terreiro*

A *Terreiro* (occasionally called the *Roça*, a plot of land) is where a Candomblé house of worship rests. Usually concrete, but sometimes earthen, it is a place, a concept; it is the source of life. The collection of Terreiros in Brazil makes up a part of Africa mythified. Each Terreiro is like an African island in a foreign land; it is a re-creation of Africa. It is no more than an island; yet it incorporates the whole of Africa, because the Orixás are there. They came from Africa to dance with their sons and daughters in this alien environment. Their very presence brings Africa to this strange yet somehow familiar land. Now, during the coming and going of everyday life, the Afro-Brazilians can learn to cope with their *saudade* (a Portuguese translation of the African word *banzo*, a profound nostalgia and longing for Africa, for times in the distant past). Thus they can once again begin to sense harmony between themselves and the natural world. In this manner, Candomblé activity in the Terreiro within the African-Brazilian form of life becomes radically participatory.

In the center of the Candomblé ring is a pillar, about which the entire ceremony revolves. Like the Capoeira Roda, the pillar and the Candomblé ring metaphorically make up the center of the universe. Numerous colors are present: chiefly white, but there is also an abundance of black, yellow, red, green, shades of blue, and a few other hues. These colors are prominent in the Yoruba tradition of the Nagô nations in Africa that make up the principle source of Salvador's Afro-Brazilian philosophical-religious practices. Many of the symbols, colors, and meanings in the Terreiro are also found in a typical Capoeira Roda. In fact, capoeiristas have associated their art with Candomblé since at least early nineteenth century. Action in the Capoeira Roda and the Candomblé Terreiro circle evince significant similarities. Some Orixás are often evoked during action in the Capoeira ring. The most common links are *Ogum*, warrior god and patron of metal, *Oxossi*, the hunter, always holding a bow and arrow, *Xangô*, Orixá of lightning and thunder and husband of various Orixás, who metes out justice, *Exu*, the trickster and messenger between the living and the spirit world, *Oxalá*, king of wisdom, good judgment, and faith, *Yemanjá*, queen of the sea, and *Iansã*, queen of tempests (see appendix A). Many capoeiristas are also Candomblé faithful; consequently they are intimately tied to their personal Orixás. Moreover, the various dance steps enacted during sacred ceremonies in honor of the Orixás are much like multiple variations of the Capoeira Ginga. The *atabaque* creates Capoeira rhythms; it also evokes the Orixás. Subtle variations of *atabaque* rhythms bring about changes in Capoeira action; they also serve to evoke different Orixás during Candomblé ceremonies.

Tourists witnessing a tailor made Candomblé session can hardly distinguish between complex polyrhythms created by *atabaques* and other percussion instruments. Yet when a beat is slapped out honoring *Ogum*, feet step lively in response. In the twinkling of an eye the pattern of *Xangô* or *Oxum* emerges, and the feet shift into a new rhythm without skipping a beat. *Yemanjá* then enters the scene, and hips swing and sway reminiscent of an undulating Ginga (Martins 2000). In every rhythm, syncopation predominates to the extent that there is a sensation of off-balanced flow that is confusing to the tourists, who can do no more than gaze in awe. Actually, tourists are not always welcome at genuine Candomblé ceremonies, and if they are, photographs are usually prohibited—except in those artificial Candomblé performance designed especially for foreigners. In fact, in the Casa Branca there is an announcement that reads in Portuguese and English: "This is a place of worship. It is not an arena for spectacles."

As religions go, representations of various Orixás during ceremonies in the Terreiro might give Candomblé the appearance of a polytheistic religion. But in the strict sense it is not. For, there is a supreme deity, *Olorum*, along with a pantheon of spirits, the Orixás. During Terreiro proceedings, Orixás descend and enter the bodies of designated individuals. They induce trance-states, when *Ilê* and *Aiyê*, here and the *otherworldly*, particular place and cosmic space, come together. These spirits or deities do not make their presence known solely during proper Candomblé moments, however. Everybody manifests tendencies in their everyday behavior that are attributed to their personal combination—usually three in Salvador—of Orixás. In this manner, everyday life includes the Orixás at every bend in the road; it entails practicing philosophy in the full sense.

My *Pai-de-Santo* (literally, "Father-of-the-Saints," somewhat comparable to what may be called a "Candomblé Priest") goes by the name of Hermes—quite appropriately named, since he is gay. During my second visit with him, I was told that my everyday personality was distinctively of the nature of *Oxalá* and *Xangô*. However, he wasn't sure about my third Orixá. This means that when I am *Xangô* acting, he is the Orixá doing my moving about and thinking and talking; and the same goes for *Oxalá* when he is acting through me. Hermes determined my accompanying Orixás after he once again tossed the customary *búzios*. The *búzios* are a collection of sixteen small shells (cowries) corresponding to the sixteen eyes of *Ifá*, goddess of divination (though she is a rare commodity in Brazilian Candomblé practices). They are thrown by a *Pai-de-Santo* or *Mãe-de-Santo* (Candomblé Priestess) on a specially prepared surface, and after proper ceremony in order to determine one's Orixá guardians and one's physical and spiritual qualities. After contemplating the position of each *búzio* and the pattern they made up in concert, Hermes discovered that my third Orixá was *Oxum*. She is a vain, self-centered woman, in contrast to my other two Orixá guardians who happened to be male. Big disappointment!—since, with a lingering sense of chauvinism, I wanted to consider myself exempt from *Oxum's* female attributes. Later, I was told during an informal discussion with Hermes that I should not consider my third guardian in a negative light, since she complemented my other two Orixás in order that I might maintain a harmonious balance within myself, with others, and with nature, during my everyday coming and going. Very slowly, painfully, and tenuously, I was beginning to sense what Candomblé was about.

Terreiro Particularity in Brazil

The French photographer and anthropologist Pierre Verger (1981) points out that in addition to Brazilian Terreiros as reinventions of African villages, African divinities are particularized in Brazil, within the family and the community. In Brazil, due to the diaspora, the Orixás took on a slightly to radically different nature. In every Terreiro there was a multiplicity, a grand mixture. Whatever the origin, in Brazil, the Terreiro was born from the need for Orixá cohesion among the members of the community and as a means of keeping it under cover and out of the censoring gaze of the Europeans.

During colonial times in Brazil, the word Terreiro usually indicated a space in the plantation that was somewhat secluded from the Big House or the mansion, and the slave quarters, the Shanties, where the slaves could be left free pretty much to do their own thing. Shortly after independence in 1822, Terreiros in Salvador were constructed just outside the city limits in the dense tropical areas. Eventually the city's sprawl engulfed them. New Terreiros were then established further into the jungle. Today, active Terreiros can be found in the city and its environs of almost three million. Many more can be reached after an hour or so bus trip, where land prices are more affordable. Most Terreiros belong to a particular Candomblé community, but some are rented property. Nevertheless, all the Terreiros are interdependently interrelated in philosophy and practice, though on the surface they might appear quite different, from time to time and from one area to another. Terreiros vary greatly in size. In the countryside some consist of various rooms with ample space between them, while in the city they might be no more than a living room, according to the financial situation of the *Pai-* or *Mãe-de-Santo*. Ordep Serra (1995:132–133, 154) observes that between the 1930s and 1940s, in spite of political repression during the Getúlio Vargas years, the number of Terreiros grew by 30percent, but from 1945 to 1967 the number increased fivefold. He goes on to remark that in contrast to the touted 365 Catholic churches in Salvador—that could at best reach perhaps a couple of hundred—there were toward the end of the twentieth century almost two-thousand Terreiros.

A Terreiro community has a keen sense of sacred and profane space. This is not the same as Mircea Eliades (1959) concept of "sacred and profane." The building they call their everyday home, and the world of work and play and commuting and shopping, is profane. A Terreiro is in a manner of speaking sacred space. But its very existence implies a third term (Thirdness), Axé, between sacred and profane traditional values and modern capitalism. The Terreiro is neither exactly the one nor the other, for Axé pervades both sacred and profane and traditional and modern within the whole of Candomblé practicing philosophy. Axé is analogous to emptiness, which gives rise to all processes that render the universe what it is. Axé maintains the continuous, effervescent flow of activities in some form or other of complementary balance. Candomblistas need their Orixás in order to participate in the life-giving, cosmic force of Axé; without Axé, everything would soon become paralyzed (Machado 1999). During a Candomblé ceremony, there are three foci of Axé in the Terreiro: (1) in the space where the Orixás are moving about—they are never at a standstill, (2) within members of the Terreiro when they mount them and induce a trance state, and (3) in deceased members (*Eguns*) of the Candomblé community. When everything is lively, the entire Terreiro is impregnated with Axé (Verger 1981).

Given the special function of Axé, and since the Terreiro is a sacred space, the candomblista must leave a few things behind upon entering the premises, whether for a formal Terreiro ceremony, a periodic visit to the *Pai-* or *Mãe-de-Santo* for consultation, or simply to help with the chores. She must cleanse herself of the world's imbalance between greater good and lesser good (or evil, in the Christian sense) and the eternal struggle between them in order to enter with a harmonious spirit. At the entrance of the Terreiro there is usually water in a pot. Some of the water must be sprinkled just outside the entrance when the candomblista enters so as to cool off whatever tension existed out there. The act is repeated upon leaving. It is a symbolic act consisting of iconicity (water as cleansing image) and indexicality (cleansing to prevent undesirable elements from entering sacred space).

The Terreiro is central to the nature and function of Candomblé living.

Comprehending this form of life is for the outsider an arduous task. Anthropologists agonized over this dilemma during most of the twentieth century. Ruth Landes herself, who spent years experiencing the ways of Candomblé living, finally confessed her perplexity:

> The philosophy, the mysticism and emotionality of candomblé always puzzled me. I learned to know it by rote, the way one learns a new language in school, and I became an adept at it; but my reactions were as remote as those of an adding machine to numbers. I grew fond of the people, I admired the quality of their lives—rich as embroidered brocade—but I wanted to know more. I am convinced now that Edison [Carneiro] was right when he said the cult followers were actually good Catholics. One had to be reared in that Latin, medieval Catholicism, ignorant of modern beliefs and systems, and indifferent to them, to get at the heart and soul of the people's values. (Landes 1947:88)

Landes writes that she learned about Candomblé and the Terreiro intellectually, but she admits her failure to get the point in her heart and her guts; she learned but didn't comprehend; she knew empirically but didn't know morally and spiritually; what she had come to know she couldn't quite say; if she had somehow been able to comprehend Candomblé living in the replete sense, I suspect it would have been bodymind knowing, not merely discursive knowing.

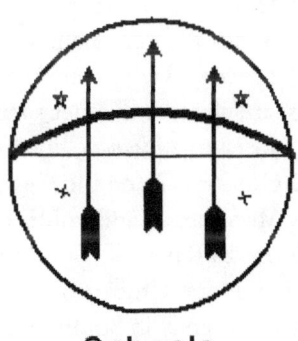

Caboclo

That much said, I wish briefly to introduce another religion, *Umbanda*, in order more effectively to offer picture of the enigmatic Candomblé form of life. I do so, since (1) *Umbanda* is interjected with a healthy dose of Candomblé; in fact, it has occasionally taken on the name "Umbandomblé" and (2) *Umbanda* is a prime example of an Afro-Brazilian homogenizing-heterogenizing process, also prevalent in Candomblé, a theme that will take on an increasingly important role from this point onward.

Tangential Paths

In 1848, French spiritism arrived to the shores of Brazil. Spiritism was the work of Léon Hyppolite Denizard Rivail (1804–1869), writing under the pseudonym Allan Kardec. In a nutshell, Kardec believed: (1) in the Christian God, (2) in benign acts of charity toward the needy, (3) in reincarnation and, (4) that certain gifted souls are able to communicate with the dead. Kardec derived these ideas in part from: (1) the social evolutionary and positivist philosophy of Auguste Comte, (2) Hindu reincarnation and the Law of Karma, (3) Christian ethics, and (4) a strange mixture of rationalism, scientism, and mysticism. During the 1930s, Brazilian *Umbanda* in its various incarnations emerged out of a combination of Kardec's spiritism, Candomblé, and Amerindian or Caboclo religious spirits (Brown 1986; Warren 1968, 1970).

Umbandistas, however, tend to downplay the rationalist-scientist side of Kardecism and upgrade the spiritist-mystical-mysterious side. Basically, Umbanda includes many of the common Candomblé Orixás in addition to the pantheon of Catholic saints and the godhead. It also places emphasis on the Caboclo spirit (Amerindian deities commonly under the command of the hunter Orixá, *Oxossi*). It includes, as well, the *Preto-Velho*, the image of an old-black man, incorporating the spirit of wise old slaves who have healing powers, and the *Preto-Safado*, the image of a crazy-black man, incorporating the spirit of nutty old codgers, full of malícia (Ortiz 1978:71–76). But there is a difference between West Africa Orixás and the Orixás adopted by Umbanda beliefs. Orixás from West Africa are immanent spirits of nature. Bantu beliefs, including spirits of the deceased who roam the world occasionally communicating with mediums, are closer to Kardec's spiritism.

In fact, Umbanda is closer to *Macumba*, chiefly of Rio de Janeiro and Bantu culture, than it is to Candomblé and the West Africa cultural tradition. Thus the combination of Macumba, Candomblé, Caboclo practices, spiritism, and Christianity give rise to this new hybrid religion, Umbanda. Especially as a result of its French input, Umbanda has gained popularity among the middle-classes, and more recently in Southern Brazil, and even Uruguay and Argentina. However, when all is said and done, Umbanda is neither Catholic nor African nor Caboclo nor spiritist, and at the same time it is all of them; this characteristic it shares with Candomblé (Berkenbrock 1995:159–161).

Until recently almost 90 percent of the Brazilian population professed faith in Catholicism. African slaves were baptized into the Church, though many or perhaps most of them were unconverted to the Catholic faith. They had been ripped from their cultural roots, and with nothing else to replace them, many slaves embraced European ways, outwardly at least. Yet there was a longing for long lost roots—*saudade*, within the alienating Brazilian environment. Consequently, certain aspects of ancient African religious beliefs managed to survive against all odds. And today they thrive, as African-based religions such as Candomblé or the spiritist-based Umbanda religion. For example, by 1987 the number of Catholic churches in Brazil had fallen to somewhat less than 50,000, while the number of places of diverse forms of Afro-Brazilian worship reached 450,000. Significantly, the expansion of Candomblé, Umbanda and other Afro-Brazilian beliefs since Brazilian Independence has more than kept up with expansion of urbanization in Salvador and throughout Brazil. Indeed, over the past decades the most prominent of these beliefs have gradually been taking on status as national religions along with Catholicism (Johnson 2002:156–159; Kloppenburg 1961, 1964, 1992; Lépine 2000).

The road, however, has not been easy. And it has come at the expense of tension and conflict between the most prominent alternative beliefs. Umbanda became popular among Brazil's black population of the developed urban areas to the south. Since umbandistas among the black population do not seek to preserve their African cultural patrimony in a pure form, Umbanda has often been looked upon as a whitened religion—sometimes contrasted with black magic, supposedly of Candomblé origin. Diana Brown (1986:146–147) points out that the 1934 law that permitted Umbanda and other non-Catholic practices placed practitioners of Umbanda and Afro-Brazilian religions in a double bind: in theory, registration allowed them to practice legally; in fact, however, it could not attract the attention of the police and hence increase the likelihood of harassment and extortion. Registered or not, Umbandistas continued to incur severe police persecution in Rio, as did other Afro-Brazilian religions in the Northeast. Nevertheless, by as early as the 1950s, Umbanda was practiced by people from all walks of life, and regardless of color, race, social or geographical origin. Although today many Umbanda followers are of European descent, Umbanda has no fixed social class boundaries, and most of its followers are still poor. The simplest explanation for this is that most of the Brazilian people themselves are poor. Since Umbanda developed its own outlook on life, a kind of mosaic of elements from various beliefs, it can lay claim to a form of transcendence that enables it either to replace the Catholic traditions or to maintain faith in Catholicism as a complementary religious sense of life (Freitas and Silva Pinto 1956; Leich 1980; Matta e Silva 1969). Actually, middle class Umbanda is quite unique. It is neither exactly an infusion of African traditions nor impoverishment of mainstream Enlightenment European society, but something different emerging from the interstices. It is, as we shall note in part III, the most dynamic form of heterogeneous practices.

CANDOMBLÉ, UMBANDA, AND AFRO-BRAZILIAN IDENTITY

There is within the very nature of the Umbanda world vision, as there is in the Candomblé vision, a vague and ambiguous identity. This identity, with its roots in Brazil's slave society, created a tension between tendencies and propensities pulling in different directions that is at heart a matter of incongruous, contradictory complementarity according to my use of the terms above.

For example, Kátia M. de Queirós Mattoso (1986:107–124) tells us that slavery in Brazil left a greater multiplicity of cultural practices than in most areas of the Americas where slavery was practiced. This multiplicity, however, was the yield of a complex ambiguous picture. The master customarily gave the slaves a blessing at the appropriate moments like the good Catholic patron he would like to be; at the same time he enforced the concept of brutal labor with the threat of lashing and flogging. The master presented the image of a sympathetic father figure with the well being of the slaves in mind; yet he literally worked them to death, and at a moment's notice he would dole out harsh treatment much as he would his livestock. How could the slaves react to these mixed messages? By creating a mirror-image of their master's ambiguity. They played their master's game in order to cater to his role as benign patron; they created subtle deviations from the game whenever possible in order to maintain a modicum of their African humanity. On the surface they became the kind of slave their master desired; deep down they deceptively undercut their master's two-faced dealings whenever they could. We have our now familiar contrasts on the part of the slaves: conformity and resistance, submissive appearance mixed with deception, loyalty on the surface coupled with subterfuge at covert levels. The slaves' behavioral patterns became ambiguous, like their master's. Both patterns existed side-by-side: they were incongruously complementary. But since the slaves' ambiguous responses in large part depended on whatever their master apparently had in mind at a given moment, they could have no masterplan giving them a fixed guide for attitudes and action. They had to live in a state of uncertain expectancy; they had to improvise according to whatever the context presented.

This is to say that in a strictly defined sense of fixed identity, the slaves seemed to have no identity, because, given the nature of their constant improvisation for survival purposes, they were always becoming something other than what they were becoming. In this respect, from one vantage point playwright and Afro-Brazilian activist Abdias do Nascimento (2002), and from another, Serge Gruzinski (2001), argue that the label "hybridism," popular among postcolonialist scholars, doesn't do the trick when accounting for some sort of subaltern identity (however, see Canevacci 1996; Werbner 1997). There is no hybridization (conformity) that might culminate in the surface appearance of homogeneous cultural processes, for there is also dehybridization (resistance) and a move toward heterogeneity. During the colonial period the Africans resisted cultural imposition by the Portuguese. At the same time, their resistance against the threats and restrictions of the dominant culture was accompanied by efforts to conserve their own culture. This resistance underlying apparent conformity to European ways and resistance for the sake of conserving African ways entails acts of what I have labeled elsewhere cultural guerrilla activity (merrell 2004). Cultural guerrilla subversion through conformity and resistance became a defense mechanism vis-à-vis a hostile world. It allowed them to survive as a human community.

So it might appear that the Africans had some sense of identity after all! But it was not identity in the positive Cartesian-Freudian sense of the ego in contrast to and in perpetual struggle with everything that is non-ego. Neither was it identity in terms of some collective sense of us as a presumed fixed, homogeneous bloc against them. It was identity as a rough-and-tumble, perpetually transient fusion of apparent conformity and conventionality (in order to survive) and resistance (self-assertion through negative action), a cultural guerrilla posture. Roger Bastide compares what I have labeled this conformity and resistance in Brazil to the situation of Haiti, which won its independence and the elimination of white domination in the beginning of the nineteenth century. As a consequence of Haitian independence, Voodoo developed into a specifically and originally Haitian form of worship, characterized by innovation and dynamic variation:

> The Negroes no longer had to fight against the Europeans' desire to assimilate them. They were not obliged to erect that double barrier of social resistance [such as we find in other Antilles or on the mainland] against racial prejudice on the one hand, and the imposition of Western values on the other. [...] The Haitian Negroes had no longer anything of the sort to struggle against, and their religion could thus more easily adapt itself to changing conditions—which, inevitably, soon took place in the infrastructures of the peasant communities. (Bastide 1971:131)

For Afro-Haitians, comparable to Afro-Brazilians, it was not a matter of our homogeneity against their homogeneity. The Africans' religious practices were already thoroughly heterogenized, or mesticized, according to Abdias do Nascimento (1979).

This very important issue reveals a quandary inherent in the tendency among today's scholars who allude to "global interconnectedness" and "local effects" (Leitch 1996), or "global designs" and "local histories" (Mignolo 2000). In spite of their professed anti-essentialism, some of these scholars still fall prey to implicit essentialist abstractions (Loomba 1998). In other words, they often characterize local histories by use of abstract, universal terms. In so doing, they create a reductive, entrenched, stultified form of what we might term "homogenized heterogeneity." Mignolo himself, it seems, has become aware of this problem (Mignolo and Schiwy 2002), as have other critics of the global/local dichotomy (see the essays in Mudimbe-Boyi 2002; also the lively debate on universals, hegemony, and contingency in J. Butler et al. (2000).

Meanwhile, back to the topic at hand, with respect to Candomblé life, soon there were...

WINDS OF CHANGE

In 1960s something strange, but perhaps inevitable, began happening. Emigration intensified from the Northeast (poor Brazil) to the Southeast (modern and industrialized Brazil). Many of these emigrants brought Candomblé with them. It soon influenced Umbanda practitioners, and many of them began converting to Candomblé and abandoning Umbanda (Birman 1995; Prandi 1991).

The movement gained a head of steam that brought about two significant changes: (1) it began leading some Umbandistas back to their roots, considered by many to be the true, original, more mysteriously sacred, religious matrix from which Umbanda once emerged, and (2) the older Candomblé tradition found a more benign economic situation, since its religious ceremonies required significant expense and the newly integrated umbandistas were on the average more financially comfortable. All this occurred at a time when there was an effort among many middle class citizens to return to the presumed original roots of Brazilian culture. Intellectuals, poets, students, writers, and artists participated in this new enlightened quest for identity, which in many cases eventually found itself at the front doors of the old Candomblé houses in the city of Salvador (Berkenbrock 1995:119). Traveling to Salvador for consultation with a *Pai-* or *Mãe-de-Santo* became fashionable. It seemed to satisfy a need to fill the vacuum left by modern secularized lifestyles in the industrialized cities to the South (Oro 1993; Frigério 1989; Prandi 1991).

As mentioned, Candomblé practices are often divided into various nations according to the ethnic origins preserved in the rites. The ancient African cultures that have contributed most to the development of the current nations of Candomblé were brought from the Sudan cultures of the Gulf of Guinea (Yoruba and Fon, presentday Nigeria and Benin), and the Bantu cultural areas (presentday Angola, Congo, Gabon, Zaïre, and Mozambique). However, a clear-cut distinction can no longer be made between them (Costa Lima 1984). For instance, in the state of Bahia during the nineteenth century, the Ketu nation (including Nagô practices) and the Yoruba language predominated, although there were other mixed strains from Western Africa. Over the years, meanings of many Yoruba words used in the religious ceremonies were lost, and the sacred songs could no longer be effectively translated. The Angola nation, chiefly of Bantu sources, assimilated some of the Orixás and many of the initiation practices of the Yorubans. During the process, the Angolan ritual language, originating from the Kimbundo dialect, also became quite untranslatable. To further complicate the issue, worship of the Caboclos, considered by the Africans to be the most genuine Brazilians, was also of primary importance to the Angolans. Thus Caboclo religious elements were mixed with both Angolan and Ketu elements (Gonçalves da Silva 1999). Consequently, Afro-Brazilian religious practices now present a virtually undecipherable picture. The heterogenizing process continues.

A question arises, then: How have these heterogenizing peoples, the Afro-Brazilians, been conceived by the dominant society, and how has this conception of them changed over the years?

Chapter Seven

Hegemonic Pressure

DILUTING RACE AND ETHNICITY

Shortly after abolition of slavery in 1888, the dream of a white European Bahia free of African influence was born. This dream followed on the heels of European-based scientific racism that was quite popular in Brazilian intellectual circles. The delirious vision, stemming from racism, of deporting all free Afro-Brazilians to Africa after the 1835 Muslim rebellion in Salvador came to naught due to prohibitive cost. Other attempts to displace blacks to other areas of the country proved problematic and ineffective as well (Reis 1993).

Nevertheless, there seemed to be a faint glimmer at the end of the tunnel for the white Europeans after all. By the turn of the twentieth century, anthropologist Raimundo Nina Rodrigues was conducting pioneer studies of African culture in the state of Bahia. His conclusion? The African race was destined eventually to disappear through miscegenation. Gradual submersion of Afro-Brazil within midstream European culture became the utopian dream. European immigration in order to *embranquecer* (whiten) the race became the practical task at hand. "Whitening" was Brazil's answer to doctrinaire scientific racism that grew out of nineteenth-century European Social Darwinism and Comtean Positivism. In Brazil this doctrine obviously grew, in part, out of the fear among elite citizens of the black population whose increase was far outrunning that of the whites (Fonseca 2000). Whitening implicitly included the idea of a Brazilian populace that would be racially mixed, for sure; but the mixture would be so diluted by a heavy infusion of "whiteness" that it would hopefully take on a surface appearance of Europeanness (homogeneity). Moreover, since Candomblé did not enjoy the status of a legitimate religion, the European elites "may have hoped that it, like the Afro-Brazilians themselves, would gradually lose its ethnic edge, curve back, and whiten into the national population without leaving any scars" (Johnson 2002:90). At the same time, the whitening project conveniently made way for the creation of the "racial democracy" myth—about which more below.

However, whitening never really caught sail in a benign wind and failed to make substantial headway. Attracted by Brazilian enticements offered in the name of immigration, Europeans flocked to the states of Rio de Janeiro and São Paulo, and more preferably to the southern climes of the country where cooler temperatures prevailed. They generally shunned the northeastern part of Brazil, where Afro-Brazilian ethnicity was concentrated. Nevertheless, the dream of a white Brazil wouldn't be denied. By the 1930s anthropologist Donald Pierson (1942) observed—and thus soothed the widespread wish—that Bahia's population was indeed becoming whiter. It was just a matter of time, and all would be fine in the land of virtual paradise. The "white hope" lingered on.

During this same period, Gilberto Freyre (1946, 1959, 1963) began propagating his "racial democracy" theme. Under Freyre's watchful eye and prolific pen, Brazil took on the image of a harmonious melding of three grand races and cultures, African, Amerindian, and European. Freyre envisioned a close relationship between Portuguese landowners and African slaves culminating in intense miscegenation. The problem is that in the estimation of some Brazilians, Freyre provided what was considered "social scientific backing" for the whitening doctrine, even though Freyre never overtly propagated whitening. Throughout the colonial period and during more than a century of independence, the three races were supposed to have learned from one another. In the process they gained appreciation of ethnic differences and became increasingly tolerant, thus making way for racial democracy that would soon reach a happy conclusion. The process of whitening would eventually resolve whatever racial problems continued to plague Brazil.

So, whitening would supposedly bring a solution to the so-called Negro problem with the creation of a racial democracy. Yet, the idea of "whiter is better" prevailed. When all is said, one must concede that if the miscegenation process didn't exactly transform Brazilian society into a genuine racial democracy, to Freyre's credit, his work powerfully acknowledged the importance of African culture to Brazilian society. However, psychologist Ronilda Ribeiro (1998:242) remarks that ironically Brazil was the last American nation to abolish slavery, and the first to claim status as a racial democracy. Anthropologist Ordep Serra (1995:163) points out that even though Freyre's racial democracy is pure myth, and in spite of the fact that he is a Lusophile, putting Portugal in a largely undeserved positive light, at least he called attention to admirable aspects of Brazilian national identity (see also Degler 1971; Ferreira 1998; Francisco 2000; Nogueira 1985; Skidmore 1974). From a more radical vantage point, Abdias do Nascimento (2002:141) goes so far as to proclaim that Brazil with its mythified racial democracy is like Mexico—where one party ruled from 1929 to 2000—a "perfect dictatorship," the label Peruvian novelist Mario Vargas Llosa once used in reference to Mexico.

A brief sketch of Brazil's plurality of cultures might at the outset lead one to embrace a variation of Freyre's thesis and spread a homogeneous umbrella over Brazil's obvious heterogeneous particulars. Robert Levine, for instance, describes contemporary Brazil in terms of its diversity. The country, he says,

> includes more persons of African descent than any country except Nigeria, and more Japanese than anywhere outside of Japan. More descendants of Arab peoples live in Brazil than anywhere outside the Middle East. Large numbers of Brazilians have ancestors from places as disparate as Italy, Jamaica, Poland, Germany, Switzerland, Korea, and the Confederate States of America. The largest Roman Catholic nation on earth, Brazil is also home to millions of evangelical Protestants as well as Buddhists, Muslims, Mormons, European spiritists, Sephardic and Ashkenazic Jews, and followers of the pantheon of animistic religions brought to Brazil in the slave ships from Africa but still very much alive today. (Levine 1997:3)

The trouble is that increasingly finer degrees of heterogeneity don't guarantee homogeneity. In qualifying these two terms at a later stage of this inquiry, I shall argue that marginalized groups throughout Brazilian history have found it the way—perhaps the only way—to survive. How have they survived? To recapitulate my now familiar theme, through the outward show of conformity— manifesting assimilation and accommodation of the dominant culture that makes every effort within its power to enforce its particular brand of homogeneity. But at the same time by creating subversive cultural guerrilla acts of resistance disguised as that very conformity. Resistance maintains traditions insofar as possible and in the process creates increasingly diverse heterogeneity (Viana Filho 1949). I might also point out that while Néstor García Canclini (2001:96) writes of hegemony and resistance, I prefer conformity and struggle or resistance. Conformity is the outward appearance—the havenots enter into interactive negotiation with the haves—while resistance is cultural guerrilla activity—the havenots covertly engage in subtle subversive activity.

Actually, Freyre romanticizes his own notion of Brazilian heterogeneity. The problem is that in doing so he sets up his notion of cultural plurality on the basis of racial and ethnic dualisms. Granted, on the one hand, Freyre concedes that racial and ethnic interrelations created not contradiction but a spectrum of differentiations. However, on the other hand, he doesn't embrace all sides of the picture equally. His lingering Eurocentrism slips through the fissures here and there. Consequently, in the eyes of some onlookers Freyre implicitly aids and abets whitening. When his sentiments are tested and he is forced to make a choice between modernity and tradition, he opts for the latter. He does so, since he is for a society seeped in the Luso-Brazilian attitude of tolerance and a liberal embrace of any and all cultural practices from Africa and the American soil. Unfortunately, Freyre's concept of tradition emerged as differentiation resulting from a set of cultural polarities. But now, in addition to Brazil's colonial distinctions, there is the polarity of modernity and tradition. This amounts to two monolithic, homogeneous forces in perpetual clash, with no genuinely dynamic pluralism involving heterogenizing processes (Ortiz 1985:93–103). Indeed, Abdias do Nascimento (2002:83) writes that ultimately Freyre was not so much for racial democracy as he was for the hoary idea of "whitening."

However, I must emphasize that it was chiefly due to Freyre's influence that scholars turned increasing attention toward Afro-Brazilian culture, and particularly, to Candomblé life. Congresses held in Recife in 1934 and Salvador in 1937 focused on Brazil's African heritage. The second congress specifically called for an end to the persecution of Candomblé. Religious intolerance persisted, but the 1930s, at least, saw increasing interest in the country's Afro-Brazilian cultural strain. President Getulio Vargas's *Estado Novo* marked resurging pride in Brazil's cultural heritage—though often for no more than populist, propaganda purposes. During this time Candomblé entered the spotlight, center stage. Shortly thereafter, scholars such as Donald Pierson (1942), Edison Carneiro (1964, 1978, 1981), and Ruth Landes (1947) began creating lines of communication between the scholarly community and Candomblé leaders.

ETHNIC AWARENESS EMERGES

In spite of its newfound visibility, Afro-Brazilian culture failed to shake off its subordinate role. Granted, police repression declined somewhat. But the negative attitude toward Afro-Brazilian religious and cultural practices remained. Moreover, given Brazil's highly touted tradition of racial tolerance within a hierarchical, paternalistic and patronizing society, Afro-Brazilians' awareness of their ethnic heritage was slow in coming. Actually, Brazilian reality remained a giant step behind Brazil's reputation for tolerance. This was revealed in a study in the 1960s supported by UNESCO for the purpose of showcasing Brazil as an example for other countries to follow. As it turned out, the country's racial democracy proved to be so much myth (see Francisco 2000; Hasenbalg 1994; Hellwig 1992; Marques 1996; Nascimento 1977, 1979, 2002:136–139; Ojo-Ade 1998; Ribeiro 1997:190–193; Sansone 1992, 1998, 2003; Twine 2000; Wade 2003; Winant 1992).

Still, Afro-Brazilian consciousness definitely made its presence known. Various Afro-Brazilian resistance movements appeared in the country at large. To wit, the *Frente Negro Brasileira* (Brazilian Black Party) was organized during Getulio Vargas's *Estado Novo*, but he soon banished it. Abdias do Nascimento formed his *Teatro Experimental do Negro* (Experimental Black Theater) during the 1950s, the *Centro de Cultura e Arte Negras* (Center of Black Culture and Art) was organized in the early 1970s, and the *Movimento Negro Unificado* (Unified Black Movement) in the late 1970s. On the Bahia scene, in 1949 a group of stevedores organized the *Filhos de Ghandy* (Sons of Ghandi), a carnival society (or *afoxé*). The *Filhos de Ghandy* introduced Candomblé chants and rhythms into their carnival processions. Soon afterward, Candomblé, Capoeira, and Samba song and dance began finding a more prominent place in the national cultural scene. From that point onward, the Brazilian Carnival gradually took on a more visible veneer of Afro-Brazilian culture. One could perhaps say that this increasing visibility culminated with Getulio Vargas's declaration in 1953 that Capoeira was the country's national sport. Samba schools were organized in Rio de Janeiro, and they began taking on an increasingly important role during Carnival time. Finally, in the 1970s Bahia's equivalent to the black movement in the United States began to emerge (Hanchard 1994). This movement was highlighted in 1974 when the first *Bloco Afro* appeared (a *bloco* is an organization participating as a cohesive singing and dancing group in the carnival). I refer to the influential *Ilê Aiyê bloco* (the name means "home space" plus "universal or cosmic place"), which brought Black African pride out in the open (Machado 1999).

It also induced the charge of discriminatory practices and racism by some members of Bahian white society—imagine that! The irony of this charge was all too evident, and it failed to invoke the expected outrage from the white society at large. Since that time, African visibility has become prominent during carnival proceedings—though some might argue that, on the negative side, Afro-Brazilian Carnival expressions have generally been coopted by the white elite (Guerreiro 2000:57–114). In fact, the theme for the 2002 Carnival in Salvador revolved about the city's African heritage, and the theme for 2003 focused on *Baianas* and *Acarajé* (*Baianas* are Afro-Brazilian women who dress in Candomblé fashion and sell *Acarajé* (food of the Orixás) on the streets of Salvador.

An important factor that contributed to increasing Afro-Brazilian ethnic awareness is the interdependent interrelatedness of Capoeira, Candomblé, and Samba within the larger Brazilian society. Capoeira and Candomblé rhythms, movements, and choreography share certain features with feverish Samba moves. Samba, "dance of the body articulate," as Barbara Browning (1995:ch. 2) describes it, probably had its beginning in rhythms and dance steps known as *batuque*, and it passed through other rhythms called *lundu* and *maxixe*. The *batuque* is a type of drum used to evoke the dance step. *Lundu* and *maxixe* were derived from *batuque*, with influences from the Spanish dance, *fandango*, and probably a little *polka* during the nineteenth-century (Vianna 1999:27–28). Samba's erotic nature initially shocked Europeans. As far as they were concerned, it offered little in the order or aesthetics. They considered it merely repetitious and monotonous. The problem is that they didn't understand the polyrhythms or the subtlety of the footwork. They couldn't differentiate between slight variations of drumbeats and body movement—a common reaction when Westerners come into contact with African rhythms (Blacking 1995). I can personally testify to this inability when attempting to play a Capoeira instrument while learning the song not by memorizing a text but by listening to it and trying to sing it during the Roda, to maintain awareness of the other instruments in order to become aware of the subtle differences of rhythm they were following, to correlate the songs syncopated rhythm with that of the instruments all of which flowed according to their own beat, to catch the subtle cues sent out by the Mestre who was playing the lead Berimbau, and all the time trying to follow the moves going on in the Capoeira ring. Keeping tabs on these diverse activities was an enterprise in frustration. This, indeed, is called "multitasking" in the most radically concrete sense!

Samba de Roda, I have suggested, complements the Capoeira Roda. It also complements the circular movement of Candomblé ceremonies within the Terreiro. Like Capoeira Rodas, the Samba Roda separates inside from outside, microcosm from macrocosm, a zone of safety from the vicious outside world, and "we" from 'them." Samba de Roda is performed by a group of participants who form a ring. They sing, using percussion instruments and clapping their hands. A woman enters the ring, makes a few moves, and the audience responds enthusiastically. She then challenges a member of the audience, who enters the ring. And the contest begins. Each person tries to outdo the other person with her footwork, body movement, sly sensuous or malicious facial gestures, and verbal banter. Then there is a change of partners, and the drama repeats itself. At some point a man present might shout: "Fora as saias!" (All skirts out). Then he and another man enter the ring, and roughneck tactics begin. This is *Samba Duro* (hard Samba). It consists of a vague continuation of the Samba step, but with body contact in the form of the dancers' efforts to trip each other with wide sweeps of their feet. The movements are now even more reminiscent of Capoeira play, and the Samba that breaks out after a Roda (Browning 1995:ch. 3). I might add that following some Rodas in the Salvador area, the Mestre often gives the order, and everybody forms a circle for a Samba de Roda performance. When this occurs with my Capoeira group, I find it quite fascinating, at least until I'm invited to enter the ring, an offer the Capoeira enthusiast should never refuse. So I enter, tentatively and reluctantly. And, as you can guess, the crimson sign of embarrassment inevitably overtakes me, as I stupidly flop around.

Until the post-World War II period, Capoeira, Candomblé, and at times even Samba were often considered lowerclass forms of recreation for Afro-Brazilians and poor whites. Mestres Bimba and Pastinha had helped dispel this image with respect to Capoeira. In the 1940s and 1950s, discovery of Candomblé's therapeutic effects brought it to the attention of dominant white culture. Eventually Umbanda, which grew out of Candomblé, began gradually taking on an aura of respectability (Ligiéro e Dandara 1998). Meanwhile, Samba schools in Rio de Janeiro and their participation in the Carnival became institutionalized. Some white middle-class citizens eventually began appropriating these previously denigrated lowerclass practices. It was now becoming quite chic to patronize Umbanda, Samba Schools, and whitened Capoeira Regional clubs, and even occasionally to participate in them. Consequently, marginalization of these lowerclass cultural activities began gravitating toward mainstream culture. This occurred especially after Capoeira garnered prestige outside Brazil, Candomblé was touted as a tourist attraction, and Samba became tantamount to national identity as Brazil took on the label, *O País do Carnaval* (the Carnival Country) (Brown and Bick 1987; Fry 1982; Risério 1981).

So, Capoeira, Candomblé, Samba—cultures within the dominant culture; worlds within the world. Cultures of conformity and resistance through mock playing-fighting, through a religious-philosophical form of life, and through dance of the most dynamic sort. There is sameness within difference, continuity within discontinuity, appearances of homogeneity that tend to conceal complex heterogeneity. Experiencing one of these three activities is vicariously tantamount to experiencing them all. In a certain sense, living one is living all; it is practicing philosophy; it is vibrant pluralism; it is a dynamic scintillating, fluctuating process of many ethnic propensities and proclivities compounded into one cultural whole. Unfortunately, these practices have been liberally romanticized, exoticized, and even mythified, as witnessed by Nascimento (1979:87) and others in the popular saying: "We have Africa in our kitchens, America in our jungles, and Europe in our living rooms" (from Nina Rodrigues 1977:15). It is impossible to think that, not without a note of cynicism, recent Brazilian President Fernando Henrique Cardozo once confessed he was also a product of Brazilian kitchens, jungles, and livingrooms. He was, of course, using the popular expression in Brazilian culture. "A foot in the kitchen" was originally used to denigrate people of black heritage, who were relegated to the presumed lowly status of household servants. Cardoso, availing himself of the racial democracy myth, alluded to his own mixed origins, thus giving the expression a positive connotation. Africa, of course, entered the kitchen through the servants' door. The fact remains that figuratively and literally speaking, what goes on in the kitchen is of the Afro-Brazilians' doing. Literally speaking, because the Brazilian cuisine is of marked African influence, and because music and rhythm emerged from the kitchen. And figuratively speaking, because there, the Afro-Brazilians have learned how outwardly to conform to the dominant society's standards yet engage in covert practices of resistance (Fryer 2000, Guerreiro 2000). The kitchen-jungles-living rooms, Nascimento tells us, don't reveal that abominable distinction whites made of their black stereotypes in the quip: "Branca pra" casar / Negra pra" trabalhar / Mulata pra" fornicar" (White women are for marrying / Black women are for working / Mulattas are for fornicating).

Let me make a quick retreat from this unbearable image and get back to the topic at hand.

Which Africa Are We Talking about Anyway?

As a consequence of the Spanish conquest of the indigenous people of America, and after the Spanish Dominican priest Bartolomé de las Casas vehemently defended the Amerindians' rights as full-fledged subjects of the Spanish monarchy, the Catholic Church decided their souls were worthy of salvation. During one of his arguments, de las Casas mentioned that there were other candidates for slavery, namely Africans, whose physical strength and natural habitat would render them more fit for strenuous labor under the tropical sun than the Amerindians. Whether or not he meant his passing suggestion as a serious proposal, the Spanish Crown jumped at the opportunity (Hanke 1949, 1959). Thus began the nightmarish manifestation of humankind's most horrendous trait: the capacity to inflict pain, suffering, affliction, and death on one another.

As pointed out above, the slaves showed remarkable survival skills, considering the odds. They were sold like cattle. Wives were separated from husbands and children from parents. Slavery caused confusion among the vast diversity of African cultures that were chaotically thrown together. To make matters worse, the European slave owners tortured, massacred, assassinated, and brutalized their slaves to the maximum. Suicides were common; escape was always on the agenda; births were very low. Yet, their misery eventually led to solidarity. Slaves of comparable languages and ethnicities usually managed to find common ground. Through lines of overlap between their ethnicities, they created mixed ethnicities. They reestablished human bonds, and recreated traditional practices, at every step of the tortuous way (Berkenbrock 1995:81–82).

During the nineteenth century, Nagô slaves of the Yoruba-speaking population of West Africa became the majority in Bahia. Finding themselves brought together in new and virtually unbearable surroundings, the Nagô people along with other African groups pooled their cultural resources to create a confusingly complex mixture of religious practices. These practices, from the very beginning, were uniquely Afro-Brazilian. They were not merely transplanted from African to American soil. I should add that besides Candomblé, other religion-philosophies emerged with a diversity of rites and local names derived from different African traditions: *Xangô* in Pernambuco and Alagoas, *Tambor de Mina* in Maranhão and Pará, *Batuque* in Rio Grande do Sul, and *Macumba* in Rio de Janeiro (Bastide 1978; Carneiro 1981; Corrêa 1992; Eduardo 1948; Ferretti 1985, 1986; Motta 1992).

However, contrary to an emergent opinion, there was no monolithic or homogenous Nagô culture. In Bahia, fundamentally there were two Nagô nations, Ketu and Ijexá, and there were various and sundry forms of what was usually considered "Pure Nagô" culture. Actually, the idea of an original Nagô expression can be no more than figment, for all was in the beginning and continues to be thoroughly mixed. Indeed, recently anthropologists have somewhat arbitrarily categorized the Salvador strain of Candomblé as "pure Nagô," and many of the candomblistas took up the idea with the assumption that they were re-Africanizing their religion. Good intentions do not always yield the desired results, however.

Re-Africanization was and is basically a search for lost roots. It was provoked in part by the virtual impossibility of coming to grips with and giving account of the numbing complexity evinced by the convergence of numerous African world visions and their combination with Catholic images and concepts. Since the Nagô tradition in Bahia seemed to have garnered more than its share of whatever reputation the descendents of Africa could manage to corner, this was the tradition highlighted as Candomblé origins of the purest sort. However, Beatriz Dantas (1987:122) points out that collective Afro-Brazilian memory has re-created African cultural practices and institutions following a supposedly pure Nagô model. In part this collective memory might have remained faithful to its presumed African origins for the sake of bringing about a symbolic form of cultural resistance. But only in part. The idea of "pure Nagô" is a re-mix of various religious strains from Africa.

Nevertheless, the issue of "re-Africanization" was heatedly discussed in the "II Conferência Mundial da Tradição dos Orixás e Cultura" (Second World Conference on Orixás and Cultural Traditions), convoked in Salvador, Bahia, in 1983. There, it became quite clear that a power play for Nagô hegemony was in effect, since there was hardly any input from other Afro-Brazilian cultural and religious expressions. While some participants in the conference conceded that religious practices of people whose ethnicity was non-Nagô and non-Yoruba could be found among those who purportedly engaged in pure Nagô practices, such ethno-linguistic interrelatedness most often went unacknowledged. The general assumption had it that the re-Africanizing process culminated in a presumed legitimation and qualification of Nagô Terreiros, and that Nagô Terreiros embodied African roots in their most pristine form, while other ethnic practices went ignored. Rather than re-Africanization, perhaps the new wave should more specifically be termed "Nigerization", or "Nagô hegemonization" (Serra 1995:62–67, 114–116).

Julio Braga (1988:88) writes that the re-Africanization of the Afro-Brazilian religious and world vision was "profoundly prejudicial" against knowledge of other Afro-Brazilian people, such as the Bantu, who had their own world vision that was comparable on many points with the Nagô world vision. Re-Africanization failed to serve the interests of Angolan-Brazilian culture, and indeed, the Angolan alternative suffered as a consequence of the re-Africanization movement. Angolan expression and the expression from other parts of Africa could not help but become to a degree stigmatized, and in the most extreme cases, orphaned, since they were barred from the central matrix of Afro-Brazilian cultural activity. It's as if the entirety of African culture were reduced to merely one expression—albeit a major one at that. In sum, the attempt at a reapproximation to Africa has not been as enlightening as the billing has often had it.

Why the need to re-Africanize and consequently artificially homogenize Afro-Brazilian Candomblé culture in the first place? It was most likely a search for some sort of purity motivated by an attempt to nurture an emerging sense of pride and prestige in the peoples of African origin—in this light recall the motivating force behind Capoeira Angola. But which purity? The complexity of African cultures thrown together presented virtually insurmountable odds against the possibility of homogenizing Afro-Brazilian culture. There were many Orixás and their corresponding Catholic personages. This mix of Catholic and African religious images might have once been necessary for survival purposes. But according to the re-Africanizers, that was no longer the case. Thus the Orixás must be liberated from their Catholic baggage. They must merge with the pure Nagô model of Afro-Brazilian culture.

As a consequence of this sort of re-mixing, whatever purity there might have been was blemished by the syncretism of Orixá and Catholic saints. Early Catholic priests and many African Candomblé practitioners tried to bridge the gap between Christianity and African beliefs. As mentioned above in passing, they found remarkable similarities between certain Orixás and Catholic saints, the Virgin, and Christ. To mention a few for the sake of illustration, *Xangô*, Orixá of fire, lightning, and thunder, was linked to Saint Jerome. *Oxalá*, the greatest of all, became the Christ-like Orixá. *Yemanjá*, queen of the seas, was often interrelated with the Virgin Mary, as was *Oxum*, lady of fresh water rivers and lakes. *Iansã*, the elderly goddess of the wind and storms, often takes on the role of Saint Barbara. *Ogum*, Orixá of iron and war, finds his counterpart in Saint Anthony and sometimes Saint George. The so-called syncretistic combinations of Orixás and Catholic images eventually became quite prevalent in Afro-Brazilian religious practices—as a means for disguising the Orixás in order that the blacks' original beliefs might survive (Greenfield and Droogers 2001; see appendix A). However, the re-Africanizers saw syncretism as no more than ...

A Passing Phase

Simply put, syncretism is purportedly a religious practice that had Orixás hidden behind Saints. It is Candomblé mixed with Catholicism to yield a faith unlike anything either in Africa or traditional Catholicism. But the re-Africanizers held that syncretism had seen its better days: it had emerged, crested, and declined in accord with the ebb and flow of the cultural tide. And now, it should be forgotten altogether.

According to some accounts, throughout the history of slavery in Brazil, there have been three general phases of Candomblé: (1) syncretism (fusion or juxtaposition of Candomblé with Catholicism); (2) whitening (especially with the Candomblé offshoot, Umbanda); and (3) re-Africanization—a purported return to the practices long lost origins (Carneiro 1978, Querino 1978, Reis 1988). In this regard the history of Candomblé roughly patterns the three Capoeira transitions: (1) dissimulation, in order to survive during slavery and up to the 1930s; (2) Capoeira regional (popularization, whitening, and folklorization of the art); and (3) a re-Africanization of sorts—the recent resurgence of Capoeira Angola.

Actually, I would suggest that with respect to both Capoeira and Candomblé, there can be either the one phase or the other, or there can be both, or neither, depending on the inclination of the beholder. In this sense, cultural blending rather than distinguishing features became the norm. Given the complex nature of cultural blending, a push toward re-Africanization could not go to completion in spite of the re-Africanizers best of intentions, for there can be no genuine return to original purity. There can be no return to that long lost imaginary garden of paradise, for innocence, once lost, cannot be recaptured. Consequently, the dissimulation stage of Capoeira and the syncretistic stage of Candomblé can be conceived as a blend of both the one practice and the other. They are both what they appear (singing and dancing, strange Catholicism) and they are other than what they appear (mock fighting, Candomblé rites). At the same time, they are *neither* the one *nor* the other, for since they are always becoming something other than what they were becoming, at any moment they can take on a novel countenance. At this juncture I must say that I can't overemphasize my use of Other and Otherness throughout this inquiry in a non-essentializing way. Other and Otherness, as I expect will emerge in full force as the pages of part III unfold, is a matter of that spaceless space, that emptiness, between the *eithers* and the *ors*, that includes both the one and the other and neither the one nor the other (on the non-essentialism of the Other, see Loomba 1998; Werbner 1997).

Given this contradictorily complementary cultural blend, survival in Brazilian slave society became a matter of the slaves' carrying within their mental and corporeal memory many possibilities of action, reaction, and linguistic response within myriad possible situations regarding their masters. Many of these possibilities are contradictory and ordinarily mutually exclusive, for the slaves must be on their toes and at the best of their wits in order to perpetuate their way of life. They must be ready to act and react and respond with both honesty and deceit, to practice both good behavior and guile, to both support and whenever necessary to subvert the system. In this manner, mutually exclusive possibilities at any given moment stand a chance of erupting.

There are none of the customary dualisms here (as we shall also note in part III, this pattern falls in line with the terms *homogeny*, *hegemony*, and *heterogeny*). The slaves' actions, reactions, and responses were devised in such a way as to give the appearance that they were matters of *either/or* imperatives for the masters. But they were not. Actions, reactions, and responses were on-the-spot improvisation with whatever devices were available; there was no stock set of programmatic strategies for coping. However, since the slaves' masters were prone to making distinctions within the master/slave hegemonic system, they were attuned to dualistic thinking. Consequently, within this system, the masters eventually pushed for a whitening or folklorization of both Capoeira and Candomblé, as if the practices were caught within a master/slave, dominant/subservient, or black/white dichotomy, and could be homogenized. The masters set for themselves the task of accommodating (acculturating) the subservients to the dominant society with a healthy injection of new (white) blood and respectable (white) cultural practices.

Even if this process could be brought to completion, it would not be a simple dualistic fusion of subservient practices with dominant practices with the accompanying creation of a harmonious, homogeneous society. Subservient memory would inevitably persevere; history would continue to exercise its force; there would always remain vestiges of the grand split between those who have and all the rest, the havenots. This effacement of the past and the same time its retention entails a re-invention, a re-creation of the past, and it is also a re-invention of culture that can't help but bring along all the baggage of the past. What has been lost is lost; yet, similarities and differences hang on; they resist blending into a continuous, homogeneous, non-contradictory amalgam. There is actually another problem. With respect to Candomblé, the re-Africanization movement is also what could be called a yorubanization process and hence at the same time a descaboclization, descatholicization, and desbantuization process, all of which, if the process could achieve its goal, would actually render Brazilian Candomblé quite un-Brazilian (see Prandi 1999).

In sum, Candomblé, like Capoeira, retains a community orientation. It is a sort of: "Penso, porque sou a consequência do meu meio," I think, because I am the consequence of my circumstances; or, "Existo, porque o outro existe," I exist, because the Other exists (Vallado 1999). There is no rugged individualism in the dualistic sense of "me" against "them." Any and all goings on are a matter of the entire community—because the community has never been entirely dissolved in the dominant culture. As we shall see below with increasing force, the nature of Candomblé is multiply complex rather than simply dualistic. This is not immediately apparent. Since when one begins studying Candomblé one apparently confronts pairs of opposites, one tends to conclude that what one has is an elaborate set of binary distinctions. Not so, however. Between the one and the other there is always a mediating third term, much in the order of Peirce's Thirdness. The third term creates two binaries, but each of them sports its own third, and so on. Symmetry breaks down, disequilibrium erupts, a bifurcation point comes into view, and a Third emerges; many Thirds emerge. I would suggest that in the Peircean sense it's a matter of Secondness emerging from Firstness and Thirdness playing its role as mediator.

Why is the third term necessary? Because that wily Candomblé rogue, Exu, remains outside the group. Exu is not part of the inner circle usually consisting of more or less sixteen Orixás that make up a given Candomblé community's pantheon of divinities. He is somewhere else, somewhen else. With respect to the combination of sixteen or so Orixás, Exu is a sort of accident. He brings tidings of the unexpected, disorder, potentially chaos. He is always able to push his way between and through any and all dualisms. He is the Other Other in addition to the One and the Other. His role is comparable to that of Thirdness bringing Firstness and Secondness together and mediating them in the same way that Thirdness itself becomes mediated with Firstness and Secondness (recall Figure 4). Exu keeps things open, dynamic, effervescently flowing, intermittently, consonantly, and dissonantly rhythming. He keeps successively finer heterogeneous differences from solidifying into homogeneity. He makes sure languages and ethnicities never fall into lethargy. He is, in short, purveyor of Axé.

In view of Exu's role in creating the perplexingly variegated combination of languages and ethnicities making up Afro-Brazilian religious-philosophical practices, a further word on the notion of syncretism would seem to be in order.

Chapter Eight

Does Syncretism Give an Adequate Account?

WHY THE PROBLEM PERSISTS

Syncretism of two or more religions is a complex issue that has engendered considerable debate and controversy. The question now at hand focuses on the relevance of syncretism to the trio of terms I have often evoked during this inquiry: interdependency, interrelatedness, and interaction.

Somewhat like Catholicism, there are two levels of existence in the Candomblé worldview: *Aiyê* or the physical world, and *Orum* or the supernatural realm. What exists in the one has its correspondence in the other. *Orum* governs *Aiyê* by means of the Orixás, and Exu. Exu's function is that of a mediator opening up lines of communication between Orixás and earthbound humans, roughly in the order of mediation by the Virgin and the saints. *Olorum* is the Lord of *Orum*, and hence also of *Aiyê*—he has been compared to the Christian God, and in this sense it can be said that Candomblé is actually monotheistic. *Olorum* is source of three forces: (1) *Iwá*, possibility of existence; (2) *Axé*, dynamic spirit or force bringing whatever is emerging into existence into existence; and (3) *Abá*, affording purpose and direction to *Axé*. Together, *Aiyê* and *Orum* form a complementary union that provides equilibrium about which the sense of life rotates. Everything is interdependent, interrelated, and interactive. Notice that the *Olorum*'s three forces seem to pattern Peirce's categories, namely, Firstness as possibility of existence, Secondness as having emerged into existence, and Thirdness as future oriented direction, if not to say purpose. Whether this analogy is mere coincidence or not is not the question here; I simply wish to highlight the importance of Threeness that includes a middle term, in many aspects of Brazilian culture; it implies nonlinearity and perpetual change, germane to the idea of process (Moura 2000). This lends credence to the idea of another cultural logic according to the premises of this inquiry.

Berkenbrock (1995:63–66) enumerates what he believes to be the basic characteristics of Afro-Brazilian religions that maintain links with Catholicism: (1) faith in a supreme being (*Olorum*), (2) belief in life after death, and (3) belief in the existence of spirits. However, as mentioned, one of the chief characteristics that set Afro-Brazilians apart from Catholicism is their tendency to make no categorical distinction between sacred and profane, which falls in line with their sense of continuity between human and natural, between the individual and her ambient. Yet, the Christian sacred/profane distinction was not entirely unknown in Africa. There are records revealing that Catholic missionaries were sent to the Congo in the sixteenth century. From the seventeenth century on, some of the slaves coming from that region arrived in Salvador, Bahia, already baptized Catholics. In this respect, syncretism didn't originate in Brazil, but rather, in its early incarnations it was brought from Africa.

Nevertheless, from the very beginning the Catholic Church dictated its will, disrespecting the religions of the Africans insofar as that was possible, much like the Romans who disrespected the early Christians. In the middle of the eighteenth century, Pope Benedict XIV declared that, in spite of the pagan traditions, African slaves possessed souls and should become subjects of God as well as their King and their owners. However, over the generations they had managed to engage in clandestine practice one of their most profound cultural practices, originally called *Kandombele* —of Angolan origin, meaning to pray, although the blacks of Salvador were chiefly Yoruba speaking people from the West coast of the continent. What now goes by the name of Candomblé as syncretized with Catholicism saw its birth during the colonial period. And especially in Salvador, it grew to maturity during the first half of the nineteenth century.

Fayette Wimberley (1998:81) outlines three different forms of syncretism: (1) one religion served as a mask for the other, with each retaining its original belief structure (in many cases the primary focus of devotion was the African deities, and Catholic statues and other trappings were mere façades to avoid police persecution); (2) both religions coexisted side by side, and were used at different times by the same devotees for similar purposes (devotees could attend Candomblé ceremonies on Saturday night and continue their worship at Catholic Mass on Sunday morning; both served similar religious purposes); and (3) two religions were blended into a new and unique creation (Candomblé communities combined beliefs and rituals of several African ethnic groups with similar Catholic components). Although Wimberly's account is considerably richer than the oversimplified, dichotomized uses of the term in some literary and cultural studies—as well as Berkenbrock's types of syncretistic mixes—it is, nevertheless, in need of some fine-tuning. Bahian scholars of Afro-Brazilian culture, strangely ignored by many comfortable mainstream North American and European scholars, can help broaden our perspective considerably in this respect.

The effort toward re-Africanization has been in effect especially since the 1970s. This includes an attempt to go back to a purer, unsyncretized form of African practices and leave Catholicism in the wake: a place for each and each in its proper place (Prandi 1999:98–100). In light of this development, Sérgio Figueiredo Ferretti argues that the creation of syncretism and its transition to re-Africanization actually consists of five stages: (1) separation of Catholicism and African practices, or non-syncretism; (2) parallelism or juxtaposition such that the two practices are separable (an either/or affair); (3) mixed practices, such that they become inseparable (a both-and affair); (4) convergence of the two practices, such that there is no longer either the one or the other (a neither-nor affair) but something else emerges; and (5) re-Africanization, or separation, once again, such that things presumably fall into their proper place and are thereby purified. Ferretti's five stages are not limited to simplistic either/or categories, in contrast to many anthropologists who remain within a binary, language-driven rendition of syncretism (Ferretti 1999:113–124; also Droogers 1989; Epega 1999:163–165).

It bears mentioning that Ferretti includes two elements overlooked by Wimberly, thus offering a more complete picture of syncretism: (1) total separation of the two practices, as if they were autonomous of one another, and (2) re-Africanization. I will follow Figureido Ferretti's more general formulation of syncretism, while giving special attention to the idea that one practice conceals the other one for the purpose of creating the appearance of conformity that hides covert resistance.

Syncretism through Conformity and Resistance

Illicit practices disguised as acceptable behavior are common to syncretism. Very simply put, syncretism is deception through the appearance of a cultural practice (of conformity) that masks over another practice (of resistance). We've seen this before, in our discussion of Capoeira. The very survival of the slaves' patrimony depends on deception; everyday coming and going depend on it; life itself depends on it. Time marched on, in the colonies, and so went life. It bears mention at this juncture that actually, elite white Brazilians engaged in their own form of deceptive practices with respect to more dominant countries in the Old World. In 1817 European treaties forced the Portuguese Crown to limit the slave trade. But Portugal, in cahoots with African Muslims, began engaging in illegal slave traffic. The British—with hypocritical indignant outrage, and confident over their successful "Black Legend" denigrating Spain and its forging a colonial empire—began exerting pressure on the Portuguese to cease their illegal practice. Later, in 1850 the now independent Brazilian nation put forth the "Eusébio de Queirós Law." This was a document implicitly allowing for subtle continuation of the slave trade under the watchful eyes of the British, by means of deception. Under the cover of the 1850 law, Brazilian slave traffic lords in the now independent nation began engaging in acts of deception to pull the wool over English eyes. Such acts eventually gave rise to an expression that is occasionally used in Brazil today, a century and a half later: "Para inglês ver" (For English eyes only) (Fry 1982). The idea was to present the appearance of nonslavery while what was in practice was a subtle form of slavery. Indeed, the slave traders were in conformity with, yet they resisted, the English in ways familiar to those acts of capoeiristas and candomblistas with respect to their Portuguese and later Brazilian lords.

During the second half of the nineteenth century, gradual liberation of Brazil's slaves began in earnest. It was approximately at the same time that in Africa Òyó, the Capital of the Yoruba people, came under the domination of the Dahomey (presentday Benin). This resulted in a significant number of Yoruba speaking slaves transported to Salvador, including many of their priests. The capital of Brazil had by this time been transferred to Rio de Janeiro. Nevertheless, the slaves continued disembarking in Salvador. As a consequence, the influx of Yoruba peoples in the nineteenth century gave Salvador a unique Afro-Brazilian mix. This helps explain heightened West African influence in the area.

It's usually the same old story, wherever and whatever the context. Repression breeds accommodation and at the same time resistance, and resistance within a repressive system becomes possible solely through deception, through the will to persevere, through struggle or cultural guerrilla tactics. Nothing remains what it is. Alternatives in the process of their becoming incessantly present themselves to create Otherness becoming (Braga 1988:29–41). The notion put forth here is doubly significant, since physical objects don't and can't represent the Orixás. Divinity can't simply be represented mimetically or metaphorically; it is also represented contiguously or metonymically. Manifestation of the Orixás is what it is; it is not a replacement for something else, nor does it stand for something it resembles. If Candomblé Terreiros sport images of Christ, the Virgin, and numerous saints alongside images of a collection Orixás, that is no evidence that the Orixás bear similarity with certain Catholic images and hence their place in Afro-Brazilian culture is legitimized. I repeat: Orixás are what they are, no more, no less. As such, their manifestation consists of their entering and mingling with and mediating human vessels, the designated candomblistas, who have been especially prepared for the occasion.

With this brief digression, back to the problem of syncretism.

QUALIFYING THE STRAINS

In a nutshell, Ferretti's typology of syncretist practice within Candomblé living takes on four general forms in today's unique Salvador scene:

(1) Catholicism and the combination of diverse Afro-Brazilian religious strains may coexist side by side such that one religion is practiced at certain times and places and the other at other times and places (Ferretti's "parallelism"). Believers of the two practices say they have no problem with the distinctions of both Catholicism and Candomblé; the points of divergence and contradiction between the two religions are not viewed as of any serious consequence.

In my own conversations, people from Salvador who liberally engage in now one practice, now in the other, tell me they believe in both, that all religions are good even if they are completely different, and that they derive comfort and solace from both Catholicism and Candomblé, though in different ways. Dare I compare this attitude to that of one of the most level headed of philosophers, Hilary Putnam? Putnam writes that when in the 1950s, "I thought of myself as a philosopher of science (although I included philosophy of language and philosophy of mind in my generous interpretation of the phrase "philosophy of science"). Those who know my writings from that period may wonder how I reconciled by religious streak, which existed to some extent even back then, and my general scientific materialist worldview at that time. The answer is that I didn't reconcile them. I was a thoroughgoing atheist, and I was a believer. I simply kept these two parts of myself separate" (Putnam 1992:1). Along comparable lines, in my experience, many Afro-Brazilian candomblistas maintain an outward show of Catholicism (accommodation) while were the truth to be known, their heart would be found to lie elsewhere, in Candomblé (covert resistance).

(2) One religion masks the other religion, while both remain virtually unchanged. In certain areas around Salvador by the end of the nineteenth century, the Orixás were on the surface, while trappings of Catholicism remained under cover (Ferretti's *mixing*). However, this mixing was subject to persecution, since the two religions were to be maintained entirely distinct—according to surface appearances, at least (Ferretti's separation).

In this sense Abdias do Nascimento writes that syncretism, rather than fusion, was a cultural struggle for survival. True fusion existed only between African religions from the Yoruba and Bantu regions. Post-slavery theories of syncretism, he goes on, are more in the order of folklorization (Nascimento 2002:161–172).

(3) The two religions may merge into an interactive whole that presents the becoming of something that is radically other than what was becoming in the two religions when maintained relatively independent (Ferretti's "convergence").

Putnam observes that knowledge is always incomplete. In this respect, it is open to amendments, alterations, and even radical revolutions (Putnam 1992:1). Formal interviews with Candomblé practitioners bear this out. When asked about syncretism, they invariably resort to a logic of yes-yes and no-no. They concede that they are Catholics and in the next breath they concede that they are not Catholics, and they say basically the same of Candomblé. In this sense, Catholicism and Candomblé are different yet unified. It is a matter of saying yes to the one and no to the other, or yes and no to both, or the assertion that neither is pure and you can't separate them, yet you do separate them. In other words, candomblistas don't always think in our customary logic and reason but through vague both-and and neither-nor modes of sensing and thinking. This flies in the face of the re-Africanizers, who are trying to eradicate the one and purify the other once and for all (Sanchis 1999). Actually, Ordep Serra writes that Candomblé isn't any more syncretic than Catholicism anyway; so interaction between the two is a sinuous, multiply-bifurcating two-way street, not one-way and linear. Moreover, he finds inconsistency from Terreiro to Terreiro, and from Candomblé to Macumba and other Afro-Brazilian strains. But this doesn't bother the faithful a whit. They are not like scholars of intellectual bent who quiver in the face of contradictions. With hardly any compunctions at all, they willfully embrace *both-ands* and the *neither-nors*. In this respect, the idea of syncretism as a "confused mixture" has it all wrong (Serra 1995:194–199, 285–286). A confused mixture for whom?—we might wish to ask. "Confused" implies contradictory elements, but there is no contradiction as far as the Candomblistas are concerned. Rather, there is what I have dubbed incongruous, contradictory complementarity.

(4) Attempts to recover ancient African patrimony in its pristine form can likewise never be complete, since vestiges of Catholicism and perhaps Caboclo beliefs cannot be entirely eradicated (Ferretti's "re-Africanization").

As briefly mentioned, many re-Africanizers see syncretism as nothing more than a strategy for survival during slavery and the years after abolition, but it no longer has any meaningful function. Consequently they wish to move on toward a more pure African expression (Consorte 1999). Nascimento writes that the "process of syncretization among African religions was of an entirely different nature from the interaction between the official state religion, Catholicism, and African worship. It is misleading to suggest that syncretism occurred between Catholicism and African religions, because the implication is that the exchange would have occurred on a level of equality and spontaneity" (Nascimento 1979:104). In reality, "African religions were outlawed by a colonial regime which knew that in order to maintain complete control over blacks they must enslave not only their bodies but also their spirits.... What scholars have called 'syncretism" between Catholicism and African religion was really a cover under which Africans continued clandestinely to practice their own religious worship. It is a tribute to the ingenuity of the Black people in preserving their own cultural heritage in the face of Aryan cultural repression: not, as Brazilian official history would have it, a symptom of liberalism and generosity of the colonial white aristocracy" (Nascimento 1979:105; see also Henry 1987; Ortiz 1980; Serra 1995).

Ogum/São Jorge

This summary reveals my obvious leaning toward Ferretti's idea of "convergence," given my proposal for the radically interdependent, interrelated interactivity of Candomblé life. Candomblé life is interdependent, interrelated interactivity, for the Orixás have no meaning without candomblistas, and vice versa. Together, they create a union between *Orum* and *Aiyê*. The candomblista resides in *Aiyê*, and at the same time she, along with the entire Candomblé community, embodies something of *Orum*. In other words, there's a little of one or more of the Orixás within everybody at all times and in all places. Each person is a plurality of manifestations and forces of nature.

Xangô / São Jerónimo

Good logic and reason would seem to dictate that Orixás and physical humans could not coexist, since they belong to distinct processes. Yet, Orixás and humans do not have completely separate existence—which would seem to render them likely candidates for syncretic fusion—for they were never categorically separated in the first place. In a strange manner of putting it—if you will bear with me—Orixás and their human counterparts are both one and they are divided, coalescently contradictorily speaking. And at the same time they are neither one nor are they divided, complementarily speaking, for they are always in the process of becoming. Orixás depend on human subjects for their process of becoming Orixás; human subjects depend on Orixás for their process of becoming human; without both processes, *Orum* and *Aiyê* could not continue to maintain their tenuous balance. Obviously, binary logic becomes impotent, which gives linear thinking fits. But it is no cause for consternation, as far as Candomblé life is concerned. In a Peircean manner of putting this, if I may, parallelism, mixing, and separation involve Secondness in terms of the One (Catholicism), the Other (Candomblé), and the Other of the Other (syncretized Candomblé practices). However, the process hardly proceeds beyond Secondness, since all aspects of the diverse religious practices presumably retain their previous either/or characteristics. Convergence, in contrast, introduces mediating Thirdness. This process brings diverse practices together and fuses them such that there is neither the One, nor is there the Other, nor the Other of the Other, for something new is in the process of emerging (i.e., Exu's role). Re-Africanization, for better or worse, attempts to reinforce either/or distinctions anew. As such, I would respectfully suggest that it is somewhat of an unfortunate return to Secondness.

Obviously, if the various sorts of syncretistic practices outlined in this section existed at the same time, confusion would be inevitable. According to many reports, that was the prevalent Candomblé-Catholicism scene: confusion. Yet it still seemed to present no problems, as far as Afro-Brazilians' religious life went. Of course, there is evidence of personality clashes among leaders and conflicts between groups due to differences of beliefs and ceremonial methods. But with respect to the apparently logical inconsistencies inherent in syncretism—logical in the classical sense, of course—there seemed to be no quandary. Life went on, and the Afro-Brazilians survived as best they could (Consorte 1999;Wimberley 1998).

Since spirit possession is at the ritual core of Candomblé, a few more words on the function of the Orixás in Candomblé ceremonies is in order before proceeding to further discussion of syncretism.

CONVERGENT COMBINATIONS

Above all, Candomblé consists of a set of precepts, rules and regulations, and rituals and practices that make up a broad world view. It is a general means by which the Candomblé faithful confront natural processes and other human communities as well as members of the home community, drawing from energy existing within body and mind. The Orixás don't exist outside body and mind—or put more effectively, bodymind—since in Candomblé and Asian religion-philosophies, as well as indigenous American cosmologies, there is no strict Cartesian distinction. I write bodymind, as in part I, because I cannot overstress the importance of the body's ways of kinesthetics and somatics (kinesomatics) in Candomblé and Capoeira and other Afro-Brazilian practices. In Candomblé philosophy, balance and harmony among conflicting tendencies, and bodily and mental health, are of utmost importance (Verger 1981:108–111; also Barros and Leão Teixeira 2000; Nina Rodrigues, 1977:47).

Steeped in my background study and teaching of the physical sciences—which later could not help but influence my graduate studies in the social sciences and the humanities—in July 2000, I consulted with my Pai-de-Santo, Hermes, and expressed my difficulty in adapting to and getting a feel for my designated Orixás. He gave me a knowing grin and linked with me after a throw of the *Búzios*. The sixteen *Búzios* are thrown only after the proper words to the Orixás have been uttered in the original Yoruba language. After the búzios come to rest they form a pattern. This pattern is made up of the configuration and interrelationship between the búzios according to whether each one of them ends up on the curved, closed side, or the somewhat flat, open side. The pattern they form can tell a story about the subject in the weeks, months, and years to come, but only if she conducts her life in balance with her Orixás—that are most often three in number though the number may vary from patient to patient. So ultimately it is up to her: how she conducts her life in concert with the Orixás (Sales 2001).

Hermes told me my inner conflict was serious, and that I needed to get in tune with my feelings instead of trying to rationalize everything. Still skeptical,

I asked him why my main Orixá was *Oxalá*, and why were my other two patron spirits *Xangô* and *Oxum*. They possess conflicting characteristics and appear quite incompatible. How was it that, within my own physical and psychological make-up, could I incorporate so many contradictions? How could I ever hope to maintain any balance whatsoever? His response was that these were my Orixás because that's just the way it is, no ifs, ands, or buts. At the time of my birth, he patiently explained, there was a collusion of these particular Orixás, and I have been playing out the struggle of tensions all my life and that it was basically up to me—with the aid of the Orixás, if I remain faithful to their call—to come to terms with myself and become one and comfortable with myself and my world. The first step in this process was a *banho de limpeza* (cleansing herbal bath). Obviously, his answers were hardly any solace, and they certainly didn't satisfy my intellectual curiosity. It seemed a relatively quick-fix somewhat equivalent of psychoanalytic babble between patient and doctor during an interminable series of sessions.

Shortly thereafter I returned to Purdue University. It took me almost a year of frequent meditation on that strange experience for it finally to sink in. But since I hadn't taken my *Pai-de-Santo*'s advice to give myself a *banho de limpeza*—at that time, in Midwestern United States, I couldn't have found the proper herbs anyway—there were those lingering questions as to whether I might have missed something important. Was I lacking in a proper combination and dosage of Axé by way of my trio of Orixás? Were my mind and body out of kilter, incapable of maintaining a healthy balance, in a dismal state of disequilibrium? The very thought of my pondering over the questions went against the grain of my intellectual upbringing. Looking at my dilemma from my logico-rational self, it was all so absurd, even silly. Yet, somehow, it seemed bodymind was hinting at something else. I tried to pay attention, but I couldn't get into the proper flow. Everything seemed askance.

That was then. Now, after various *banhos*, numerous sessions with Hermes, and much meditation on the problem, perhaps I have eventually become somewhat more attuned to myself and my condition since those trying times. Perhaps. At least one side of me would like to think so. At the same time, my rational hyperanalytical side continues to balk at the very idea. It might be because I have been unable effectively to heed my inner Other and its kinesomatic, bodymind messages. And yet, in a sense I've heeded this inner Other, for it has occasionally surfaced and buffered my obsessive intellectual curiosity. Why did it all appear so strange to me for so long? Why does it still appear strange? Why can't I simply give in to whatever that inner Other side of me was telling me? After much mind-wrenching over the problem, and during some of my quite extensive readings on the issue, my rational hyperanalytical side once ran into the following.

The power of Axé is contained within and transmitted by elements in the vegetal, animal, and mineral realms that are grouped in three categories: (1) "red blood" from the animal realm, the vegetal realm (*dende* or palm oil of deep-red consistency), and the mineral realm (copper), (2) "white blood" from the animal realm (semen, saliva), vegetal realm (sap), and mineral realm (lime), and (3) "black blood" from the animal realm (ashes), vegetal realm (dark juice from certain fruits and vegetables), and mineral realm (charcoal, iron). The manner in which Axé transmits these three types of blood depends, once again, on the circumstances and one's faithfulness to one's Orixás. Axé is thus a power received, communally shared, and distributed by daily as well as ceremonial practices, with imagistic concepts and elements serving as vehicles. Axé allows one's Orixás to fulfill themselves through one's maintaining a proper balance with one's animal, vegetal, and mineral environment (Vocks 1997; Wafer 1991).

I hardly need write that after thinking about these interrelationships a disenchanted form of estrangement engulfed me anew. The discursive rendition I was taking in stroked my intellectual vanity. At the same time, my inner sense of bodymindedness began falling by the wayside. That was logical enough. After all, I was now far away from Bahia and what I had thought of as its strange magic. Presumably with a renewed sense of objective detachment, I could now think about these issues and hopefully write about them like a good scholar should. So I tried to analyze them and articulate them. But the words didn't come out as I expected. I wasn't into it, bodymindedly speaking. Then, after more reading and considerable bewilderment, there was more. And things became even stranger.

According to Candomblé philosophy, each individual has an Exu messenger-guardian, in addition to two or three Orixás. One must always strive to maintain one's Orixás in balance so as to maintain a proper force or spirit (Axé). The Orixás do not simply compose a pantheon of deities conjured up by people in need of some mythical power that transcends human existence. Rather, in their composite they make up a coherent cosmology. Everything, including you and me and the human community and the animal and vegetable and mineral realms and the entire universe, is immanently interrelated in a vast self-enclosed space. There is no transcendence, for whatever the cosmos was becoming, is becoming, and will have been becoming, including the individual self, becomes from within. All is immanently interrelatedly, interactively, interdependently self-organizing. This extraordinary form of holism flies in the face of our most cherished objectivist, logico-rational principles. It grates on our eyes when we read it and on our ears when we hear about it. It leaves us with a furrowed brown when we try to make heads or tails of it.

Yet, there it was, staring me in the face. What I eventually came up with, and meekly offer for your contemplation, is the following.

Process within the Big Picture
Holism: One's subjective self and one's inner feelings, one's objectivizing self and one's thoughts, the whole of one's self and one's community, one's self and one's community and the world, all must be held together in one package.

But you see? There I go again. There can be no package at a single spacetime moment if everything is becoming something other than what it was becoming, if everything is process. So there is no self in the fixed, essentialist sense. Nor is there any identity of self or of community that remains the same over time. Nor is there a world that confronts the self and community in the same way from one spacetime juncture to another. There is just everything in interdependent, interrelated, interactive flow, like the oceanic channels contemplated from a space shuttle perspective. The point is that emphasis must be placed on a most important facet of Candomblé life: one must take Candomblé on its own terms, not as some mystical, quaint concoction of fetishisms, myths, rituals and rites, and magical beliefs. Thus, there is nothing in opposition or contradistinction to anything, for everything complementarily flows into everything else.

Thus also—to revive the topic from previous sections—relatively simplistic binary notions of Catholicism and Candomblé, and of a syncretistic pairing of the two, simply can't fly. The idea of syncretistic binarism is by and large the product of linear, analytical, nominalist thinking. It links certain facets of Candomblé cosmology with certain elements found in Catholic doctrine on a one-to-one basis. It tells us essentially that there was a Candomblé image that the Afro-Brazilians found comparable to a Catholic image, and they linked the images. Then another linkage made itself known, and then another one, and so on. The problem with this form of syncretism is that Candomblé is not merely a Catholic sort of religion. To a greater extent than Catholicism, even medieval Catholicism, Candomblé is an entire way of life, a holistic cosmology. With respect to this cosmology, there is no primordial text, no foundational center. Candomblé cosmology is a form of life within which everything is within everything else; everything is intimately interconnected with everything else; in a manner of speaking, everything literally is everything else. Thus the entire cosmology is like a sphere whose center can be anywhere and whose circumference is nowhere. Since everything is within everything else, there is no absolute sameness or identity, no hard-core individualism, no absolute distinctiveness. Everything is like everything else and at the same time it differs from everything else.

I eventually sensed that contingency is of the nature of Candomblé life such that whatever happens to happen is as if it were not more than a shot in the dark. I write "as if" for it is not really a shot in the dark if the individual and his Orixás maintain a healthy balance, however tenuous. There are no algorithms for generating Candomblé living. Everything at every moment can threaten to fall into chaos and at the same time it can promise renewed order. This is a genuine form of Peircean Firstness: everything is interrelated with everything else such that virtually any one of a plethora of possibilities stands a chance of emerging at a given spacetime juncture. Yet after some things possible have emerged into the light of day, there is apparently a tinge of causality, since within a particular context what there is, the One, comes into contact with some Other. This is Secondness: the interaction of what is with something else. But if there were no more than that, the door would surely soon be closed and the process would come to a screeching halt. There must be, in addition to Firstness and Secondness, mediating Thirdness: interdependency of all that is becoming such that the something becoming would be emptiness were it not for everything else collaborating to bring about the becoming of that something. In this manner, there is none other than creative improvisation at each step of the way (Risério 1996:40–44, 103–105; for an excellent account of a comparable form of life, see Abram 1996).

The inherent processual nature of Peirce's categories can perhaps be more effectively illustrated through Exu's basic nature.

EXU: THE IDEA OF SYNCRETISM CONCRETELY EXEMPLIFIED:

Exu from within oversimplified Catholic teachings is a malignant force. In fact he is often linked Exu with Satan, and he is still so linked in Umbanda and other Afro-Brazilian religious strains.

This is erroneous. Exu satanized as evil in contrast to good is Exu transformed into what he is not. Exu is no Satan. There is no Evil One in the Candomblé cosmology (Serra 1995:156–157). Truth/falsity and good/evil binary values belong to the language of customary Western forms. Candomblé will have no truck with this logic. A proper sense of Exu implies a general philosophy of life, and life in its purest form is both positivity and negativity mediated by the emergence of newness. This vague qualitative rather than strictly quantitative logic of life is just what it is: process. Hardly more should be said. According to Candomblé tradition however, Exu is a mediator and messenger interacting between the Orixás and worldly beings. He is who helps make Axé happen. Consequently, he existed before all the other Orixás; he existed before the world order. In fact, he is of the nature of life itself. He incessantly brings about the emergence of novelty; he is the supreme improviser from what often appears to be chaos created by his own hand (Barbosa 2000; Trinidade 1985).

Exu is a cunning customer. You never know if his countenance is genuine or fake, if the twinkle in his eye reveals empathy or malice, whether the twitch of his eyelid is just that or if it is a calculated wink, whether his popping up now here, now there, is an aid or a trip-up. You never know, that is, unless, like the equally wily Capoeira master, you know precognitively. Friedrich Nietzsche (1968:289) observed: "Before judgment occurs there is a cognitive activity that does not enter consciousness." The Capoeira master has the capacity to know, without the need consciously to reason out his knowing. He just knows, before consciousness has had time to make its move. He knows, because it's in bodymind, not in the relatively torpid, linear workings of mind alone. At this level, there is no sharp boundary between memory and imagination, tacitness and intentionality, voluntary and involuntary, for everything is interrelated. In other words, Exu is the embodiment of incongruous, contradictory complementarity. The Capoeira master knows this, because he has Exu qualities.

From a particular point of view Exu might be regarded as evil, though tenuously so, because he always shows an ingratiating ludic streak. At the same time, he is dubiously good, though his actions would lead one to believe otherwise. He is also, like Mercury, a messenger and mediator between the Orixás and mere mortals. Privy to the codes that govern the designs and actions of the Orixás, he is in a position to play the role of patron saint, though he rarely does so, because he is too busy manifesting his talents as trickster. Take him seriously, and you get burned. Ignore him, and he'll slap you in the face when you least expect it. Try to play his roguish game, and he'll turn the tables on you when you're off guard. Resign yourself to whatever fate he chooses to mete out, and you'll lose all vestiges of control and self-control. You can never win for losing whether you try to play his game or not. Exu is like the syncope of the Brazilian Samba beat: he is the moment of emptiness. He is like what Duke Ellington once said of the Blues: it is sung by a third person who is not there (Sodré 1997:17). Exu is resistance in process: a Samba of ironic ecstasy, shifty ebullience, screaming silence, a cauldron of effervescent bubbles, an in-your-face smile (Lamego 1934:87; Sodré 1997:47–49).

Exu's image is a mythical sign, a supreme expression of sly conformity and conflict. He is the projection of the Africans' longing for freedom beginning with the first cargo of slaves that made the trip to America, longing that is self-perpetuating up to the present and will endure into the unseen future. He is a presence that throws caution to the wind and defies rigid codes and formalities and impositions of neocolonial and postcolonial states. Whatever stereotype is slapped on him, he negates; whatever identity is attributed to him, he flouts; whatever history he is crammed into, he rebuffs.

Exu is the quintessential rebel against customs, conventions, and norms. In Brazilian Candomblé he is guardian of a loose, vague sense of Africanness, negritude; he is a slippery link between past and present as he wiggles his way into the future. Exu as everybody's Exu is nonetheless the only Exu who cannot be charged with lying down and syncretizing with some Catholic saint or deity. Indeed, since the good Fathers didn't know how to classify him, given his resistance toward the holiest of images, equation between him and the Devil was inevitable. But as I have emphasized, there is in Candomblé no good/evil dichotomy. If within Christian thinking Exu must find a place, it can be within none other than the virgule between good and evil. He creates an enigmatic coalescent collusion of sacred and profane, culture and nature, civilization and barbarism, and everywhere and nowhere and everywhen and nowhen. As illustrated in figure 13, Exu is never simply either the one or the other, nor is he literally speaking both the one and the other.

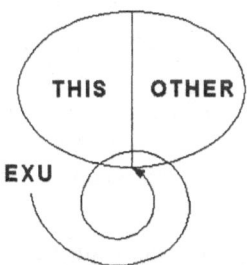

FIGURE 13

In this respect he is like Firstness illustrated by the line of demarcation in figure 13. Exu is at the sime time either the one thing or the other. He is either Satan—according to the Catholic Fathers—or he is not—in genuine Candomblé philosophy. In this respect he evinces Secondness. And at the same time Exu is neither the one thing nor the other, for he is the supreme expression of the world in its process of always becoming something other than what it was becoming. In this respect Exu is like Thirdness: mediator, moderator, source of complementarity between all tendencies, and carrier of novelty that never ceases emerging into the light of day. Put all these roles together, and Exu is living paradox, the paradox of life itself, life within process, or semiosis, which is another way of saying paradox.

In this manner, Exu is a model of freedom, evidenced by his mental agility and his physical plurality through a diversity of appearances. By way of his incessantly changing space-time situatedness, he perpetuates a sense of selfhood that is at one and the same time self-preserving and self-transmuting. He is self-preserving in his unwavering refusal to submit himself to any set of fixed defining characteristics, and he is self-transmuting insofar as he resists any and all labels that might conceivably be attached to him. He appears comfortable with himself but he is not; he makes everybody squirm when he gives them a sense of helplessness and at the same time he leads them to an understanding of their strengths. In part because of Exu, candomblistas become resigned to their weakness, and so they conform. In the same breath they become aware that they are of indomitable will, and so they resist. In this regard, Exu is the spirit of those communities of escaped slaves, the *quilombos*: the people resisted and freed themselves of their chains and now they submit to the collective will; the collective will manifests bellicose resistance even though it is of the most benign form of conformity. It bears mentioning that the equivalent of Brazilian *quilombos* could be found throughout the American colonies—going by the name of *palenques* in Cuba, Mexico, and Colombia, *Cumbes* in Venezuela, and *maroons* in Jamaica, the Guyanas, and the United States. The Brazilian term comes from *kilombo*, originally from *Umbundo*, a Bantu language. In a very real sense, the *quilombos* are a copy of the African *kilombos*, reconstructed by the slaves in an effort to recreate Africa in the Americas and to defend themselves from their enemies (Bastide 1971; Carvalho 1995; Freitas 1982; Moura 1981; Ratts 2000; Vasconcelos 1995).

When one meditates on Exu's pluralistic personality throughout time and space, one cannot but garner a sense of particularity within an image of the most general sort, a generality that paradoxically and enigmatically allows a plethora of diverse particular manifestations perpetually to emerge at what might seem to be the most inopportune of moments. Exu is dynamic, courageous, and aggressive; at the same time he is instrumental in perpetuating harmony among the Orixás, among Orixás and their human subjects, and between Orixás and nature. He is charged with the responsibility of maintaining harmony and unity in spite of the fact that he is always in the act of disrupting the apple cart to create apparent chaos.

Exu lurks around in the back alleys, the side streets, and the dark corners. He is neither inside home nor Terreiro nor is he outside, in the open streets where the big, wide world of social, political and economic institutions exercises its dominion. Yet he is everywhere. He embodies neither order nor disorder. Yet he embodies both. He is neither friend nor adversary. Yet at any moment he can don the mask of either of them and play out the role magnificently. He unites and he polarizes; he is playful and simultaneously dead serious; he is a fighter yet his pliability, his suppleness, gives rise to the idea that he is always giving in to the pressures that be; he is hard as rock yet he is fluid, slipping and sliding in and out of every situation. He exists on the borderline between the either and the or; he is always in the margin (see figure 13). That is how he seems to be nowhere at all, yet he is omniscient. Putting all Exu's qualities together, one must conclude that he is a supreme sign of resistance. He is a radically heterogenizing force for religious freedom, social freedom, and rebellion against norms and restrictions. I might add that this role is also taken up by *Pomba-Gira*—female counterpart to Exu found chiefly in Umbanda—who creates confusion where homogeneity was thought to exist (Lody 1995:80-85; Teixeira 1975).

Obviously, Exu constantly changes: he is process exemplified. But his changes are uneven, and they seem unfair, because he changes the rules of the game as he pleases. He is restless energy manifested, and a master of multiple paradoxes; yet it is he who keeps things alive, through Axé. Since he makes it possible for Axé to circulate, if treated with consideration (offerings), he reacts favorably. Indeed, in a manner of speaking, Exu is the most human of all Orixás, for he is neither totally evil nor totally good. He is everywhere, for he is the eternal intermediary between men and women and the gods. For this reason, in all Candomblé ceremonies his offering, called *Padê* (re-union), comes before all the other offerings. Through *Padê*, Exu is called, saluted, greeted, in order: (1) to summon the other Orixás, and at the same time; (2) to remove Exu so that he doesn't disturb the ceremony with his tricks.

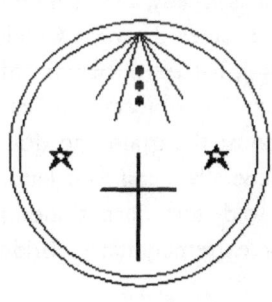

Oxalá/Christ

Exu is responsible for maintaining a balance of exchanges between the various character traits of the three or so Orixás each person possesses. He often provokes conflict to foster balance and mediation, for without conflict there is nothing to balance and mediate. Everything that is thus joined with Exu subsequently multiples, separates, and transforms itself. Everything that is in incessant change, which is to say everything, period, is the consequence of

Exu's dynamic role. He is the very personification of the transformation principle. His day is Monday. He is associated with the now and the future—I write "now" and "future" instead of "beginning" and "end", for there is no beginning and ending; there is just perpetual change. His color is dark purplish blue, color of the mystery of procreation. His animal is a canine friend; one of his plants is the cactus—that should give you an idea. He is often involved with sex, lascivious sex as well as fertility, that borders on what may be taken by the outsider as lewd. Significantly, regarding this theme, he often wears a hat similar to a phallus. In fact, there can be no sensuality without Exu.

Yemanjá/ Virgin Mary

According to the Candomblé tradition, Exu's candomblista son or daughter—a person one of whose Orixás is Exu—has the following psychological characteristics: strong, agile, dynamic, untiring, overflowing with vitality. She loves the pleasures of life, she is greedy, always hungry, and she has a liking for alcoholic beverages. If she imbibes during a Candomblé ceremony, she always spills a little of the drink for Exu's benefit. She is happy and mischievous. She likes to play tricks, hide objects, tell lies, and above all, she takes pleasure in always going against the grain and doing things the wrong way. She loves to shock people, liberally using four-letter words for that purpose. She is untidy, and she loves to disturb parties and meetings. However, if it is to her advantage, she can be extremely hard working, efficient, untiring and obstinate.

All told, I would suggest that Exu is possibility, actuality, and necessity through contingency manifested; he is a fusing and confusingly voracious swirl of Firstness, Secondness, and Thirdness; he is porter that which makes life life. It is he who takes one by the hand and gently, mischievously, cunningly, abruptly, or even viciously, moves one into the undulating, effervescent whole.

At this juncture I cannot resist the temptation to reveal Paul Johnson's account of one of the yearly celebration of Yemanjá, goddess of the sea, on

February 2 in Rio de Janeiro. It was commercialism gone wild, pop culture globalized, havenots making their resistance known; it was Candomblé postmodernized to the hilt. Homage paid to Yemanjá had been organized in the form of a Rolling Stones concert. The announcement of this event in Maracanã stadium, the world's largest, had it that Christians have long viewed Exú as the Devil; Exú is a son of Yemanjá; the Stones have been viewed as diabolical, and even recorded a song called 'sympathy for the Devil. Hence, Stones-to-Devil-to-Exú-to-Yemanjá: the Stones show honors the goddess of the sea! (Johnson 2002:145). Johnson tells us that during the procession some dancers fell into a Yemanjá trance, as pandemonium reigned. Some businessmen "watching from high-rise windows shook their heads in disgust, while others were delighted and descended to join the party with bottles of their own brands of spirits" (Johnson 2002:145). He concludes with consternation over how easily the Rolling Stones were transmuted into part of Candomblé's system of classifiers, granting the orixá Yemanjá massive powers of synecdochic extension: Yemanjá as the part signifying the whole of not only the sea and maternity, but now even of English rock-n-roll bands" (Johnson 2002:146). I would suggest that during this event the Rolling Stones, and Yemanjá as well, flowed in and out of the figure 13 process, which is Exu's playground. On so doing, they made shambles of classical logic dictating that everything has its proper place and that everything must remain in its proper place. This Rio scene is a far cry from Candomblé living as I have tried to narrate it to this point. Yet, the scene alludes to the bigger world, a world that, as becoming is more apparent in light of complexity physics, chaos theory, and information flows, is processual through and through (Davies 1988; Pagels 1988; Penrose 1989; Stewart and Golobitsky 1992; merrell 1998). This, I would like to believe, is the message Candomblé philosophy implies.

Perhaps a discussion of various Orixás and their particular qualities might afford a better sense of the Candomblé world vision.

Some Other Orixás

Oxalá enjoys syncretism with Christ. He is the holder of the progenitor of both male and female power. In contrast to Exu, he shuns all violence, disputes, and fights. He likes order, cleanliness, and purity. White dominates whenever he is present, and his day is Friday. His children should wear white on this day. Like *Oxalá*, they are benevolent and paternal, wise, calm, patient, and tolerant; they are slow, closed, and cold; they are also obstinate, and work best when in silence.

Oxalá has two forms when manifesting himself through an initiate: Oxaguia, the young warrior, and Oxalufa, the old man who leans on a silver cane. Oxalufa is fragile, delicate, and subject to colds because he always feels cold. He makes up for his physical fragility with a great moral force, and his objective is to realize the human condition in its noblest expression. He is faithful in love and friendship. The Oxaguia type is a young, pugnacious warrior. He is usually tall and strong, but neither aggressive nor brutal. He is happy and loves life deeply; he is talkative and playful. At the same time, he is somewhat of an idealist. He jumps to the defense of those who need justice, the weak and the oppressed. He is proud, craves for glorious deeds, and is sometimes a sort of Don Quixote. His original thoughts usually anticipate his times. Oxaguia is the beginning, the East where the sun rises, and Oxalufa is the setting, the West where it sets.

Oxum/Our Lady

Yemanjá is the mother of some of the most important Orixás—Ogum (of iron, a blacksmith), Xangô (fire and thunder warrior), Oba (of water and a female warrior), Oxossi (the hunter), and Oxum (the eternal feminine, of springs, streams, lakes, and all fresh water)—who were born from an illegitimate affair. Traditionally speaking, she also enjoys a syncretic affair with the Virgin Mary of the Catholic tradition—the parallels, and even the illegitimacy of her children is suggestive. Yemanjá is deeply revered in Bahia. In fact, a cult of fishermen emerged around the image of Yemanjá that eventually became well nigh independent of Candomblé ceremonies. She is often depicted as a mermaid with long black hair. She is mother of the fish, so to speak, and through the sea image she represents fertility. She loves flowers and is usually given seven open white roses, which are thrown to the sea in thankfulness on February 2, the day of her commemoration. Her color is white and blue. During Candomblé ceremonies the person representing her wears bead fringes hiding her face and holds a round silver metal ritual fan in her hand with a mermaid cut in the center.

Yemanjá's children are imposing, majestic and beautiful. They are calm, sensuous, fertile and irresistibly fascinating. Yemanjá's daughters are especially good housewives and mothers. They are excellent educators, and they are remarkably generous. They are known to raise other people's children when they feel the need to do so out of their love for all children. Yet, when offended, they do not forgive easily, and they are possessive and very jealous. Since Yemanjá guides the formation of her childrens' individuality, which exists basically in the head, she is present in all rituals.

Oxum depicts the image of beauty, femininity, grace, charm, and sensuality, along with a dose of spice and coquetry. She is the matron of love, and of the rivers and lakes; as such she complements Yemanjá's mastery over the seas. She is quite vain, and takes pleasure in embellishing herself with perfume and jewels, especial made of copper, the metal with which to cast a spell over her husband, Xangô—actually her second husband, since she had previously cohabited with Ogum. She protects women during their periods of pregnancy, and wives who suffer cruelty at the hands of their husbands. At the same time, she loves to party, dance, and entice men with her charms; the fact they that they might be married doesn't deter her a whit. She is a close friend of Yemanjá and Exu, her protector. Her color is yellow and her day is Saturday. She has been linked with the Catholic images of Our Lady of Candeias, Our Lady of the Conception, and Our Lady of the Apparition, all of the Brazilian Catholic tradition.

**Iansá/
Santa Bárbara**

Oxossi's day of the week is Thursday, his colors are light blue and green, and he has often been syncretized with Saint George, and occasionally with Saint Sebastian. According to legend, he was once King of the Ketu nation, where he dedicated himself to hunting and often lived for prolonged periods in the jungle. While in the wilderness, he cohabited with Ossaim, who taught him the medicinal value of many herbs. Consequently, he is known as lord of the jungle. He is a provider, as a result of his hunting skills, and given one of his most outstanding characteristics, physical nimbleness and agility. For obvious reasons, Oxossi and Ogum, lord of iron, metallurgy, and war, whose chief characteristics are virility and violence, are brothers.

Xangô, so the legend goes, was King of one of the principle cities of the Yoruba speaking people. He is lord of lightning and thunder; he metes out justice to all, and he is marked by vanity, royalty, wealth, power, and at times by violence. His colors are red and white, and his day is Wednesday. Syncretically, he is usually interrelated with Saint Jerome and Saint Peter—since he is said to guard the gates to the heavens. Like Exu, who established justice and has the power to establish and re-establish cosmic equilibrium, he can be cruel, especially to those who step beyond the cosmic laws. The sons and daughters of Xangô are large of stature, vigorous and energetic, but with a tendency toward obesity. At the same time they are charismatic, able to attract others to their way of thought and sentiment. The problem is that they sometimes become arrogant and haughty, and as such they don't realize that their very charisma can lead them to harm those people that are most attracted to them if and when they take a violent turn toward others. On the other hand, when those who are closest to Xangô don't pay him what he considers to be proper respect, he can become vengeful.

The process of Orixá manifestation in the Terreiros and in worldly affairs is like water. It takes on the contours of whatever contains it, whether smooth or rough, of variable contours or not, whether there is meandering or rippling or choppy or violent flow or not. Water and Orixá processes are continuous, homogeneous, and completely pliable, incessantly flowing and changing form. Yet, on the surface, there may be no indication whatsoever of change. The surface, if smooth, affords a mirror-image of that which lies outside it, and a balance between inside and outside may be forthcoming. In contrast, if the surface is rough, discordant, dissonant, and tension-ridden, violent interaction may ensue. The waters, whether placid, smooth, effervescent, or unstable and heaving, set the mood of the interdependent, interrelated, interaction between the Orixás and their children.

As I briefly revealed above, during a Terreiro ceremony, certain Orixás return to earth and take possession of key initiates dancing about the center of the Terreiro. An Orixá, according to the prevalent image, mounts the person who was born with some of the characteristics of that particular Orixá. This has a dramatic effect on the initiate. Her entire body jerks violently as if she were the victim of a bolt of lightning. Supporting female onlookers, called *Quedes*, are always around the circle with a watchful eye, and they immediately jump in to assist her in the event her body completely collapses. She will be helped to an adjacent room, while the other initiates continue around the circle, in counterclockwise direction, as if nothing out of the ordinary had transpired. Once the Orixá has incorporated her on earth, she assists her victims of diaspora in America. She protects them from harm, cures ailments, and grants their pleas—if made with contrition and for noble purposes.

Spirit possession can be a shocking experience for a newcomer to Candomblé ceremonies. During my second Terreiro experience, a *Filho-de-Santo* (Son of Saints, or priest-apprentice), a large, corpulent man of around 250 pounds, suddenly collapsed, striking his head sharply on the concrete floor. I feared he might be seriously injured, but a couple of Quedes—both women, as are all Quedes—rushed in, apparently unconcerned over his physical state. With great effort they helped the man to his feet, and ushered him away and into another room to prepare him for re-entry as his designated Orixá. A half hour or so later an elderly woman was possessed with such violence that she lost consciousness. The Quedes placed her on the floor, face up, and covered her with a sheet. Once again, I couldn't help but register my concern, and asked a few people around the circle if she was all right. They didn't respond. The *atabaques* soon ceased their drumming and the proceedings were temporarily halted. But the people paid the unconscious soul no mind. They simply stood around talking, gossiping, and joking, as if nothing had happened. After some ten or fifteen minutes, the initiate began showing some life. She was helped into the room to the back, and the ceremony began anew. After a while I noticed that the Filho-de-Santo had appeared at the doorway and slowly entered the circle, eyes glazed. He was obviously still possessed. Slowly he entered into the rhythms of the ceremony and resumed dancing in the circle. Later, the elderly woman entered the room and also resumed her dance in accord with the Orixá that had possessed her.

I should not omit further mention of Olorum, the grandest deity of them all. Olorum incorporates the whole universe and, as pointed out above, has three powers: Iwa, Axé, and Aba. By combining these three powers, Olorum transmits them to the Orixás, and Exu carries them to Olorum's earthly inhabitants. When everything is operating harmoniously, the universe maintains its balance. For obvious reasons, Olorum enjoys no representation in the form of some visual or material image. S/he is considered pure spirit. I once asked my Pai-de-Santo why Olorum never mounted anybody during Candomblé ceremonies. He responded with an all-knowing laugh. I persisted. He finally told me Olorum carries so much force that if it entered a mere human, he would explode into a million pieces. I met his explanation with rapt silence; I believe he understood my empty response.

I provide only a few sketchy examples of the Orixás for the purpose of affording a glimpse of the reputed process of uniting images from supposedly otherwise incompatible religious practices (for images linked to the above discussed and other Orixás, see appendix A).

Chapter Nine

More Complex Than Meets the Eye

IMMANENT DIVERSITY

Elaborate rituals of worship practiced in West Africa by a professional priesthood had to be curtailed, altered, and often transformed quite radically in the new American environment where plantation owners and their intermediary strong-bosses exacted rigid demands on the slaves. When one becomes aware of the inhuman conditions to which the slaves were subjected, one begins wondering how it might have been possible for the slaves to revive any of their traditional customs at all. With great difficulty, one must assume, some aspects of the ceremonies survived, especially when Pais- and Mães-de-Santo of a particular deity had been transported to Bahia and managed to construct a modest temple to their Orixás.

The west coast Africans, most notably, had a predilection for selling royal rebels into slavery in order to get rid of the authority base of their enemies. This occasionally served to create a small group of slaves in Brazil who were well versed in the religious rituals of the royal pantheon. Survival of ancient traditions was in this way somewhat enhanced. However, even without the help of enslaved priests and royalty, many daily rituals in Africa carried out in the household somehow managed to survive. These more limited ceremonies did not require the services of a professional priesthood or the elaborate and costly preparation of traditional temple rituals. They were family affairs, and if by chance some or most members of a family found themselves within communicating distance from each other, they might be able to renew their customs. Individual slaves or freed men and women could engage in domestic worship and invite neighbors to these clandestine ceremonies, thereby preserving at least a few aspects of their homeland (Agier 1998).

Early anthropologists up to and including Bastide emphasized Candomblé's ethnic aspects. Customarily seeing Candomblé as an Afro-Brazilian religion, they focused on specific African traditions within it. Recently, in contrast, revisionists have argued that Candomblé leaders have used ethnicity and concepts of ethnic purity as propaganda for the purpose of attracting followers. This has created a competitive "generic spiritual marketplace" somewhat reminiscent of Evangelist tactics in Protestant religions. Candomblé consequently becomes politicized and organized into networks that come into conflict with one another (Barros and Leão Teixeira 2000; Epega 1999; Ferretti 1995; Gonçalves da Silva 1999; Prandi 1999).

Michel Agier cites the example of Vila Flaviana, a Salvador Candomblé Terreiro that reopened in the early 1990s after having been effectively closed since 1940. Vila Flaviana reveals that Candomblé culture is polyvalent and extremely complex. The Terreiro's reopening under the leadership of Valnizia P.O., a young Mãe-de-Santo and great-granddaughter of the Terreiro's founder, reveals the intricate set of tensions and self-organizing networks that pervade those aspects of present-day Candomblé that have become politicized. Agier writes:

> At least three elements comprise this complexity and, at the same time, pose problems for the analysis of Candomblé. On one level, the conversion of the faithful and the training of their leaders can be studied as individual responses to affliction; they can be viewed from the perspective of social and, particularly, familial networks. On another level, an examination of Vila Flaviana's history reveals the gradual development of a political network within the house based on the family and spiritual relationships that its *mãe-de-santo* and her close associates cultivated with one of the principal Terreiros of Salvador, a network that eventually tied Vila Flaviana to various individuals and groups linked to the local black movement. Finally, and closely related to the second, there is a third network consisting of ethnologists and "friends of the house" interested in the success of the enterprise of restoring the Terreiro, at its origin an informal and popular process. It includes students and teachers at the local university, white people (I wondered what they were doing there) who regularly attend Afro-Brazilian ceremonies, and black activists in search of spiritual and cultural identity (the guys and women in dreadlocks). Personal affliction, politics, and spirituality thus mingle in the motivations of those who frequent the Terreiro, which is firmly anchored in modern urban society. (Agier 1998:134–135)

With one eye attuned to these vigorous social networks and their interaction and another eye on divergent interpretations of this radically changing heterogeneous situation, it may be possible to appraise the dynamics of the so-called syncretic process. In order to do so, a brief historical survey of alternate interpretative strategies will be necessary.

Problematic Interpretations

I argued above that early Afro-Brazilian studies were dominated by racial overtones. Nina Rodrigues argued shortly after abolition that the African race, of which the Yoruba (Nagô) ethnic group was the most advanced, had its own spiritual life. Candomblé from the outset was thus classified in terms of a hierarchy of "races" or "ethnicities," with the Nagô people occupying the upper echelon. Among these early scholars, Edison Carneiro launched one of the most ideologically charged early interpretations. In his first books, dealing with black religions and Bantu blacks from Angola, Carneiro had no qualms about establishing a hierarchy among different religious practices. This concept of "superior" and "inferior" forms of Candomblé pervaded his active role in the second *Congresso Afro-Brasileiro* (Afro-Brazilian Conference), held in Salvador in 1937. It also influenced his aid in founding the *Uniao das Seitas Afro-Brazileiras* (Union of Afro-Brazilian Sects) (Carneiro 1981).

Candomblé in Brazil thus became a re-invention, a religion re-invented by black slaves. This re-invented religion was a mind-numbingly complex heterogeneous combination of many elements from Africa. As radically heterogeneous, Candomblé seemed to support the idea that it was not a religion in the usual Western sense. In its specifically Brazilian incarnation, neither did it exist in Africa, where there were different cultures and languages and different collections of divinities organized according to the form of ritualized ceremonies practiced by each community (Braga 1988:53–60). Brazilian Candomblé was a disparate collection of whatever the Africans could re-invent from their past, combined with Catholic and Caboclo elements. There was by no means any standard form of ritualized ceremonies, but rather, whatever could be re-constructed was elaborated on-the-spot with whatever happened to be at hand (Vocks 1997). After several generations of racial miscegenation, the concoction became so confusing as to render a race-based taxonomy to account for syncretism patently absurd (Ortiz 1980:97). In spite of all this complexity, there was a push to create a religious form along the imaginary lines of Yoruba purity, which was considered the ideal.

When in the 1930s certain Terreiros began propagating the idea of Yoruba purity, Melville Herskovits also adopted the Candomblé ethnicity thesis. He had engaged in ethnological work on ancient Dahomey in West Africa. He then became aware of diverse African sacred and secular cultural interpretations among Afro-Brazilian people. It influenced him profoundly. He came to believe that the Afro-Brazilian world made up a relatively autonomous, homogeneous subculture that could be most adequately studied in terms of its African origins. It was as if for Herskovits there was hardly any syncretism to speak of. Or it was as if his idea of syncretism was of the first sort listed above, following Ferretti. I allude to separation, according to which Candomblé effectively masks any Catholic elements that might be lingering about such that they are of no consequence. Thus there is no syncretism in the ordinary sense. Rather, Candomblé managed to maintain its Africanness in spite of prohibitions set up by the Catholic Church (Herskovits 1943, 1966).

Roger Bastide's and Pierre Verger's works focused principally on the idea of African "acculturation" into the Portuguese-Catholic tradition. The notion of acculturation is even less syncretically oriented than Herskovits' interpretation as separation—though they both fall within comparable ethnic or racial frameworks. The problem with acculturation is that it is almost exclusively a one-way street: from subservient culture to dominant culture. In particular, Bastide alludes to what he labels "compartmentalization" of Afro-Brazilians that separates them, the subservients, from the Other world inhabited by the dominant or hegemonic society. Compartmentalization allows the Africans to live comfortably and presumably without conflict within their own world and within that of the dominant European culture. This interpretation is somewhat in line with Ferretti's separation in conjunction with parallel syncretism. Coexistence of African religious worlds and the Luso-Brazilian religious, social, political, and economic world entails no form of static dualism, however. Within compartmentalization, it may be possible for the Afro-Brazilian to oscillate between participation in her ancestors' traditional way of life and at the same time take a somewhat active role in the larger society, under the watchful eye of her superiors who are the caretakers of that society. In this manner, the Afro-Brazilian can be Western and non-Western; she can be a candomblista and a Catholic; she can be herself and take on the role of the Other—which might stand a chance of becoming her own inner Other. The problem now is that this might also prime her for the philosophy of whitening, which was to make its appearance around the next curve in the pluralistic Afro-Brazilian cultural flow (Bastide 1978).

But I shouldn't write Bastide off so handily. His posture is exceedingly more complex than I have revealed to this point. Actually, he distinguished between two types of acculturation: formal and material. The material variety is consciously brought about. It is open to the view of all; it at times tends to enter into the arena of ideological give-and-take; and it entails explicit content of thought. Formal acculturation is more occult. It consists of transformations that are more profound and subtle than those that meet the eye or are of consciously derived thought and attitudes. It involves feeling and sensation, affective proclivities and propensities that through repetition and habituation have submerged into and within attitudes and behavior such that the individual is no longer consciously aware of the whys and the hows of her feeling and sensing and acting in the way she does. She just does what she does because that's the way she does it.

This is tantamount to a Catholic automatically making the sign of the cross when traveling in a city bus that happens to pass by a church. It entails properly entrenched, habituated, activity the body—or kinesomatic bodymind—engages in while leaving the conscious mind free to engage consciously and actively in other matters—much like when bodymind is in the act of driving a car while conscious mind, as if disengaged, is, talking to a friend in the seat to his right, catching a few lines of the morning newspaper at the stoplights, engrossed in thought over a business engagement that evening, or whatever. It is all a matter of bodymind doing what it does, tacitly, without the need of the mind's intervention. It is tacit doing within a form of life. It is practicing philosophy within a general sense of one's place in the world. In other words, it is knowing how, as discussed in chapter 3. The problem is that Bastide takes this form of mindlessness or kinesomatic bodymind thinking and acting to be linear and logical, in the best of Western ways. He exercises a slash between form and content, thought and feeling and sensing, and he goes on to classify things either on the one side or the other of the virgule.

Thus Bastide's "essentializing compartmentalization" is at the heart of his writings on Afro-Brazil. As a result, he completely loses sight of process; he can't quite come to acknowledge perpetual change in the cultural phenomena he studies. Indeed, as Agier writes, Nina Rodrigues, Carneiro, Herskovits, Verger, and Bastide "generally concurred in foreseeing the disappearance or dilution of Afro-Brazilian religions during the process of modernization and the development of a "non-ethnic society" (Agier 1998:136). But, as I have suggested and will argue more acutely below, rather than a whitening of the whole of Brazilian society into a homogeneous, nonethnic culture, just the opposite occurred. I might add as a final note in passing that Leslie Desmangles prefers the term "symbiosis" over syncretism, which includes both the one pole and the other and neither the one nor the other, depending upon to the viewpoint. As will become evident, this is close to the thesis put forth in the present inquiry (Desmangles 1993:74–77, 113–114, 123–124, 168–169).

TRANSCULTURATION AND OTHER ENIGMAS

Allow me a brief turn to Ferretti's third form of syncretism: mixed syncretism. According to this form, two religions may merge into an interdependent, interrelated, interactive whole that presents the becoming of something that is radically other than what was becoming in the two separated religions.

This strikes one as comparable to the concept of "transculturation," developed by Fernando Ortiz (1940) from studies by Bronislaw Malinowski (1940) and expanded in the work of Angel Rama (1982). Ortiz understands by transculturation the process of transition of one culture into another through the merging, confluence, coalescence, and fusion of two or more cultures. Transculturation is not simply a matter of one culture engulfing another culture in amoeba fashion. That would be more akin to acculturation of a subservient culture by a dominant, hegemonic culture that would bring about the deculturation of the subservient culture. Unlike acculturation, the concept of transculturation implies the mergence of cultures such that something new and creative begins its process of becoming. Cultural offspring take on many of the characteristics of both of their parents. Yet they are to a greater or lesser degree different than either of their parents. They are something that has never before emerged in exactly the same way—recall the above words on mediating Thirdness and the emergence of novelty regarding the fourth form of syncretism listed above, *convergent* syncretism (combinations of Firstness and Secondness). This new creation is not a mere mechanical, or at worst an aleatory, agglomeration of elements from each culture. Nor is it a mosaic in which one can identify now this, now that, and so on. Simply put, it is something different and new. Transculturation can be the result of conquest and colonization, but it can also involve interdependent and mutual assimilation and accommodation, and diffusion and hybridization.

Cultural reality implies perpetual change and transfiguration. Nothing cultural ever remains the same. Some facet of a particular culture might appear the same, but if so, that sameness is in the eye of the beholder; it is more imagined and invented than encountered, more fabricated than found. Memory, nostalgia, longing for past times, myths and distant golden ages, are deceptive. Duplicity, montage, collage, bricolage, and simulacra, might appear reminiscent of things previously experienced. But they are usually illusory. Impressions and thoughts that seem as real as can be and fixed for all time are chimeras of hopeful hearts and wishful minds. The only thing that doesn't change is change itself. In other words, everything cultural is processual.

What has this to do with syncretism? Above all, the idea of process is an indictment of the very idea of syncretism that tends to focus on either separation or parallel dualist ethnicities making up Candomblé. At the same time, process aids and abets syncretism as mixture and as convergence, but only insofar as they are perpetually changing. As mentioned, dualistic syncretism, tacitly lending support to racist and whitening utopias, has been censured by the re-Africanists—following the fifth form of syncretism: re-Africanization.

Nevertheless, critics of re-Africanization theorists claiming Candomblé is a unique ethnic expression counter that re-Africanizing theories actually have detrimentally influenced Candomblé leaders. This is likely an exaggeration (many revisionists overrate the impact of works by Bastide, Carneiro, and others that occasionally find their way to the shelves of the more textual-minded Mãe- or Pai-de-Santo). It is more plausible to assume textual culture is paid relatively little mind by those who swim within the current of popular culture, including Candomblé and Capoeira. In Agier's words:

> Rather than indicating that Candomblé has been directly inspired by anthropologists, the presence of such books serves to legitimize Terreiros whose leaders can point the names of former priests. In these volumes; it also lends legitimacy to those who read and write about Candomblé. While anthropologists have contributed to the ethnic discourse of Candomblé leaders, their work has had little or no influence on the faithful; after all ritual apprenticeships involve hierarchical social relationships, oral communication, and gestures, not book learning. In any case, the faithful remain, in their majority, people who do not read or read little. (Agier 1998:136)

Yet, some scholars continue to envisage a syncretic form of Afro-Brazilian culture as relatively static, unified, and largely autonomous of the larger Brazilian culture. It would be utopian to suppose Candomblé has simply remained what it once was. Yet, the view of Candomblé as a fixed sort of ethnicity through syncretism continues to have an attraction on entrenched scholars, and recently arrived ones as well.

A 1993 publication of *Meu tempo é agora* (My Time is Now) by Mãe Stella, the current Mãe-de-Santo of the Salvadoran *Ilê Axé Opó Afonjá* Terreiro, is especially revealing. Head of the most orthodox and Africanist and even re-Africanizing Bahian Terreiro, Mãe Stella offers an ideological and minutely prescriptive correction of the so-called errors of both scholars of Candomblé and faithful members within Candomblé. The faithful usually give in to a presumed syncretic mixture with neither qualms nor regret, and carry on with their worship. Scholars either applaud this or try to recover long lost African purity they see—or at least think they see—in the way Candomblé should be practiced. It is ironic that anthropologists must now compete with Candomblé spiritual leaders whose prestige once depended on how those same anthropologists' effectively promoted them. The fact is, however, that Mãe Stella's efforts constitute part of a broad network of Candomblé ethnic expressions that now mediates the relationship among ethnographic writings, anthropological theory, and daily Candomblé practice, agencies that include the *Comitê de Defesa das Religiões Afro-Brasileiras* (Committee for the Defense of Afro-Brazilian Religions).

The last couple of decades have seen the development of a social and political anthropology of Candomblé that reacted against those who based their studies on the concept of mythology. The pioneering work of Vivaldo da Costa Lima and his associates (1984), for example, drew attention not merely to the myths, rites, and legends of Candomblé, but to the hierarchy of offices, personal and family conflicts, and the legitimization of sacred and lay power within Candomblé, all of which he analyzes as a broad social group. Costa Lima concludes that Candomblé is neither primitive nor is it a religion to be practiced only during certain specified times and places. It is a *holistic* religion-philosophy for everyday living. Moreover, since it doesn't distinguish between good and evil in the Christian sense, it tends to attract diverse sorts of individuals who have been socially marked and marginalized by other religions and non-religious institutions (see also Santos 1976; Sodré 1983).

This testifies to Candomblé's embrace of a cultural world that includes ghetto alleyways as well as broad central avenues, the underworld as well as flashy shopping mall commerce, street vendors of ripped-off goods as well as established businesses, and those who have walked through prison doors as well as apparently upright and respectable citizens. Saints and sinners, the blemished and the pure, the ugly and the beautiful: all are joined in an apparent homogeneous yet profoundly heterogeneous community. If Candomblé liberates the individual, it is also capable of liberating the entire community.

I do not wish to imply that Candomblé has a message to hand out to each and every one of the world's communities. Candomblé is no more and no less than its own message. Since Candomblé is not a religion based on the Sacred Word of some Supreme God in the manner of Christianity, it offers no salvation as the ultimate goal, nor is it infused with a missionary zeal to save the human race. What is of importance is the concrete issue of life with respect to each individual: illness and pain, unemployment, lack of money, food and shelter. In this sense, Candomblé might be touted as a religion based on a sort of magic that leads one out of the temptation of reason, science, technology, and all the trappings of modern consumerist society. It could entice those who no longer believe in the meaning of an enchanted world that has lost its magical charm. The important point is, however, that Candomblé holds no utopian promises, no grand totalizing visions of the future, no entry into paradise for the faithful. It just attends to the issues of concrete everyday life. Brandão (1980, 1986, 1989) suggests in his studies that popular religious expressions in Brazil are of the nature of enchantment and that we remain disenchanted with respect to their belief patterns. I would respectfully disagree. The nature of our own belief in the magic of technology is of the same sort of logic as that of enchantment (see in this regard Bennett 2001; Latouche 1996; 1998, Spretnak 1999).

So much for ramifications and pitfalls of syncretism, at least for the moment. From this point on, I will focus on Candomblé from within its own sphere of influence in an attempt to come to grips with the process involved. And I say process, for process it is. In the universal process of maintaining a tenuous balance of the Orixás, and due to the dynamic mediating force of Exu, nothing, absolutely nothing in the universe, stays the same. With a sense of process in mind, let us return to a broader consideration of Candomblé life.

Chapter Ten

Process: Perpetual Change within Stability

Reconciliation of the Apparent Conflict

Candomblé is a practical, here-and-now belief system, dedicated to the uncertain certainties of life more than to the certain uncertainty of death as in Catholic and most Christian teachings. It is, as Pierre Verger (1981:67–68) aptly describes it, "exaltation turned toward life and its continuance," as opposed to a religion of salvation directed toward the hereafter. Consequently, Heaven, Purgatory, and Hell are alien concepts regarding the Candomblé way. Rather than chain the body and soul to an unknowable Christian paradise, Candomblé resonates with the power to improve people's condition during their brief passage through this life. Thus Candomblé has potent appeal for the descendants of Africans as well as for an increasing number of Brazilians of European ancestry. When I write the "people's condition" I don't allude by any means simply to economic and consumerist standards, but rather, to their sense of well-being with respect to themselves and their surroundings. Of course, if money and material possessions come along as a byproduct, perhaps so much the better; but perhaps not, depending upon how a particular individual is able to handle her/his increased purchasing power.

Candomblé, then, is basically centered on practical issues. In a manner of speaking, it is unapologetically hedonistic, even though a large number of its practitioners are mired in poverty. It revolves around the resolution of everyday trials and tribulations we are all caught up in, whether rich or poor, white or black. Unlike religions focused obsessively on salvation of the soul when the day of reckoning happens to come around, the Candomblé belief system is quite unconcerned with the afterlife. Its cosmology distinguishes the world of mortals from the world of spirits, and communication between flesh and blood humans and Orixás as the means to an end. The idea of some nebulous hereafter hardly enters into the picture. Focus remains on the here-and-now, on real-world problems—physical health, balanced human relations, hearty sexual life, and spiritual well being. In another way of putting the matter, the candomblista is both actor and participant with and within nature, rather than a detached spectator.

Regarding actual Candomblé practices, as typical of an oral culture, every Mãe- or Pai-de-Santo is always changing some aspect or other of her/his ceremonial performance. The Orixá garb s/he directs each participant to wear, and to an extent even the ceremony itself, is never what it was—although if the Mãe- or Pai-de-Santo is criticized for invariably interjecting differences into the proceedings, s/he most likely denies s/he has deviated from the standard norm. In fact, in Candomblé is a tradition that always deviates somewhat, with the incessant introduction of new elements at every step of the way. Since the deviations are usually minimal and subtle, the process at any given moment in time and place is neither what was in the past nor is it what was not in the past; it moves along a new line of becoming that marks out something different, something new. In this manner, the process seems caught up in ambivalence. It is a to and fro oscillation from one possibility to another, with no end in sight (Braga 1988).

Once again it becomes apparent that articulation of process is notoriously elusive. Perhaps one of the most adequate ways of conveying the idea of process is by alluding to its nature of interdependency, interrelatedness, and interaction. Everything—actually the term is a misnomer since there are actually no things—is interconnected—also somewhat of a misnomer, since connectedness according to common conception needs things that can be connected—with everything else, in a holistic flow of cultural phenomena . Still elusive, I'm afraid. Perhaps the best I can do is reiterate my qualification of process I suggested at the outset of this inquiry: culture is unceasing practice, practice is continuous process, and process is ongoing change within space and through time. That, of course, is an indirect approach toward a sense of process.

Another Digression
Holism, again, that intangible notion I mentioned in the previous paragraph that is shunned in many circles these days. And interconnectedness: usually avoided, given its vague nature. However, allow me to attempt summarizing holism and interconnectedness according to some terms from the vocabu-

lary developed in this inquiry—while for the moment eschewing standard Candomblé vocabulary:

(1) Everything is interdependent, interrelated, and interactive with everything else.
(2) Nothing is permanent, and everything is impermanent.
(3) Nothing is of no consequence whatsoever; rather, everything provides some function within the whole of the processual flow.
(4) Nothing is simply meaningless, for everything has its perpetually altering place in the whole of the flow.
(5) Everything is immanent, within nature; nothing can exceed or lie totally outside nature.

Since all that is in flux, and since everything is interconnected with everything else, what I have termed "kinesomatic bodymind," in conjunction with its world, must be an ecological matter.

Why ecological? Because just as bodymind is perpetually becoming, so is nature. This is to imply that bodymind's interdependent interaction with nature alters, even though to a virtually infinitesimal degree, nature's process. As a consequence of this interaction, nature reciprocally alters bodymind's process. If bodymind is at peace with itself and of good health, nature responds benignly; if bodymind perceives and conceives itself and nature in negative terms, the interactive process can be none other than negative. "Walk, and the clouds walk with you; smile, and the birds in the trees respond; talk, and nature dialogues with you." I offered this suggestion, even though it is so simple that it is dumbfounding, and so profound that it appears embarrassingly childlike. Just as individual bodymind is in communion with its immediate surroundings, so also entire communities with respect to nature. Candomblé life is living with and within animal, vegetal, and mineral realms, which is to say that it is living with and within the community and the interconnected whole of nature, and in addition, with and within anything industrious, insidious and destructive human hearts, hands and minds may happen to produce. Candomblé as a truly holistic affair has no use for the Western equivalent of objectivist, nominalist doctrine, for it incorporates a thoroughgoing realist philosophy. Everything, whether sensed and perceived or merely felt and unsensed, is taken for real. Actually, Western science is at its roots not entirely divorced from this notion. Gravity, electromagnetic fields, black holes, and many of the more elusive subatomic particles cannot be directly perceived. Solely their influence on their surroundings can be detected. If we still wish to call Western science a science of reality, then Candomblé is a cosmology of reality in its own right. If we wish to conceive of Western science as objective—though this has been hotly debated over the last half-century—then Candomblé, within its cosmological sphere of influence, is as empirical as can be.

At the same time, Candomblé is, as philosophies can become. Even here we find affinities with the roots of Western science. If we consider the nondirectly observables of science as the products of some sort of philosophical idealism, then Newtonian gravity belongs to one reality, Einsteinian gravity belongs to another reality, and as far as that goes, the ancient Greek universe, Copernicus's universe, Newton's universe, and Einstein's universe, belonged to different worlds, different realities. At the same time, in their composite, all these realities make up part of the whole, part of the sphere of all possible realities that have been, that are, and that will have been conceived. Candomblé is one of these realities. In this respect it is its own world. A chief difference is that Candomblé entails some inner awareness of the whole, of the range of possibilities (from emptiness to Firstness as discussed above), while empirical science presumably remains obsessively attuned to the phenomena at hand in spite of any and all postulated unobservables.

For obvious reasons, I have no time to delve into the ardent debates on science as objective and rational, science as subjective and constructive, science as alternative modes of knowing, and science as either factual knowledge or relative knowledge. I would hold that the important point to make here is that cultural knowledge of whatever sort, as a whole, must be taken from within and according to its own premises and practices. For cultural knowledge is inert and of little consequence until it emerges within cultural practices. Along these lines, Eugene Halton (1995) makes the most important point that if we conflate nature and culture and mind and body, then we must admit that just as our interpretations are the product of our own constructions, so also we are constructions of nature, for we are in nature and nature is in us. (With respect to debates on relative and objective knowing within science and without along the lines suggested here, see Bernstein 1983; Cartwright 1983, 1999; Devitt 1997; Farrell 1994; Feyerabend 1987, 1999; Goodman 1978; Goswami 1993; Gutting 1999; Fine 1986; Haack 2003; Hacking 1999; Hollis and Lukes 1983; Krausz 1989; Laudan 1996; Margolis 1991; Pagels 1982; Putnam 1990; Smith 1995; Stove 1982; Wright 1992.)

ACTOR-PARTICIPANTS WITHIN THE WHOLE

Regarding actor-participants knowing with and within nature, Candomblé certainly fits the bill. It is more than a conjunction of rituals, rites, and magical practices. It is a form of life in the full sense. It requires a tight-knit interconnected community, with its own form of conventional practices, in addition to what demands the larger societal institutions may exact on it.

I have argued that since the time of slavery, through Candomblé and kindred cultural practices such as Capoeira, oppressed Afro-Brazilians as a community have been able to keep their traditions alive through conformity and resistance. As would be expected, the merging of conformity and resistance has not been an easy task. In spite of the miscegenation of multiple African ethnicities into a community of resistance, there was always a tendency toward fragmentation, as various benign and a few antagonistic enclaves tended to spin out and away from the central cultural core. Miscegenation took place chiefly between Nagô and less populous groups from West Africa, on the one hand, and the Bantu peoples from the Equatorial region on the other hand. There was an interpenetration of cultural compatibilities and a few relative incompatibilities that eventually gave rise to emergent, novel religious groups, most of them sporting some Caboclo or Amerindian influence and some of them, especially Umbanda, tinged with spiritism. These sects are quite foreign to the spirit of Candomblé that originated in the Benin Sea area of West Africa and especially among the Nagô (Yoruba) and Jêjê (Dahomey) peoples. Among the less traditional Terreiros, a mixture of Angola (Bantu) and Caboclo (Amerindian) traits can be found. Taken as a whole, however, these diverse practices are one, in their interconnectedness. This interconnectedness has little to do with analysis, discourse, and intellection. It isn't known explicitly, for it is chiefly a matter of feeling. It just is; it is what Candomblé practitioners do; it is practicing philosophy.

Candomblistas, as practicing philosophers, are immanent, within the whole of their religious, ethnic, cultural, and natural world, within the processual flow (i.e. the five features of interconnected holism outlined in the previous section). As such, they make no overt distinctions between what is Candomblé in the pure sense and what is not (Catholicism, Caboclo, Umbanda, or whatever), or what is cultural and what is natural. They do what they do as if it were the most natural thing to do: they *are* what they do and what they do is their world. For example, my experience with my Pai-de-Santo, Hermes, who practices at a Terreiro (*Ile Ase Odé G'Mim*) located in the small village of Areia Branca about an hour and a half from Salvador by bus, doesn't conform to most scholarly accounts of Candomblé. Hermes is no scholar. He enters into no debates over the status of the religion-philosophy, and political activism leaves him cold. Yet in his Terreiro on some occasions he performs his interpretation of what the re-Africanizers would likely call "pure" Candomblé ceremonies. On other occasions he offers his conception of a Caboclo ceremony—his principle Orixá is *Oxossi*, the Caboclo influenced hunter—depending on the needs of the community. When I asked him about this, however, he told me standard Candomblé and Caboclo Candomblé are not separate; they need each other. He went on to give concrete examples about members of the community who were able to harmonize with the group and with nature only after experiences both strains of Candomblé. I left with the feeling that each ceremony by itself is lacking something. Together, however, they are a unity. The fact that they can't both be practiced simultaneously is due to our own physical limitations. The Orixás' world is a continuous whole, and unlimited by time and space. As far as Hermes is concerned, the Orixás are not interested in nor do they make any distinction between standard Candomblé and Caboclo Candomblé. Consequently, it is as if the two strains were complementary, or in the terms of this essay, coalescently, contradictorily complementary.

In contrast, the story among intellectualizing, re-Africanizing scholarly works leaning toward some idealized form of pure Candomblé usually has it that since the Bantu in Brazil were presumably less rebellious and hence more accommodating and acculturable into the dominant society, they were chiefly responsible for integrating and syncretizing Catholic saints with their corresponding Orixás. Thus, for example, their trance-states came about by the grace of particular Orixás, often accompanied by Catholic entities. As far as pure Candomblé goes, however, there should be no otherworldly spirituality involved. The experience should be a matter of the living forces of nature coming into communion with a particular human individual and bringing her into the flow of the totality. Unfortunately, the story continues, the very idea of syncretized trance-states can give rise to the idea of otherworldly Christian dogma, and even spirit mediums comparable to Kardecist doctrine. This tends to taint what might be considered genuine Candomblé practices. It can even encourage Candomblé practitioners to spin out and away from the tradition to form their own cults. The result can be a corruption of so-called pure Candomblé. Consequently, the notion of a syncretized trance-state should be avoided (Aflalo 1996; Berkenbrock 1995). I might add that even though Hermes remains quite aloof from the mainstream Terreiro communities and their debates, I see no indication of corruption due to syncretism in his practice. Rather, I sense that he intuits the nature of Candomblé for what it should be, with no need for debate and no desire to take sides with any of the political issues. Simply put, his interpretation of the Candomblé form of life is fundamentally extratextualist. He feels and senses it bodymindly. I have become aware of his feel for his art when during ceremonies he seems to border between consciousness and trance—even though a Pai-de-Santo never effectively enters into a trance-state. He is there, in the ceremony, but he is not there; he is aware of his brute physical surroundings and he is almost elsewhere. He seems to teeter at the edge, where bodymind, self, and world become one.

Actually, the trance-process raises the role of body, of kinesomatic bodymind, to its limits. It effectively dissolves any and all distinctions. There is no thisworldly and otherworldly, here and there, we and the others. Since the trace-process as a process dissolves distinctions, language loses its predominant role. In this respect Barbara Browning (1995:48) reflects on Candomblé choreography and ritual when she writes: "It is not meant to be read. It is not meant explicitly to suggest. We are the suggestion of divinity." In this manner, bodymind during the Candomblé ceremony suggests divinity. It doesn't actually or metaphorically become divinity. There is not simply a metaphorical image with a symbolic (linguistic) meaning attached to it. Metaphor implies that the subject both is who she is and at the same time she is somebody else: she is one of the Orixás, for example Oxum. It is not merely a matter of this person here dancing like Oxum and hence, metaphorically speaking, therefore she is Oxum. The process is considerably more complex than that.

In the very least, the metaphorical interconnection between Oxum and a candomblista entering into a trance-process is comparable to Peirce's category Firstness coupled with Secondness. Firstness qualifies something as what it is, no more, no less. It enjoys no interdependent, interrelated, interaction with anything else. But there must be at least a hint of something else, Secondness: the subject is what she is and she is also *not* only what she is; she is Oxum, the Other. Hence, when Oxum mounts her subject and that subject enters the trance-process, there is more than metaphor, or icon. There is, in addition to metaphor, implication—indexical—cause-effect (but interrelated and nonlinear) or part-whole, container-contained. The Candomblé subject as bodymind is a container, a vessel; she comes into indexical interrelation with the Orixá, Oxum in this case, who possesses her. This indexical nature of the trance-process is outwardly an either-or affair, for sure. But there is more. Something is becoming, which is neither the One nor the Other but something else, becoming. It might seem that first there was the subject, a vessel or container, then Oxum, the contained, mounted her, and she became both who she is and Oxum, and that's that.

But that's still not really all there is to it. The subject is not who she is without her context, which includes the entire community involved in the ceremony, and the whole of nature. And as Oxum, she is not who she is without the entire pantheon of Orixás, and the whole of nature. The either/or of the indexical or metonymical nature of the trance-process is no linear cause-effect affair. Rather, everything is the cause and it is also the effect of everything else. There is not simply an atomistic "I" or 'this." There is holistic "we becoming" and "everything else that is becoming."

In other words, Thirdness and symbolicity eventually also enter the scene. Thirdness enters, because the subject and Oxum could not metaphorically or iconically have become one nor could they metonymically or indexically have become container and contained without mediation by means of which they are becoming something other than what they were becoming. If Firstness engenders its Other, Secondness, then the One and the Other engender their Other Other, Thirdness. This Other Other is the becoming of something Other than the One or the Other: it is neither the One nor the Other but something else. It is inner Other becoming, both metaphorical and metonymical, both iconic and indexical. At the same time, it is somehow neither the one nor the other but something else: emergent Thirdness. In other words, it has emerged from within the imaginary (Firstness, iconicity) and the physical (Secondness, indexicality, Other than the First) context, and begins its process of becoming Other than the Other, mediator and moderator (Thirdness, symbolicity, agent of interconnectedness). The initial moments of the flow of the trance-process, including Firstness and Secondness, iconicity and indexicality, have no need of language. But finally, Thirdness, symbolicity, language, enters, and offers its meditative function in order that the process might move on.

How can we get a better handle on this idea of process in light of Candomblé as practicing philosophy? I'll attempt a few possible answers from a Peircean view. But a word of warning: abstractions will inevitably enter the scene, given the nature of the problem. (In constructing these abstractions I by no means wish to judge the relative value of Nagô Candomblé in comparison to other Candomblé ways, but rather, I attempt to account for their differences through use of Peirce's Firstness, Secondness, and Thirdness. Nor do I presume the ability to give the definitive interpretation of Candomblé. I very modestly suggest an alternative to the diverse interpretations now in print.)

What Sort of Cultural Mix?

As noted, the greatest influx of Africans of Nagô origin occurred during the nineteenth century. However, in 1770—and surprising as it may seem by comparison with the history of slavery in the United States—the first ambassadors were sent by the King of Benin. In 1824 the Benin nation was the first to recognize Brazil as an independent state; France and England soon followed suit. Ties between African states, especially in West Africa, and Brazil, were always considerably more extensive than ties between Africa and Spanish America or the United States.

Pierre Verger (1987) documents the first celebration of a deity transported directly from Africa in 1780. Overt syncretism of African deities with

Catholic images began soon thereafter. Verger writes that syncretism was from the very outset encouraged by various Catholic clergy. The clergy hoped this would facilitate conversion to the Church by way of stories regarding the lives of the saints, and further, that it might soften the slaves' tendency toward rebellion against their sorry condition. The slaves apparently accepted the invitation to syncretize, since under the guise of Catholic practices it would allow them to camouflage their own forms of worship. Various black fraternal societies soon emerged, perhaps most notable of which was the *Irmandade de Nossa Senhora da Boa Morte* (Sisterhood of Our Lady of Good [Atoning] Death). Some representatives from these societies even traveled to West Africa to established ties with fraternal societies on the home continent. A local homogeneous Afro-Brazilian culture within the larger heterogeneous dominant culture that was striving to institute homogeneity was by mid-nineteenth century creating the flux and reflux characteristic of Brazilian society since that time. However, according to various scholars, there remained a striking difference between the Bantu or Equatorial African relative acculturating, assimilating, and accommodating mentality, and the mentality that entailed relatively more resistance and rebellion among the Nagô and other peoples from West Africa (Goulart 1975). How can we account for the difference between the Bantu way and the Nagô way as they were re-invented in Brazil? I offer the following as a suggestion for your consideration.

The Bantu mentality allowed for both Candomblé and Catholicism, in the fashion commonly touted as syncretism. On the one hand, practices were both the one thing and the other, as a contradictory combination and fusion, though the contradiction presented no problem since in the two practices' combination they became as if one practice. The One practice camouflages the Other and the Other the One. On the other hand, in a noncontradictory mode, at a moment's notice either the One practice or the Other could dominate and in the process place the other practice under closely guarded cover. This now contradictory, now noncontradictory mixture of two homogeneous yet incompatible practices becomes subversive at one level, and at another level it pays homage to binary, linear, logic.

Putting Candomblé and Catholicism into one ball of wax in this manner slips a knife into the backside of classical logic by creating a noncontradictory, both-and condition as if it were as natural as could be. Yet by doing so it pulls either the One or the Other of any pair of alternatives into the light of day, thus paying homage to the Principles of Identity and Noncontradiction. Linear, binary thinking is both applauded and given a thumb down. In this manner, the both-and mode creating the appearance of homogeneity usually manages to prevail—albeit while doing a cover up of the underlying tension between incompatibles. The either/or mode allows for the appearance of whichever practice is most advisable under the circumstances. But the idea of "now this alternative, now that alternative" at different times and places creates disharmony and heterogeneity as a relatively mild subversion of the dominant culture's effort to impose homogeneity. In a nutshell, this, I would suggest from my readings, is the Afro-Brazilian Bantu cultural tendency.

Then what is the Nagô cultural tendency among Afro-Brazilians? It entails the Bantu tendency in the sense that it includes the *both-and* and *either/or* modes. In addition, it entails the more radically subversive neither-nor mode. How does this come about? Consider the Nagô *neither-nor* mode this way. In the Bantu mode, two cultural practices can exist side-by-side as the consummate odd-couple; yet each member of the couplet is no more than a possibility. Actualization of either the One or the Other does not ordinarily, and should not, come about during the same time and in the same place. There can be no more than now the One, now the Other, and so on, as described above. Hence as possibilities, two apparent incompatibles can become the strangest of bedfellows; as actualities they should never meet face-to-face on equal terms. There is no problem here, not really, from within the purview of classical logic. There is really no rape of the Noncontradiction Principle as long as A and Not-A are no more than mere possibilities. If A pops up at one time and place and Not-A at another time and place, there is still no problem. What is now A is not Not-A, and what is now Not-A is not A. If the Bantu way tends to becomes rebellious, it might abolish A (Catholicism) with a wholehearted embrace of Not-A (Candomblé), or vice versa. Or it might make an outwardly brash show of both A and Not-A as some sort of confusing syncretic mixture, which would undoubtedly bring down the Inquisitorial guardians' wrath full force—recall, in this regard, the discussion of figure 13. So far, so good.

Now comes the quirkiness. The Afro-Brazilian Nagô way usually has no need of an incongruous mixture of A and Not-A as two incompatible and, according to prevailing assumptions, relatively fixed practices. That would be too easy, too reasonable, too logical. The Nagô way is more slippery. It says "No" both to A and to Not-A. So, what is there? What can there be, if everything is negated? There is nothing, no-thing, if we take the existence of some-thing to mandate what there must be and is at a given point in time and place. There is no-thing following the Nagô tendency, for all that is, is in process. Everything is perpetually becoming something else (Berkenbrock 1995).

Process: within the interconnected whole. Process hints that what there is, is not what is becoming, for what is becoming never is, in a fixed sense. It hints that there is neither what there is nor is there not what there is, but rather, some-thing different, novel, perhaps hitherto unheard of, is always making its entrance onto the stage of universal flux. Flux and reflux. That is the Nagô world view in its most dynamic incarnation. It is saying neither A becoming nor Not-A becoming but always the becoming of some-thing other that what was becoming. The Nagô way says that either the One or the Other is impoverished; it says that both the One and the Other is fine as far as possibilities for everyday practices go, but they can't make their presence known without actualization into some either/or dualism; it says it also needs the neither and the nor. This neither and the nor is a fluctuating, oscillating, scintillating, effervescent process of what manifests itself to a greater or lesser degree as perpetual creativity, novelty, and yes, perpetual resistance and rebellion. Yet, like the either/or mode, there is a show of assimilation, accommodation, and conformity, by way of deception, always the element of deception. Deception is a cultural guerrilla shuffling and slithering, clever maneuvering while slipping a knife blade between the dominant culture's ribs. It is a means of maintaining tradition in the face of powerful attempts to snuff it out; it is a means of getting one's way come what may; it is a means of survival when conditions dictate that survival value is virtually nil. In this regard, it is not that the candomblistas aren't capable of or don't comprehend Catholic principles and thus syncretize them with Candomblé practices. Rather, they are engaging in cultural guerrilla warfare in one of the few ways available to them. (In this sense, if you wish to allow a little credence to my suggestion regarding the difference between Bantu Afro-Brazilian tendencies and Nagô Afro-Brazilian tendencies, a re-Africanization of the Nagô way cannot recover what once was, but what was and is always becoming something other. Thus the dilemma re-Africanizers remain caught up in; thus the common ground, after all, between the Nagô way and the Bantu way.)

How can the survival value of both the Bantu way and the Nagô way be more adequately qualified? If the concept of syncretism doesn't quite cut the cake—as we have observed, and will note in more detail below—then what alternative accounts for Afro-Brazilian staying power might we have at hand? For a preliminary step toward an answer to this question, allow me another digression—into further abstraction, for better or for worse—in order to take a look at .....

AFRO-BRAZILIAN PRACTICES AS GUERRILLA CULTURE

Bastide often comments on the ability of the black population during the Colonial period in Brazil simultaneously to live in two different worlds and still avoid tensions and conflicts. Ordinarily, there would be the conflict of contradictory values as well as the demands of the two societies that are incompatible on many points. The Afro-Brazilians, however, provided loose-and-limber *Included-Middles* to subvert the classical logical taboo in the venerated name of the classical *Excluded-Middle* imperative. Let me try to account for this by way of Peircean process philosophy and with the aid of some Brazilian scholars.

As the anthropologist Roberto DaMatta (1995:270) puts it: "A virtude está no meio" (Virtue lies in between [two contradictory values]). Indeed, it's what's in the middle that counts, for that's where effervescent, scintillating emptiness, or Axé if you will, brings about the emergence of what is perpetually new and fresh; it is the fountain incessantly pouring forth differences that can make a difference; indeed, it is what's behind the life principle of the universe. DaMatta studies contemporary Brazilian culture at large. Nevertheless, his model applies quite well to the particular Afro-Brazilian condition, past and present. In demonstrating how Brazilian culture subverts classical dichotomies of logico-rational thought and cultural practices, DaMatta draws from Victor Turner's (1974) studies of social dramas. Turner focuses on historical events, rituals, and social practices rather than institutions and beliefs. In so doing he effectively accounts for concrete cultural practices and what they mean to the people who engage in them (in this regard see the collection of essays in Gomes et al. 2000).

DaMatta presents various case studies illustrating how Brazil's individualistic/personalistic and egalitarian/hierarchical cultural traits emerge and operate simultaneously, and in the process, otherwise irreconcilable contradictions break down. Most commonly, scholars use the terms "personalism" and "paternalism" as well as other kindred labels in reference to the whole of Latin American societies. DaMatta demonstrates how Brazilian culture subtly and effectively operates within the interstices between conflicting categories—much the same could be said of Spanish American societies as well. One of his most notorious examples is found in *Carnivals, Rogues, and Heroes* (1991), where he interprets the ritual of reversal known as "Você sabe com quem fala?" (Do you know to who you're speaking to?). This occurs when a subaltern is conversing with a superaltern and crosses the line of proper respect for those of citizens of presumed 'superior" status. Then a quick rebuke from the superaltern, "Do you know who you're speaking to?," is necessary in order to put the subaltern in his proper place. As would be expected, subaltern Brazilians find this little ritual demeaning, for it is most often used by people who wish to assert their position of authority and importance by way of family, friendship, wealth, social standing, and work-related ties. What relevance does DaMatta's interpretation hold with respect to the topic under discussion? That for any two apparently dichotomous cultural phenomena, there is always a third possibility—or Thirdness if you will—that which can emerge from the middle. So the middle is to be included rather than excluded after all.

For example, in his study of the Latin American scene, John Beverley (1999:123) wants to dissolve what he sees as the subalternizing binary consisting of the distinction between those who are dominant and those who are subservient. Well and good, it might seem. But actually, there is no real binarism in the first place, if, like DaMatta, emphasis rests on what's in-between. Within the in-between, there is always a Third that can at any moment come into play. In fact, that's part of the problem: "The subaltern classes, by definition," according to Antonio Gramsci (1971:57), "are not unified and cannot unite until they are able to become a state." Before the collection of human subjects can become unified there must be some unifying force, and that force emerges with a state's emergence. Granted as well. But if upon cornering their share of the spotlight the subaltern classes and groups have to become essentially like the superaltern classes and groups, then in a sense the old ruling classes and the dominant culture inevitably win, even in defeat. How does one effectively move from the negativity of subaltern consciousness to hegemony? As if the problem were a matter of dualism? That is the question posed by Néstor García Canclini's (1995) and Homi Bhabha's (1994) critiques of the subaltern/dominant binary (see especially Friedman 1997). It is also behind Angel Rama's (1982) idea of transculturation, and Florencia Mallon's (1995) effort to read back into the historical record the effective presence of peasants and peasant communities in the constitution of the modern state in Peru and Mexico. I would suggest that by and large their answers to this question are unsatisfactory, at least with respect to Candomblé life as I have described it thus far. In this light, Beverley (1999:137) goes on to write:

> Gramsci tends to equate the subaltern as such with the categories of the "traditional," the "folkloric," or [most often] the "spontaneous." However, García Canclini thinks it is necessary to abandon the categories of "subalternity" and "hegemony" altogether, because, in his view, the subaltern can be conceptualized as a subject-position only in relation to a sense of "traditional" or "popular" culture that has been overthrown by modernity. As another alternative, Mignolo (2000:14–15), suggests use of the term "colonial semiosis" rather than Ortiz's and Rama's 'transculturation" in order to dispel the "colonizing notion" of "traditional" or "popular culture." I would be inclined to agree with Mignolo: the concept of "popular culture" is loaded down with too many essentializing and colonizing overtones.

The subaltern/dominant dilemma raises its ugly head when hegemony is crammed into a presumably fixed pigeon-hole. Actually, there are at least two forms of hegemony—if not more. Both of them, if taken in the ordinary dualistic fashion as linear binarity, actually depend on nonlinear triadicity (see figure 14). How so? First, before there is anything at all there is possible emergence (Firstness, or the upper leg of the tripod). In the Candomblé vision Axé, or emptiness, holds the possibility for the becoming of whatever might becoming at a given space-time juncture. After what might have emerged has emerged, there is the dualistic formal, mechanical, and relatively fixed type of hegemony (Secondness, or the left leg of the tripod). And there is the flowing organic, contextual, processual, open hegemony. This is hegemonic process. It allows for neither one static interpretation nor its opposite interpretation, for there is always mediation such that something novel is in the process of emerging (Thirdness, or the right leg of the tripod).

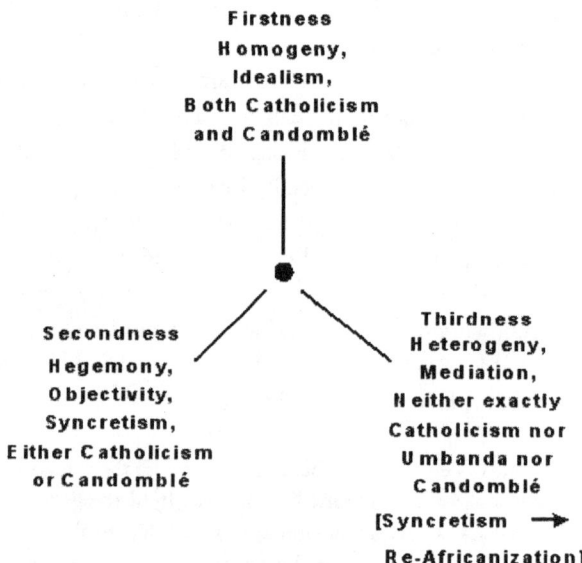

FIGURE 14

CULTURAL PROCESS TRIPOD

We have in figure 14 some of our now familiar terms; we also have their variation in homogeny, hegemony, and heterogeny. The prefix homo- aids in qualifying the sphere of Peirce's category Firstness. It consists of a union of possibilities into a harmonious package without any pair of opposite terms having (yet) emerged into the light of day to begin their age-old combat. Hetero- helps qualify the sphere of category Thirdness. It is made up of actualized terms that have either become bored or exhausted as a result of their incessant cultural guerrilla warfare, their accommodation and struggle. Consequently, it is in the process of beginning a potential reconciliation of virtually any and all differences. Hegemony, of course, signifies authority, predominance, the preponderant influence of one community or social class over others—with a greater or lesser degree of contestation and negotiation in the Gramsci interpretation of the term. The suffix, -*geny*, indicates a manner of emergence, origin, organic becoming without reaching the stage of already having become. This becoming, I would suggest, is of the nature of the pathway leading from zero, emptiness, or Axé if you will, up to Peirce's Firstness.

Placing this formulation in symbols (see figure 15) as they will be further discussed in chapter 12, the transition is: $0 \rightarrow \emptyset \rightarrow \sqrt{} \rightarrow + \rightarrow - \rightarrow \Psi \rightarrow$ FIRSTNESS. In other words, the scheme entails the process of what for lack of an appropriate label can be called *pre-Firstness* (zero, Axé, emptiness) which is in the process of becoming one of a number of possible manifestations of Firstness (or possible signs) by way of "noticed absence" or the "empty set" ($\emptyset$). This noticed absence implies acknowledgment that where there is nothing there could be something as a possibility having become actualized. Next, there is an oscillating equivalence of the square root of minus one ($\sqrt{-1} = \pm 1$), where possible Firstness can interact with some possible Other (or the possible sign with its possible object) to bring about the emergence of some possible Secondness. The process then flows into some form or other of a possible symbolic representation (i or Ψ), or possible Thirdness. In other words, possible Firstness and its possible semiotic object become possibly mediated by Thirdness. Now, the initial process can emerge into the light of day as one of the possibilities actualized as a physical or mental manifestation of concrete Firstness, which then moves on toward concrete Secondness and Thirdness. In other words, figure 15 is a semiotic prelude to actual signs (i.e., figure 14, following figure 4)] as they emerge during the process of everyday living (see Baer 1988). This formulation remains inordinately abstract. This the only way it can be. For the figure can do no more than spell out the possibilities for sign actualization within an imaginary realm—the word in quotes is appropriate, I would suggest, given its exemplification by the "imaginary number", $\sqrt{-1}$.

I would like to think that Firstness (the range of possibilities within homogeny) and Thirdness (the mediating role within pluralistic heterogeny) are by now quite obvious. I also would hope the illogicality of homogeny and heterogeny is a point well taken in light of the above pages. The problem likely lies in the middle term, hegemony. The term is common enough in much scholarship going by the name of cultural studies, and in postcolonial and neo- and post-Marxist talk. But when situated within the context of this inquiry, problems arise. I have opted to place the term within the bag of binary thinking generally in line with classical logical principles. How can this be? The very idea of contestation and negotiation between subalterns and the dominant society is dynamic, and constantly open to change. There is no stasis, no intransigence, no simple binarity. It would appear that even here we have processual flow. A few words regarding this problem are in order, then.

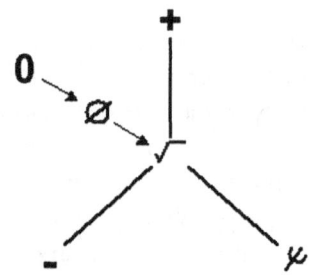

FIGURE 15

FROM AXÉ, 'EMPTINESS', THROUGH THE 'INCLUDED MIDDLE'

A Case in Point
Consider a person of the upper echelons in the social hierarchy who, while driving through the streets of a crowded city, runs a stoplight. In Brazil, the United States, and Western societies in general, ideally the law of the road applies to all citizens. All individuals are theoretically on an equal basis, for according to the legal system, egalitarianism rules. Young and old, rich and poor, movie stars and common folks, politicians and ordinary citizens, are all expected to obey the law. Nobody is exempt.

However, in Brazil, "decent" and "respectable" people often successfully subvert this universal order according to the legal system. In the situation of our driver who broke the law, if a police officer confronts her and begins addressing her as he would any other citizen, he may at some point have to contend with the haughty, indignant, offensive move DaMatta so effectively analyzes: "Você sabe com quem fala?" (Do you know who you're speaking to?). The implication may be something like: "I'm a friend of so-and-so, who is a friend of so-and-so whose cousin is Secretary of Internal Affairs; so I am not just any ordinary individual; I am a person of status, and I demand respect of the likes of you." The traffic offender now becomes the socially offended, and may then release the clutch, leave a little rubber on the pavement, and speed away as if insulted. Or the officer may meekly apologize for his error and carry on with his duties elsewhere with citizens of lesser status. In other words, the officer didn't address himself to any ordinary citizen, to just an ordinarily individual equal in the eyes of the law to all other ordinary individuals. He addressed himself to someone who saw herself as a *person* of worth, of social status. The modern idea that all citizens are equal under the law was not for her; her place was in traditional Brazil, where so-called respectable people were at the top of the heap. She was not just anybody; she was somebody.

In this manner the otherwise intransigent dichotomy, individual/person, and with it the interdependent, interrelated dichotomy, egalitarian/hierarchical, became vague. The representative of the law took a person for an individual, as would be appropriate in an egalitarian society. That would be standard procedure in an egalitarian society. However, the person in question considered herself not on a flattened horizontal cultural plane and of the same value as all other citizens, but at the top of Brazilian traditional hierarchical society delineating between those of greater value and those of lesser value. The apparent dichotomy, individual/person, was no longer a mere binary but both the one term and the other term came into play within the same spatial and temporal social setting. There was no longer exclusion of a third alternative between the dichotomous pairs, for something emerged to make its presence known.

What was that something? It began as pre-Firstness (figure 15), the possibility of our person turning the tables and asserting herself as a person in a context that would ordinarily call for equal treatment of all citizens as individuals. The dichotomy quickly melted; an individual emerged sporting a person's countenance; a person pushed her way into a context calling for individuals; and what shouldn't happen according to social conventions but could happen as a possibility in fact happened. This Third alternative gushed forth from 0 (Axé, emptiness) as a possibility that became actualized within a particular cultural setting with the possibility of mediating between two poles of the presumed dichotomy, individual/person. The dichotomy teetered, and tumbled. Consequently, the Principles of Non-Contradiction and Excluded-Middle made their exit, and something emerged from the in-between as the Included-Middle to make its play.

With this abrogation of classical logical operations in mind, we can appreciate DaMatta's observation:

> For generations, Latin America has had its share of observers, who like to prove that the continent is a true logical disaster. More precisely, it's a sociological disaster. The problem is that these observers rarely question their own starting point. They assume their position to be logical and precise to the extent that they are part of a system capable of defining itself with a word (capitalism, modernity, progress), two or three well-known concepts (usually made up by the observers, and on their own terms), and only one sort of logic—the excluded middle (the *tertium non datur* of the ancient philosophers)—that does not allow apples and oranges to mix. But none of this works for the so-called Latin American reality. (DaMatta 1995:270)

During everyday coming and going within what is called Latin American reality, what is or should be, is not, and at the same time there is both what is or should be, and there is not, and there is neither what is or should be, nor is it the case that there is not what there is or should be. This abrogation of ordinary social logical principles enters the scene at the levels of pre-Firstness, and then proceeds to Firstness, Secondness and Thirdness, and vagueness and distinction and imprecise generality, and homogeny, hegemony and heterogeny (figures 14 and 15). There is no simple "A or Not-A." Rather, in DaMatta's example, there is "Do you know ... ?" which includes what would otherwise be excluded from the binary equation. There is no mere sense of democratic individualism, because social hierarchization manages to remain on the scene and they both become convenient and somewhat comfortable yet antagonistic bedfellows. Thus there is inclusion of the equation "Both A and Not-A" (homogeny or possibility). There is no mere exclusion of a middle term between the horns of the opposition, but emergence of one and perhaps many alternatives; consequently the "Neither A nor Not-A" (heterogeny) mode has its day. There is individualism and there is personalism, and there is egalitarianism and there is hierarchization. It's all there during each day of life in DaMatta's Brazil as a "sociological disaster"—but with salutary rather than malignant connotations in DaMatta's conception.

Brazil's "Do you know ... ?" is somewhat comparable to that expression in the United States, "Who do you think you are talking to?" The latter commonplace phrase, however, places sharper focus on the subordinate individual in an effort to shove him down to what is considered the proper social level; the former, in contrast, throws the spotlight on the dominant person and in the process elevates her appropriately. Nevertheless, "Who do you think you are talking to?" is somewhat the social counterpart of Brazil's "Do you know ...?". The chief difference is that in the United States the individual is all-important. Everybody is first and foremost an individual. She possesses an individuality that stands out above and beyond all other individualities insofar as its owner is capable of winning whatever socio-cultural game is being played out: to be "Número uno" is of utmost importance, for one must triumph at all cost. In Brazil, a person is with much greater frequency a person by virtue of birth, or if not, by a long and successful career likely involving a series of "Do you know ... ?" encounters; and now, she is surrounded by individuals who must pay her proper respect. In Brazil, when appropriate social distinctions are to be reaffirmed, the person must rise to the highest possible peak of the social terrain, in contrast to the United States, where the *individual* must find her place (see Barbosa 1992:75–77).

Anthropologist Howard Wiarda (1974:214) observes that Latin America in general is an extraordinary place, where "virtually all the systems of society that have ever governed [human] affairs continue to exist." Wiarda attributes this peculiarly Latin American characteristic to the absence of any genuine social revolution, which has permitted the continuing coexistence of Thomism, divine-right monarchy, feudalism, autocracy, republicanism, liberalism, and all the rest. In a comparable vein, the Brazilian social scientist Oliveira Vianna (1934:91–92) calls Brazil the "showcase of an ethnographic museum." Putting these images together, we have tenuous suggestions of pre-modernism and modernism and postmodernism all wrapped up in a rather incongruous and tension-ridden package; yet when Brazil is at its best it is a remarkably harmonious social concoction. Brazilian social analyst Sergio Buarque de Holanda (1935) labeled his society of the 1930s that of *homen cordial* (cordial man). That's how it might have appeared, in the days of whitening and according to the myth of racial democracy. But the cordial-man notion conceals the fluctuating, scintillating, whirlwind of cultural processes beneath the surface, always ready and willing to spew forth from the Included-Middle. Consequently, I would tend to prefer the idea of Brazil as an incongruous, coalescent melody of ethnic tensions perpetually in need of complementary harmonizing.

In sum, "Do you know ... ?" makes use of the authoritarian base of Brazilian culture, and at the same time it reveals dynamic interplay between the terms in figures 14 and 15. It de-equalizes and re-establishes presumed social identity. It is a rite of separation or distinction; it re-fortifies symmetrical relationships, and above all, it negates; it says one cannot occupy the social pigeon-hole one is trying to enter, that one must not try to take leave of one's so-called inferior standing. It entails verbal and gestural imposition. It is a matter of imposing one's will on others through amiable, informal, indirect and subtle nuances, by means of a large dose of word play. It is a game with explicitly and implicitly defined rules, where the winner is invariably the person of higher status. This authoritarian base of Brazilian culture has been the target of Capoeira and Candomblé conformity and resistance, of the cultural Other, of guerrilla culture, from the very beginning. Cultural guerrilla interaction has effectively subverted the either/or pressures of authoritarian Brazil. In the process ordinary logical principles have been trashed for a more subtle other logic, a logic of the Included-Middle. This lies at the very heart of Brazilian culture as a whole. Brazilian culture, like all cultures, follows a logic that refuses analytical chopping into fixed categories.

SPECIFIC BOTH-ANDS AND NEITHER-NORS WITHIN CANDOMBLÉ LIVING

In my experience with Candomblé life in Salvador, I have been told by practitioners: "Yes, we go to Mass, because we're Catholics, but we also participate in Candomblé ceremonies, because they help us solve our problems, and, well, they're just beautiful; we feel something in them that we never feel in the Catholic Church." There seems to be no problem here, no concern over what would ordinarily be taken as an inherent contradiction. It would appear that homogeny, hegemony and heterogeny are in a dynamic interdependent, interrelated, interactive, incongruously complementary process. One might also suspect at the outset that here we have Ferretti's "parallelist syncretism." Then, on second thought one might tend to conclude that it must be "convergentist syncretism." So, what is the answer?

In light of the interrelations in figures 14 and 15, consider this. As far as candomblistas are concerned, Catholicism and Candomblé are both acceptable, as possibilities for actualization in either the parish or the Terreiro. In this case the binary Principle of Non-Contradiction inheres. However, in their everyday coming and going these people evince the making of neither-nor behavior. In their Portuguese speech patterns outside the home, they customarily evoke Catholic values and Christian images; at home, Candomblé values and images often emerge. If they have the money they might pay a visit to the doctor practicing Western medicine; the next day they might consult with a Mãe-de-Santo, and purchase the necessary herbs that will take their place among other items in the kitchen. On Friday, a son or daughter of *Oxalá* might properly dress in white and eat soul food of the Orixás—served in many popular restaurants on that day—yet when seated before the meal mumble a few words of thanks in the Catholic tradition. This is not simply syncretism in the customary sense. Catholicism and Candomblé practices in each case are in the process of continually becoming some-thing other than what they were becoming. They are no longer the Catholicism and Candomblé culture they were, but some-thing else, some-thing different, some-thing new. The most notable example of this process is found in the community of Mães-de-Santo and Candomblé practitioners who wash the steps at the Church of the Senhor do Bonfim during January of each year.

When neither-nor liminality becomes trickster, the Exu of classical logic, what's between the eithers and the ors, or the otherwise *tertium non datur*, opens itself up to new possibilities. Either/or Excluded-Middle binary rules and regulations somewhat of the sort meted out by Xangô's system of justice and Ogum's war and vengeance are for the time being of no consequence: we are now in the arena of myriad possibilities. We have been transported into Exu's playground, where the hitherto unimaginable always stands a chance, however remote, of popping up somewhere and somewhen. Now it's not simply what goes around comes around, but whatever was in the process of going around is now coming around in a slightly to radically different guise. It is coming around to offer something fresh, something new, that is not simply there for the taking by the most aggressive macho mind and body around in order to make it his and his alone, for in order that it may emerge there must be participation. Whether we know it or not and whether we like it or not, we are by no means neutral spectators; we are actor-participants in the grand drama of processual becoming. There is no becoming without the whole of the world's actor-participants and each and every actor-participant stands no chance of beginning her becoming without the whole of all actor-participants, and that includes the entire world, from the Orixás to subnuclear particles to the most remote galaxies. Two important points are to be made at this juncture. First, the neither-nor liminality I have articulated is very fundamentally the sort of African sensibility found within Capoeira, Candomblé and other Afro-Brazilian cultural practices, and indeed, in the whole of Brazilian cultural (Chernoff 1979). Second, my choice of the Greek Psi symbol was not merely arbitrary: it is figuratively a three-pronged fork symbolic of Satan; it also commonly accompanies Exu images as illustration of the erroneous syncretic fusion brought about by early Catholic.

Yet, I can't simply leave things in this state of mumbo-jumbo. In an effort more adequately to articulate the alternative cultural logics I speak of, I turn once again to DaMatta.

Homey Comfort versus Street Smarts

With DaMatta, one should assume that qualifying Brazil as a scandalous contradictory mélange of tradition and modern liberal and neo-liberal ideas will be looked upon as a symptom of impropriety and inadequate interpretation. Yet, there is more than an iota of truth to the qualification. In DaMatta's words:

> Everyone knows that in Brazil (as throughout Latin America) everything is "out of place." But why wouldn't it be? And what logic presides over this apparently prelogical untidiness? This is precisely the question that hardly anybody asks! And for this reason the Brazilian tradition and the institutional framework that it legitimates becomes such a tremendous mystery. Nonetheless, the puzzle begins to make sense when one reflects about the place of favor, of patronage, and of personal relations in the Brazilian social system, contrasting their importance with their role in liberalism. One then discovers what was tacitly known, that the personal relations and impersonal rules on which liberalism is based exist within mutually exclusive, although complementary, social spheres. (DaMatta 1995:274–75)

Liberalism and neo-liberalism in Brazil is a matter for government and the world of economics—egalitarian ideals of modernism, highlighting the individual. This, in a metaphorical sense, is life in the Street, public life, the life of Individuals. In contrast, values of patronage—traditional hierarchical social processes—place emphasis on the Person of social prestige and the "Do you know ... ?" syndrome. This is metaphorically speaking culture within the Home. Such private domestic life emphasizes traditional family, friends, and associates. Individual and Person, Street and Home: not only does each set of values carry a different weight; they customarily move in very different spheres. My allusion to Street and Home evoke DaMatta's (1991a) concept of "modern" Brazil, Street Brazil, the competitive world of wheeling and dealing based on Enlightenment thought and the elusive equality of any and all individuals, and traditional Brazil, Brazil in the Home, where a Person is of worth according to birth, upbringing, and proper education. DaMatta's "Do you know ...?" entails interdependency and interaction between Street life, where everybody is an Individual, and Home life, where special individuals take on the status of Persons. This recalls once again the Included-Middle between Individual and Person, when the applecart is overturned and an Individual suddenly puts on a Person face even though the context calls for Street life. In fact, DaMatta's apparent dichotomy between Street and Home is mediated by what he calls the "Other World," an Included-Middle where Street space and Home space fuse and become confused. In this Other World are both Individuals and Persons and Street and Home, and, given the Included-Middle principle, there is neither the one pole nor the other pole of the dichotomy, for something else, possibly something new, always stands a chance of emerging.

In a comparable vein, Roberto Schwarz suggests how a type of circular logic often emerges in Brazil:

> Precisely because I am a liberal in Congress (i.e., as recognized in national public life), I have the right to be a slave-holder or a paternalist at home! To use the very example of Machado de Assis [Brazil's première late nineteenth-century writer], it is precisely because Machado is "a combative journalist and an enthusiast of the proletarian intelligence, of the classes," that he may also be (within the system that separates the streets and the home) the "author of chronicles and commemorative pieces on the occasion of the marriage of imperial princesses ... a knight and eventually an Official of the Order of the Rose". (Schwarz 1977:21)

The knight's behavior in the Street might seem to confer the right to be the opposite at Home. Would this be a personal inconsistency or a deeply rooted manifestation of a system that does not operate in linear terms and is not, in fact, governed by a single set of rules? Such would be the case of the knight's complying with the rules. At the same time, the knight subverts those rules at a higher level where the tacit assumption exists that at this level the rules don't apply. They don't really apply, for the conditions are different. In other words, the rules apply at the level of the individual and egalitarianism (the knight's public life—in the Street), but they don't apply at the level of the person and hierarchical culture (the knight's private life among family, friends, and nobility—in the court or the Home). As we shall note below, this concept is germane to Latin American cultures in general and specifically to Capoeira and Candomblé life.

Ideally, we should study and write about Brazil from within the country's so-called illogical sociologic. The problem is that, as products of enlightenment thought, we have difficulty breaking out of our logical straitjacket. We persist in thinking logical contradictions inevitably end in mental quagmires, and we should categorically reject them. We tend to think that what is, is what it is, and it can't be anything else, period. We believe the answer to a problem must be either right or wrong, true or false, black or white. Any other alternatives leave us in muddles, so they shouldn't even enter into the picture. DaMatta, among few scholars, puts the whole matter in another way:

> We may speak of Brazil as a system of oppositions between blacks and whites with Indians mediating between the two; or between people and the government with the church mediating. Mediatorial figures are neglected in Brazilian sociology (excepting the classical work of Gilberto Freyre and Sérgio Buarque de Holanda). This has led analysts to see our social logic as contradictory when it is also triadic, complementary, and hierarchical. From a formal academic position the mulatto can be reduced to black or white, and this has been presented as an "advance" over other explanations. From a societal perspective, however, the "mulatto" is not simply the empirical result of a physical and sexual relation between "races" but also the crystallization of the possibility for encompassing opposition. Using comparative historical analysis, Carl Degler ... understood the mulatto within the Brazilian racial system as an "escape hatch"—a valve that liberates social tensions and allows for compensations. I similarly interpret the Brazilian system as *substantively functional* and exhibiting original sequences of *social compensation*. (DaMatta 1995:281)

There is a strange anecdote about an American journalist's interview with Haiti's Papa Doc Duvalier that bears out this illogical logic. The journalist asked Papa Doc what percentage of Haiti's population was white. Ninety-eight percent, Papa Doc responded without blinking an eye. How could this be? Perplexed, the American asked the Haitian how he defined white. Papa Doc answered the question with a question: "How do you define black in your country?" The journalist patiently explained that in the United States virtually anyone with black blood was considered black. Duvalier nodded and said, "Well, that's the way we define white in my country." The journalist had contextualized Papa Doc within "white" thinking, but Papa Doc upended the applecart and suddenly became "black" thinking Papa Doc. The Included-Middle yielded an unexpected turn of events.

So, it seems I'm back to square one ... again. How can I get a more adequate grip on these strange logics, these logics that have been and will continue to be the focus of my modest inquiry?

Chapter Eleven

The Dichotomies Become More Pliable

SYNCRETISM REVISITED

In an effort to answer the questions that arose in the preceding chapter, I reconsider, if you will, Ferretti's (1999) separation and mixture syncretisms. The first, he tells us, is relatively objective, while the second is relatively subjective. Objective separatedness is where the One has its Other and the Other has its own Other, the One. Like oil and water, they don't mix. When the One has been actualized it excludes the Other at that particular time and place, though their roles could be switched at the drop of a hat. Subjective mixture exists as the possibility for actualization of either One thing or an Other thing.

Mixed possibilities imply that neither the One nor the Other has been actualized; they exist in some sort of silent and tacit competition with each other, in wait of the proper moment for their emergence. With respect to syncretism, separation entails actualized icons and ritual interaction from within either Catholicism or Candomblé; mixed possibilities entail icons and ritual interaction from both religious traditions, and when some particular icon or ritual action emerges, it will evince elements from both traditions that can be interpreted as either the One tradition or the Other in parallel fashion. In order that the mixture may be so interpreted, there must be mediation between the One and the Other such that the result is neither the One nor the Other as they were in their previous incarnation, but something new, something different. This entails convergence. Thus we have, as in Figure 14, homogeny or Peirce's Firstness, hegemony or Secondness, and heterogeny or Thirdness.

According to figure 14, the ideal of the dominant society makes a concerted effort to impose a particular sense of hegemony and thus homogenize society at large. It does so at whatever cost, often with a minimum of violence and genocide, and if not, by whatever means might be deemed necessary. This is the ideal, at least as far as the dominant society is concerned. The ideal is presumably in principle possible. Possibility, of the nature of Firstness, places Catholicism and Candomblé together as alternative forms of life. They are there as possibilities, but according to the ideal in the minds of the dominant society, if and when any aspect of either of them is actualized, there must be separateness at all cost. Catholicism and Candomblé are in a twisted manner of speaking 'separate but equal," as possibilities. Now, as possibilities, if Candomblé and Catholicism were equally actualized, they would be incompatible on many points. Hence if they were put in the same bag, the Principle of Non-contradiction would be ravaged. This is taboo for the properly linear, binary-minded institutions of the domineering power groups. So if and when aspects of the two practices are actualized, they must be maintained separately. But in actual practice they are by no means equal. The One is presumably civilized, the Other is barbarous; the One is sacred and of the one and only true God, the Other is under the keeping of Satan; the One is of refined culture, the Other is vulgar and primitive—linear thinking tends to do this to people, especially when they enjoy more power than they deserve. Hence the Other must be prevented from emerging. So, repression, sometimes brutal almost beyond imagination, is the consequence. The dominant society never ceases its efforts to impose a presumably hegemonous, and overtly Catholic, way of life (Sanchis 1999).

There is among those who rule, then, an obsessive effort to maintain the two practices in separation if and when both of them may be actualized for the purpose of identifying the Other and eradicating it. We are still at the left-side leg of figure 14: homogeny at the service of hegemony. The task of the haves is now to search out and destroy any and all vestiges of heterogeny the havenots are hanging onto. One might insist, however, that there is a certain beauty in interpretations the likes of Sérgio Buarque de Holanda/s "cordial man" and Gilberto Freyre's harmonious, "New World in the tropics" where kinder, gentler landowners take on a fatherly role toward their slaves in the field, romp with slave women when possible, keep a paternal eye on their mulatto offspring, and everybody becomes one happy family. This terribly romanticized interpretation in part manages to persevere, though to slightest degree, even in the early revisionist works by Carl Degler (1971), Florestan Fernándes (1971). It also suggests that there is a certain element of dialogic give and take within the spirit of hegemony. The dominant society allows subservient society a little bit of leeway in order to keep them in line and prevent unnecessary rebellious tendencies.

However, the subservients, understandably, attempt subtly to take a mile when given an inch. As little as possible is out in the open, for maintenance of their traditional culture under the watchful eye of the dominants must by and large go undetected. The most apparent avenue open to the subservients is covert guerrilla warfare, cultural guerrilla activity motivated by overt patterns of accommodation coupled with seething resentment and resistance just below the surface. Thus egalitarian cultural homogeny becomes a pipe dream, for in spite of Catholicism's imperial pressure on Candomblé, heterogeny persists in springing up here and there.

So it is that the two practices, Catholicism and Candomblé, are inextricably mixed as actual icons and ritual interaction. What does this reveal? Orixá images openly embrace Catholic images; Afro-Brazilians focus their eyes on saints in their place of Catholic worship; but minds are elsewhere, hearing the drums and chants, feeling the dance steps, sensing the Orixás, and at times even going into trances, right there, in the Catholic Church during mass. There is both Catholicism and Candomblé as far as the Afro-Brazilians are concerned. And quite often the Orixás ultimately have their say. Yet from the dominant society's perspective, they must be and are separated. And there is no question about which practice rules: Catholicism. There is Catholicism and ideally no more than Catholicism according to the dominant society: the Other has been appropriately repressed, and that's the way things must be. Now enter the right leg of figure 14. And it would seem that syncretism takes on a new countenance.

Ferretti (1999:117) suggests that a *convergence*, rather than a relatively simple mixture, often results from what I have termed the interdependent, interrelated interaction between the two forms of life after a certain period of existence in the mixed state. In convergence there is complementation of the One with respect to the Other, and vice versa. The One and the Other are complementary in the sense that they are both there, with a portion of the One within the Other and the Other within the One. They become one form of life in the sense that they can enjoy manifestation at one point or other in time and place, though they are not both under the interpretative eye from within the same frame of reference. Both interpretations complement each other. However, this is no simple both-and affair. They are not merely mixed and mixed they will remain in static fashion. As complementary forms of life, there is neither precisely the One nor the Other, but rather, something different, something creative and new, is always in the process of its becoming. This processing is of the nature of Thirdness. Hegemony has given way to heterogeny on the right leg of Figure 14. Otherwise minute differences in the two forms of life converge and become differences that make an appreciable difference. Other elements from outside the pair of forms of life enter. They converge and merge to begin their processing in complementation with the processing already going on.

Such processing might conceivably mark the emergence of Umbanda and a whitening of certain other aspects of Afro-Brazilian culture—notably, Capoeira Regional. There has been convergence of the two forms of life, and the emergence of something new is out in the open. Prohibition and repression were reduced, and the new process is permitted, up to a certain extent. This is no indication that preconceptions, prejudices, and discrimination are no longer present. They are there, as always. The difference is that with an acceptable degree of whitening, the convergent, complementary practice has become respectable in the eyes of the cultured folks. Hence the middle-class appeal of Umbanda. Where is the relatively static, dualistic either/or syncretism in all this? Indeed, there is process more than product; there are amorphous cultural differences more than stubborn distinctions. If syncretism there must be, it is of the complex variety depicted in the whole of figure 14.

Of course some reputable scholars hold to the notion of syncretism, most notably Renato Ortiz (1978), Ordep Serra (1995), and Waldomir Valente (1977). But they do so with reservations, especially Serra, who, as we shall note, gives the notion of syncretism a sly twist so as to render it in line with what will eventually become the suggested outcome of this essay. From a synthetic vantage point, syncretism allowed for adaptation, accommodation, and survival, for sure. Yet, taking DaMatta's (1991a) *Home-Street* pair of terms into consideration, we might come to a view of syncretism not in the strict dualistic form, but as coalescent complementation—and indeed, DaMatta himself uses the term "complementarity." More about this later. For the moment, it bears pointing out that as far as the Afro-Brazilians were concerned, Catholicism was the modern way, and since it had been imposed on them from above, it must be outwardly manifested in the Street. However, on the Afro-Brazilians' Home base, the Orixás continued to do their thing. Eventually Catholicism and Candomblé converged to form an incongruously complementary form of practice that contained within itself the possibility of something else, something new.

This novelty, within certain contexts in the form of Umbanda, is a whitening of the practice. The problem is that whitening commonly brings with it the implication of what is superior and what is inferior, what according to the natural order of things should dominate and what should remain subordinate. In other words, the tendency is back toward a binarized form of hegemony. This is fine for the whiter converts to Umbanda, who take to the dynamic openness of the practice. But it doesn't go well with those who continue to covet their traditions, especially with the "black pride" movement of the 1970s. There is a reaction against the whitening, and commercialization for tourist trade, of Candomblé, and especially against Umbanda and other offshoots. Assimilation and accommodation of Candomblé to whitening was always off-key, out of balance, and terribly skewed, according to the purists. The most attractive move for many candomblistas was toward re-Africanization (Prandi 1999:100–108). This move might appear to land one squarely within hegemony once again. After all, is it not once again us against them, black against white, Candomblé purified of Catholicism and all other practices? And if the re-Africanization movement becomes dominant, would the logical consequence not be separation once again, as exemplified in the *Ilé Aiyé* Carnival Block (*Bloco*), with its emphasis on negritude? So it might seem. That reaction, however, is only the first stage. Eventually, the erstwhile subservient culture will most likely show a different face: a face more congenial and inclusive than exclusive. The watchword in the best of all worlds will be, I repeat, convergent, incongruous, contradictory complementarity.

Re-Africanization more often than not becomes skewed toward Nagô cultural practices since the very inception of the movement with a conference in 1983. It is of the Fon (Jêjê) tradition. Indeed, as mentioned, even before the turn of the twentieth century anthropologist Nina Rodrigues exalted the Nagô nation above all other groups, thus opening himself to the charge of what is called "Nigerianization." Shortly after the First International Congress of the Orixá Tradition and Culture in 1983, Mãe Stella Azevedo of *Ilê Axé Opô Afonjá* was in the process of re-Africanization of her establishment, by throwing out all Christian iconography (Braga 1988:83–88). Yet, by 1986, in the Third International Congress, she pointed out that freed slaves at first desired to whiten themselves and syncretize Catholicism with Afro-Brazilian practices, she concluded: "But, in the present times of total liberation, it is worth remembering that these maneuvers ought to be abandoned, with all people assuming the religion of their roots" (in Wafer 1991:56). Re-Africanization, as it turned out, has not only repressed Catholic elements but also Caboclo input to traditional Candomblé. Re-Africanization is thus to an extent de-Brazilianization, which, ethnically speaking, could be unhealthy. Moreover, the very idea of re-Africanization is basically top-down, since it was in the beginning anthropologist intellectuals who invented the idea (Serra 1995:144–145).

The upshot of this section is that interdependent, interrelated interaction between the three legs of the tripod in Figure 14 we have all five of Ferretti's forms of syncretism and more. We have a dynamic give-and-take between all tendencies, overt and covert, objective and subjective, individual and collective, linguistic and extralinguistic. However, merely alluding to syncretism and thus assuming there is no problem brings on the risk of evoking images of binary simplicity. I would suggest that the triadic model including homogeny, hegemony, and heterogeny gives a richer sense of Candomblé life, and kindred cultural processes. Many non- or anti-syncretic scholars are prone to admit that syncretism might be the only way that the various Afro-Brazilian beliefs could have found survival value. Yet, for the re-Africanizers, syncretism's heyday lies in the past, and it's now time to move on.

What Now Is, When It Is Acknowledged, Is Not What It Is

However one wishes to look at the issue, we cannot help but conclude that Candomblé living is a re-invention, a re-creation. This is Maria Lina Leão Teixeira's (1999) thesis. If nothing is what it is but is in the process of becoming something other than what it was in the process of becoming, then after Candomblé has passed through the stages of separation and mixture and convergence and then parallelism and separation once again, it is by no means what it was, however well-meaning and faithful the re-Africanizers, for it was, is, and will have been, always already in process. Consequently, there is no "I think, therefore I am." There is "I am becoming, therefore I am not yet."

Above all, re-Africanization is product and parcel of literate culture, written language, textuality. That is to say, once Candomblé entered the academy in the guise of Afro-Brazilian studies, it became more than a matter of anthropological studies in the sense of some exotic, romanticized, idealized, or folkloric academic endeavor. It became the focus of study by certain Afro-Brazilians of their own Afro-Brazilian cultural expressions. The tendency was to de-folklore, de-romanticize, de-idealize, and de-exoticize it. This is understandably a noble undertaking. However, during the process, Candomblé became alphabetized, textualized, and relatively stultified and fixed as a consequence, for good or for bad. The new Afro-Brazilian scholars took it upon themselves to re-Africanize their cultural practices, but in the long run they intellectualized and textualized them, making them a matter of bookish knowing.

Sandra Medeiros Epega notes that a certain disillusion began to creep in. Gradually, some observers became prone to see the re-Africanization movement as somewhat artificial and illusory. Something was lacking in this new bookish form of Candomblé and other facets of Afro-Brazilian culture. For example, in the push to re-discover their African past, an increasing number of re-Africanists left Brazil for Nigeria and other African stopping places. But they often met with disappointment. They became aware that what they expected to experience was not there at all. Rather, the language, cuisine, and general cultural traits were quite alien, and had to be internalized in much the same way one would internalize any other foreign culture. This was disconcerting. Within this new cultural setting, even the venerated Orixás appeared as if behind a mist. They were not transparent at all, but to a greater or lesser degree opaque, and had to be translated anew. The pilgrims left Brazil, looking forward to rescuing their ancestors' Axé, but they found language and cultural barriers that must be transcended before they could even begin. Nevertheless, many returned to Brazil with the status of pilgrims who had experienced the long journey to Mecca and returned with great tidings for all. Yet, in spite of the fact that re-Africanization believers in Salvador now walk in African dress with some vague notion of the motherland's culture, syncretism prevails to a degree. There is the syncretized African mix; Catholic images and commonplace gestures invariably emerge; *caboclos* also remain, as do *Pretos-Velhos*, *Pomba-Giras*, and sometimes even a satanized Exu (Epega 1999:165–166).

Julio Braga (1995:52) tells the story of Anani Dzidzienyo, of Ghana, and professor at Brown University, who was invited by the *Centro de Estudos Afro-Orientais* (Center for Afro-Oriental Studies) of the Federal University of Bahia (UFBA) as a visiting scholar. While there, he was often asked about the nature of the Orixás. This placed him in an uncomfortable position, for he, a political scientist, knew little about the religious history of his country. It was difficult for him to explain to Afro-Brazilians that as far as Yoruba culture went he was almost completely in the dark. The case of this illustrious professor is typical, Braga writes, of Afro-Brazilians who misunderstand contemporary African culture. The assumption often has it that if someone is from Africa, she must speak a native language and sing praises to the Orixás. As a counterpart to Professor Dzidzienyo's experience, Braga (1995:57) also writes of a Pai-de-Santo from Salvador visiting West Africa. He was shocked to see religious ceremonies taking place without the customary white garb and the rigid formalities customarily practiced in Brazil. In fact he took it upon himself to instruct the Africans on the proper way of conducting their religious affairs, which usually fell on unappreciative ears. One of the problems, Braga tells us, is that the Brazilian Pai-de-Santo took Candomblé to be a religion in much the Western tradition. He had lost a sense of the Afro-Brazilian practice as a form of life, as a world vision. The function of Candomblé was for him continuous with Catholic practices.

These sorts of experiences are common. They result from the tendency to oversimplify other cultures by forcing them through a sieve of preconceived notions. In recent times, many Candomblé faithful and scholars of Afro-Brazilian culture who have visited Africa have met with disillusionment. They discover that Candomblé—that is, Candomblé practices of the Brazilian sort—doesn't exist in Africa. What exists is a mind-numbing variety of deities and cults that have been adapted to cultures within contexts that are almost as varied as the deities and cults themselves. There are Orixás, for sure, but their symbolism and functions vary from region to region, and none of them faithfully conform to the images that go by the same names in Brazilian Candomblé. Braga (1995:59–60) observes that among students of Afro-Brazilian culture who have not been fortunate enough to have traveled to the continent of their origins, belief in origins that can be specified with the proper scholarly tools tends to hang on. What exists in Brazil is re-invention of the cultural traits that by hook or by crook were able to make their way across the Atlantic.

Returning to figure 14, we notice that de-Africanization or whitening falls chiefly along the right leg of the tripod, though there is never exactly a matter of either one leg or the other, for all three legs are in perpetual interdependent, interrelated interaction. Along this third leg there is *neither* the one aspect of Afro-Brazilian cultural life nor the other nor the other, but something different is always on the verge of emerging. Since whitening brings with it a tendency toward the dominant society, hegemony may at times seem to exercise its force. But the balance is precarious, and at any given moment the unexpected may pop up. Re-Africanization has appeared on the scene. This, I would suggest, has both salutary and detrimental consequences. Salutary, for it gives Afro-Brazilians a more genuine sense of themselves within the natural world and within Brazilian society. But detrimental, for re-Africanization tends toward a textualizing form of intellectualized (and rationalized, if you will) reaction against whitening, and all it entails. In contrast to this textualization, those trends within Candomblé culture that remain within the oral tradition, in contrast, are relatively less fixed by the written word; they are what they always were; that is to say, they are not what they always were for they are always becoming something other than what they were becoming. They are Candomblé culture flowing along with the flux of Brazilian culture at large. They are incessantly changing, like the whole of their natural and cultural context.

After all is said and done, however, what is good and what is bad? Should Candomblé have remained fixed since its inception with the ancient African cultural context? It shouldn't have, and it couldn't have, even if it so desired. Should it have become whitened to the maximum? Perhaps it could have been, but that is unlikely, since Afro-Brazilian movements have of cultural necessity arisen and they have taken on their own cultural force. Should there be a proliferation of Umbanda and other hybrid expressions? That might be inevitable. To an extent it is precisely what's going on in some parts of Brazil these days. Well, then, should the Afro-Brazilian just give in to flow and navigate it as smoothly as possible? That, I would suggest, is what has been going on from the beginning. Candomblé life has always been in the process of going with the flow, conforming, but at the same time setting up resistance in assertion of its own values. There was syncretism, of a sort. But it was interdependent, interrelated, interactive syncretism. All that, for survival value. And the culture survived. Then there was whitening, after Candomblé culture suffered from lesser levels of suppression and discrimination. This rendered it a tad more respectable in the eyes of the haves, and it was allowed to go its way, changing, always changing. At the propitious moment, when things seemed to be going along smoothly and even members of the white culture were making Candomblé theirs and proper, a slight eddy appeared in the stream; it then dissipated, and picked up its rhythm, becoming at times well-nigh chaotic; it bucked the flow, attempting to go its own way; it more openly asserted itself, until the entire stream was in disarray. And it continued along some newly found course. All in the name of survival, and a degree of autonomy such that it might evolve naturally.

Once again, is this good or bad? We might say that no aspect of the Candomblé process is either wholly good or wholly bad (in the Protagorean sense), but feeling and sensing and a little nonlinear, nonbinary thinking can make it so—if I may be allowed roughly to paraphrase Shakespeare's Hamlet. This is to say that if we put one thing that is neither good nor bad with something else that is equally neither good nor bad, we'll get a concoction that is of the nature of incongruous, contradictory complementarity of the sort briefly described above. This is also Candomblé life at its uncertain, rhythming best. It confirms ones suspicion that, as they often say in Mexico, "Cada cabeza es un mundo" (Each head [brain-mind] is a world). But Candomblé actually takes the equation a step further, as if to say, "Each head is a slightly to radically different world." There is allowance and tolerance for difference and diversity (heterogeny) within the community's general homogeny. The community: heterogeny within homogeny, a homogeny that is heterogenous with respect to other local homogenies within the overriding more or less homogenous culture at large (Póvoas 1999).

This difference and divergence within the community and the neither-nor mode, is perhaps no more adequately in evidence than through Exu. Exu: transporter of *Ebó*—sacrifices—from fallible human communities to the Orixás, transporter of Axé from the Orixás, and general facilitator of communication between this world and the other world. Exu mediates good and evil and all ordinary binary categories in the sense of incongruous, contradictory complementarity. Exu, deceptive, always gives the appearance of what he is not. But what is it that he is not? He is not what he appears. Then what is he? He isn't, that is, as some fixed essence or other. And he is, as a supreme example of processual becoming. He is never becoming what he was becoming but something else, something different, something novel and fresh.

While in the process of becoming what he was not becoming, Exu is always on the negative end. Granted, so was Satan as the antipode of Christ. But that is not Exu. In fact, he can possibly be whatever you say he is, yet that is not what he is. He is not even what he is not. He is neither this, nor that, nor that, nor that,... potentially to infinity. If *Orun* (Sky) plays out the function of both-and, as the composite form of everything and its Other, and if *Aiyê* (Earth) is either-or, where the division of actualized things plays out its role on the world's stage, then Exu is neither-nor. Exu knowing is like the aleatory principle as in the throw of the 16 *Búzios*. Indeed, in Brazil, 16 is quite commonly the number of Orixás selected to do their thing according to the cosmic principle within a particular Terreiro. Serra (1999:301) lists the most common set of sixteen Orixás as, in addition to *Exu, Oxalá, Yemanjá, Nanã, Obaluaiê, Oxumaré, Xangô, Iansã, Obá, Oxum, Oxossi, Logundé, Ogum, Euá, Ibeji, Iroko,* and *Ossâim* (most of which are listed in appendix A).

SIXTEEN ORIXÁS AND SIXTEEN BÚZIOS

Coming in sets of three, they make up 256 combinations, the same as the *I Ching* (Barcellos 1991a, 1991b; Serra 1999:289–302). However, this is not to say that the combinations are merely binary, as usually goes the interpretation of the *I Ching*. The principle is most explicitly trinary: There is *Orun, Aiyê,* and Exu-*Ifá*, and whatever Orixás happen to have entered the stage, Exu is lurking around somewhere, ever ready to do his trickster act. The binary scheme of things is entirely inadequate for interpreting this process, as Serra effectively argues. It is inadequate, for Exu exists outside the range of the sixteen Orixás. Where might we find him in the figure 14 scheme of things? In the central point and what is a point anyway? It is an infinitesimal nothing, nothing, and the geometrical center of the figure. It is there and it is not there; it is and it is not; it is no-thing. Or better, it is Axé; it is comparable to the Buddhist's emptiness (see merrell 2002).

In Retrospect

It is becoming increasingly evident that the specifically Christian conception of God simply doesn't exist in Candomblé culture. Candomblé has no place for a single God as sole provider, who is responsible for the well being and future salvation of all those who are of good will and act accordingly. There is no supreme transcendent deity somewhere out there. If deity or deities there may be in any religious sense, they are always and invariably here, immanent, within and the very spirit of everything that is in the process of becoming. Men and women and children are part of this process. They are within it, and they participate in the process, helping keep the things in process in balance and on an even keel. They are responsible for their own salvation.

There is in the Candomblé cosmology no otherworldliness. The goal is to find a balance in concrete everyday living, rather than preparation for some coveted place in the hereafter. Moreover, Candomblé living deviates radically from classical reason and logic, as is quickly becoming evident in this inquiry. In yet another variation of Descartes's "I think, therefore I am," Candomblé culture counterposes "I am becoming, therefore I am a thinking process." The "I am" in this latter case is not the "I am" of hard-core individualism, but rather, perhaps better put: "It is." What do I mean by that? That "it is" includes the self as an integral part; that the self of the "it is" can never be apart from that which gives it life and perpetuates its process of becoming within the cosmos' becoming; that the self and all that is becoming forms a vast community—a communing whole—of vegetal, animal, and mineral realms within which the self remains inextricably submerged.

This implies a nonmaterialist sense of value. In Candomblé culture, value emerges from Axé, and the nonmaterial richness of Axé brings about the cosmic process by means of which culture maintains a place for the processual becoming of every-thing.

Part III

THOSE OTHER LOGICS WITHIN CULTURAL PROCESSES

Chapter Twelve

Qualifying the Process: An Impossible Task?

Now comes crunch time. I will attempt to outline theoretical support for the key terms I have been using to qualify Capoeira and Candomblé life: interdependency, interrelatedness, interaction, incongruous complementarity, conformity, resistance, homogeny, heterogeny, hegemony, syncretism, and some of Peirce's semiotic terms. The expectation might have had it that in a book of this nature I would begin with theory and end with its elucidation through a presentation of Capoeira and Candomblé. My turnabout is for a justifiable reason, I would like to think. Concrete, everyday practicing philosophy precedes its articulation. In other words, first there is Firstness; then Secondness and Thirdness follow suit. Practicing philosophy within culture is internalized tacitly, with linguistic prescriptions and prohibitions providing explicit embellishment. Given the tacit dimensions of practicing philosophy, one does what one does largely without having to load what one does down with cumbersome linguistic baggage. Now that in the previous chapters I have hopefully left you with at least a tenuous sense of Capoeira and Candomblé, I now attempt to offer a more explicit conceptual view of practicing philosophy at the interstices between the haves and the havenots of Brazilian society. I hardly need write that the discourse now takes a radical turn, as abstractions occasionally reach a screaming pitch. I must confess, however, that what I suggest in the three chapters in part III is no more than that: suggestions for your contemplation, a possible alternative way of looking at cultural practices in the broadest sense, a few ideas that can be extended further. If perhaps I have somehow been able to lift the veil, ever so slightly, to reveal what has been concealed, credit goes not to me but to my many teachers along the way.

BECOMING BECOMES

First and foremost, there is the problem more specifically of articulating the idea of *process* in view of the previous discussions of Capoeira and Candomblé living and comparable cultural practices. I by no means pretend to give Capoeira and Candomblé objective, totalizing, discursive window dressing. I only hope my change of rhetorical mode might help provide a sense of cultural process. As a cautionary note, what I have to say is no substitute for concrete kinesomatic bodymind feeling and sensing. Feeling and sensing do not lend themselves directly to textual display. They accompany concrete experience, without which we could have no ideas, thoughts, concepts, or textuality in the first place.

As a way of beginning, reconsider the trio of terms, *homogeny*, *hegemony* and *heterogeny* according to their incorporation in figure 16. The central swirl of this diagram emerges out of the passage of zero (0) into the empty set (Ø), and into the gyrating *Yin-Yang* sort of icon (as we saw in Figure 15). Zero, whose history begins with Hindu thought, is perhaps best—albeit inordinately vaguely—qualified as absolute emptiness in the Buddhist sense, especially according to Buddhist philosopher Nagarjuna. When I write "emptiness" it is by no means "nothingness" in the ordinarily Western conception. Zero as emptiness is just that: emptiness. It is empty of everything, even of itself as a sign or its acknowledgment as such or of the very idea of "emptiness". Hence the word "emptiness," like the word "Axé", cannot do justice to *emptiness* or *Axé*. *Emptiness* can be taken as both the presence and the absence of or neither the presence nor the absence of. You're free to take your pick as you so desire. In any case, I repeat, *emptiness* is not just nothing in the Western sense. It is the possibility for "everythingness"—hereafter I will write *emptiness* to distinguish it from the word "emptiness" (for further, Varela et al. 1993; merrell 2002).

Newman Robert Glass (1995) offers two views of *emptiness*. The first view entails *emptiness* as associated with phenomenology, that is, pure experience and presencing in a positive sense. The second view is associated with deconstruction, difference, and the critique of presence. How can both of these views be associated with Buddhism? If there can be more than one understanding of the nature and function of *emptiness*, exactly how are they similar and how are they different? How many ways of thinking *emptiness* can there be anyway? Glass tells us that this split can be seen between two opposed understandings of the Buddhist concepts of "interdependent arising" and *Sunyata* (or *emptiness*). Although both of these concepts begin with "negation", they end in quite different ways, one affirmative and other negative, one taking experience in the positive sense, the other denying experience as the source of knowledge (episteme). This, again, leads us to quite different positions. On the one hand, from *emptiness* comes affirmation, presence or positive interdependent arising. On the other hand, from *emptiness* comes negation, difference or negative interdependent emergence.

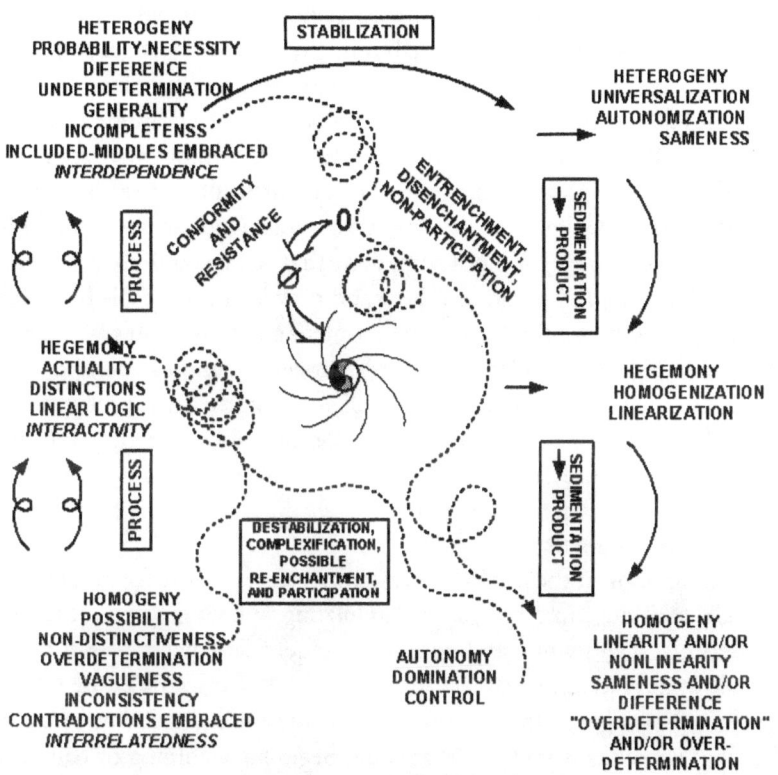

FIGURE 16

CULTURE: FLOWS AND COUNTERFLOWS

However, both approaches contain the possibility of a third working of *emptiness* not as something to be thought out (Peirce's Thirdness) but as a matter of affect, feeling, sentiment, emotion, and qualities of kinesomatic bodymind (Firstness) rather than merely mind. I would like to think a variation of this third way I adopt here is counterpart to Walter Mignolo's (2000:67) "double critique." This move entails a critique of both sides of the issue. Yet there is wholesale rejection of neither side. Rather, there is the remainder of both sides after the critique, and in addition, there is something else, something new. This condition, Mignolo writes, is necessary for an "other thinking," a "thinking that is no longer conceivable in Hegel's dialectics, but located at the border of coloniality of power in the modern world system."

Focusing anew on figure 16, from zero, we enter the empty set, or, something that just happens to be empty. It is the "noticed absence" of something that might once have been there and might once again take its place in the set, or that might never have been there but might occupy the set at some future moment. When the empty set enjoys occupancy by something, that something is never what it is as an essential somethingness. In addition to its belonging to a set, it is the becomingness of something without that something's possibility of completely becoming because it is no more than its own becomingness. In this manner, *somethingness* complements *emptiness* (Axé). Moreover, like *emptiness* (Axé), it is not something that can be pinned down and said outright. What might be said of it here and now is not what it is because it is becoming something other in another moment and at another place. Thus, as in the *emptiness* (Axé) problem, the word "process" cannot hope to do justice to *process*. So it appears I've painted myself into a corner. Or, perhaps not. At least perhaps not, if I place a qualification on the process from 0 to Ø to the central swirl of figure 16.

A FLUX OF INTANGIBLES

Take another look at the central vortex at the center of the figure. It is, metaphorically speaking, an effervescent, undulating, spiraling gush that fuses and confused black and white and combines frequencies that can spin out blue and yellow and red at its borders that in turn merge into the entire spectrum of colors. The figure emerges out of 0 or the pure possibility of *emptiness* (Axé) that becomes something that could begin its becoming or had been in the process of its becoming but is now absent and unavailable to occupy the empty set. Then the dance begins unfolding. And becoming is initiated.

How does becoming become its becoming? By an act of choice and selection on the part of some participating agent as an actor rather than a mere spectator in the grand drama of cultural becoming. First, the participant chooses and selects something, and then something Other than the first something. In their most primitive form, this something and its Other is like black and white. If there is a moment of whiteness (comparable to playing Capoeira "with the crystal ball"), then it reflects all colors and absorbs none. The combination of all those colors yields whiteness, which is potentially all colors, and it is no color. If there is a moment of blackness in contrast with whiteness (like the mere possibility of playing Capoeira "In the Dark"), then it absorbs all colors and reflects none. The absence of any and all reflected colors yields darkness, which is potentially no color, and it is—it contains—all colors. Put all this together and you have *both* all colors *and* *n*o colors, and *neither* all colors *nor* no colors. The scintillating, interactive flux of black and white gives rise to the emergence of all colors, first yellow, blue, green, and red, and then all the rest. From this strange concoction, the becoming of all things colored introduces us to the interrelations outside the central swirl of figure 16, and from there, we can choose and select from the range of possibilities the making of a world, our world.

What do I mean by all this? Assume we have a*n apple ima*ge in mind. It initially appears in the guise of an icon (a sign of Firstness that is like that with which it can possibly interrelate). If we put the image in the form of an utterance, we might have "this is an apple." There is the 'this," a symbol functioning like an index (Secondness, as indicator of the sign) that draws our attention to the icon, the image of an apple. And there is "apple" as a solitary word (Thirdness, a symbol) in search of a sentence and a text in order that its function as a sign may be brought to fruition. The sign, "apple," interacts with the index and the icon through the connective and the article "is an" to compose a sentence, a string of symbolic signs.

We might say: (1) the icon is in the image of a schematic diagram that depicts or is similar to something (a positivity, or a sign); (2) the index relates to in terms of what the icon is not (negativity, or a semiotic object); and (3) the symbol and its interpretant (meaning through the participating interpreter's collaboration with the sign) brings the is and the is not together and mediates between them in such a way that there is *both* the is *and* the is not and at the same time there is *neither* the is *nor* the is not. We sense the apple image as an apple, while deep down we know full well that it is not an apple but a somewhat impoverished image of an apple. We can talk interminably about this apple image and any number of absent apple *images* and actual apples and the word "apple" and other words having to do with apples. Or apple can be a particular type of apple, a Jonathan apple. Or apple can depict a symbol common to student-teacher interrelations in elementary education. Or it can be a candidate for all-American cooking. Or it can relate to folklore, to New York City, to a line of computers, to the endearing phrase "You're the apple of my eye," or to "He's a bad apple," and so on. As such it is not merely an apple image, an apple, or an "apple," but enters into an entirely different field of discourse. We can do all this to signs and more, and then more, virtually without end. And we may become increasingly confused in the process. We no longer know we know but know many ways in which we perhaps know not but we are not really sure because the *not* is now many steps removed from that most fundamental initial not. So, finally, let us return to that fundamental not—as if we could, yet let's suppose we can.

If the icon *is like* something or other, a positivity, and the index *is not* what the icon *is*, a negativity, then let us provisionally call them "+" and "−" for the purpose of illustration. If the sign emerges out of *emptiness*, or *no-thingness*, then it enters into the range of anticipations and expectations and hopes and desires and fears of *some-thingness*. It is initially experienced as *some-thing* that is like *some-thing* else that might bring on pleasantness or unpleasantness, depending upon the experiencer and the context. But now we are a far cry from mere *emptiness* (Axé). It is like going from zero, 0, to the empty set, ∅. Zero is just zero. It is empty of everything, including even an indication of the mere memory of numbers. The empty set, in contrast, is what it says: something, *some-thing* that happens to be empty. It is the noticed absence of *some-thing*. So we have pure *emptiness* (Axé), "noticed absence", and the plus and the minus. What has been left out of the picture is the sign's meaning or *interpretant*. The icon (or sign or *representamen*) as Firstness, and the index (or semiotic object) as Secondness, needs a symbol (or a sign with its meaning or interpretant) to perform the role of Thirdness, of mediation.

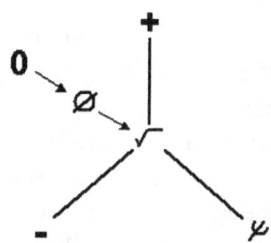

FIGURE 15a

**FROM AXÉ ('EMPTINESS')
TO NOTICED ABSENCE,
AND THEN TO THE THIRD WAY**

Consider the becomingness of the being of Peirce's Firstness, Secondness, and Thirdness, and the being of their becoming in light of figure 15a. The imaginary number, $\sqrt{-1}$, a combination of the central icon and the negative sign, is undecidable. Like the notorious Liar Paradox, its solution is neither legitimately +1 nor −1. Yet the number is used in relativity theory, quantum mechanics, computer logic, and many engineering problems. It must surely be irreal, since it cannot correspond to anything recognizable in our material world. Yet its use in symbolically accounting for our material world according to contemporary Western science tells us that it must be somehow real. At one and the same time the imaginary number embodies what is (+1) and what is not (−1) without any possibility of deciding which should be foregrounded and which backgrounded. There can be no more than oscillation between two self-contradictory values.

Mathematicians using the imaginary number usually designate it as i. This is for convenience sake. The symbol i has *neither* positive *nor* negative sign. It is in a sense neutral. It is *just what it is*. It is *neither* positive *nor* negative, yet in contradictory a manner of speaking it is *both* positive *and* negative. By the same token the role of the interpretant (roughly, meaning) as mediator and moderator and media minimizing agent, is, in and of its own accord, *neither* positive *nor* negative and at the same time *both* positive *and* negative. So it's déjà-vu all over again. In this vein, and for the purpose of this inquiry, I use Ψ to depict the mediation of + and − in the becomingness of a sign.

FAREWELL TO CLARITY AND DISTINCTION

I would suggest at this juncture that in spite of our wish for logical cogency and rational aplomb, we invariably fall into inconsistencies at one step or another in the long walk of our everyday affairs. But this is not necessarily a problem. It is what makes us human, perhaps all too human. And occasionally, quite unfortunately so.

But let's try to leave our coveted humanity behind for a moment. Upon so doing, nothing has any real biased self-seeking, self-indulgent, ego-centered value. There is nothing, no-thing at all, for everything, every-thing is mere possibility; that is, *every-thing is* possibly in the process of becoming, without *any-thing* having (yet) actually become. It is all like the mathematical "i" or "Ψ." What *is* in the positive sense is related to what *is not* in the negative sense, though under other circumstances the *is not* could have been the *is* and the *is* the *is not*. The positivity and the negativity are given an undecidable oscillatory "$+/-/+/-/+/-/... n$" value at the core of the sign map where "$\sqrt{}$" is found, which just *is*. It is *neither* positive *nor* negative and at the same time it is *both* positive *and* negative. The icon "$\sqrt{}$" is comparable, if I might suggest, to T. S. Eliot's "still point" where the dance unfolds:

> Neither from nor towards; at the still point, there the dance is,
> But neither arrest nor movement. And do not call it fixity,
> Where past and future are gathered....
> ... Except for the point, the still point.
> There would be no dance, and there is only the dance. (Eliot 1943)

In the timeless 'still point', or "$\sqrt{}$", about which "+", "−", and "Ψ" gyrate, we have the counterparts to *emptiness* (0), the "empty set" ($\emptyset$), and Firstness,

Secondness, and Thirdness. In other words, the still point is like the center of the Buddhist wheel the center of which is timeless and motionless, while the wheel is in perpetual movement in time.

All this must appear inordinately abstract and quite irrelevant. But I would suggest that the map of information processing I am presenting is germane to the topic at hand. In the first place, the map is necessary, for the sign cannot on its own emerge from *emptiness*. The semiotic participant must already have some notion or other of what has been in the past, what might be in the present, and what the future holds in store. This involves anticipations, expectations, hopes, desires, and fears regarding the noticed absence (the empty set) to be filled with one or more of the virtually unlimited range of superposed possibilities. In other words, the *apple* image is an apple, because "An *apple* (icon or image) *is* an "apple" (a symbol) *is* an *apple* (as indexed) *is* an apple (the actual article)." But at the same time it *is not* an apple, since "an "apple" (symbol) *is not* an apple (icon or image) *is not* an apple (as indexed) *is not* an apple." So we have a plus side and a minus side. But there is no solution to the quandary regarding what is and what is not, at least within this most primitive of domains, unless we consult Ψ, which is *neither* the one *nor* the other and *both* the one *and* the other. In any event, we see that the not cannot be absent in the sign's processing. Given the not, we must concede that nothing is fixed and everything is impermanent. All is flux, including identity and self-identity, even including the "I" or self itself.

The notion of impermanence implies that there is no fixed self or self-identity, no enduring subject that knows, or object that is known. The hopeful idea of a fixed, rugged, hell-bent-for-leather individual self is a pipe dream, an illusion. Obsession with the idea of a separate self, captain of its own ship, clawing and punching and scratching for "what's in it for me" with little regard for anyone or anything else, is a dead-end alley. What's in the present meditation on signs for all of us is the suggestion that the self is in an incessant process of emerging as is the world plus the self, the world minus the self, the world and the self as Ψ. The self, the ego, the "I," have no independent existence. Rather, they are perpetually in the process of emerging with the emergence of everything else. In essence there is essentially no essence, matter is of no matter, and never mind mind. There are no grounds for any of all that. There is only 0 and $\sqrt{}$ and "+" and "−," all of which makes up $\sqrt{-1}$, which we have incorporated into Ψ. Our groping for permanent grounds or for anything else of durable countenance can only end in frustration. (Regarding the underlying assumptions of the above from Eastern as well as Western scholars, see Griffiths 1986; Iida 1980; Jacobson 1983; Kalupahana 1986, 1987; Loy 1989; Nishitani 1982; Odin 1996).

Hence, "*Is not* an apple" *is not* an apple." A distinction is made between a sign and what it *is not*. It *is not* an apple. All right. The distinction comes to the fore. Since an apple image is not an apple, meaning obviously isn't in the image (icon) or the apple (the physical object). Since the 'this" is not an apple, meaning isn't in the reference or indicator (index) of the sign. Since "apple" is not an apple, meaning isn't in the word (symbol). If we assume there is no apple in some participant-interpreter's mind, we're left with a dilemma: meaning is neither seen nor read, nor is it in the mind nor the sign nor in the world out there. Where is it, then? I would suggest that it's in the entire context; it's in the mediated (co)dependent interrelations; it's in the pattern, the patterning. With respect to meaning as outside mind and sign and media and that to which the sign refers, Hilary Putnam (1981, 1983) offers some knock-down arguments I can give only passing mention here (for further reading, see merrell 1997).

A question likely arises why do we need some off-the-wall logic to account for all this? Actually, all we have to do is take a look at the world's and life's uncertainties, which pattern the uncertainties of our knowledge of ourselves and our world. To put it bluntly, we have reached the end of objective certainty, if we contemplate: (1) the implications of Capoeira and Candomblé life, Buddhism, the concept of practicing philosophy, and general cultural processes to which I have alluded throughout this inquiry, (2) the importance of Kurt Gödel and other logicians and mathematicians regarding their limitations on human thought according to which we invariably fall into either inconsistency or incompleteness or both (DeLong 1971; Kline 1980; Nagel and Newman 1958), and (3) contemporary physics, especially regarding complexity (especially Horgan 1996; Pagels 1982, 1988; Penrose 1989; Prigogine 1980, 1997; Prigogine and Stengers 1983; Smith 1995; also merrell 1998, 2000a, 2000c).

Limited time and space do not allow me to enter into the details of these intricate labyrinths. However, I will attempt to further qualification of figure 16 in light of the general implications of (1) through (3).

It's a Contingent Life

Consider, one more time if you will, the trio of terms, *homogeny*, *hegemony*, and *heterogeny*. As suggested above, homo- qualifies the sphere of Firstness: a union of complementary coalescent contradictories into a harmonious package in terms of sheer possibilities. Hetero- qualifies the sphere of Thirdness: sets of actualized terms that within indeterminately variable contexts are always in the process of becoming something Other than what they were becoming. The suffix, *-geny*, implies a manner of emergence, organic becoming without reaching the stage of already having become.

Refocusing on figure 16, homogeny makes up a continuum of possibilities. Nothing is actualized, not yet at least. There are no distinctions, no lines of demarcation, no boundaries, no Other, no Otherness. Everything is there as a continuous—hence in principle potentially infinite—set of possibilities. The sphere of homogeny is of the form of virtually unlimited interrelatedness. It is the "utter vagueness" of which Peirce often wrote. Thus, within homogeny, overdetermination is the order of the day. From homogenic possibilities through *emptiness* and the absence of actualities by the emergence of distinctions from *emptiness*, virtually anything can possibly give rise to anything else at some time and place or other. As a consequence, inconsistencies within the sphere of homogeny can become virtually compatible, at least until they enter the light of some hegemonic day. Once again, the classical Principle of Noncontradiction is thus rendered impotent. Both one entity or sign and another otherwise contradictory of incompatible entity or sign can exist side-by-side quite comfortably. This is no problem, however, for nothing is actualized to make the inconsistency readily apparent. All is no more than possible. But, considering virtually unlimited contexts, past, present and future, there is no determining what might stand a possibility of emerging. What at one time and place might be considered contradictory and hence categorically barred, at another time and place might be considered as normal as can be. Is the Earth the center of the universe? Or is the Sun the center of the universe? Or is the center perhaps somewhere else?—It's a matter of who lives when and where and what corpus of thought they buy into (Goodman 1978).

Hegemony is not simply a polarity between haves and havenots, dominants and subservients, superalterns and subalterns. Through contestation on the part of the havenots and their negotiation with the haves, it contains, within itself, effervescent, scintillating possibilities. These possibilities include emergent images, interrelations, and ideas giving rise to renegotiations of norms and values. This is no simple binary matter of Secondness with respect to hegemony. It intermittently highlights Firstness and Thirdness while subjecting Secondness to alterations and reforms. A certain sense of identity may make its appearance during these exchanges. But if identity there be, it is no more than ephemeral, transient, a minuscule and barely distinguishable area within the entire flow of things.

In this vein, hegemony entails distinctions marked out, actualization of what there is—or at least what there apparently is. It is the onslaught of digitalization and linearization at their best and at their worst. Here, classical logical principles usually manage to put on their best show. There is apparent Identity; Contradictions are customarily taboo; and Excluded-Middles are usually maintained at all cost. Hegemony is more often than not taken as the author of binaries, dualities, Manicheisms. Everything actualized—and imaginary unactualized things as well—is subject to strict demarcation: here/there, then/now, master/slave, dominance/subservience, self/Other, male/female, rich/poor, superaltern/subaltern, and so on. Here, the idea of "incommensurability," as in Thomas Kuhn's (1970) "scientific revolutions," becomes an issue in terms of nontranslatability, incompatibility, unintelligibility, and the impossibility of effective communication. Here, Gayatri Spivak's (1988) subaltern apparently can't speak and scholars can't listen, because they live in totally different worlds. Here, the much used and abused concept of syncretism can usually have its day. However, all is not always well in the utopia of a definite place for everything and everything in its place. Hegemony is also the field of interaction, conflict, contestation, and negotiation. At any moment the possibility of the unexpected stands at least an outside chance of making its apparent existence manifested. Then, things may be up for grabs once again, and something from the virtually infinite range of possibilities (homogeny) can bring on something different, something novel, something new.

When novelty happens to pop up from the sphere of homogeny to take what might seem to be its rightful place within hegemony, it is primed to enter the arena of heterogeny, where clear-cut Manichean distinctions become fuzzy differences. Differences are at freedom to proliferate, and become increasingly finer until they are hardly distinguishable. For, the long history of surprising turns of the screw and the arising of novelty from homogeny to create change and often havoc and chaos within hegemony creates the notion that, actually, nothing is fixed, for everything is flux. Flow, meandering streams, sidewinding whitewater stretches, rushing flood stage chaos, are, apparently they have always been, and quite likely they will always be, of the nature of the universe. Comfortable fixtures in our perceived and conceived world are no more than minuscule islands constantly eaten away by the vast sea of chaos surrounding them.

Within heterogeny, full-blown language practices arise. Now, there is the possibility of metaphor, metonymy, irony, malapropisms, spoonerisms, hyperbole, portmanteau words, and myriad other strange making rhetorical devices. Nothing is ever exactly what it was. Within this process, underdetermination is always ready to make its play. Whatever might be considered the one and only interpretation of whatever there is at one time and place can possibly be subjected to another quite incompatible interpretation at another time and place (first, the Earth as center of the universe; at another time and place, the Sun as center; now, the center as relative to the frame of reference). Consequently, there are no necessary Excluded-Middles. Given the myriad concoction of possible times and places and their contexts, there is no predetermining what theory, interpretation, or general form of life might emerge. There is mediation between hegemony and hegemony through heterogeny to bring about the condition wherein whatever happens is in the process of becoming: there is no Being, only a being of becoming and a becoming of some possible being that never quite finishes its becoming. (Basically, the concepts overdetermination, underdetermination, inconsistency, and incompleteness to which I allude come by way of philosophy of science and logic found in various guises in Quine 1969, Norwood Hanson 1958, 1969, Michael Polanyi 1958, Putnam 1990, Goodman 1978, and Feyerabend 1975, and most especially, Gödel's incompleteness proofs [for further, merrell 1997, 2000C, 2003a]. In this light, and given the general implications of [1] through [3] at the end of the previous section, it would seem that behind contemporary mathematics, science and philosophy, and the various practicing philosophies discussed in this volume, there are certain common features. If this is so, the search for alternative cultural logics and ways and means of construing alternative cultures should be deemed a worthy enterprise.)

In sum, everything heterogenous is interdependent, a characteristic that complements the interactivity of hegemony and the interrelatedness of homogeny. Everything is interrelated, interactive, and interdependent through the merging of Other, the Otherness of the Other and the Other of that Otherness. This is not merely a matter of some Self here and some Other there. The line of demarcation between Self and Other within the sphere of hegemony becomes something" rather than merely nothing—or at least nothing in the usual Western sense of the word. Or perhaps better put, it becomes *emptiness*, which is to say that it is something yet it is not something: it is *emptiness* (for illustration, look ahead to figure 17 if you wish). The interdependency of everything and every Other suggests that the celebrated subaltern can speak after all. She speaks, and if the superaltern—member of dominant social circles—can listen, she listens. But she is able to listen only after undergoing a long, painful, mind torturing process of initiation.

Contemplate, for instance, the role ideally—and in many to most cases actually in my estimation—played out by Subcomandante Marcos of EZLN and the indigenous Chiapas peasants (Marcos 1995). Marcos lived among the indigenous people for some eleven years before the Zapatista rebellion began January 1 1994, the same day NAFTA went into effect. He learned their language and their form of life insofar as possible. He did not enter the Chiapas jungle with the purpose of gathering them around him and leading them according to some ideology hitherto unknown to them. Rather, while learning their ways, he dropped suggestions here and there, and finally, they took the lead for themselves while he became their spokesman. His role was that of a mediator between the Zapatistas, the larger Mexican society, and the neoliberal world. Thus the mask, in order to resist becoming the typical charismatic revolutionary hero in the mold of Che Guevara; thus his originally concealing his identity, in order to prevent his being highlighted with respect to the indigenous people any more than necessary. Did the subaltern speak to Marcos? Had Marcos learned to listen? I would like to think so, at least inasmuch as communication between subaltern and superaltern can become possible. Incidentally, John Beverley (1999:26–29) writes that most talk about subalternity regarding the Latin America scene is no more than so many concepts without content, preconception devoid of intuition, theorizing in ignorance of first-hand experience, language divorced from the concrete physical world. I tend to agree.

Homogeny proceeds from *emptiness* to the empty set and toward the possible emergence of something. Hegemony is the consequence of actualization of something from the empty set. And heterogeny makes of the categorical somethings within hegemony manythings (recall figure 15a). Homogeny, I cannot overemphasize, is comparable to Peirce's Firstness, hegemony to Secondness, and heterogeny to Thirdness. Firstness has benign tolerance for inconsistencies, and Thirdness allows for virtually unlimited Included-Middles. Classical logical principles find a somewhat contentious home in hegemony. Thus, when scholars within postcolonialism, poststructuralism, and postmodernism make inordinately vague allusions to logics going by various and sundry strange labels, these logics cannot fall exclusively within the customarily defined philosophy of hegemony. They are, in line with the premises of this inquiry, logics of inconsistency and vagueness (within homogeny) and of incomplete formalities, universals, and generalities within heterogeny (see table 2).

Actually, I should take a further step to suggest that not even in the hardest of sciences do we find logic always used in the strict sense, as Henry Harris (2002:48) observes: "I do not think that one can hope to understand (science) unless one appreciates that ..., however formal its symbolism may sometimes become, it is not an exercise in logic. When some philosophers talk about the logic of scientific investigation ... I can only suppose that they speak metaphorically." Compare this statement to quantum physicist Louis de Broglie for whom "in the region of the inexact sciences of human conduct, the strictness of the definitions varies inversely as their applicability to the world of Reality" (Broglie 1939:281). Well and good, one might conclude, for the human sciences cannot be held to the same rigorous criteria binding the hard sciences. However, elsewhere he writes that even the physical sciences "are not that much less applicable to reality when they become more complete and, although we have little inclination to be paradoxical, we could hold, contrary to Descartes, that nothing is more misleading than a clear and distinct idea" (Broglie 1953:219; see also in this respect Broglie 1960:131; Bridgman 1951:9; Heisenberg 1971:81; Jeans 1959:1).

HOMOGENY	HEGEMONY	HETEROGENY
Emptiness → Empty set	Empty set → Something	Something → Many things
Continuity	Distinctions	Differences
Boundarylessness	Boundaries, as nothing	Boundaries, as 'some thing'
No Other	Otherness, Other	Mediated Other
Alinearity	Linearity	Nonlinearity
Interrelatedness	Interaction	Interdependency
Overdetermination	Relatively fixed categories	Underdetermination
Inconsistency	Relative clarity and distinction	Incompleteness
No absolutely necessary Noncontradiction	Classical logical principles	No absolutely necessary Excluded-Middles
Both-And	Either/Or	Neither-Nor

TABLE 2

ON THE INTERCONNECTIONS BETWEEN HOMOGENY, HEGEMONY, AND HETEROGENY

When Process Becomes Tenuously Stabilized
At the left-hand side of figure 16, process is chiefly the name of the game. Conformity and resistance, as I have used the terms, entail cultural process is at its best. Human interrelations, interaction, and interdependence are never what they are for they are always becoming something else.

However, we must not forget that hegemonic pushes and pulls are part of this process. Hegemony is never a static affair. The will to dominate and the equally ubiquitous will toward contestation and negotiation—emerging out of accommodation and struggle—are germane to all cultural processes where relatively closed, Manichean hegemonic affairs tend to exercise their force over open homogenic-heterogenic processes. When hegemony manages to have its way, a move toward stability ensues. Collection of many differences into presumed universal categories flattens those differences to sameness—that is, the homogenizing force of globalization exercised by multinational corporations in the name of neo-liberalism servicing the new world order. Sameness of signs and their meanings introduces entrenchment, embedment, and automatization, of cultural practices such that they threaten to become robotically acted out. Individuals lose their interrelatedness and interdependency with respect to one another, as they begin gravitating toward autonomy. Individualism and the assumption of individual identity take on increased importance; classical logical principles increase their power; linearity begins to predominate; culture strikes out on a path toward homogenization; everybody tends to assume common likes and dislikes, common values, common patterns of behavior. All this follows on the heels of a move from left-side to right-side heterogeny as illustrated in figure 16.

Putting this conception of things within Capoeira and Candomblé life, as deceptive cultural guerrilla practices of conformity and resistance became increasingly refined and heterogenized along the left-side during the colonial period, they tended to become embedded, entrenched. They became part of the capoeiristas' and candomblistas' repertoire of "knowing how" to make do with what there was by means of creative improvisation. Then, if the dominant culture manages to exercise its force, these practices would tend to become further entrenched such that gradually deception and resistance would tend to fade away, and practice would fall increasingly in line with society's demands. The slave would now behave like a good slave should, in conformity with the rules handed down, while the will to resist would by and large fall by the wayside. The havenots would know their place and obediently place themselves squarely within it. Now, there would be a clearly defined right way and a wrong way, good and evil, and all the other Manichean distinctions, for the tendency would have gravitated downward along the right-side of figure 16. However, to the dominant culture's chagrin, things don't always work out as planned: within hegemony a tendency toward resistance always manages to persist (Gomes da Cunha 1998).

It bears mention that the three-way movement in figure 16 opens Mignolo's occasional—and unfortunate—inclination toward linear thinking. For example, he maintains that 'the Americas, contrary to Asia and Africa, are not Europe's difference but its extension" (Mignolo 2000:51). Granted. However, Mignolo's use of the term "difference" lies between the two homogenies in figure 16.

In contrast to Mignolo, and with due respect, I allude to differences within heterogenies. Left-side heterogeny remains open and nonlinear; it is processual. In contrast, right-side culturally imposed heterogeny is relatively closed, linear, and governed by rigid social categories of thought and behavior.

Within the context of contemporary society in general, as a consequence of the transition to right-side practices as illustrated in figure 16, eventually disenchantment in the sense of Max Weber (1965) begins infiltrating. Enchantment with the unexpected, the fresh and new—wellsprings of creativity—begins waning. Interest in local differences that make a difference and peculiarities of practice and idiosyncrasies of behavior fall out of focus. This is because homogenization at the right-side of figure 16 on the global level becomes increasingly prevalent. Product begins taking priority over process. How does this transition begin to occur? On the left side, when hegemony remains dynamic and it continues to create differences within heterogeny. Within left-side hegemony, differences ideally bring importance to local practices and their uniqueness with respect to any and all other local practices. However, if there is pressure exercised on the havenots by the haves, hegemony can become crystallized in proportion to its increasing dominance, and sameness comes to the fore. This implies a move toward right-side heterogeny, hegemony, and finally homogeny, imposed from above by the dominant forces in society. Right-side homogenizing pressure compels individuals within the community to become convinced that the good life can be found in maximizing sameness of behavior and sameness of commodification among all citizens. Obviously, global pressure from big industry, technology, and multinational corporations are right-side homogeny's greatest allies. However, along with industry, technology, and global trade comes waste as the product of production, and with it, the overriding force of entropy—a move toward decay and disorder. Thus the squiggly arrow moving from left-homogeny of pure possibilities and right-side homogeny the product of sameness imposed by the dominant society evince the tendency toward liberation through resistance underlying surface conformity. Indeed, it would seem that Afro-Brazilian Capoeira and Candomblé responses to imposed standards and norms are not unique; they are examples of a general human tendency. (Regarding the preceding, I follow arguments in Carmen 1996; Latouche 1996, 1998; Sachs 1999a, 1999b; Robert 1999; Rivero 2001; Esteva and Prakash 1998. These scholars' works tend to support my suggestion that right-side homogenizing processes have been in effect in Brazil and the Spanish American colonies from the very beginning. As Darcy Ribeiro [1997:60] observes, the Portuguese slave empire appropriated the slaves' minds as well as their bodies by indoctrinating them into the system and bringing them to believe their role was to carry on like good slaves, for that was their natural lot in life. In other words, global pressure and rhetoric tended to proceed from left- to right-side heterogeny and toward right-side hegemony, where each slave is considered the same as all slaves, or where each consumer is hardly different from any other consumer.)

If right-side hegemony continues to exercise its hold, the broad highway moves downward toward homogeny. But this form of homogeny is a far cry from its left-side counterpart. Rather than virtually unlimited possibilities for actualization, it is actualization homogenized and automatized, such that any and all individuals fall into the marching order dictated from above. Rather than left-side overdetermination as the process giving rise to novelty, it is a form of overdetermination more akin to the Freudian sense of the term: everything is jam-packed into one handy, albeit neurotic and even paranoid, conceptual scheme and way of doing things, and if something doesn't fit the scheme, it is Procrusteanly whittled down and forced into its proper place. Rather than interrelatedness, there is a humdrum coming and going of individuals as if there were atoms caroming about in the same fashion toward a common goal. Instead of vagueness and tolerance of apparent contradictions, there are dogmatic, hegemonic binary logic rules. Autonomy, domination, and control are the watchwords.

Conditions of sameness and identity, dualistic symmetrical relations, and equilibrium of stabilized forces rarely last long, however. Such conditions, as mentioned, are no more than tiny islands soon dissolved by a billowing ocean of disorder. When disorder raises the ante, wins the pile of chips, cashes them in, and proceeds to spread the booty everywhere and anywhere, destabilization, complexification, and the possibility of re-enchantment inevitably emerge. The subsequent path follows a sinewy route back toward left-side hegemony. The ride is wild, with much diverging and converging, involution and convolution, serves and sways. It is radically nonlinear; it is liberally marked by periods of fluctuation tending toward chaos, as well as a few ephemeral moments of order bearing promise of things to come. Once left-side hegemony has been re-entered, however, a healthy proliferation of differences that make a difference, dignity for local practices within the global whole, and modest narratives instead of totalizing grand discursive narratives, can once again emerge. Proper process in line with natural fluxes and flows is begun anew.

Now, re-enchanted Capoeira deception can come to the fore, as the dominant society becomes the target of conformity and resistance. Now, equally re-enchanted Candomblé life can persevere as before, holding to tradition while creating the appearance of obedience to the norms handed down by the dominant society. Now, Afro-Brazilian ethnicity can maintain its heterogeny within homogeny in spite of pressures to conform. Limited time and space don't allow my addressing another important issue: the confusion throughout much of Brazilian and Spanish American history between "American consciousness" and "Creole (American born Spanish, white Portuguese) consciousness." In Mignolo's (2000:65) words, "American consciousness" is confused "with one of its historical manifestations: the 'hegemonic' imaginary of the Creole intelligentsia within the subaltern location of Latin America in the order of the modern/colonial world system." Putting Mignolo's words within the context of this inquiry, "Creole consciousness," disguised as universal "American consciousness," has historically pushed the naturally evolved left-side heterogenic popular expression to the right-side, forcing it into the modern homogenic mold. The two-way street of conformity and resistance as depicted in interactive left-side-right-side movement, in contrast, helps keep the process open.

The question now is: How has this processual view fared among scholars of Afro-Brazilian culture?

Chapter Thirteen

Attempting to Refine the Figure Further

Is It Syncretism or a Sociological Disaster?

The view toward Afro-Brazilian-White-European interrelations has been radically transformed over the years. Nina Rodrigues's evolutionary thesis marched in step with the social Darwinist ideology of his day. It entailed the inferior folks' adoption of, adaptation to, and acculturation into the superior society. This way they could hopefully become proper and upstanding citizens. Roger Bastide's culturalist thesis retained many precepts of the "inferior/superior" posture, though it embraced a two-way road of mutually interactive influences from both sides of the virgule rather than acculturation as a one-way street along which the subservients are brought conveniently in line by their submergence into the dominant culture. Bastide and many of his followers held to the idea of mixture, conjunction, and/or a harmonious fusion of ethnicities into a syncretic whole (Ferretti 1995:41–46). This mix, conjunction, or fusion accompanies a move from the possibilities of hegemony to a dynamic form of hegemony as illustrated by the left-side of figure 16 (see leg 1 of figure 17).

Others scholars, along the lines of Pierre Verger, contended that the two ethnicities simply don't mix (Verger 1983:45). In the case of Candomblé and Catholicism, the two practices remained separate; at the same time, they existed in parallel or juxtaposed fashion (leg 2 of figure 17). This thesis brings dynamic hegemonic interrelations creating heterogenic divergences and differences into a struggle between haves and havenots. When heterogenic interaction remains dynamic and the havenots keep cultural processes open to change, gravitation to right-side heterogeny can be relatively slight. Such is the way of Umbanda, especially as Diana Brown (1986) conceptualizes it. In contrast, when the haves of the dominant society exercise an iron-hand rule, they can initiate the process of bringing about a transition from dynamic left-side heterogeny to relatively static right-side heterogeny (figure 16). They do this by imposing stultifying, coercive, exploitative, and at times racist and fascist, right-side hegemony. However, as we've noted, since human nature is always becoming something other than what it was becoming, heterogeny often doesn't simply stop at the right-side. Instability opens up the chaotic swirling road back toward the left-side. There may be overriding pressure on the part of the haves to push things along in their favor.

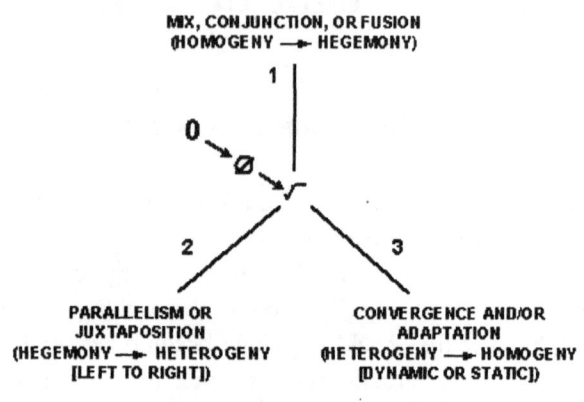

FIGURE 17

THE THIRD WAY, INCLUDING FORMS OF SYNCRETISM

If the haves continue to exercise their force, they may even be able to impose right-side homogenization. When they manage to do so, sameness begins ruling over difference, and likeness becomes the norm over upstart variations. Everything tends to become a bland remake of what the haves dictate. As one might expect, Jean Baudrillard's (1983a, 1983b, 1988) forms of simulacra can begin to predominate on the contemporary cultural scene. Here, we have overdetermination for sure. But, as suggested, it is Freudian in the sense that everything is packed into a predetermined and preestablished mold. It is overdetermination, in contrast to left-side overdetermination depicted in figure 16 in the guise of cultural behavior that always invites the emergence of interpretations that are distinct and perhaps even inconsistent and incompatible with currently held interpretations. Thus convergence (depicted by leg 3 of figure 17) ultimately brings about bifurcation points that can give rise to overdetermination, and hence the possibility of spiraling, converging, diverging, renovating pathways toward a renewal of left-side hegemony and heterogeny, or overdetermination, with its subsequent linear, Manichean, authoritarian imposition of homogenic sameness.

Or, if the re-Africanizing concept of "Nagô purity" might conceivably become the order of the day, a relatively crystallized form of homogeny could ensue, along with a hegemonic pure/mixed dichotomy. Everything of worth would be deemed pure, and whatever might be thrown into the pot of stew as some form or fashion of syncretism would be up for contempt. Quite obviously, 'superior/inferior" categories would remain in force. The chief difference is that pure and mixed Afro-Brazilian practices would replace white race and black race. Although to an extent purity is a creation of the wishful thinking of some anthropologists and other intellectuals and scholars, drawing from early work by Bastide and others, the idea has been criticized by various observers (Dantas 1982, 1987, 1988; Fry 1982, 1986). In fact, upon witnessing the rather gaudy paraphernalia involved in the supposedly pure Nagô ceremonies, Peter Fry (1982:14) remarks that some might refer to it as chic, but he only sees it as kitsch.

Kitsch is the word bantered about in postmodernist circles. *Postmodernism*, the word that often evokes the image of heterogeny in its most outlandishly differentiated and complex forms, threatening to implode at any moment. And the term *heterogeny*—move from linearity to alinearity to nonlinearity, from a hegemonic place for everything according to proper and respectable logical principles toward tangential alogical pathways (see table 2). When Roberto DaMatta (1994:125) alludes to Brazil as a "sociological disaster," I suspect he is thinking of homogenic and heterogenic rather than hegemonic aspects of Brazil. But a sociological disaster cannot come about except through the lower echelons of the middle zone in figure 16. This is where complexification occurs, with unpredictable fluctuations and eventually destabilization and disorder. Here is where the center makes its home, from 0 to $\emptyset$ to "+" and "–" and then to the emergence of objects, acts, and events into the material world as we know it from within our particular cultural milieu. Here, the process of becoming begins its journey toward what it will have been becoming. Can the hoary concept of syncretism really account for all this complexity? Is not complexity, with its contemporary implications of order to fluctuations and disorder through bifurcation points and back to order too much to ask of syncretism, a term that all too often evokes dualistic thoughts and provoking us to binary simplicity? Is syncretism really all there is?

Obviously, in view of previous chapters, I would like to think not. Let us return to the DaMatta inspired dictum "It's what's in the middle that counts" with respect to his essay on Street and Home (1991a, 1995). Brazilian traditional values continue to stand strong and stalwart in the Home. These are the values handed down by the Portuguese hierarchical colonial order. The key terms are paternalism tending toward a patriarchal setting. Just as the religious order consisting of God above and Christians below, with the Holy Spirit, Virgin, and saints acting as mediaries, so also with the family consisting of father and children, with mother as mediary. In family businesses, the plantation, and government, from local municipalities to the top, a comparable hierarchical order tends to hold. There is security to be had for those who conform to these values. There seems to be a natural place for everything and everything seems conveniently to fall into its proper place. That is the up side. The down side is that until 1888 slavery was part of this order. Once slavery was abolished and the Afro-Brazilians where thrown into the world somehow to fend for themselves with hardly any preparation, with nostalgic sugarplums of a harmonious past dancing in their heads, it became quite convenient for the dominant class to invent what was called "racial democracy." The down side is also that, once modernity gained a firm foothold among Brazilian elites and middle classers, and whenever the threat of instability made its presence known, authoritarianism—and even totalitarianism and fascism—seemed to be the most feasible answer. Witness the periodic waves of military takeovers in Brazil and throughout most of the Latin American nations during the twentieth century. At any rate, DaMatta's Home order has been willing and capable to makes its presence known from the beginning to the present.

The other side of the coin sports the Street, that cold, cruel world outside the cozy confines of the Home. This is where Western modernity has made its gains. Modernity, with its Enlightenment ideals, its democratic all-are-created-equal myth, its mystique of indefinite progress upward and onward through systematic development of our god-given natural resources, its obsessive individualism, and its competitive dog-eat-dog capitalism. Here is where DaMatta's individual stands equal with all other individuals before the law. In the Home of the haves, everybody is a DaMatta person, and each person enjoys status. Even though a respectable person confronting some individual on the Street on an equal basis at the outset, if that individual oversteps his bounds, he is quickly put in his place with a "Do you know who you're speaking to?" challenge. Nevertheless, when the modern world is at its best, hierarchies are flattened, all individuals outside the Home are equal, and the toughest of them all wins and takes top prize consisting of money, power, and prestige (it's definitely a game rather than play). That is the up side—in case one might wish to look upon this condition in a favorable light. The down side is that the condition breeds insecurity, and threatens to end in neurotic behavior, with all its ramifications. The down side also is that, once again, when the powerbrokers have their way, racism, totalitarianism, and even fascism (along the right-side of figure 16) can ensue. Above all, the very dream of unlimited development and progress leads all peoples of the world to the idea that "first world" status can be just around the corner. For decades, Brazilians have dubbed their nation "the country of the future" (Zweig 1960). This future, unfortunately, continues to recede into the horizon. (I write this in spite of recent optimistic reports—see the special issue of the weekly magazine *Veja* 35 [19], 2002).

Yet, all is not as Manichaean as the Home-Street pair of words might indicate. To paraphrase DaMatta, it's what's between Home and Street that counts. And what's in between? A border, an imaginary line of demarcation. This is a socio-cultural counterpart to a line in the mathematical sense: infinitesimally thin, a mere nothingness, of hardly any importance if it were not for the whole picture that renders if all-important. The dividing line is virtually nothing. Yet, like 0 of figure 17, or linguistically speaking like Homi Bhabha's (1994:36–39) "third space," the dividing line contains, within itself, the possibility of everything. What is that everything? In DaMatta's conception, it is *both* Home *and* Street, and *neither* Home *nor* Street but something else, something different, something new, for the Home-Street mentality keeps contradictions together (Ferretti 1995:60). How can we account for that everything? We can't, logically and rationally speaking. We can't, because everything is a continuous range of possibilities, potentially unlimited in extension. There is a way of getting a sense of the middle, however. I would suggest that perhaps a sense of the middle by way can be had through certain Brazilian everyday practices as outlined by Roberto DaMatta, Roberto Schwarz, Lívia Barbosa, and Mériti de Souza, among others.

I allude to that charming yet shifty and shady practice of *jeito*.

It's Also How You Get Things Done That Counts

"Tem jeito ou não tem jeito?" (Does he have that special knack or cunning about him or not?). That is the question dividing the adroit, skillful, dexterous, sly, shrewd, subtle, clever, nimble, quick-witted, astute, perspicacious, ingenious, artful, adventuresome Brazilian from ordinary folks—whatever "ordinary folks" means, whatever "adroit,... etc". means. *Jeito* is one of the most difficult words in Brazilian Portuguese to decipher (Prado 1962). The term is confusingly polyfaceted: "Dar um jeito" (to find some singular way, make do with what you have, bend the rules a little, pull a few strings), "O jeito é" (the singular, etc. way to do it is), "É o jeito" (it's the best or most subtly clever way), "Ao jeito de" (in the particularly cunning style of), "Daquele jeito" (in that uniquely sly way), "De qualquer jeito" (any way or whichever way), "De nenhum jeito!" (no way!), and so on (for further reading see Leers 1982; Levine 1997:80–110).

The unwritten, tacit custom of the *jeito brasileiro* entails methods for using and beating the system by subtle means almost always with a note of humor, a little irony, a wink of the eye, a knowing nod, accompanied by a little malandragem and a sprinkling of malícia. It is a means for avoiding bureaucratic glitches and authoritarian and institutional roadblocks, a way to operate in the most expedient way possible. She who has the gift of jeito has that charming way about her. She always has a few tricks up her sleeve, in her creative, unorthodox, somewhat idiosyncratic way. She has that special style for communicating in a familiar, down-to-earth manner with people from all walks of life and according to what the particular situation calls for. She has a unique talent for getting things done, her way, through her verbal aplomb, the apparent ease and spontaneity in her dealings with others, and especially, her ability to twist rules and regulations to fit her purpose.

Lívia Barbosa (1992) offers an entire volume on the word and what it entails. She writes that after beating her head against the wall for some time, she realized her confused state of mind had a bearing on her incapacity to comprehend that the negative, the no in Brazil does not signify that which semantically we would ordinarily expect it to signify. She came to understand that no is not the limit. Unlike laws, cultural codes of conduct and norms do not set down boundaries fixed for all time but remain to a greater or lesser degree flexible. In short, the no is fuzzy. So also the no between the two jeitos in *Tem jeito* and *Não tem jeito* is exceedingly slippery. The no in jeito, more than perhaps any other Brazilian vocable, means "no." It might also mean "not really no and not really yes"; it might mean "perhaps yes"; it might mean "by all means, yes"; it might mean "no,... but yes"; it might mean "no,... but,... well, just no"; it might mean "*both* yes *and* no"; it might mean "*neither* yes *nor* no"; it might mean "*all* of the above"; it might mean "*none* of the above." In other words, it just means what it means, but not very clearly and not very distinctly, and at the same time it means what it does not mean, but at the same time,... and so on (Novinger 2004).

By now, finally, I would suspect, the relevance of those strange illogically logical goings on about which many of the above pages revolved is emerging into the light of day—and if not, it will be discussed further in light of figure

18. And, I would likewise suspect, the relevance of jeito to Capoeira and Candomblé life within guerrilla culture implying conformity and resistance begins hitting us full force.

Jeito can be conceived as a sort of move toward meritocracy, toward an egalitarian social setting—which flattens an otherwise hierarchical society—toward political stabilization. To the extent that in Brazil there are inequalities in the distribution of rewards, through the dialogical, egalitarian practice of jeito, resentment toward those who receive greater rewards by those who receive fewer rewards is less intense than we would expect. This is because justification of rewards is often offered on the basis of merit—the individual who is most adept at the jeito game—and not simply on the basis of a person's social status. That is, privilege earned by merit in jeito culture somehow becomes morally and politically more acceptable to most people than privilege earned by inheritance. Jeito is in a manner of speaking of the people, by the people, and for the people.

Barbosa interviewed a number of Brazilians and found that they all recognize the term and know what it means; they have a feel for its meaning. One interviewee suggested that the word is used and put into practice by all Brazilians "from the office boy to the president" (Barbosa 1992:32). Obviously it is understood and put into practice quite differently by office boys and presidents. Yet everybody understands it and uses—and often abuses—it, each in her/his own way. Jeito at once implies the maximum of generality and the maximum of particularity. It's a general way of everybody getting things done within particular circumstances and according to the ways of particular individuals. It's a unique way things get done with whatever is at hand and by creative individuals wherever and whenever. It's serious business, for one's survival is at stake, whether in the local market place, at knife's edge in the *favelas*, over a brandy discussing a million dollar business deal, or at the conference table while engaging in political decisions that will affect the lives of millions. It's the business of showing off one's ability to give a sly wink while distorting ordinary social, political, and economic customs and habits. It's straight talk, and it's talk peppered with irony, cynicism, mockery, parody, satire, and word play of all sorts. It's a carnival of words and gestures, of signs becoming more signs.

The subtitle of Barbosa's volume, *The Art of Becoming More Equal Than Everybody Else*, is revealing. The individual who has jeito usually manages to get his way because there is that certain way about him. That way is as charming as it is repulsive, as attractive as it is revolting, as captivating as it is reprehensible. But it is the way of all who know how to become more equal than their fellow citizens. More equal? The very phrase incorporates jeito logic. If some are more equal than others, then there is no genuine equality, and if there is no genuine equality, then some cannot be more equal than others. That is the beauty and the banality of the word and its practice. Jeito implies a continuous spectrum of equality. In a manner of speaking, all Brazilians are born into the possibility of jeito equally, but some soon find themselves chained by the jeito of others because they knew not how to cultivate their god-given talent for becoming more jeito equal than others. Indeed, we definitely have more than mere dualism in the process of jeito practices. All this appears inconsistent, even paradoxical. And so it is. In Barbosa's (1995:47) words, jeito "is a symbol of our institutional disorientation, incompetence, and inefficiency as much as it is a symbol of our cordiality, street smarts, and conciliatory character. It reasserts our traditional marriage with a relational and traditional worldview and our equally unending affair with an individualistic modern ideology."

In fact, Barbosa constructs a three-term set of categories for depicting jeito culture. On the left side we have the Favor (tradition), on the right side, Corruption (modernity), with Jeito in the middle (compare to the landscape evinced in figure 16). Corruption is corruption, within whichever context, and after granting the terms polyvalence, I will assume we are all in agreement regarding its meaning. But what is favor in this respect? Portuguese colonization of Brazil, based on monopolization of the land, gave rise basically to three social categories: lords, slaves, and free men, who were in fact dependent upon the proprietorship of the lords. Relations between masters and slaves were relatively well defined. Relations between lords and free men were for the most part that of dominant and subaltern. Any benefit that might be forthcoming to the free man was by way of some form or other of favor from those who wielded power. Favor was the general form of social mediation, more appealing and more in line with the practices of jeito than slavery. It is understandable that the institution—we must call it an institution, so embedded in everyday practices as it is—has found its way into Brazil's literature, most notably in the works of nineteenth-century novelist Machado de Assis. Favor formed and gave flavor to the national life of Brazil, and it perseveres to this day. It is present everywhere, in politics, industry, commerce, professions, skilled and unskilled labor, and at the soccer stadium, in the restaurant, and in the home. Brazilian cultural critic Roberto Schwarz writes:

> Slavery gives the lie to liberal ideas; but favour, more insidiously, uses them, for its own purposes, originating a new ideological pattern. The element of arbitrariness, the fluid play of preferences to

> which favour subjects whatever it touches, cannot be fully rationalized.... Favour in turn implies the dependency of the individual, the exception to the rule, ornamental culture, arbitrary pay and the servility of labour.... [Favour] governed both patronage and gratitude. The symbolic compensation was perhaps a little out of tune, but not ungrateful. (Schwarz 1992:22–23)

Schwarz goes on to suggest that from the very beginning of Brazilian history, favor falsely assures the weak that somehow they are not really slaves, in spite of their subservient position, and it assures the powerful that their position of superiority is secure. Each needs the other, both in their complicity recognize their place in the social game of make-believe-that-you-are-not-really-like-this, and the centuries of slavery are conveniently conjured away. Yet this "recognition sustains an extraordinary complicity, made even worse by the adoption of the bourgeois vocabulary of equality, merit, labour and reason" (Schwarz 1992:25).

In Barbosa's favor-corruption polarity with jeito falling in the space between the two, favor takes on a positive connotation with respect to corruption as the lesser of the two evils, so to speak, relegating corruption to negative connotativity. Favor at least implies reciprocal action, although it is understood that one party enjoys an advantage over the other. Corruption, in contrast, is a one-way street: one party wins and the other one loses. Since jeito can be an either/*or* affair, but also either *both-and* or *neither-nor*, it can be either of positive or negative connotation, or both, or neither. There is a leveling effect in the jeito custom. In many cases there might not be a clear distinction between superordinate and subordinate; in others the distinction might be there but it becomes diffuse and cloudy during acts of jeito; in yet others the tables might be overturned with respect to superior/inferior categories. For these reasons jeito can to a certain degree take place between players of the game who hardly know each other, while favor is usually solicited solely among associates, friends, and relatives. Moreover, petition for a favor demands a relatively formal setting, while jeito can take place most anywhere: at home, at play, at work, in the street, restaurant, and so on.

The distinction between jeito and mere corruption might appear clearer than that between jeito and favor. But in practice, confusion ensues. Jeito is subtle and discreet. Corruption, though customarily an under-the-table operation, is relatively straightforward, in addition to the fact that it usually involves a larger sum of money, power, and prestige, a greater infraction of the law, and a more scandalous infringement of social conventions. Consequently, corruption tends to widen the gap between haves and havenots, dominant and subservient, powerful and subalterns, while jeito often, though not always, has a flattening effect. The general jeito attitude is: 'today he is more equal than I because his jeito was in better rhythm than mine, but tomorrow it may be my turn." Jeito is not the sole possession of some individuals and inaccessible to others. At any given moment the sharing is unequal, but in the long run, jeito exercises a certain equalizing tendency.

Still, the Dice Are Loaded against the Havenots
Roberto Schwarz (1987, 1990) writes that from the very beginning of modern Brazil, favor provided a mediary function between masters and slaves and free laborers. Masters were white and slaves were black, and, depending on the area, many of the artisans and skilled and unskilled laborers were white. This presented a conflict, since the haves and the havenots could not be divided conveniently into whites and blacks. The answer to this problem emerged by way of what was called the "favor." It was liberally doled out to the white laborers, but rarely to the blacks, whether free or slaves. The favor was granted, and the recipient was indebted to the grantor until due time for payment to be forthcoming. In this manner the distinction held. Yet the White laborer was given at least some token form of membership as potentially a *person*, rather than merely an individual, like the slaves and Black laborers. That is a plus for the White underclass citizen. The negative comes when he begins treading ground too far in the direction of respectable persons among the haves, and he is slapped back in his proper place.

So, we have masters and slaves and the Others, and whites and blacks and Others, and persons and individuals and Others. The Others are neither masters nor slaves, neither respectable persons nor black individuals. They are in between, in a sort of cultural limbo. Up to and throughout the nineteenth century, they occupied a no man's zone within a paternalistic, patriarchal, authoritarian society. In more recent times, they have carried their load as recipients of mediation within a democratic setting where ideally everybody is flattened to the same egalitarian level. But not really, for there are the blacks who are merely individuals (within modern Street life) and the white upper crust consisting of persons (within traditional Home life), while those in between are neither exactly genuine persons nor are they simply individuals. They are neither engaged in Street interactivity nor can they gain legitimate entry into the Home hierarchy like respectable haves. They are the Other. Jeito practices can give them a degree of respectability, but when they get to smart for their own britches, they are rejected for their effort.

According to Mériti de Souza (1999), there are modern formal laws (DaMatta's Street) dictating freedom and equality and emancipation for all. And there are informal pre-modern or traditional practices and rules of conduct (DaMatta's Home) that say it's all right to continue doing what you've always been doing as long as you exercise lenience, tolerance, and play the role of a good father-figure to those under your custody—in other words, be a good Buarque de Holanda "cordial man." Formal laws stretch themselves to the maximum in order to fit daily comings and goings. Informal rules of proper behavior give a subtle wink of the eye when formal laws are cited, and life goes on through constant improvisation according to whatever context happens to pop up. The individual on the Street is free, equal to all other individuals, and can be all she can be, since she is protected by the constitution. However, she is not really an individual according to modernity's promises, because she is constantly reminded of her inequality by some person from the Home front. The upright person may be all she is through her family stature. But she constantly has to be on her guard against some upstart individual who may think he is one of her kind.

This situation is reminiscent of the maxim developed in Spanish America during colonial times: "Obedezco, pero no cumplo" (I obey but do not concord or comply, or, I pay homage and lip service to God, King, and Spain, but the sordid affairs of everyday life call for other, more practical measures, that I choose to apply according to the demands of the particular moment). If you consider yourself a good and decent person, then you profess your allegiance and obedience to the formal laws of the land; yet, when confronted with the concrete, everyday life's encounters, you fail to comply and engage in a little jeito, and favoritism. It's not that you're evil or an inherently bad citizen. The law has things right, and it merits respect. However, it just doesn't apply within those ever-changing social contexts where give-and-take improvisation is the order of the day. If you are no more than an individual, you can still be as patriotic as the next guy. So of course you obey. But since you are no more than average, and above all, since the system has really done very little for you, you fail fully to comply whenever the opportunity arises to take advantage of whatever situation presents itself. On the Home front, you comply with tradition; hence you look the other way with respect to formal law. On the Street, you might outwardly obey formal law; yet behind the scene another story can be told, for you do what you have to do to beat the system a little. And what's between obeying and complying? Just that: the in between. It's "what's in the middle that counts." "I obey but I do not comply" obviously entails a pragmatic paradox like the "Be spontaneous" injunction. If you consciously and willfully obey the injunction you don't comply, because in doing so you aren't spontaneous. And if you just naturally happen to immerse yourself in spontaneity, you don't comply either, because you don't take it upon yourself to obey. You're apparently damned if you do and you're damned if you don't.

Mériti de Souza calls the workings of jeito a "perverse logic." This seems to complement DaMatta's qualifying Brazil's subtle, nondualistic "middle way" as logical unruly. Actually, there's nothing perverse about the logic at all. De Souza and DaMatta apparently had classical logical principles of Identity, Noncontradiction and Excluded-Middle in mind when they wrote what they wrote. But if we read de Souza and DaMatta closely, we realize that their allusions to "perverse logic" reveals that their inclination is actually toward an entirely different logic, an illogical logic of the sort outlined above through figures 15, 15a, 16, and 17.

During everyday cultural life, Brazilians use this illogical logic at the drop of a hat, because it's second nature to them; it's in their bones, so to speak. They use it, because it's the most natural thing to do. Like cultural illogical logic in whichever society, it's practicing philosophy. Regarding cultural proclivities and propensities, cultural illogical logic is heads and shoulders above the dream of fixed identity, maintenance of consistency at all cost, and the incapacity to allow alternatives to emerge from between the horns of culture's most cherished dichotomies. If Brazilians—or the citizens of any country for that matter—held tight to classical logical precision and order, that, indeed, would be a disaster. DaMatta tells us time and again in his writings that Brazilians have a special knack for maneuvering in and out and over and under contradictories apparently with the greatest of ease. The implication is that the rest of the West had better wake up to the music before it's too late. Brazil and Spanish America have from the beginning been coping with cultural complexity of the sort the rest of the West never experienced until the past few decades.

THE WAY OF SOCIOLOGICAL DISASTER
The particularly Brazilian knack for coping is exemplified through novelist Jorge Amado's Dona Flor in *Dona Flor and Her Two Husbands* (1969 [1966]). Dona Flor's first husband, Vadinho, died, but he continues to visit her. Vadinho, is a roguish, adventuresome, unpredictable, terribly sinful and terribly exciting, macho character. Her second and present husband in the flesh, Teodoro, is polite, proper, and pragmatic; there is for him "a place for everything and everything in its place." Which of the two should she choose? Her phantom, but sensuously exciting, husband, or her rather droll flesh and blood husband? She chooses not to choose. She opts for the two of them and lives a life of contradiction,... no of complementarity,... that's not quite it either,... no,... they become fused in her mind, a hybrid,... so she must realize a synthesis, no? Not that either!... Never! Then what is it? It's by and large indescribable. It's a scandal of reason, a rape of the senses, a slaughter of what ordinarily goes as good logic and good taste. It's multiple times and

spaces and everything causing and bringing about the emergence of everything else.

Dona Flor reveals a fundamentally irresolvable paradox in standard logic and practical reason when she decides to embrace both husbands and thus create the best of all possible worlds, in deciding not to decide, choosing not to choose. This is itself a decision and a choice, of course. But it remains a problem only insofar as linear binary thinking is concerned. Nonlinear, n-ary feeling and sensing and becoming along that other mode can live quite well with such trivial puzzles of the mind, for they follow an illogical logic, the subtleties of which the mind knows not, which the mind has no chance of knowing, really knowing, or really saying for that matter, for these subtleties are of the body, that is, of bodymind, in its scandalous, disrespectful best. Dona Flor remains in the middle, between the either and the or. If there is no linearly logical solution to her problem, and if she can't have both Teodoro and Vadinho within the same spatio-temporal context nor can she have neither the one nor the Other but some Other Other—since she has no alternative—she opts for now the one, now the other, like DaMatta's Home and Street, and person and individual, like the Afro-Brazilians' conformity and resistance.

Putting this more specifically within the context of Capoeira and Candomblé culture, consider the condition of many Afro-Brazilians of Bahia who call themselves black, and they are proud of it. This is their Home, where they find their black identity, their own tradition. There, they are persons. In the same breath they call themselves Brazilians, and they are equally proud of it. This is their modern identity of the Street; it makes up their identity as individuals in the modern Enlightenment sense. But, of course, there's a problem here. They are neither persons nor are they nonpersons nor are they individuals nor are they nonindividuals in the sense described above. One cannot say there's precisely a syncretic mix, nor is there exactly any conjunction, fusion, parallelism, juxtaposition, convergence, or adaptation according to the terms as they are portrayed in figure 17. Citizens of Afro-Brazilian culture tend to slip between the virgules, between the dotted lines. When at their best, they are self-organizing; they bring about something new, some new third way surfacing to take its place among the becomings of other third-way practices; they operate at the liminal zone, at the border, nowhere and nowhen. I would modestly suggest that what we have here is something akin to "border thinking" in the manner of Mignolo (2000:19) which he qualifies as between Darcy Ribeiro's "subaltern knowledge" and Michel Foucault's "subjugated knowledge." However, the idea of "border thinking" doesn't quite do the trick either. "Border feeling" and 'sensing" is prior to thinking, as I believe I have illustrated throughout this essay and will continue to do to the end. Limiting border issues to language ("languaging," as Mignolo dubs it) and thinking is yet another form of "linguicentrism." In Edouard Glissant's (1997:119) words: "If language is given in advance, if it claims to have a mission, it misses out on the adventure and does not *catch on* in the world." Of course! Because the extralinguistic, or prelinguistic is in advance of language (merrell 1997, 2002a).

In short, Capoeira and Candomblé practices involve neither persons nor individuals, strictly speaking. There is neither Home nor Street; there is neither homogeny nor hegemony nor heterogeny, as the phenomena have been hitherto sensed and known. Then what, pray tell, is there? Whatever there is, it is always emerging; it is novelty, vibrant flow, flux, which is to say: process. It is bodymind memory incessantly emerging into the light of day (see Martins 2000).

Chapter Fourteen

Still in Search of Process

Change and Vagueness

Theory in the humanities and the social sciences owes much of its prestige to a conception of the physical sciences that belongs to the past. I allude to the classical scientific paradigm, a Cartesian-rational, Aristotelian-categorical approach to understanding the physical world. This approach has paid dividends, to be sure. It has been one of the greatest success stories of all time. It has endowed us with the myth of unlimited knowledge growth and material progress. We can hardly argue against such success. At the same time, success can lull us to sleep.

If we briefly survey the history of our tradition from Plato and Aristotle to the present, we become aware of a persistent bias against vagueness, ambiguity, indeterminacy, and uncertainty, and above all, against change. However, in recent years, the myth of unlimited knowledge and unending material progress has slowly been revealing itself for what it is. Logic, mathematics, physics, and biology, as well as the arts, have disrupted unthinking faith in our customary notion of a world cleanly cut into sharp edge crystals of shimmering brilliance. We are now told that things inevitably become messy; they break down; they fail to perform as expected; they invariably change. Change reminds us that we must force ourselves to acknowledge the existence of flux, of pure change, of process. This presents problems for our classical modes of thought, big problems. For our noncontradictory means, models, and methods more often than not preclude such acknowledgment. It is as if we assumed that even though flux infringes and indeed invades our conventions of understanding, it is undesirable and must be avoided at all cost. Penetrating the outer limits of tradition and entering the unknown territory of flux can, of course, be a frightening experience. Understandably, it is avoided (Margolis 1991).

Another myth lies behind the myth of unlimited knowing and progress: identity. A is A and it can neither be nor become anything other than A, and that's that. Zeno of Elea takes the idea of fixed identity to the limit. He tells us that an arrow in movement is at every moment just where it is and nowhere else; hence at each moment it is at rest. Hence there is no motion. There is only the arrow, identical to itself, timelessly. According to Zeno's mighty logic, whatever is, is as it is, and so it will remain. Our experience, in contrast, knows of no such stasis. It consists of the onstreaming gush of experience that makes shambles of the very idea of a fixed world. Concrete experience tells us that the arrow flows from one place to another. The flow brings about change; change is a by-product of the flow; it is in the flow; it *is* the flow. This seems clear enough. The problem is that how ever we wish to express the process of our concrete experience, we can do no more than create vague notions, for process cannot be precisely described. When we say what our experience is, it isn't, for it is already something else.

In other words, if we take Zeno's arrow as our experience sees it, by the time we see and conceive it here, it is somewhere else along the line toward the end point. This is, of course, because according to psychological studies, our awareness of what we see is registered at around .08 to .10 second after the photons enter our retina (Pöppel 1972, 1988). We never experience what is becoming in the exact instant it is becoming what it will have been becoming. There is always a lag, a lapse, a *différance*—to use Jacques Derrida's (1973) celebrated term—between what is happening and our registering what is happening. Where is this time lag—this nothingness between here and not here, now and not now? How can we get a handle on this strangeness in our daily life? Obviously Zeno's world is considerably more comfortable than the idea of flux.

In an attempt to come to grips with this strange world of pure change, assume that at each moment the arrow is just where it is: here. But, according to our consciously sensing it, it is not here, because by the time we become conscious of it, it is somewhere else. It occupies a particular piece of space at the moment of each now. But, given our experiential lapse, that now is not now, but then. In a manner of speaking, if we put the becoming of our consciousness in the same bag as Zeno's static increments of space and time, we might say that at each moment the arrow is neither here nor there but somewhere else, and that within each spatial increment there is neither now nor then but somewhen else. "But," someone will rebut, "we might just as well say that there is both here and "there and everywhere and both now and "then and everywhen." Fine. We can do so, if we wish. From within a processual world, eithers and ors give way to both one possibility and many others as well at some future moment—the sphere of overdetermination. And they give way to neither one interpretation nor another of our experienced world, but some other interpretation altogether—the sphere of underdetermination (from figure 16).

Once again, our comfortable world becomes topsy-turvy. We are cut adrift in a raging sea with neither oars nor compass, and we lose our bearings. Things are not so dire, however. Look at our apparent enigma this way. If border there must be between here and now and there and then, it is our construct. We place a line of demarcation here and now. But actually, here and now are in the here-and-now of our consciousness in the process of becoming there and then. In fact they have already become some elsewhere and elsewhen and are in the process of becoming yet some other elsewhere and elsewhen. We can never catch any precise here-and-now by the tail and pin it down. Yet, our flow of experience tells us that we hold passing heres-and-nows in the hyperactive present while we are in the process of experiencing incoming heres and nows. I would respectfully suggest that, metaphorically speaking, the elsewhere and elsewhen are found in a line of demarcation, or a border if you will, that separates here from there and now from then. The line is neither what each of the categorizing words is nor is it not what it is but something else in some elsewhere and elsewhen. Then what is the line anyway?

Nowhere and Nowhen

A line separating something from something else is no more than an infinitely thin membrane, so fallible and so fragile. It is a demarcation that mars at the same time that it de-mars, and in this manner it de-mar-cates, making an exceedingly tenuous difference between one world and another world. It might appear that the line separates here-now from there-then and that everything must be either of the one or the other, and never the twain shall meet.

But appearances are often deceptive. The line of de-mar-cation in figure 18, however flimsy, is nonetheless that which lies between one thing and another thing. For purposes of economy, call here-now A, and call there-then not-A. The line of de-mar-cation is not A, to be sure. But neither is it not-A. So in a manner of speaking it must be A-lessness, for it is not A. If this is the case, then it must also be Not-A-lessness, for it is not not-A either. So it is A-lessness-not-A-lessness. However, as A-lessness the line possesses something in common with not-A, since Not-A is also A-less; and as Not-A-lessness it shares a commonality with A, since A is also Not-A-less. In this sense it at one and the same time enjoys A-ness and Not-A-ness. So it is *both* A-ness *and* Not-A-ness. It is also *neither* A-ness *nor* Not-A-ness. The line of demarcation, then, is in a manner of speaking "emptiness", yet it implies, within itself, the possible for the engenderment of everythingness. It is at once nothing and everything (see also Peirce *CP* 1:463–469, 5:447–457).

You will have noticed an affinity between the paragraph you have just finished and Jacques Derrida's baffling "undecidables," words that "can no longer be included within philosophical (binary) opposition, resisting and disorganizing it, without ever constituting a third term, without ever leaving room for a solution in the form of speculative dialectics" (Derrida 1981:71). In all Derrida's undecidables, the either/or is present, for sure, but the both-and and the neither-nor also manage to make their way onto the scene to create havoc with the usual classical logical principles (for further regarding Oriental thought along these lines, Huntington 1989; Kalupahana 1986).

The fissure in figure 18, then, is a hairline of identification; it is identification as a process of the one thing identifying itself insofar as it is a difference from another thing. However, just as that difference is already a different difference, so also identification is a process of becoming without the possibility of its being having become once and for all. In an interview, literary critic and cultural studies theorist Homi Bhabha tells us: "Identification is a process of identifying with and through another object, an object of otherness, at which point the agency of identification—the subject—is itself always ambivalent, because of the intervention of that otherness" (Bhabha 1990:211). So there are not merely two possibilities in eternal conflict. Between every pair of possibilities a third always stands a chance of pushing its way in through the interstices, a "third space" and a "third time" that enable other positions to emerge. This is a far cry from the customary binary classifications deployed in the construction of order in terms of the haves and havenots, those who exercise hegemony and those who are destined to remain in positions of subservience. There are now multivalent ambiguities. It is not simply a matter of the *either* or the *or*. Rather, it is a transition and transformation from an all-embracing both this, *and ... and ... and ...n* to a sly, roguish neither this, *nor ... nor ... nor ...n*, and then at some point in the interstices, something else, something different, something out of the ordinary, begins emerging (this is comparable to Deleuze and Guattari 1983).

Taking the whole of these possibilities for the practice of everyday life into account—as if that were really possible, which it is not, of course—it might be said that there is no custom but customs, no fashion but fashions, no strategy but strategies, no rule but rules, no choice but choices. A choice, rule, or strategy over another choice, rule, or strategy, is largely binary. In contrast, when attempting to consider the whole of everyday life, choices, rules, and strategies, are nonlinear, unpredictable, uncertain, for the most part inconsistent, and they evince qualities of virtual chaos and what Gilles Deleuze and Félix Guattari (1987) call rhizomicity. Almost anything can in principle become virtually anything else. But when it comes down to the nitty-gritty of actual practices, multiply variegated choices, rules, and strategies, lead to the engenderment of interrelated, interdependent, interactive, context-bound actualities that are invariably incomplete, for they could have been something other than they are and at some future time and place they will have become one of a spectrum of alternative possibilities.

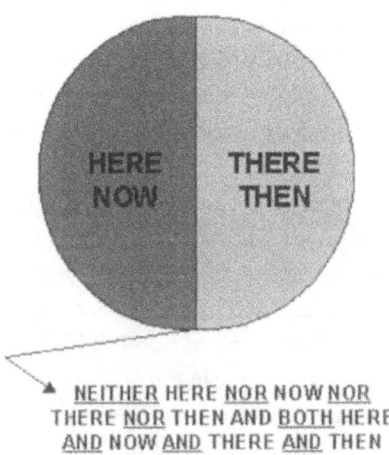

FIGURE 18

IT'S WHAT'S IN BETWEEN THAT COUNTS

In this sense the problem with Bhabha is that he gives us the postcolonial world according to the textualized, strictly linguistic word. Bhabha's narrative is extravagantly and excessively "linguicentric." I would suggest that we need to drop, once and for all, the idea that in the "beginning was the Word." First, was the bare image of a world, the world we fabricated, the concrete world of our kinesomatic bodymind feeling and sensing and experiencing. Then, and only then, comes the generalizing, essentializing Word (merrell 2003a; Parry 1994, 2002).

All this goes to suggest that there should be no priority of essence over existence; nor should there be any priority of existence over essence. That is to say, what is could always have been other than it is, and it will have been one of the myriad possibilities of that other: flux, pure change, process.

What emerges in practice does not become what is, for there is no "is" and there is no "it," as Gertrude Stein would put it. That is, there is no is equal to what is, that is not what it is not, and regarding what is and what is not, there is nothing else that can be. There is only process, the becoming of some nostalgic order of being. But that being is nothing except that it is no more than the being of the becoming of what will have never become what it is and nothing but what it is. Traditional humanistic values seem to fall by the wayside, if they do not disappear entirely. Dissemination, dispersal, diaspora, deterritorialization, reterritorialization, and scintillating, effervescent, vibrant, rippling near-Brownian movement at the hairline: each actor on the flowing stage is like a point in n-dimensional space and nonlinear time that can fly off in one of many directions, and whatever may have happened is no necessary indication of what will have happened in the future, for the future, as much as the past, resists closure.

Within process, it becomes a matter of "I participate therefore I am becoming." The idea of an individual self is seen as so much of an anomaly. The idea of the subject also wanes, since there is no such fixed category and since it does not reside in some determinable space-time juncture. As we have observed, participation in Capoeira and Candomblé life is processual through and through. I will address this topic in part IV, but for the moment, I remain on theoretical terrain in an effort better to account for the process itself.

How Is Process a Benign Rather Than Malignant Sociological Disaster?

Hegemony in the genuine Gramscian sense is not simply binary Secondness. It is a convergence of present possibilities of Firstness and future exigencies of Thirdness. In spite of assumptions to the contrary, hegemony, like homogeny and heterogeny, is process, not product. It is process beginning its becoming pigeon-holes of categorization set down by the interaction of Secondness (Laclau and Mouffe 1985). The problem is that these pigeon-holes simply can't stay put. They begin to ooze, to melt into one another. They begin giving way to process. This beginning of process manifests itself even in the physical sciences, that, as Joseph Agassi (1975) puts it, is perpetually "at war with itself," it is science "in flux."

Perhaps the most succinct way to put the issue is by evoking a scene from what is known as the "paradox of induction," developed by Carl Hempel (1945). In a nutshell, the tale goes like this. We generally assume all swans are white, and go about our daily affairs. As far as we are concerned, it is simply true to say "all swans are white" and false to say "some swans are nonwhite," and that's that: case closed. It is an either/or binary matter. We have an ingrained feel (Firstness) for the whiteness of swans, and we could hardly feel otherwise, unless in some imaginary world. However, a certain explorer down under in Australia, namely, Captain Cook, once found—that is, sensed (*via* Secondness) and interpreted (*via* Thirdness)—some black swans. Henceforth the categorical borders suffered a change. Knowledge of swans shifted. It became the case that most swans, but not all, are white; those nonwhite, that is, black, swans can be found in a remote region of the globe, Australia.

Actually, it shouldn't be at all shocking that all swans are white did not withstand the test of time. In fact, it was to be expected, in view of the above discussion on the sphere of all possible possibilities. When considering the range of all possible events, seeing and saying must imply the statement: 'swans are white and they are nonwhite." One pole of this contradiction was held true during one period of human history, the other pole during another period. So if the statement "swans are white and they are nonwhite" is taken to be atemporal, then the statement "Swans are either white or they are nonwhite" is atemporal in another more limited sense, for either one or the other is viewed as immutable, depending on the time and the place and the folks involved. However, we also have the implicit statement: "It is neither the case that all swans are white nor is it the case that no swans are nonwhite." That is to say, previously it was the case that all swans are white, but it is now the case that most swans are white. And it was previously the case that no swans are nonwhite but it is now the case that some swans are nonwhite, specifically, those that are black.

From this rather unkempt sphere where seeing and saying are neither timelessly one thing nor the other but potentially something else, temporality emerges. Given our temporality, there is one thing at one time and another thing at another time, with both things thrown into the same bag as part of a vast ocean in constant self-organizing movement wherein it is perpetually becoming something other than what it is. So we have at one extreme the assertion (1) "*Both* white swans *and* nonwhite swans." At the other extreme, we have (3) "*Neither* exclusively all white swans *nor* no nonwhite swans". And in the middle, (2), there is the principle "*Either* white swans *or* nonwhite swans." Assertion (1) is the sphere of unactualized possibilities in harmonious intermeshing, no matter how contradictory, two is basically the sphere of classical logical principles, and three is the sphere of emerging novelties between the either and the or. In this manner, (1) is qualified as exceeding vagueness; it is fraught with contradictions any number of which can over time be actualized, and (3) is marked by generalities arising from the particulars actualized from one and passing through (2).

Following Hempel's paradox, (3) is invariably incomplete, since there is no knowing when and where something new and different will emerge to take is place between two already actualized general conceptualizations. Hence

(3) is underdetermined heterogeny, since between any two general terms or statements there always exists the probability somewhere and somewhen of something else emerging. In other words, the system is perpetually moving toward the completion of its own continuity without the prospect of ever realizing that goal. Given the above considerations in view of figure 16, (2) is under most circumstances the dwelling place of binary practices (hegemony) as they are customarily articulated: there are either the haves or the havenots, locked in an apparently eternal, timeless, synchronic struggle. And (1) may be labeled homogeny, since, if it contains all possibilities for actualization, it must be exceedingly vague.

Focus obsessively on (2), and you have the pathway of least resistance the somnambulistic yes-sayers customarily tread. Allow your attention nomadically to wander over (1) and (3), and you begin to resonate with the tossing, rolling, heaving tide of process, which includes cultural guerrilla strategies of conformity and resistance regarding Capoeira and Candomblé practices. Within (1) and (3) you are coming to an awareness of the unspecifiability of this resonance. You can't clearly and distinctly say what you think about the hegemonic cultural milieu outright. At best, you can only feel it, empathize with it (the contingency of Firstness). Perhaps by more luck than management, you might be able to bring it into rapport with your general understanding (the sociocultural world of Thirdness). As a result, you might find yourself on the path of conformity and resistance.

Find yourself is actually an overstatement. For if you are in the habit of bucking the waves, kicking against the pricks, swimming cross-stream, you engage in your somewhat subversive activity because of your gut feelings and proclivities. Your behavior will be what it is because that is how you feel, often without your ability precisely to articulate your actions and reactions. It is as if you were a natural born cultural guerrilla out to shake things up a bit. In short, you practice conformity and resistance. On so doing, you can help create what might be called a 'sociological disaster," for sure. But actually, it is no disaster at all. It emerges from an alternate logic, what might be called a sociological illogic, the likes of which you have learned to master.

Process, Product, and Incongruous, Coalescent Complementarity
The upshot is that the flux of experience never ceases to slip out of the grasp of standard logic, linear thought, models presuming completeness and consistency, and orthodox analytical methods. In experience, what appears, is already other than what it is. It is always sliding into our scintillating, undulating, effervescent flow of appearances. What seems to be is not; what is, is not what it is; there simply is no "is." Unless we come to terms with this very important point, we stand nary a chance of comprehending Capoeira or

Candomblé, or any other cultural process for that matter. Process is accessible to us solely through our flux of experience, not by way of stultifying, fixating, thought. (For further in support of this notion about which the remainder of this chapter revolves, on inconsistency regarding our world see Melhuish 1967, and Rescher and Brandom 1979; on phenomenology see Merleau-Ponty's massive *opus* 1962; on Asian thought see Hayward 1984, 1987, Lockwood 1991, Smith 1995, and Walker 2000; on perception and the "quantum mind," see Zajonc 1993; on perception of light see Weiss and Haber 1999; and in general regarding these themes, see merrell 2003a, 2004.)

Awareness of the elusively paradoxical nature of experience demands a break with our tradition predicated on the unambiguous character of the world. Granted, our traditional conceptual scheme has its place. But it also has its severe limitations. It behooves us to admit to so much and embrace experience in its most basic form. Our Aristotelian-Cartesian, rational-logical, relatively static corpuscular-mechanical, linear-analytical means and methods are fine, as far as they go. But they don't go far enough. They take up only a small part of the whole of human knowing that includes feeling, sentiment, intuition, and emotion. This whole of human knowing includes the more subtle levels of experience within the spheres of homogeny and heterogeny, while our Aristotelian-Cartesian heritage encompasses little more than hegemonic linearity.

Full-blown process goes against the push of traditional Western ways and means that tend to focus obsessively on product—review, if you wish, the italicized terms and their complements in figure 16. Process, as ongoing change in space and through time, is onstreaming. It always opens itself to future possibilities within the homogenic sphere; it readily embraces many alternatives that present themselves at any given moment from within the heterogenic sphere; it knows no fear of incompleteness and inconsistency; it offers a general yet vague picture of perpetual scintillating, undulating, and sparkling, effervescent change. Product, in contrast, demands nothing less than clarity, distinction, and precision, strung along in linear fashion. It prizes either/or thinking—toward right-hand hegemony in figure 16—and relegates fuzzy ideas and living to the trash bin; it waxes ebullient over the hoary gap between the eithers and the ors and will allow nothing to come between them.

The mind understandably usually prefers product and avoids process. Product follows standard logical imperatives; process tends to subvert them. Product is hard-core, rational thought; process seems to be the arena of soft-minded feeling and sensing and intuiting—however, it has reasons unknown to the calculating mind. Product is clarity and distinction; process in comparison seems fuzzy, vague, and ambiguous—though it is of a subtlety resisting clear and distinct ideas. Product is the hard-nosed macho way; process in comparison seems fickle—nevertheless, it has its own purposes. Product is proud, self-determined mind; process often looks like it follows the body's weak-kneed ways—but they are actually limber and elusive. Product touts itself as the best show in town; process faithfully sticks around to mop up the mess after the crowd leaves—yet it is picking up bits and pieces of knowledge for possible future use. As I suggested in the Preface, we are concrete, embodied individuals within our respective culture, all cultures are unceasing situated practice, practice is continuous process, and process is ongoing change within space and through time. Product would kill process and stake it out in the sun to dry it.

However, process and product cannot exist autonomous of one another. They coalesce in incongruous, contradictory complementarity throughout the flux of experience. What product is, was process a minuscule part of which became segmented and actualized. In terms of product, hegemony on both the left and right side of figure 16 perpetuates itself insofar as possible. In so doing, it remains a sorely impoverished remnant of what it once was, and it becomes lodged in its habitual pathways of least resistance, unaware of the myriad possibilities that it could enjoy and of the actual alternatives that could otherwise present themselves. Tradition in the West has it that product rules over process. And why not? After all, it is the yield of Identity, Noncontradiction, and Excluded-Middle when at their best. It aids and abets the venerable myth of indefinite and virtually unlimited progress by means of the proper application of logic and reason. It is realization of the goals envisioned by Enlightenment dreams. It is emancipation from darkness and ignorance into the shining rays of material prosperity, and the good life for all. According to this tradition holding tight to Identity, Noncontradiction, and Excluded-Middle, if there is good there must be evil, right is offset by wrong, pain is always lurking around and waiting for the opportunity to replace pleasure. For every force there is an equal opposite force: that is the iron law of linear, binary thinking.

Like the horse and the carriage, you can't have proper functioning product without process. Product and proper logic play out their role solely in consequence of their presumed antithesis, process. But without process, there could be no product at all. If the move is toward product via diligent application of proper reason and logic, it can be achieved because there was that virtually infinite expanse of possibilities, many of them mutually exclusive, awaiting selection and actualization within some world or other and according to indefinitely varying contexts. Selection and actualization can be achieved solely when accompanied by the emergence of alternatives, by the proliferation of heterogenous, underdetermined, yet perpetually incomplete, alternatives that often creep in when least expected. If nothing could contravene what is given by hard rock reason and logic, there would be no change, no novelty, no amelioration of standard practices in order to bring about a better product. In short, progress would be halted in its footsteps.

Indeed, without process, noncontradictory answers could not be forthcoming in the first place. Regarding possibility and selection, the very notion of myriad possibilities implies that every possibility must have its negative side somewhere, and each and every act of selection implies that something that goes unselected is what the selected is not but could otherwise have been selected. Process by its very nature includes the possibility of linear, binary series. And, in addition, it is more, much more. If there is assertion in good linear fashion, something, many somethings in nonlinear fashion, have been denied. If it is possible to assert the non-existence of something, then the possible non-existence of many things, virtually an infinity of possible nonexistent things, must be implied. In order to argue for the implausibility of some possible things that are denied because of their inconsistency or incoherent character, a hard-line argument must be set up for those things' inconsistency and incoherence; hence they are given some sort of existence by the fact that a set of sentences has been generated with which to deny their plausibility. In this manner, what is most plausible and purported to exist can be asserted only by the denial of what is purportedly less plausible and hence relegated out of existence—this problem, of course, has plagued philosophers since pre-Socratic times.

Paradoxical formulation of all possible possibilities—the selected in conjunction with the unselected—and actualization implying what could have been actualized but was not, applies as much to the principles of Identity, Noncontradiction, and Excluded-Middle as it does to whatever world a given culture might have made. Process, as depicted in figure 16, does not deny Identity, Noncontradiction, and Excluded-Middle at all. Far from it. It includes them as a subset. Pleading for process merely as disordered flow is no way to expand the view of cultural logics. Expansion of the view must preserve and at the same time subvert; it embraces and at the same time it practices infidelity; it asserts and in the same breath it denies; it incessantly pulls new practices from the included middles of old practices. In other words, cultural logics are joyously contradictory.

ON WHAT'S BECOMING

With the idea of cultural "sociological illogic" in mind, consider the notion of incongruous, coalescent complementarity within the relatively identitiless, selfless, egoless, self-contradictory, flux of experience. This is by no means to imply contradiction in the strict sense of a surface that is at one and the same time green all over and blue all over. The flux of experience gushes forth in space and through time, and when taking time into our purview, a surface can be in the process of becoming something other than what it is now becoming. Artists have been keen on teaching us so much for well over a century.

In this sense, a surface can be both green and blue within the temporal process (homogeny, inconsistency, from Firstness to Secondness). A surface could have appeared green within one context but it now appears blue since the context changed. In this sense, from within that rush of time bringing about concept-dependent change, we can say that it is neither green nor blue, for it is now becoming something else rather than either its green-becoming or its blue-becoming (from Secondness to Thirdness, heterogeny, incompleteness). In a word, the phenomenon in question might be called "grue"; it is an incongruent coalescence of complementary green and blue viewed by way of process logic within an incessantly changing culture. It is the process of one's becoming aware of some color (Firstness), then identifying the color as "green" or "blue" or perhaps in some bizarre case "grue" (Secondness) in terms of that color's difference with respect to all colors, and indeed, to all things and processes within one's world (Thirdness). This flux of experience leading to identification and articulation passes from homogeny to heterogeny in a continuous flow, as if it were as natural and simple as can be. But actually, it is a mind-numbingly complex processual matter. The term "grue," by the way, comes from Nelson Goodman's (1965) "New Riddle of Induction." I would suggest—as I have elsewhere—that the consequences of his "riddle" lie behind all forms of sensory experience and behind cultural life in general (see Hacking 1993, 1995; Hesse 1969; Stalker 1995; merrell 1997, 2003a, 2004).

When in everyday living we engage in conversation in contrast to the static image of the printed word, or when we look at an animated picture in contrast to an unanimated one, we are primed for becoming in tune with change. But this is nothing out of the ordinary. For we are at each and every moment to a greater or lesser degree in tune with change, even when we contemplate the static impression of a printed word or a still picture. Awareness is never at a standstill. We participate with it in the coming in and fading out of appearances. If we accept what appears (hegemonically) classifiable and at the same time we render it dynamic within the (homogenic) flux of experience such that it is already (heterogenically) in the process of becoming, we are dispensing with our customary world. And we find ourselves embracing Non-Identity, Contradiction, and Included-Middles. Within the world of Identity, what is, seems present, and it lends itself to experience. Within the world of Non-Identity, what appears present, is absent, for it is passing on as something other than what it was when it was becoming present to experience. What seems present is the appearance of changelessness from one moment to the next; what is continuously passing on swims in the flow of pure change. In other words, there is a coalescence of presence and absence, of hegemony and homogeny-heterogeny, such that there is both presence and absence and there is neither presence nor absence. Consequently, there is both affirmation and denial: what is, is identical to itself, and it is becoming other whereby it is not identical to itself.

All this injects a massive dose of fear in even the most stalwart cultural observer. But what is the alternative? If wherever we are we construct for ourselves a comfortable world of certainties, we can happily flit here and there with the illusion that we are in control. If we negotiate our way through this world, giving a little here and taking a little there, we can become quite smug. We think we are the kings and queens of the hill. However, we will have lost sight of the fact that this world is of our own making, a world actualized according to our desires, a world of our own hegemonic preference that we deludedly project out toward an apparently secure future. Futile dreams.

Reality Can't Simply Be Hog-tied

After all has been said and done, we must concede that reality, when coupled with temporality is, like Exu, deceptive. It allows us to think we know it, but we don't. No matter to what degree we know it, we only manage to know what it is not, for in some respect it is always something other than what we think of it.

Like the prisoner in Plato's cave allegory, the only way we can become convinced that our knowledge is illusory and that we have been deceived by the world is by placing what we previously took as our knowledge and we now take as illusion against what we now take as our knowledge. In other words, only by taking what we thought we knew as illusion and what we now think we know as truth can we take what we know as truth against what we thought we knew as illusion. What we think we know we can genuinely think we know only insofar as it interdependently, interrelatedly interacts with that reality we thought we knew but now think we knew not.

Tell Plato's prisoner the world he perceives and conceives isn't the legitimate world, and you will likely be confronted with blank, unknowing stares. As far as he is concerned, the world is what he thinks it is, and that's that: he knows not that he knows not. Tell the Newtonian scientist space is curvilinear and Riemannian rather than straight and Euclidean, and she will call on the scientific community to run you out of town on a rail. Tell the god-fearing Christian about the virtues of the Aztec deities, and he will shake his head in pity of your naiveté. In all cases the world they think they know is the world that is: there's nothing more to the matter. Actually, Plato's prisoner, Riemann, and the Aztec priest are also to a degree right, and they are to a degree wrong. Moreover, they are all, as are we, to an extent deceived by reality.

We are all to an extent deceived, because reality embodies a chaos principle that takes precedence over any ordering principle that might happen to make its presence known—in view of recent complementary physics and chaos theory. The "chaos principle" (or perhaps we should say the "Exu principle") includes the range of all possibilities, within pure homogeny, from within which what might be taken for what is can reveal itself (on the left-side of figure 16). That which might be taken for what is, emerges into the light of some cultural form of life as Other than what was taken for what is—Plato's prisoner becoming aware of the deception. At the outset, things appear ordered into eithers and ors: the hegemony principle. Then differentiation begins its push toward the ordering principle, where what is taken to be what is becomes more and more finely qualified. So we have in somewhat of a new light: (1) homogeny, or the range of unordered possibilities where no distinctions are made; (2) the long, strong arm of hegemony in an effort to keep things under control; and (3) heterogeny, or ordering, but with many alternative possibilities or probabilities presenting themselves at unexpected curves in the road. From chaotic homogeny, hegemonic order arises, and ordering heterogeny aids and abets hegemonic order, if and when possible. Everything is accounted for. Not so?

No, not really. What about the movement in figure 16 from the left-side to right-side heterogeny and downward to hegemony, and from hegemony to homogeny? If we construct our world, then that world can become entrenched to the extent that it is taken as the only possible world. Our experience sinks out of consciousness and becomes sedimented; it becomes part of our tacit, automatized sensing and doing. Likewise, if order is hegemonic and the ordering principle is heterogenic—since within a given set of cultural practices, new ways of sensing and perceiving and conceiving and talking and doing never cease to pop up—then there must be a two-way street between left-side heterogeny and right-side hegemony and homogeny (the squiggly arrows in figure 16). For example, some unexpected idea appears in the flux of experience during everyday living as if from nowhere. The newly emergent idea suggests a more efficient way of doing things. The idea is given a chance to prove itself, and it passes the test. A new concept is born. Then it is refined and moves upward onto the stage of heterogeny. As it becomes commonplace in daily practices, its place within the flow of culture eventually falls out of the conscious awareness of its participant-actors. In other words, entrenchment occurs (by the downward arrow, and the right-side of figure 16). The way of doing things eventually becomes so much a part of cultural flows that it is used and perhaps abused as if it were what really is, instead of a construct. If this entrenchment becomes deeply sedimented and automatized, some commonplace comings and goings may no longer need mind's patronizing role. The body—kinesomatic bodymind—now just does what it does in virtual automaton fashion, with the assumption that it can fend for itself—the new way of doing things is taken for what is; the world simply could not be otherwise.

This process is as common as our going through the sedimented motions of walking, riding a bicycle, driving a car, and so on. It all becomes a matter of our knowing how to do what we do. We do it without further ado, naturally, and confidently. In other words, in the beginning the motions emerge, and carefully we must do this instead of that, here and now instead of there and then (within chiefly binary practices). In time, the motions become fine-tuned, and with repetition, we become so proficient in bringing them about that we no longer have to be aware of these motions when we walk, ride a bicycle, drive a car, and so on (see Polanyi 1958, and merrell 1995b, 2000b, 2003a). In complementary fashion, if enchanted Capoeira and Candomblé are whitened and properly homogenized within the dominant culture, they can threaten to become sedimented and disenchanted —white guy rough-and-tumble Capoeira regional with hardly a vestige of its sources, or white middle class Umbanda. If this occurs, transformed forms of Capoeira and Candomblé practices can become entrenched to the extent that they compel one to go through the proper motions within whitened culture as if it were the only way, blind to any and all alternatives from the past.

During the process of sedimentation, there is a ubiquitous danger: the move toward right-side hegemony and downward toward homogeny can become tantamount to totalitarian force. I allude to the highly touted "globalization" phenomenon. The assumption has it that the ultimate goal of global pressure is worldwide homogenous culture. During globalization by multinational corporations and developed nations, hegemonic distinctions become increasingly finer to the extent that they are rendered well-nigh unidentifiable. Many cultures threaten to become one culture: a grand "McDonaldization" (Westernization) of the world (Latouche 1996; Ritzer 2000). It might appear to many onlookers that the good life is finally available to all. The world's citizens are now free mindlessly to go about their daily grind in soporific bliss. This would be tantamount to a move toward overdetermined hegemony and a simulacration of everything and everybody at the lower right-side of figure 16. Yet, citizens of the globe would be under the illusion of freedom of choice. It would be as if to say, "But of course, we all like "Coke" (or whatever other globalized product for consumption) for Coke would have become the standard. The relentless homogenizing campaign waged by Coca Cola to flatten heterogenous differences would have by and large slipped below the level of consciousness (Ortiz 1994:161–171).

I realize I stretch customary usage of the term "hegemony" to the limit here and elsewhere. However, when the term merges with "homogeny" and "heterogeny" within cultural flows: (1) distinguishability between one term and the other two becomes virtually impossible; (2) distinguishability between individual and community fades; and (3) all interdependent, interrelated interactivity becomes fused and confused to the extent that awareness of the nature of hegemony wanes. Now, in order that the pump can be primed and the process can begin anew, Plato's prisoner becomes aware of the deception, Hegel's slave becomes aware of his condition, and in everyday living we become aware of other possible ways of doing things.

This state of affairs risks culmination in utopia, *1984* or *Brave New World* style, but with a major difference: through presumably democratic processes rather than totalitarianism. Think about it. If multinational enterprisers have their day and reduce the world's cultures to a homogenized soup of humanity, what will we have? Virtual chaos. How so? If distinctions proliferate until they become so fine as to be hardly detectable, then indifference rather than difference will become the name of the game. A mindless sense of indifference will eventually prevail. Such a state of affairs will not be simply a matter of just one damn thing after another, for from one thing to another there is no difference that really makes a difference. Our differences will have become as fine as the flow of McDonald's whipped ice cream out of the immaculate stainless steel machine. Within such a milieu, there will be no possible surprises, for there will be nothing against which to gauge the surprise. There will be hardly any chance of our becoming aware of differences that are other than what we expected so we can become primed for alterations of our standard ways and means within our everyday practices. Within the homogenic mish-mash of indifference, there will be no more than bland sameness. This sameness will be tantamount to chaos, since there will be no meaningful differences. Within the chaos principle, virtually everything and anything will be possible. But we will be aware of few of the possibilities, and we will hardly ever become authors of any of the possibilities actualized, as long as we remain confined within our prison-house of bland, amorphous dough within right-side homogeny in Figure 16. There, at the ultimate extreme, we have the final stage of the Second Law of Thermodynamics, maximum entropy. Fortunately, however, as long as we are around, this state of affairs will never be reached.

What do I mean by this? I mean that such homogenic completeness and consistency are not for us. If they were, we would ultimately have fixity, and death. For example, Serge Gruzinski writes in so many words that the push of globalization is capable of "homogenizing" (my term) cultural complexity. He specifically cites the Spanish *Law of the Indies* as the Crown's grand design to create a replica of its imaginary idealized societal superorder—right-side homogeny (Gruzinski 2001:93–96). With due respect, I would beg to differ. I believe the above pages reveal that right-side homogenization can never go to completion, for process sooner or later brings in a renewed note of complexity and heterogeny; otherwise culture would come to a halt. From another point of view, Samuel Huntington's (1996) celebrated "clash of civilizations" assumes broad, quite homogenous cultural systems defined along ethno-religious lines. My problem with this idea is that a clash presupposes relative fixity between two or more entities. It is much as if there were intransigent, untranslatable (homogenous) cultural paradigms as products rather than process. Since paradigms offer few lines of mutual understanding, the only alternative is closed minds, wagging tongues, clenched fists, and a fight to the bitter end.

Otávio Ianni (2000:83–87) effectively argues that Huntington's thesis is predicated on an "Occidental backlash" over the resistance to globalization. This, he writes, is as fundamentalist a view as any other fundamentalism. It implies the dream of cultural fixity. Ianni reiterates the thesis suggested time and again in this inquiry that cultures are process. In other words, fixating right-side homogeny in figure 16 invariably melts into process, while disordering tendencies lead back to left-side possibilities. This is to say that local processes bring about change in globalizing pressures. Consequently, what looks like hegemonic globalization "is often only a means of domesticating the West, sometimes by reducing the West to the level of the comic and the trivial" (Nandy 1998:108). Indeed, I would suggest that if we wish to think globalization, we'll have to come to terms with overdetermination and inconsistency and vagueness and underdetermination and incompleteness, along with our fleshless generalizations.

How, then, can we come to more adequate terms with this homogeny-heterogeny-hegemony trio? Perhaps by returning to certain aspects of Capoeira and Candomblé living for some illustrations of the cultural logics I have been propounding. But first, let's take another look what makes Brazil Brazil: ambiguity, vagueness, and incongruous, coalescent complementarity, necessarily ingredients for a sociological illogic.

Part IV

CAPOEIRA AND CANDOMBLÉ AS CULTURAL LOGICS

Chapter Fifteen

Brazilian Haziness

Elusive Ambiguity

To recap, from emptiness to Firstness we have the overdetermined range of possibilities. Many possibilities are unavoidably contradictory and even mutually exclusive, if and when they might be actualized into Secondness. Secondness allows clear and distinct either/or bivalency insofar as possible. And Thirdness is the underdetermination of actualized Seconds in the sense that whatever there is will at some curve in the cultural stream give way to something else. Taking this into consideration, we are forced to concede that Thirdness is ultimately ambiguous. It is an incongruously, coalescently, complementary combination making up a triadic process.

Ambiguity. Outside literature and the other arts, its reputation has suffered considerable setbacks. Linked to uncertainty, indeterminacy, and duplicity, it has been severely judged as the product of sloppy and even morally bankrupt thinking. Yet all things considered, Thirdness—ideally, clear and distinct language use—especially with respect to its temporal nature, is actually shot through and through with ambiguity. As a case in point from that most rigorous of disciplines, physics, what is light according to the quantum account? It comes in the form of photons. What is a photon? Does it have wave nature or particle nature? It can be of wave nature when left alone; it is of particle nature when entering into interdependent, interrelated interaction with whatever is becoming in its immediate environment. So, what is our understanding of a photon? Physicists tell us that it can be now a wave, now a particle, and now once again a wave, and so on. Yes, but what is a photon, really? It is both wave-like and particle-like, and it is neither wave-like nor particle-like, as you wish. Or perhaps you might want to call it something else entirely. You might call it a "wavicle"—that was actually seriously proposed during the early days of quantum theory. As such, it is neither exactly wave nor particle but something else (Smith 1995). There is Firstness and Thirdness to our photon that simply will not allow us the comfortable either/or distinctions common to ideal Secondness. Yes indeed, ambiguity.

Of course we need not consult a theoretical physicist to account for ambiguity. We find it in the processes of our everyday world. Let us cast our eyes on the surface of a swimming pool on a hot and sunny summer day. What do we see? Focally speaking, we see dancing, scintillating water, and trembling pastel tiles distorted by the water. Subsidiarily or peripherally, we see the surrounding ambient. The empiricist philosopher would tell us that we see water, tiles, and refracted light, nothing more, nothing less, the combination of which makes up an object that goes by the name 'swimming pool." We see the phenomena *as* water, tiles, and refracted light, and in almost the same blink of an eye we see that it is a swimming pool. Entrenched within our habitual, sedimented ways of perceiving and conceiving, we automatically interpret the phenomena.

There is plenty of ambiguity here. Our sense and conception of water possibly includes a shimmering surface in the sunlight, and much more besides; our sense and conception of tiles possibly includes distorted images due to the refraction of light from the water in a swimming pool, and much more besides. Our sense and conception of refraction possibly includes the result of gazing at swimming pools, and much more besides. Water, tiles, and refraction can have a vast array of interpretations within different contexts, some of them apparently incongruous and even contradictory. Ambiguity is not simply defective thinking, nor does it imply a lack of intellectual rigor; it is with us in every walk of life, whether we know it or not and whether we like it or not. The phenomena of our daily activities are multivalent, not merely bivalent. Nevertheless, caught within our habitual ways that usually demand clarity and distinction, we tend to pack our sensations and interpretations into convenient pigeonholes. This simply won't fly, especially when contemplating cultural practices the likes of Candomblé and Capoeira.

THE BRAZILIAN PUZZLE

We have noted how Brazil has traditionally been a society of patronage, malícia, jeito, malandragem, and favor, among a host of other things. Take favor, once again. Those who have power, prestige, and money liberally dole out favors to those who do not so that they will remain perpetually in debt. They cannot repay their debts in the form of money, labor, and shows of proper respect so as to gain a degree of cultural autonomy, for their patron makes sure the favors outweigh the debts cancelled.

Cultural guerrillas occasionally subvert this formula. In 2001 there was a popular TV soap-opera by the name of *Porto dos Milagres* (Port of Miracles) in which a humble fisherman, Guma, rescued the patron's son who had lost his way in a small craft at sea during a violent storm. A favor had been rendered and the patron and richest person in town, Félix Guerrero, was the benefactor. Now he owed Guma a debt. He offered him a generous sum of money in order to erase the debt and then some, such that now Guma's owing Félix a favor would be implied. To his surprise, Guma refused Félix's gesture, saying that his people customarily did what they could to help each other out with no expectation of any reward. Guma's subaltern community is predicated on cooperation. The patron's traditional society is hierarchical, held together by patronizing glue. This created a dilemma for Félix. He felt compelled to pay his debt to Guma in order to maintain his lofty position in the social hierarchy. But Guma refused the reward. As a result Félix found himself in an untenable situation, and as time went on he became more and more vindictive toward Guma, because in his estimation, Guma had spit in the eye of his prestigious image.

Favor and debt, favor/debt, is basically bivalent thinking. However, a third, some mediary function, is necessary in order to complete the triadic spiral. We find such triadicity in DaMatta's work. He constructs three-tiered sets of spatial interrelationships that compose three complementary worlds: for example, we have observed his Home, Street, and Other. The Home world is tradition, the intimately personal world, where everyone enjoys her/his own identity and is recognized for it. This world is governed by loyalty, friendship, and family ties. It is a hierarchical world of subordinates and superordinates, of those who have and those who don't, of those who command and those who obey. Street life is a matter of the laws of the land as drawn up by the national constitution and legal codes. It is the arena of competitive, survival of the fittest capitalism, where all citizens are supposedly created equal and where the individual is anonymous, just another atom careening about in interaction with all other atoms. While the Home incorporates tradition, holding to vestiges of pre-Enlightenment societies, the Street is the product of modernity's Enlightenment dreams of a rational administration of human societies and emancipation for all (Hesse and DaMatta 1995).

One might incline toward the assumption that the North American community is homogenic, egalitarian, individualist, and exclusive (when entering hegemony), while Brazil is heterogenous, unegalitarian, relational, and inclusive (when entering hegemony). That interpretation would be too dualistic.

Within Brazilian hegemony, as mentioned above, there is a flattening effect on the Street and the tendency is toward homogeny, while the Home is hierarchical; hence hegemony tends to homogenize the heterogenous, but heterogeny nonetheless endures—through conformity and resistance.

Then there is DaMatta's "Other world." If I may deviate somewhat from DaMatta's interpretation in view of some of the above discussions, the Other world is the line of demarcation, the border, separating distinctions as in figures 2, 3, and 18. The border is neither here nor there nor now nor then, and at the same time it is both here and there and now and then. A person of unique value is distinguishable from a mere individual who stands alongside all other individuals, all of them of virtually the same value. Tradition is distinguished from modern Brazil. Vertical, hierarchical societal structure is distinguishable from horizontal, democratic society, and paternalistic human interdependent interrelationships based on cutthroat capitalist competition. The Home is a safe haven, while the Street is dangerous. In the Home, those who by birth, by virtue of experience, or as a result of honors bestowed on them, command respect and usually get it; in the Street he who does unto others before others do to him gets ahead (DaMatta 1995, 1997:76–78).

It would appear that one world is virtually the polar opposite of the Other: bivalence rules, dualism is the name of the game, and Secondness pervades, but not really. Whereas Enlightenment ideals are on the minds of lawmakers and written into Brazil's legal documents, corporatist, hierarchical, authoritarian tendencies remain from days long past. One of the most telling indications of this is in the custom of favor and indebtedness. This infusion of certain aspects of Home life into the Street world is possible, since the border, DaMatta's Other world, is both non-Street and non-Home. Thus Home life and Street world have something in common: they are what the Other world is not. But there is more, infinitely more so to speak. The Other world is both non-Home and non-Street, and the same time it is neither non-Home nor non-Street. As such, it can serve to tap into the virtually unlimited sphere of Contradictory possibilities of Firstness. And it can interject an indeterminate number of alternative possibilities into the Included-Middles of Thirdness to create differences, novelty. Such is Brazilian society: it is Western and, at the same time, it is not Western and it is non-Western and African and a little Amerindian and streaked with some Arabian. But not really, because Brazil is Western. Perplexing, all this. Jacques d'Adesky (2001) effectively argues in this regard that although the current Brazilian Constitution calls for a multicultural society in which all ethnicities are afforded equal treatment, nevertheless, tradition, including favor, clientelism, and whitening, continue almost unabated.

AMBIGUITY AND THE OTHER LOGIC

Brazil is one of the most multiply ambiguous cultures around. Consequently it is perhaps the supreme example of DaMatta's Other world in action. One of the most telling tales of the country's ambiguity is found in Marilena Chaui's conformity and resistance that I have made use of time and again in this inquiry. Let us see more specifically how conformity and resistance work.

From 1500 onward, Portuguese and Amerindian cultures converged and became pluralistic. Since at least 1549, Africans and Portuguese and Amerindian cultures did the same, but on a more massive scale, given the increasing Portuguese population and the importation of somewhere between 3.5 million and 5 million slaves from Africa. From the beginning, Brazilians, and Spanish Americans as well, lived under a canopy of ambiguous messages. The Iberian crowns handed down a set of laws. They were often rather idealistic documents drawn up by visions depicting how the colonies should be in the future; they were not practical documents specifying how daily affairs should be conducted according to the actual state of the colonies. Thus, from the very outset, there was a distinction between the ideal and practice, what ought to be done and what was actually done. This ambiguity has prevailed to the present.

An example: Chaui (1986:67–69) tells us that when the Brazilian government recently offered mass housing projects, the people decided it was an offer they could afford to refuse, and they constructed their own houses on whatever vacant lots were available. They re-invented the imposed idea of what a Home should be. The imposed idea was from above and hegemonic; the re-invented idea was from below and heterogenic. For them, Home was a little spot between Street and hegemonic Home. It was neither Street nor Home in the hegemonic sense; it was Other— "it's what's in the middle that counts." This is a popular cultural logic, a logic that creates lines of communication according to the will of the people in rebellion against hegemony. Another case in point: humor. The Brazilian military dictatorship (1964–1985) took on the responsibility of promoting popular culture. It patronized and financed the carnival, soccer (World Cup in 1970), and religious festivities. The intention was basically for mass support, to attract tourists, and to improve its international image. Nationalism reached a screaming pitch, and the flag became sacrosanct. All was hegemony, and everything was to be taken on a serious note, like an orderly military parade.

But jokes abounded, as if it were carnival time: conformity and resistance putting on their act. There was the satirical Samba verse: "Who discovered Brazil / It was Cabral, it was Cabral / On the day of the Carnival." To the hegemonic "Brazil, love it or leave it," came the response "Will the last person out please turn off the lights?" (Chaui 1986:89–105). This is jeito engendered cynicism with a touch of malandragem in the face of hegemonizing culture. Working class families made a show of conformity to hegemonic rules and regulations in order to survive, and with a dose of jeito they engaged in resistance practices. In these and other examples, there is more than a conceding nod toward binarity; there is the third zone, the third space, where the Other resides, in the processual flow of jeito, that creates conformity and resistance (see also Sodré 1999:258–264).

In Brazil and Spanish America, as a result of a dichotomy between ideal laws and rules of conduct and actual everyday practices, a split between private and public domains, between saintly composure in the Home- and Street-wise roguish conduct outside, also led to that notorious maxim of the Spanish colonial period, "I obey but I do not comply," briefly mentioned in chapter thirteen. At the outset the maxim appears to be basically a binary affair. "I obey" brings along the baggage of the City-of-God image. "I do not comply" puts one in the cutthroat, in-your-face, City-of-Man environment. But it goes much further than that.

For instance, Capoeira and Candomblé culture's conformity and resistance tactics are to an extent of the "I obey but I do not comply" sort. A white Brazilian counterpart to this maxim is the Afonso Arinas Law of 1951 prohibiting overt discrimination against Afro-Brazilians. So was discrimination hitherto abolished? Not really. Well, then, how did the dominant class circumvent the law? They created their own, racist oriented, cultural guerrilla tactics. One notable move is found in newspaper want ads. They began avoiding terms explicitly referring to "blackness" and "whiteness" such as "Não se aceitam pessoas de cor" (Colored people will not be accepted). They overtly implied so much, with phrases like "de boa aparência" (of good or respectable appearance), or "gente bonita" (good-looking people) (Guimarães 1995, 1997; Nascimento 2002:122). The haves seeking servants to do their work for them obeyed the law, but they didn't genuinely comply. After 1951 there was much debate over the letter and spirit of the Afonso Arinas Law, for sure. Yet, when push came to shove, noncompliance tended to prevail. It reminds one of that infamous Brazilian saying: "Para os amigos tudo, para os inimigos a lei" (Everything for your friends, the law for your enemies). Rephrasing this, one could say in a negative spirit: "the Afonso Arinas Law? Yes, in principle and as far as we 'respectable folks' are concerned. Noncompliance with the Law? Yes also, in practice with respect to those Other people." Along these lines Neusa Maria Mendes de Gusmão (1998:55) writes of a poor, landless rural family member who told her that if a large land tenant doesn't feel the need to comply with the law, then there is no need of municipal laws, nor is there any need for state or national laws.

This now reminds one in a negative light of Kant's "Argue as much as you want and about what you want, but obey!" (Kant 1983:54). Interestingly enough, Kant's advice is cited and discussed by David Owen (1994:17–21) with respect to reason and rationalism. However, hard-core Cartesian reason should not be the issue, but rather, varying styles of reasoning (Hacking 1983, 1985). We pick and choose from our repertoire of styles of reasoning whether at work, in the home, in the street, or at play. The very concept of Cartesian reason is predicated on a couple of quandaries. First, it involves the *tu quoque* argument: belief in reason requires a leap of faith as irrational as any other belief. If one wishes to found one's knowledge on reason, one errs. For reason enjoys no fixed, irrefutable corner stone (Agassi 1975; Bartley 1984). Second, according to Enlightenment principles, society must provide the wherewithal for the citizens to act freely. Ideally, to act freely, all citizens must act morally and responsibly. If they are all mature, they stand a chance of doing so. But if some of them are immature, they may fall into immoral and irresponsible behavior.

Obviously, a society of only mature citizens, all of whom behave according to rational imperatives, is a pipe dream. If the dream were realized, quite conceivably, drab sameness and indifference would prevail. Brazil—and each and every other country for that matter—are far from this dream. In Brazil, where malandragem (of the nature of a street-wise, wily, cunning, and deceptive individual) can create havoc, as well as other practices in the order of malícia, jeito, and favor, such practices can throw social ideals out of kilter. Yet, when at their best, they can help flatten and equalize society. The process of this flattening and equalizing, however, does not yield the bland product envisioned by the dream of a society liberally greased by logic and rational behavior. It is society ambiguously flowing along by way of dynamic interpersonal interdependent, interrelated interaction. This, I would suggest, applies to respectable Brazilians' noncompliance with the Afonso Arinas Law as well as to cultural guerrilla tactics in Capoeira and Candomblé living and other forms of life among the people (see in a comparable light, Goto 1988:41–44; Oliven 1982:29–31; DaMatta 1997:148–155). In this latter sense, "I obey but don't comply" creates interplay between order and disorder, with some new order emerging out of the virgule presumably separating them. This makes shambles of the notion of cultural binaries. It is like the havenots saying: "I obey, like a good citizen." And at the same time they say: "But I don't comply, for I practice jeito—or malandragem or whatever—and thus engage in cultural guerrilla activity. But this is not all bad, for in so doing, I collaborate with other like-minded members of my community to bring about something different, something new, and keep the process alive."

THE UBIQUITOUS MIDDLE

There is no simplistic dualism in a socio-cultural milieu of multiplicity, nonlinear and asymmetrical hierarchization. With a nod to DaMatta, between private life and public life, the Home and the Street, there is the both-and and the neither-nor offering an undeterminable concoction of alternative responses many of which are forthcoming in daily practices whenever and wherever.

Consequently, relations inherent in the triadic concept of the sign engulf customary polarities (colonizer/colonized, lord/serf, private/public, home/street), while the Other lurks within the virgule; it is behind the scenes, at any moment willing and ready to make its appearance and, like Exu, disrupt the action, whether to a minimal or devastating degree. Both the one horn and the other horn of the opposition used to account for the Latin American cultural scene are essential, for sure. Yet, neither the one nor the other can be absolutely prioritized. In the first place, the One term of the presumed binary needs the Other One—they are codependent—and in the second place, a third term, in fact many alternative terms, can at any given point make their presence felt either explicitly or implicitly.

The upshot is that when there are ambiguous role models, conduct is equally ambiguous. Or to put it in some of the pet terms in this essay, *coalescent, congruent, complementary* conduct is the response to ambiguity. In this respect, the implications of DaMatta's apparent Home and Street dualism placed in the light of "I obey…" give us a sense of nimble swaying, swerving, syncopated jeito practices outside, yet inside the law. "I obey" is equalizing, individualizing, and modern, while "I do not comply" remains hierarchizing, a matter of person, of tradition. Jeito practice flies in the face of behavior dictated by the code of rules and regulations such that the hierarchy of Home interrelations is flattened, and equalizing Street interrelations are hierarchized. DaMatta points out that in jeito culture, the idea of obeying all the rules is considered fit only for dimwits. If you're on your toes, you find ways to subvert legislated codes of conduct. On the one hand, in the non-personal sense you must obey the law like everybody else, but as a proper person of respect due to your family pedigree in your Home atmosphere, you must be above these non-personal laws. On the other hand, personal interrelations allow you to distinguish between yourself and merely anybody, so ordinary equalizing behavior within Street life becomes hierarchized.

It hardly needs saying that all this follows a different logic, a logic of flow and ambiguity and vagueness and mediation, where what's in the middle counts, where between one horn and the other of an opposition something can always emerge from within the Included-Middle (DaMatta 1997:82–87). As Brandão points out (1989:17–22), the Home and Street pair of terms does not create binarity; it creates complementarity. A combined logic of opposition and complementarity is in operation, especially during cultural happenings such as jeito practice, and, of course, during all facets of Capoeira and Candomblé living. And yet, binary dualist thinking manages to hang on regarding to Latin American scene. In addition to Glen Caudill Dealy's (1992) excessively dualist interpretation of Spanish America, a perusal of Ménendez Pidal (1966), Inman (1942), and West (1957) will shed more light on the problem. Indeed, Marilena Chaui (1986:109–117) observes that Brazil is like other countries where what might be called different languages (i.e., Baroque, Enlightenment, Romanticism, Positivism, Modernity, Postmodernity) are brought together in our contemporary milieu. All these countries pretend to forge the nation and create national identities. But a nation is not a thing; it has no essence. It is a practice, and the language is the language of everyday life, of conformity and resistance.

Ambiguity, the process that ever so tenuously keeps Brazil's perplexing culture in motion. And conformity and resistance, the supreme Brazilian manifestation of ambiguity. A sociological disaster all this? Yes, if by logic we are speaking of the classical variety. But an emphatic "No!", if by logic we mean living and breathing practicing philosophy within cultural flows. There is no disaster at all, in the subtle Brazilian sense. There is sociological illogic allowing for creative improvisation and subtle coping in the best way possible with whatever one has at hand. A return to Capoeira and Candomblé with respect to this theme might behoove us.

Chapter Sixteen

Capoeira, Again

HEGEMONY, CAPOEIRA STYLE

Letícia Vidor de Sousa Reis (1997) argues that the popular story about Capoeira as a form of black resistance against white rule since the time of the *quilombos* is the fabrication of wishful but misplaced hearts and minds. From the very beginning Capoeira as an art form attracted not only rebellious captive slaves and escaped slaves, but also free blacks and not a small number of whites.

Sousa Reis points out that, paradoxically, at the same time whites were attracted to Capoeira; it became in the eyes of the dominant class a threat to society. Consequently, persecution began at the same time Capoeira began to take on a little whitening here and there. Capoeira was mesticized within mainstream culture in the eyes of its practitioners; yet it was pushed to the margins of culture by conservative elements in the colonial hierarchical order. Thus, over the generations blacks and whites as well have continuously invented and re-invented the Capoeira tradition. Criminalization of the art form toward the end of the nineteenth century was a social construction, a "re-invention of tradition" in the words of Hobsbawm and Ranger (1983). The same can be said for its liberation, when it was to an extent whitened in the 1930s and 1940s finally to take on the status granted it by Getúlio Vargas as the only genuine Brazilian sport. Much the same occurred in the 1970s, when it became officially recognized and was integrated into mainstream society.

Capoeira in this manner takes on a multiplicity of faces. This left-side (figure 16) heterogenous activity was practiced by slaves, escaped slaves, free blacks, blacks conscripted into the military who used it as a form of combat,

Pardos (mulattoes), and by whites as a pastime, European immigrants fascinated by the art, and gangs of both blacks and whites among lower class urban dwellers for the purpose of assaulting and looting. Criminalization of the art was an effort to bring it under government control; it was a covert attempt to homogenize Capoeira's heterogeny (along the right-side of figure 16). Whitening was a second attempt at homogenization. The final and most successful effort to make Capoeira "respectable" came in the 1970s, when it was to an extent de-marginalized. Nevertheless, Capoeira has usually managed to resist the imposition of right-side homogeny; it has obstinately, and often with considerable effort and duress, remained basically heterogenous. If we grant the art's nature as re-invention, a social construct, we must at the same time emphasize the perpetuation of its heterogenous nature. In this manner, Capoeira's various manifestations make up an incongruously, coalescently contradictorily complementary whole. Its logic takes on our now familiar both-and and neither-nor characteristics in addition to its either/ors. It has maintained its radically pluralistic nature (Morse 1993; Cândido 1993; Fry 1991).

Capoeira Angola and Capoeira Regional Revisited

Capoeira's negative image during the first part of the twentieth century was used to justify its widespread persecution, since it was considered no more than a crime under the laws of the land. When Mestre Bimba, was granted a license to teach Capoeira, it began finding its way into the academies of physical education. Under Bimba's tutelage, there was a concerted effort to turn the art into rational, intellectualized and erudite, highly competitive sport, in contrast to what was then considered in Salvador a popular black expression. This couldn't but help create a heterogenizing tendency. The envisioned sport would be neither black nor white, or perhaps better, somewhat more black than white in order to bring about a general whitening effect. As such, it would be neither African nor purely a matter of martial arts nor music and dance and song nor a competitive struggle nor agile gymnastics nor a brutal show of strength along with the acrobatics. It would be an ethnic form, a hybrid mixture of white and black ethnicities.

What usually goes as whitening philosophy during the latter years of the nineteenth century and the twentieth century up to around the 1950s was designed eventually to snuff out African influences in Brazil. In this respect Mestre Bimba's strain of Capoeira entailed a certain degree of whitening, to be sure. But in Capoeira Regional and to an extent in Brazilian culture at large, ethnic distinctions managed to hold on. In other words, the white elite dreamed of a homogenous Brazil, racially and ethnically speaking, such that it would eventually become considerably more white than non-white. A little Afro-

Brazilian cuisine would be acceptable, even with a dash of Amerindian ingredients. National festivities would be allowed to retain their massive dose of African cultural manifestations with a sprinkling of Caboclo influence. The musicality and rhythmic voice inflections characteristic of Brazilian Portuguese would remain a matter of national pride also, as well as Afro-Brazilian music, dance and art. But, following the venerable Enlightenment pie in the sky, social, economic, and political administration, and work efficiency, would hopefully be European through and through (Skidmore 1974; Degler 1971; Fernandes 1971). Over the long haul, white, erudite culture would prevail, and Brazilian culture would be homogenized as far as possible (at the right-side of figure 16). Still, Bimba insisted on heterogeny regarding his interpretation of Capoeira Regional.

Mestre Pastinha reacted against Bimba's mesticizing or partly whitening the art. He campaigned for what we might call "African purity," while disseminating his philosophy of Capoeira Angola in contrast to Bimba's Capoeira Regional. Strangely enough, both Pastinha and racist whitening proponents denied mesticizing, but for opposite reasons. Pastinha's goal entailed a return to Afro-Brazilian roots in search of a genuine expression of Capoeira—and by extrapolation, of the Afro-Brazilian culture in general. The anti-mesticizing posture of white racists entailed a program for gradually erasing undesirable elements within popular Brazilian culture and replacing them with desirable white elements from the dominant culture. In other words, Pastinha's vision implied homogenizing of one sort (toward the left-side) while the white racists envisioned homogeny of an entirely different sort (toward the right-side).

Bimba saw no problem with mesticizing what he considered more of a competitive struggle than anything else. Pastinha emphasized deception, malícia, an encounter of wits, and even at times jocular good fun, instead of out-and-out combat. Above all, Capoeira for Pastinha was a matter of profound corporal learning; it was kinesomatic bodymindness, not mind-over-body according to the occasional conception. In fact, Pastinha is known to have declared that good capoeiristas do not move their body, but, in a manner of speaking, let their body be moved by the 'spirit." Some of his disciples contend that playing the instruments, bellowing out the chants, and making the proper moves, must be learned while Capoeira action goes on. This learning must take place within the body. It is far removed from learning by rote memorization, through books or videos, or while frolicking in the beach. The Roda is the classroom, the Mestre is the High Priest, playing instruments and chanting and allowing the body to do what it does in making Capoeira moves provides de flow of action, and in the process individuals become fused into a community. In this manner, upon re-Africanizing and homogenizing Capoeira,

Pastinha introduced a magical, sacralizing dimension to the art. Indeed, Pastinha's Capoeira Angola took on an almost religious and mystical nature.

Sousa Reis (1997:106–129) argues that, in spite of Pastinha's best of intentions, he actually re-invented a tradition. He attempted to recoup the ancient African ritualized practice of the art and in so doing ended up mythifying it. He re-made it not into what it had been, for it was always in the process of becoming something other. As a result of his efforts, Capoeira Angola became known as the "purest" form, because it was the most re-Africanized. This presupposes that there must exist what the *angoleiros* might consider an "impure" form of Capoeira. And what would this impure form be? By and large, Capoeira Regional, mesticized Capoeira. Thus it would seem that we have yet another set of cantankerous dichotomies: pure/impure, African/non-African, Angola/Regional.

This artificial dichotomization goes even further. Some whites denigrated Capoeira, both Angolan and Regional, as a "black thing." It became the target of adjectives involved in white prejudice and preconceptions: disorderly conduct, a matter of emotion rather than intellect, illogical rather than logical thinking, an activity of bums, illiterates, lazy good-for-nothings, street gangs, and in general, loiters, idlers, thieves, and accosters. These whites continued to look upon Capoeira as a no account, marginalized activity that ran the spectrum from a pastime by those who had no taste for cultured sports and recreation to rigorous training for the purpose of robbing, looting, assaulting, and raping. Yet, from the very beginning some whites, often from the margins of society by at times from the respectable folks, engaged in the art along with the blacks—although this was more prevalent in whitened Capoeira Regional than in Capoeira Angola. So the dichotomies tend to become somewhat fuzzy and ambiguous.

Moreover, dichotomous haziness emerged even within the purest of Angola practices. As we have noted regarding Candomblé, and as Waldeloir Rego (1968) writes with respect to Capoeira, the re-Africanization of Afro-Brazilian culture from the 1930s onward and especially during the 1970s and later tended to devalorize Angolan culture in favor of what were considered the more "advanced" and 'superior" cultures of northwestern Africa. Candomblé especially emphasized the Yoruba language and the tradition of the Ketu-Nagô nations, while Angola Candomblé was avoided because it was less developed and less pure. In contrast, Capoeira Angola finds its roots chiefly among the Bantu people of equatorial Africa. What became negative in Candomblé became positive in Capoeira Angola. If Capoeira Angola re-invented its tradition, then Candomblé did likewise, although the traditions were partly at odds (Dantas 1982). But that is not all. Candomblé's purity is somewhat blemished by mutual influence between African Candomblé and

Caboclo Candomblé—that adopts elements from the Caboclo or Amerindian cultures (Braga 1998). The dichotomies thus become multiply frizzled. A case in point: Mestre Rapôsa is one of the most radical Capoeira Angola purists in Salvador; yet his chief Orixá is Oxossi, customarily associated with Caboclo culture, and he is a passionate supporter of the Ara Ketu Institute, that maintains ties with its West African roots.

The Apparent Dichotomy Qualified

Still, distinctions continue to persist between Capoeira Angola and Capoeira Regional. Both forms entail a search for identity. However, while Capoeira Regional's notion of identity is more inclusive, Capoeira Angola focuses to a greater extent on black identity. While the former focuses less on its historical tradition, the latter goes back to its origins in order to reconstruct past practices. While the former becomes increasingly eclectic, incorporating elements from other forms of combative arts, the latter sticks to its noncombative origins. While the former paid the price of co-optation into Brazil's political rhetoric, the more conservative latter remained by and large apolitical. Consequently, the admittedly murky opposition, black (Angola)/white-Mestiço (Regional), still manages to win sympathizers and provoke antagonists.

If we look at this shadowy dichotomy from the vantage point of the terms constructed for this inquiry (in figure 16), the situation becomes considerably less dichotomous. There has been a tendency toward whitening in Capoeira Regional, largely because of its martial arts-like nature. This pushes it toward right-side heterogeny, and to an extent keeps the sport open to change, for it remains by and large underdetermined. Capoeira Angola, in contrast, striving to maintain its (re-invented) past, stays close to left-side heterogeny, and eases ever-so-slightly into left-side homogeny. Consequently, it tends to become overdetermined, in contrast to Capoeira Regional's underdetermination. It would appear that as overdetermined, Capoeira Angola would present virtually uncountable possibilities—including negative possibilities, improvisational play-like possibilities—in comparison to relatively underdetermined Capoeira Regional, which is basically limited to positive and rule-governed, game-like possibilities. In this sense, one might assume that Capoeira Regional's relatively probable outcome in the face of certain prevailing conditions would limit it, since the outlandishly contradictory, the bizarre and illogical, the strange and peculiarly inconsistent, would be by and large barred from its practices. And so they are often barred. Since Capoeira Regional is predicated on rule-based competitive struggle, oppositions tend to prevail between prescribed and prohibited action. But there is never a closed, no holds barred situation, for strategies still allow for a degree of improvisation. Nevertheless, given Capoeira Regional's eclectic character, the competitive game tends to gravitate toward right-side heterogeny. This is because as the purportedly rational, intellectualized form of Capoeira, freewheeling play, rampant deception, picaresque moves revealing that the capoeirista is someone other than her appearances would lead one to believe, are less common than in the more creative Capoeira Angola.

Capoeira Angola practice involves deception and malícia played to the hilt. Presumably drawing from Angolan sources, ideally, this art form should be a prime example of left-side heterogeny and downward. This would seem to limit freedom of creativity and improvisation, since ideally the *angoleiro* must remain faithful to the old ways. Not necessarily so. Like all historical artifacts, the sources of pristinely pure Capoeira are irretrievable in their original form. Also, because, as a consequence, the tradition has been to a degree re-invented; so it liberally allows for change. Thus Capoeira Angola's theoretically enjoying access to myriad possibilities, whether contradictory or inconsistent or paradoxical, affords the creative freedom one might want. All told, Capoeira Angola patterns both re-invented tradition and black ethnic re-Africanized culture. It entails adherence to a presumed past and at the same time openness to innovation. Since it is to a degree both the one and the other, there is freedom, and at the same time there are restrictions set by the imagined tradition. This both-and character of Capoeira Angola qualifies its nature as overdetermined. As such, it is always becoming something other than what it was becoming.

Capoeira Regional is basically neither black nor white, and neither a martial art nor not a martial art, strictly speaking. It is neither traditional nor modern, neither play nor fight. Rather, it is, like Capoeira Angola, always becoming something other than what it was becoming. This is the case, for, given the basically neither-nor nature of Capoeira Regional, something is always in the process of emerging between the one horn and the other of the distinction or opposition. Consequently, Capoeira Regional is more complexly mixed than Capoeira Angola. Capoeira Angola is mixed, of course, but mixture is more prominently highlighted in Capoeira Regional. In other words, Capoeira Regional is a more thoroughgoing hybrid form. As such, it is also a re-invention, or better, the re-inventing process of something that has not yet arrived rather than of some tradition in the long lost and irretrievable past.

What is the upshot of all this? That the opposition black (Angola)/ white-Mestiço (Regional) is no opposition at all, but rather, it is incongruous, coalescent complementarity. Within Capoeira in general, disciples of Mestres Bimba and Pastinha continue to perpetuate their distinctions. Capoeira Angola, devalued during the 1960s and 1970s when Capoeira Regional came on strong, was revalued during the 1980s and 1990s with the re-Africanization movement among academics and proponents of African purity. Today, the Capoeira scene is a mixed and confusing bag. "Reconstructed purity" is the ideal name of the game in some quarters, while a pragmatic form of whitening still makes a gallant attempt to wax dominant once in a while. At the same time, there are Capoeira schools in increasing number that mix the two styles, to the chagrin of the purists (Sousa Reis 1997).

Capoeira, qualified in terms of the interrelationships depicted in figure 16 and its implications, gives us a sense of multiple ambiguities, and the incongruous, coalescent, contradictory complementarity within the Brazilian cultural scene as a whole. Complexity is there to stay, and nonbinary, nonlinear logic is always in play. The whole scene gives rise to cultural process of the most ebullient possible nature.

Chapter Seventeen

Candomblé, One More Time

THE SYNCRETISM IDEA

Julio Braga (1995) takes pains to show us how Candomblé represents an undeniable focus of resistance: (1) religious resistance to the pressures of the Catholic Church; (2) resistance in terms of a representation of Africa in Brazil; (3) resistance to standard European medical practice; and (4) resistance to legal means of enacting repression of the Terreiros. These manifestations lead to the idea of a profound, unbreakable spirit found in a large number of the Afro-Brazilian people throughout the country's history.

In regard to religious resistance, we have, of course, that common label "syncretism." Today, most Terreiros are sprinkled with a few Catholic images, and many of the Catholic churches, constructed by slave artisans, bear some Candomblé images that were slipped in unbeknownst to the European architects and construction engineers. For example, the church of Rosario in the Pelourinho district of Salvador, constructed specifically by slaves and for slaves, sports a baroque column replete with a profusion of infant angels, saints, and a tangle of foliage. As one's eyes travel from top to bottom of the impressive artwork, one meets with a surprise. What do we have here? Why, it's an African Orixá figure, holding up the entire structure! Cultural guerrillas put on over on the dominant culture.

This is syncretism, for sure. It is usually taken as the fusion of ordinarily incompatible religious elements. As I have argued, there are problems with this concept of syncretism, however. *Yemanjá* doesn't really dovetail with Our Lady. Nobody would imagine that Our Lady is married to the Senhor do

Bonfim (Lord of the Good Ending), or Christ, who is often syncretized with *Oxalá*, as the husband of *Yemanjá*. *Xangô* is often syncretized with Saint Peter, who according to the local tradition was crucified. But there is nothing comparable to any crucifixion of *Xangô* in the African legends. Syncretism seems to be no more than a matter of rough analogy. This, at least, is Roger Bastide's interpretation (1955).

However, classicist and Candomblé specialist Ordep Serra writes that the Greek equivalent of the word "syncretism," *synkretismós*, was originally used to designate a political coalition between otherwise adverse factions. Later, the word was used in philosophical discourse to signify any artificial conjunction between ideas coming from distinct theoretical perspectives. This has to do with a mixture of divergent, sometimes even mutually incompatible, elements. Given this connotation, the word entered religious studies and became common in anthropological theory as a fusion of cultural phenomena that are different, and even antagonistic, into one phenomenon. Yet the two phenomena making up the fusion are often conceived in terms of their original meaning: the word "syncretism" is politicized. In Brazil, syncretism fell into almost exclusive use regarding the presumed fusion of Catholic icons and African religious elements. In fact, Serra uses the term *mixórdia* (mixed order, ordered mixture) to qualify the process. There is confusing mixture yet there is order, for things still keep their proper place (Serra 1995:196–197).

Serra, however, dubs this no more than a "confused mixture of diverse heterogeneous beliefs." It really explains nothing. He proposes, in contrast, that syncretism in a more precise sense should be considered an "intercultural structuration" which correlates mythical models and liturgies that may also engender new modes of perceiving and conceiving religious images. This implies a principle of union, for sure. But it is a union of both the one set of religious images and the other set into a whole that, when it is engendered upward, becomes neither the one nor the other but something uncommon to both sets of religious images. In this manner, the Africans practicing now Catholicism, now Candomblé, saw no pernicious contradiction at all. There was no call for concern. It was rather a matter of becoming as comfortable as possible with the new religious context in the Americas, while at the same time retaining traditional practices insofar as that might be possible (Serra 1995:197–198).

However, this does not really cut the cake either, if one of the two sets of images is prioritized, as in the case of Nina Rodrígues's (1935) studies. Nina Rodrígues writes of the blacks' "fetishist animism" that renders them largely incapable of understanding the more profound precepts of Catholic dogma; hence they needed syncretism as a sort of pedagogical crutch to aid

The Igreja dos Negros (Rosario), constructed by slaves for slaves

them in relating what was common knowledge for them with the new, alien, and exceedingly more complex Catholic concepts. The problem is that this interpretation implies racism.

A Matter of Incongruous, Coalescent Complementarity

What I would suggest, with due respect to Serra, is that there is neither exactly a fusion nor a practical—call it pedagogical if you wish—combination. Rather, in the terms of this essay there is interdependent, interaction between the one set of images and the other such that incongruous, coalescent complementarity emerges.

This is to say that in the so-called syncretistic image there is the one set of images and there is the other set of images, contradictorily speaking. The whole concoction of images can exist side by side as possibilities within the overdetermined sphere of Firstness or homogeny (I refer once again to figure 16). They are there and ready to be selected and appropriately distinguished. When so selected and distinguished, they enter the domain of hegemony, where any and all categories are at least for now acceptable and generally accepted as part of a given culture's imperatives. There is representation here, and there is resistance to the representation—Julio Braga's second form of Candomblé resistance. This resistance simply cannot remain content with what is given, imposed, inculcated, and even brutally shoved onto the African slaves. There is consequently a process of migration toward the underdetermined sphere of Thirdness, or left-side heterogeny. Here, there is neither the one set of images nor the other set, but rather, emergence of something new within the two horns of the opposition. The Principle of Included-Middles comes into effect. There is conformity, for the Africans have embraced Catholicism—as if to say "I obey"—and there is resistance, for they hold onto their tradition, "but I don't comply". There is obedience and noncompliance, and there is also disobedience and compliance. There is neither the one nor the other but something else, something unlike anything in Africa. In this respect, those who in recent decades have fought for re-Africanization of Candomblé and a return to its original purity are in a no-win situation. The past is gone; it is irretrievable. And the present offers incessant change: process. If syncretism there must be, it is process, not product.

Then there is Candomblé resistance against standard European medical practice. From the very outset Candomblé as physical therapy, psychiatric counseling, and a means for coming into a spiritual balance with other members of the community and with nature, was labeled witchcraft, useless fetishism, or primitive and irrational responses to natural maladies, by Western medical practices as they existed during the times. The explicit goal was to civilize the Africans by indoctrinating them with rational, scientific medicine—or at least what was considered scientific at the time. In the Europeans' effort, whether well meaning or not, and whether the means were humanitarian or brutally cruel, there was massive misunderstanding on the part of both parties. The Africans did not see the value of this strange new science called medicine, so they managed also to hold onto many facets of their own tradition. The Europeans, from their point of view, tended to integrate negative interpretations of the Africans' Orixás and the concepts they implied into their own Catholic and scientific cosmology. Consequently, Exu, messenger, mediator, trickster, and he who keeps guard on the household, was due to his role as trickster associated with evil and Satan. Moreover, bells and percussion instruments used to call the Orixás became for the Europeans no more than the hubbub typical of child-like, primitive religions. *Búzio* tossing was looked upon as so much superstition; so also with the use of amulets. Interrelations between *Xangô* and lightning and thunder, *Ogum* and iron, *Yemenjá* and the sea, *Oxossi* and hunting, and so on, were considered no more than the product of naïve imagination (Braga 1995:131–134).

Braga compiles trial testimonies given during prosecution of Pais- and Mães-de-Santo to show how the people within their oral tradition were coherent in the accounts of Candomblé practices and rational in the organization of their thoughts. Nevertheless, documented comments on testimonies offered during depositions made liberal use of pejorative adjectives, thus affording hardly any credence to the Africans as witnesses to Candomblé ceremonies. The effect was inordinately negative. Braga maintains that this is viable proof of the prejudices, presuppositions and preconceptions of the times. The Africans were undoubtedly aware of this manipulation of their coveted religious worldview. Yet, as subalterns, they hardly had any alternative but to grin and bear it (Braga 1995:125–145; see also appendix B).

Grin and bear it, they did. But they did not simply consign themselves to silence and passivity. They engaged in subtle cultural guerrilla resistance. It was a polite nod when the European master offered medical advice, and then off to commune with the Orixás and remedy one's ills by traditional methods. Robert Vocks (1997) gives ample demonstration how the Africans brought whatever herbal medicines they could from the homeland, they learned from the Caboclos or Amerindians, and they took to using native Brazilian herbs in place of unavailable African herbs by analogies between them, and usually by hook or by crook they met with success—actually, since the two continents were once joined, much Brazilian and African flora bear close relationships. The African slaves used what they had at hand, and if there was nothing, they improvised. Improvisation, in fact, became the chief modus operandi among

Candomblé practitioners, and it persists to this day. They perpetuated their tradition however they could. They conformed through resistance and they resisted through conformity.

The *Ogã* as Agent of Mediated—Yet Not Quite Coopted—Resistance

Candomblé from the beginning found yet another form of resistance within conformity in their *Ogãs*—initiates who act as dignitaries of the Terreiro. *Ogãs* perform a very important role in Candomblé ceremonies. I have left this role to the final chapter on Candomblé for a specific reason. The role beautifully illustrates the breakdown of either/or categories; thus it falls in line with the theoretical premises that guide part III of this inquiry.

Due to repressive measures brought about by the police force representing the political system, Pais- and Mães-de-Santo eventually created patronage networks with certain sympathetic members of the white society, many of them of high economic and social status, to serve as spokespeople and protectors. These white representatives of black Candomblé communities became known as Ogãs. The Ogã is usually a prestigious individual. He is often—though not always—white and from the dominant society. When he is appointed as an Ogã, an honorary member of the Candomblé community, he brings social, political, and economic support. He also serves as a mediator between the Candomblistas and police, politicians, and the white society. Through the Ogãs's function, it becomes possible that whites and Afro-Brazilians might hold hands in a rather tension ridden form of cultural symbiosis. It is a somewhat uncomfortable symbiotic interrelationship however, because the white Ogãs recognize the power Orixás hold over black consciousness, and they obviously realize that it would be expedient to bring this powerful hold on the Afro-Brazilians' mind into interrelationship with the dominant society by way of their own mediation (Kraay 1998:15–16).

The danger, of course, rests in the possibility that the Terreiros might become co-opted into white society—as at times it seems to have been the case among Umbanda groups (Chaui 1986). However, this usually doesn't happen, as the Candomblé faithful quite effectively resist infiltration of white elements into their ceremonies. In other words, the Terreiros generally maintain their re-invented world of the Orixás intact—albeit within the process of becoming—while availing themselves of protection by way of mediation offered by their strategically chosen white spokespeople, the Ogãs (Silveira 1988).

Julio Braga, among other scholars, emphasizes the fact that the Ogãs by no means invariably came from the upper echelons of exclusively white society. That idea, he writes, has unfortunately become a commonplace assumption among scholars. Actually, a number of Ogãs were black and of humble origins. They were selected specifically because they could sympathize with the unfortunate plight of the Candomblé communities and their worship, and at the same time they could collaborate and participate in the activities, for they had the Orixás "in their blood," so to speak; the Orixás made up part of their ethnicity. In most of these cases, selection of an Ogã revolved around prestige within the Afro-Brazilian society, renowned wisdom, and certain notable charisma. These Ogãs might not have been capable of playing the role of protectors and mediators as effectively as the white Ogãs, but their ethnic identity offered other advantages. Regarding the Ogã as protector, Nina Rodrígues writes:

> The persecution directed toward the Candomblés, and the bad reputation they had as primitive fetishist cults brought about the need for strong and powerful protectors that would be capable of guaranteeing police protection. These protectors, that might be initiates into Candomblé or not, though in either case they must be believers of Candomblé, or at least manifest sympathy for the Candomblé cause, receive in return for their service the title of Ogã. (Nina Rodrígues 1935:70)

Qualifications for the position of Ogã obviously included certain social prestige within and outside the religious group, independently of the social situation of he who carries the title, be he black or white, rich or poor—and, I might add, since Afro-Brazilian culture is traditionally patristic, Ogãs are invariably male. This necessary social standing takes on increased importance in view of the fact that

> the Ogãs make up a specific priesthood; they are masculine members of candomblé that never enter into trance [never participate directly in the ceremonies] and take care of administrative, financial, and diplomatic affairs, such as preparation of the ceremonies. Within the structure of the cults in Bahia, this priesthood was maintained in all its complexity, becoming a special branch of the organization: certain whites that had acquired elevated official social status and who sympathized with candomblé practices took on, as Ogã, the function of protectors of the cult. (Silveira 1988:182)

The Pais- or Mães-de-Santo did not select Ogãs. According to tradition, the

Orixás selected them. It was strictly a spiritual affair. Once an Ogã was selected, he must purchase a very special chair, usually ornately hand carved, usually with silk lining, to be placed at the right side of the Pai- or Mãe-de-Santo during Candomblé ceremonies. The Ogã could be consecrated only after the chair had been purchased and placed in its proper position. In this manner the chair occupied a very special point at the periphery of the circle around which the Candomblé ceremony rotates (Bastide 1973:325).

It has become obvious, in light of the above, that the religious function carried out by the Ogã requires much time and expense. There is considerable sacrifice. The Ogã, especially if white, is often set up for rebuke from members of the white society for lending sympathy and support to this "wretched fetishist cult." Nevertheless, if he expects to carry out his duties properly, he must go to bat for the Candomblé community, protest the injustices, negotiate with political authorities for police protection and for cessation of police repression at the command of prejudicial civil authorities, and keep an eye on bureaucratic measures that might be detrimental to the interests of the Candomblé community.

In short, the Ogã contests and negotiates. Insofar as possible, he maintains his former social standing: there is conformity. At the same time he fights for Candomblé rights: there is resistance, sometimes not very passive. As a general rule of thumb, the Ogã conforms; thus he has a foot within hegemony (from figure 16). He also resists, with the other foot within both homogeny and heterogeny. As mediator, he oscillates between homogeny and hegemony and between hegemony and heterogeny. He is part Exu, injecting massive doses of malícia into the dialogic give-and-take. When necessary, he becomes black, white, or Mestiço. He can now take on an African purity role, now a whitening philosophy role, whichever serves his purpose best according to the occasion. He now becomes the voice of the dominant class, now the subservient class, in order more effectively to make his point. He becomes a man for all possible reasons, an advocate within diverse cultural logics (Braga 1998).

Thus the Ogã is both inside the Candomblé community and inside the dominant society. This is the stage of possibilities of interdependent, interrelated, interactive resistance within conformity. At the same time he is neither exclusively of the one community nor the other. If the Ogã is effective in creating subtle strategies of resistance, the emergent means and methods used within the context of ordinary social conventions are more often than not unexpected, always presenting a new angle that sets the dominant society back on its heels, creating situations with which the white community doesn't know how to cope. Conformity and resistance: two faces with the same mask, or two masks intermittently placed on the same face, according to how you wish to take the phenomenon of Ogã-ship. Without the incongruous, coalescent, complementarity inherent within the office of the Ogã, Candomblé survival value would have been more severely limited.

BRINGING LEGAL STATUS TO CANDOMBLÉ LIFE

As noted in part II, Candomblé up to the 1970s was subjected to every imaginable form of persecution, discrimination, and rejection, usually by the letter of the legal codes that had been written by whites and intended to be for the benefit of whites. In large part due to the persistent work of Edison Carneiro, Arthur Ramos, poet Gilka Machado, dance artist Evos Vobesias, novelist Jorge Amado, and Professor Donald Pierson of the University of Chicago, the virtually nonexistent status of Candomblé changed.

This change came in the form of issues pressed by the above-mentioned scholars and artists in conjunction with a few newspaper reporters—although most newspapers, co-opted by the hegemonic society, followed the hard line approach and proposed eliminating Candomblé practices. This work awakened rebellious sentiments among the Afro-Brazilians, even though they had no means institutionally for expressing their grievances. Eventually, legislature was enacted allowing for the existence of alternative beliefs alongside the official religion, Catholicism. But I'm getting ahead of myself. Allow me to summarize the story provided us by Julio Braga, albeit in piecemeal fashion due to limited time and space.

In the early part of the twentieth century, Candomblé was labeled a "fetishist practice" and a "false medicine." This alone would be enough to strike a note of fear, ire, and contempt in the hearts and minds of devout Catholics. However, although Brazil's first Constitution of 1824 declared the Catholic Church the official religious doctrine of the land, it permitted other religions as long as they confined their activities solely to houses designed specifically for worship. It seemed quite clear that there should be no persecution of alternative beliefs, even though they might be considered "fetishist." Candomblé as medicinal and therapeutic practice, however, was another story. Here, the boundary between sacred and profane was infringed, at least according to the Catholic way of thinking. The Catholic way assumed that Candomblé as medicine entered into competition with secular medical and pharmaceutical professions in the dominant society; hence Candomblé medicine should be barred. In reality, the Candomblé way was something else.

In the first place, the Candomblé way was the product of hegemonic or binary thinking of the right side of figure 16. Candomblé as a holistic worldview was actually in competition with no other institution, social class, or political dogma. It simply was what it was in and of itself. It was a matter of left-side homogeny and heterogeny. When put into practice, it became process, process in the manner of perpetually bringing the whole of all tensions into interaction such that there was neither the one characteristic of the patient nor the other nor the other, and so on, but rather, emergence of something else hopefully capable of a more healthy balance. In a nutshell, this is Candomblé medical practice. It was a matter of finding a balance and dynamically keeping it, while the practice was in the process always of becoming something other. It was not a matter of patient with symptom here and remedy there and the remedy must eliminate the symptom, all of the nature of binary thinking. Candomblé medicine is holistic: patient and symptom and natural remedies are all in interdependent interrelation with one another but for some reason or other a healthy balance has been lost, and the task at hand is to re-establish the balance.

In the second place, the dominant class saw Candomblé medicine cutting into the market, and called for legal measures to prevent competition through alternative religious beliefs. This is binary capitalist thinking; indeed, it is protectionist thinking. Of course the rhetoric focused on witchcraft, primitive magic, as well as the use of teas made of the most "vulgar" and useless plants in the vicinity, as part of the Candomblé peoples' purportedly false medicine. Yet, the fact remains that what the dominant society clamored for was perpetuation of Western medical practices and economic protectionism. There was no knowledge of, nor was there any sympathy with, this alternative medicine. There was no awareness that this form of medicine was so radically different from their accustomed Western variety as to be virtual incompatible with it. Consequently, Candomblé medicine was simply dubbed "false" (Lühning 1999; Rodrígues and Caroso 1999; Serra 1999).

The social composition of Bahia during the first half of the twentieth century saw Candomblé relegated to the status of what the dominant class called a "vulgar spiritism" and "illegal practice." This was at a time when another aspect of the whitening policy, the highly eclectic hybrid religion, Umbanda, was enjoying increasing respectability. Umbanda was considered "high spiritism," while Candomblé practiced this vulgar or low spiritism—that includes a gamut of other qualifiers such as witchcraft, charlatanism, and black magic. A clash of social classes was obviously behind this view, since Umbanda was whiter, having attracted quite a few middle class believers. This high/low categorization obviously served to aid and abet the dominant mode of dichotomous thinking (Braga 1995:154–165).

During the 1920s and 1930s, newspaper and magazine reports usually favored the dominant society's view supporting police action designed severely to restrict and prevent Candomblé observance altogether whenever and wherever possible. Obviously the publishing houses feared political repression if they didn't conform to the dominant view, and reporters feared for their jobs. During moments of greatest persecution directed toward Candomblé communities, it became imperative that they organize themselves in Western fashion as a unified block in order to combat their oppressors. Organization began in 1937 with the *Second Congresso Afro-brasileiro* (Second Afro-Brazilian Conference). Edison Carneiro led the proceedings, as petitions were made to various government officials from the Governor of the State of Bahia downward.

Shortly thereafter, the *Conselho Africano da Bahia* (Bahian African Counsel), made up of Pais- and Mães-de-Santo and Ogãs, was organized for the purpose of taking African based religions outside the jurisdiction of police discrimination and brutality. On August 3, 1937 the organization changed its name to *União das Seitas Afro-Brasileiras* (Union of Afro-Brazilian Sects), with representation from each Candomblé Terreiro that would take on the responsibility of pressing the police and political authorities to end abuses of the Terreiros and candomblistas (Braga 1995:168).

Eventually, the Terreiros acquired legal status. Most noteworthy, during the 1980s, with the program of re-Africanization, the Orixás as symbols of Africanism became symbols of Bahian culture in general. Images of the Orixás began popping up everywhere, in public places, in business establishments, in white and Afro-Brazilian homes alike, and they became one of the principal themes during Carnival time. Whitened Umbanda and other eclectic religious expressions found a home in Rio de Janeiro and further south, but they never met with the same success in Bahia. There, Candomblé became the chief alternative. But, as in the case of Capoeira, there was no return, nor could there have been a return, to the original pristine form of Candomblé. Candomblé, Candomblé and its ongoing interrelated interaction with Catholicism, Candomblé and Caboclo expressions, Candomblé and popular art, political rhetoric, and everyday life, and Candomblé commercialized for tourism, were always in the process of becoming something different. In this regard, Serge Gruzinski (2001:58–61) writes that all cultures have always been in flux to one extent or another; there is no such thing as a stable beginning, a rock-solid foundation. In other words, in all cultures there is always mixture. In sum, today's Candomblé is underdetermined, incomplete, and always in the act of becoming. As a holistic religion, a therapeutic practice, and a general view of the world, it enjoys homogenic underpinnings. After engaging in legal resistance, Candomblé was in the process of becoming mainstream. Like Capoeira, it has consequently become increasingly complex, like all of Brazilian culture. Both Capoeira and Candomblé, by way of conformity and resistance through cultural guerrilla tactics, have improvised with whatever happened to be at hand for the purpose of survival and sanity, and in order to salvage some vestige of Afro-Brazilian ethnic identity that was, is, and will always be in the process of becoming something other (for further reading on this Candomblé characteristic, see Agier 1995; Gonçálves da Silva 1999; Leão Teixeira 1999; Epega 1999; Santos 1998a, 1998b).

I would suggest that the task now at hand for Candomblé as well as for Capoeira is to stand firm against co-optation by populist politicians, against becoming the object of commercial and tourist hype and hoopla, against globalizing pressures to disseminate heterogenically along the right-side of figure 16 and downward toward homogeny. In other words, if Candomblé and Capoeira can never fully recover their roots, so be it. They have coped in the past and they will continue to do so. However, if they allow themselves to be co-opted, it will surely result in severe blows to their emerging identity and their dignity.

Afterthoughts

You have likely questioned my compulsion to reiterate the terms interdependent, interrelated interaction, and incongruous, contradictory complementarity, among others. By no means do I offer them for your contemplation with the idea of providing a definitive answer to the excruciatingly difficult questions regarding one of the most complex cultural processes on the globe. I simply offer them for your contemplation as a possible alternative to the various and sundry theoretical postures from within the cultural studies milieu in its diverse guises.

The first set of terms—interdependent, interrelated interaction—could easily be taken for a good/bad, female/male, black/white, slave/master, and so on, dialectic. But these terms could only be construed in this manner if the second set of terms—incongruous, contradictory complementarity—didn't exist. In concert, the implication of the two sets of terms blows binary logical and classical reason to smithereens. In other words, interdependent, interrelated interaction might presumably be construed as rock-solid concepts if it were not for incongruous, contradictory complementarity, which melts them into thin air. This concert of terms keeps the idea of process alive. The concert's processual nature is especially illustrated by the Latin American cultural scene, where one is reminded of a few verses from Caetano Veloso's song, "Americanos" (North Americans), where: "White is white, black is black, and mulatta, there's no such thing. Gay is gay, macho is macho, woman is woman, and money is money. That's how rights are bargained for, granted, won and lost up there [in the United States]. Down here [in Brazil], indefinition is the rule, and we dance with a grace that I myself can't explain." In reference to Veloso's song, Hermano Vianna (1999:108) reminds us that in Latin America, 'the rule" of indefinition [between black and white, man and woman, the big house and slave quarters] is still viewed as our principal characteristic, our great particularity, that which imparts our special grace." Indefinition: another way of saying incongruous, contradictory complementarity.

Indefinition flows along in an unpredictable world, a world of uncertainty and surprise, a self-organizing world, a world perpetually blooming forth its novelty. It is a world who's only claim to being or fixed essence is the being of its becoming and the becoming of its being. The watchword is novelty, incessant novelty. Hence whatever is becoming is tinged with the image of its past becoming and it gives uncertain promise—hence often a surprise—with respect to its future becoming. This is to say that what is becoming is in the process crossing over into what it was not becoming, for it is now becoming something that is difference becoming, becoming differently. Everything is becoming some other becoming. A line is crossed; a border is transgressed; a mark of distinction falls into disarray such that there is no distinction worthy of making a distinction because what is becoming is what it was and it is not what it was and it is neither what it was nor was it not what it was. It was, is, and will have been, process, just process. This processual philosophy, I must add, finds inspiration in late twentieth-century "complexity physics" (Prigogine 1980, 1997; for some of my work bearing on the philosophy of complexity and process, see merrell 1998, 2000c, 2002, 2003a.)

Capoeira and Candomblé life is thoroughly processual. It is always in the process of change, in spite of the re-Africanizers and the Capoeira *angoleiros*, who might wish to stop becoming in its tracks. For instance, each July I leave Salvador for my yearly journey back to Purdue University where I will be going through the motions for the next nine months. Then, in May of the following year I return to the city. Everything is familiar; yet it has changed. Most striking of all, some of the Capoeira songs that as far as I know have never actually been written down, following Mestre Rapôsa's strictly oral tradition, have changed. The songs I once painfully learned sport a few changes in the lyrics, some of the voice inflections are now other than what they were, the instruments are now played with a few well nigh imperceptible alterations—even by the Mestre—and most significantly, some of the syncopated nuances have been replaced by others (or has my memory failed me?... perhaps, since memory is also process). There is sameness within difference, difference within sameness. Metamorphosis took place. I find myself having to begin learning anew. But after all, this was inevitable.

Capoeira and Candomblé life were born out of the need to cross boundaries, to erase them, and to create new boundaries, in order to perpetuate life's processes and live within them to see another day. Capoeira and Candomblé can never come to a standstill. If they did, they would no longer be worthy of their names. They would go the way of other crystallized, automatized, mind-numbing cultural practices whose change is so minimal all vestiges of enchantment have fled. Metaphorically speaking, Capoeira and Candomblé manage to hold onto their enchanting qualities for the same reason that one's rapid bodily movement can carry one away and into a vertiginous swirl. Capoeira and Candomblé emerged from apparent mimesis—movements that looked like fun and play and dance, Orixás that took on the characteristics of Catholic figures of worship—but they were actually becoming something other than their appearance—moves that could be used for defensive measures if and when necessary, ceremonies of worship that evoked the slaves' African past. After the body rapidly gyrates in clockwise and then counterclockwise direction, up high and mighty and down low and dirty, it tries to maintain balance, now to one side and now to the other side, now to the front and now to the back, with the sensation that swirling movement hasn't yet ceased. The vertigo remains; uncertainty lingers on; there is incongruity, and a complementarity of contradictory tendencies. This is Capoeira and Candomblé feeling and sensing at its best. There is neither fight nor play, neither right nor wrong, neither purity nor hybrid nor syncretism, and above all, there is neither good nor evil. Capoeira and Candomblé are all that, and more.

Spontaneity (Firstness) is an unpredictable, swirling, swerving, spiraloid. This is perhaps most typical of Exu, the trickster—perpetual disequilibrium, asymmetry, imbalance, when things seem to be flying out of control, toward disorder. Oxalá is prototypically temperate and judicial, the produce of wisdom (Thirdness)—rhythm—that brings us back to order. Exu experience is disconcerting, veering toward neurosis; Oxalá experience is a return to renewed harmony. Put the two together and you have what in the Western modernist sense might be called a "magical world," a "world of enchantment," where experience creates unlimited possibilities only the wildest imagination can hope to encompass. This is of course a far cry from our modern so-called disenchanted world, we might wish to respond with smug assurance.

And yet, perhaps our disenchantedness is not as pure as we would like to believe. For example, we presumably disenchanted know-it-alls confidently enter the virtual world of the Internet. But unless we are computer scientists, we don't have an inkling as to how what our eyes gaze at on the monitor came about. It is as mysterious and magical for us as were the guns and cannon for the Amerindians in the Caribbean when initially confronting the Spaniards with plunder, wealth, and rape on their minds. But we self-satisfied internauts do not think of our computer innards in the way the Amerindians remained enchanted with their gods and at the outset with European technology. We assume that if we so desired, we could take a few courses and master the hardware. So we think we remain disenchanted.

As Max Weber (1965:139) puts it with respect to the disenchanted, hyperintellectualizing and rationalizing Westerner:

> The increasing intellectualization and rationalization do *not*, [...] indicate an increased and general knowledge of the conditions under which one lives. It means something else, namely, the knowledge or belief that if one but wished one *could* learn it at any time. Hence, it means that principally there are no mysterious incalculable forces that come into play, but rather that one can, in principle, master all things by calculation. This means that the world is disenchanted.

Yes, in principle, there seem to be no limits. Many aspects of our disenchanted world are now formalized in mathematical symbols. According to those who hold faith in modernity's promises, in principle the entire world can be formalized, and it will be, once the scientists get it all figured out. The most disenchanted among us are confident that the coveted pot of gold, ultimate knowledge, is just around one of the curves on the Royal Road to Truth. Indeed, Weber's "rationalization" places us within an iron cage and throws away the key according to one particular assumption. However, this assumption doesn't take into consideration the possibility that disenchantment cannot help but initiate a process of re-enchantment with and from within science and technology, and to an extent the arts. This is not the same form of enchantment, yet it is enchantment all the same (see Bennett 2001; Berman 1981; Ianni 2000). Perhaps the "end-of-science" notion that has recently caught on in various academic circles could hold the key to such re-enchantment (Horgan 1996).

We think we have taken the magic out of our world and replaced it with reason. But in the final analysis we have no more than knowledge, in principle, of our world and ourselves. The problem is that this in-principle principle leaves us huddling in the cold while gazing at the big wide world out there, rather than entering into and participating with the great drama of the universe's becoming.

Appendix A

ORIXÁ	NATURAL ELEMENT	HUMAN FUNCTION	HUMAN QUALITY, ACTIVITY	COLOR	DAY	SYNCRETIC LINK
Exu	Fire	Communication	Messenger, Trickster	Red, Black	Monday, Friday	Satan
Ogum	Iron (metals)	Metallurgy, War	Violence, Virility	Dark Blue, Red	Tuesday	Saint Antonio
Oxóssi	Jungle	Hunting	Provider, Agility	Light Blue, Green	Thursday	Saint George
Obaluaiê	Earth	Medicine	Health and Sickness	Purple, Black, White	Tuesday	Saint Roque
Ossaim	Plants	Medicine	Health and Sickness	Green, White	Monday, Thursday, Saturday	Saint Benedict, Saint Roque
Oxumaré	Rainbow		Serpent, Continuity	Green, Yellow	Tuesday	Saint Bartholomew
Xangô	Lightning, Thunder	Justice	Vanity, Royalty, Wealth	Red, White	Wednesday	Saint Jerome, Saint Peter
Oxum	Sweet Water	Procreation	Fertility, Love, Vanity	Yellow	Saturday	Our Lady of the Candeias, of the Conception, and of the Appearance
Yemanjá	Sea Water	Procreation	Fertility, Maternity	Light Blue	Saturday	Our Lady of the Seamen, and of the Conception
Iansã	Wind, Tempest		Sensuality, Courage, Spontaneity	Red, Purple, Rose	Wednesday	Saint Barbara
Oxalá	Air	Creation	Creation of life, Patience, Wisdom	White	Friday	Christ, Our Lord of the Good End (Bom Fim)

A SELECTION OF THE ORIXÁS AND THEIR PROPERTIES

Admittedly, the problem is that this table of the Orixás is all too convenient. It might have some heuristic value. But its condensing the Orixás into what might be taken as a fixed set of pigeon-holes textualizes and thus does violence to their very nature: they tend to be taken as either/or affairs. Even though in a manner of speaking this condensation "democratizes" the Afro-Brazilian deities, they may be textualized so as hopefully to give them meaning, that meaning is to an extent what they are not, for they are always also something else. In fact, any and all definitions of the Orixás invariably miss the mark. They have been variously qualified as "anthropomorphized forces of nature" (Walker 1990), "vibrations of elemental natural forces" (Cacciatore 1977), "African nature spirits" (Wafer 1991), "personalized natural phenomena" (Berkenbrock 1999), the "force emerging from the head (or mind)" (Aflalo 1996), and a system of interrelationships much like psychoanalysis (Browning 1995). After all is said and done, the esoteric sense of the Orixás is virtually impossible to translate, though it can be condensed and textually analyzed. One timely observation has it that:

> Fieldwork interviews suggest shifts in contemporary understandings of orixás from those that were articulated in accounts of traditional Candomblé. Even among priests, definitions of orixás run the gamut of abstractions ... Among less articulate practitioners, the semantic field widens even further, and nonpracticing sympathizers often invoke orixás much as they would an astrological birth sign, such that the query "Who is your orixá?" functions alongside "What's your astrological sign" (Johnson 2002:171)

Condensation of the Orixás can end in such vulgarization; yet, heuristics can at least give a rough sense of their nature, that is, if one remains mindful that they simply cannot be hogtied and staked down at some particular place. With this in mind, please take the above table in whichever manner you wish.

Appendix B

SOME ASPECTS OF CANDOMBLÉ AS PRACTICING PHILOSOPHY

The proud European conquerors of this promising New World, the Americas, began trying to manipulate the nature of Candomblé practices the African slaves re-created in their own grave new world. They reduced some of the religious and philosophical underpinnings from Candomblé to Christian religious concepts. They thus rendered the slaves' religious practice an otherworldly preoccupation having little to do with the physical world or the idea of kinesomatic bodymind improvement within its natural setting by conscious and conscientious individuals and communal practices.

Candomblé's importance to everyday life was consequently masked, falsified, translated into what it never was and could never have become.

Religion. the word signifies *re-ligate*," a re-tying, re-binding, and a bringing something together with something else to establish a union that once was, but it was ruptured. And what was this union? In the Christian sense it signifies the conjunction of mere mortals and the Supreme Being, renewed linkage of temporality and eternity, finitude and infinity, and discontinuity and continuity. It implies a re-union of human souls with the Creator. This is far from the conception of Asian religion-philosophy as well as Candomblé. God defined in the West as Creator and provider, remains basically outside Buddhist, Taoist, and African thought. Asian thought and Candomblé and other African world visions are not centered around a sole Creator of all that is, but rather, they focus on an impersonal universe of interdependent, interrelated, interactive parts that are absolutely nothing—they are emptiness, empty of any and all attributes—as raw individuals. The universe's interdependent, interrelated, interactive atoms take on their function only when they enter into the flow of becoming. There is no flow unless each and every part provides its role and its function; there are no parts unless they are in the flow.

There is indeed an affinity between African and Asian world visions, especially, I would submit, found in Buddhism. Buddhist cosmology entails a world in continuous and sustaining process. All things are codependent and interrelated. This also holds for one's capacity for understanding and knowledge: one know things for what they are in the process of becoming, for one interacts with things as they are becoming. One's knowing as an open process does not simply involve believing, thinking, conjecturing, and asserting; it also involves *kinesomatic* acting and doing; in short, it involves living. In this manner, knowing cannot be conceived as simply a mental act but must be also considered corporeally and as a matter of personal action in an open-ended process of change. When one says one knows, what one knows is in large part portrayed through what one does and how one does it. There is no need to have an independent methodology with which to seek knowledge or to gain knowledge. Knowledge comes from one's interdependent interrelationships and one's interactivity with and within one's world.

In Buddhist philosophy, as in Candomblé, there is no dichotomy between object and subject; there is no abstraction of the object from the existing relationship between the subject and object as sustained by the cosmological process of reality. No abstraction of method or methodology could even arise. This lack of methodological consciousness bespeaks an underlying continuum of subject- object interaction. It has the merit of allowing close and intimate interaction between subject and object which is meaningful in producing interhuman harmony. This lack of dichotomous separation between subject and object did not produce a sufficient distance necessary for objective and rational knowledge in the abstract and theoretical sense as one would find in modern sciences. It would not be conducive to a more objective evaluation of intellectual education in scientific knowledge and its consequences for planning purposes. Nevertheless, this is what the lack of methodological consciousness means in Buddhist and Candomblé philosophy. It lacks methodological consciousness because it has something in its place, namely, the goal of achieving harmony between the human person and nature as well as among other people.

Like Buddhism, in Candomblé there is no Christian sort of deity who created everything and now keeps it all going—whether creator of the natural hierarchy of things where all has its place or the winder of a cosmic Newtonian clock. There is no deity directly responsible for human souls; rather, we are all responsible for ourselves and for maintaining our own balance with ourselves and our surroundings and ourselves and other selves. There is no distinction between subject and object and individual and community and self and other. Buddhism and Candomblé are philosophy-religions in the broadest sense.

A case in point. In June of 2001 distinguished scholar Agnes Heller delivered the keynote address at a conference at the Federal University of Bahia in Salvador. During her discussion she repeated alluded to philosophy, but obviously the references were restricted to Western philosophy. After her talk, an Afro-Brazilian, in traditional African garb, meekly suggested that in Bahia many people held a philosophy that was not entirely of the Western tradition. Without allowing him to finish, she shot back that there is only one philosophy, and it is predicated on the tradition originally established by Greek thought. Silence followed. There was respect, but apparently no unanimous consent. Obviously, on the one hand, Heller the Westerner knew how to speak, and she did so authoritatively. But was the silence proof that the subaltern simply couldn't speak? I would like to think not.

References

Abe, Masao (1985). *Zen and Western Thought*. Honolulu: University of Hawaii Press.
Abram, David (1996). *The Spell of the Sensuous*. New York: Random House.
Aflalo, Fred (1996). *Candomblé: Uma visão do mundo*. São Paulo: Editora Mandarim.
Agassi, Joseph (1975). *Science in Flux*. Dordrecht, The Netherlands: D. Reidel.
Agier, Michel (1998). "Between Affliction and Politics: A Case Study of Bahian Candomblé." In *Afro-Brazilian Culture and Politics: Bahia, 1790s to 1990s*, H. Kraay (ed.), 134–157. New York: M. E. Sharpe.
Almeida, Bira (1986). *Capoeira: A Brazilian Art Form*. Berkeley, Calif.: North Atlantic Books.
Almeida, Raimundo de (1982). *Bimba: Perfil do Mestre*. Salvador, Brazil: Centro Editorial e Didático da UFBA.
——— (1994). *A saga de Mestre Bimba*. Salvador: Ginga Associação de Capoeira.
Amado, Jorge (1969). *Dona Flor and Her Two Husbands*, trans. H. de Onís. New York: Knopf.
Araújo, Paulo Coelho (1997). *Abordagens sócio-antropológicos da luta/jogo da capoeira*. Portugal: Instituto Superior da Maia.
Augras, Monique (2000). "De iyá mi a Pomba-Gira: transformações e símbolos da libido." In *Candomblé: religião de corpo e da alma*, C. E. M. de Moura (ed.), 17–44. Rio de Janeiro: Pallas.
Bacelar, Jeferson (1989). *Etnicidade: ser negro em Salvador*. Salvador, Brazil: Ianamá.
——— (2001). *A hierarquia das raças: negros e brancos em Salvador*. Rio de Janeiro: Pallas.
Baer, Eugen (1988). *Medical Semiotics*. Lanham, Md.: University Press of America.
Barbosa, Lívia Neves de H. (1992). *O jeitinho brasileiro: a arte de ser mais igual que os outros*. Rio de Janeiro: Campus.
——— (1995). "The Brazilian *Jeitinho*: An Exercise in National Identity." In *The Brazilian Puzzle: Culture on the Borderlands of the Western World*, D. J. Hess and R. A. DaMatta (eds.), 33–48. New York: Columbia University Press.
Barbosa, Maria José Somerlate (2000). "Exu: 'verbo devoluto'." In *Brasil brasileiro*, M. N. S. Fonseca (ed.), 153–171. Belo Horizonte: Autêntica.
Barcellos, Mario César (1991a). *Os orixás e a personalidade humana*. Rio de Janeiro: Pallas.

———— (1991b). *Os orixás e o segredo da vida: lógica, mitologia e ecologia*. Rio de Janeiro: Pallas.
Barros, José Flávio Pessoa de, and Maria Lina Leão Teixeira (2000). "O código do corpo: inscrições e marcas dos orixás." In *Candomblé: religião de corpo e de alma*, C. E. M. de Moura (ed.), 103–138. Rio de Janeiro: Pallas.
Bartley III, William M. (1984). *The Retreat to Commitment*, 2nd ed. LaSalle, Ill.: Open Court.
Bastide, Roger (1945). *Imagens do Nordeste místico em branco e preto*. Rio de Janeiro: O Cruzeiro.
———— (1955). "Le principe de coupure et le comportement afro-brésilien." In *Annais do XXI Congreso Internacional dos Americanistas*. São Paulo: Anhembi.
———— (1971). *African Civilisations in the New World*, trans. P. Green. London: C. Hurst.
———— (1973). *Estudos afro-brasileiros*. São Paulo: Perspectiva.
———— (1978). *O candomblé da Bahia*. São Paulo: Companhia Editora Nacional.
Bateson, Gregory (1972). *Steps to an Ecology of Mind: A Revolutionary Approach to Man's Understanding of Himself*. New York: Ballantine.
Baudrillard, Jean (1983a). *Simulations*. New York: Semiotext(e).
———— (1983b). *In the Shadow of the Silent Majorities*, trans. P. Foss, J. Johnston, and P. Patton. New York: Semiotext(e).
———— (1988). *The Ecstasy of Communication*, trans. B. Schutze and C. Schutze. New York: Semiotext(e).
Beauvoir, Simone de (1952). *The Second Sex*, trans. H. M. Parshley. New York: Knopf.
Benedict, Ruth (1946). *Patterns of Culture*. New York: New American Library.
Bennett, Jane (2001). *The Enchantment of Modern Life: Attachments, Crossings, and Ethics*. Princeton, N.J.: Princeton University Press.
Berkenbrock, Volney J. (1995). *A experiência dos Orixás*. Petrópolis, Brazil: Vozes.
Berman, Morris (1981). *The Reenchantment of the World*. Ithaca, N.Y.: Cornell University Press.
Bernstein, Richard J. (1983). *Beyond Objectivism and Relativism: Science, Hermeneutics, and Praxis*. Philadelphia: University of Pennsylvania Press.
Beverley, John (1999). *Subalternity and Representation: Arguments in Cultural Theory*. Durham, N.C.: Duke University Press.
Bhabha, Homi K. (1990). "DissemiNation: Time, Narrative, and the Margins of the Modern Nation." In *Nation and Narration*, H. Bhabha (ed.), 291–322. New York: Routledge.
———— (1994). *The Location of Culture*. New York: Routledge.
Birman, Patricia (1995). *Fazer estilo criando gêneros: possessão e diferenças de gênero em terreiros de umbanda e candomblé no Rio de Janeiro*. Rio de Janeiro: Universidade do Estado de Rio de Janeiro.
Blacking, John (1995). *Music, Culture, and Experience*, R. Byron (ed.). Chicago: University of Chicago Press.
Bohr, Niels (1961). *Atomic Theory and the Description of Nature*. Cambridge, U.K.: Cambridge University Press.

Bola Sete, Mestre (1997). *A capoeira Angola na Bahia*. Rio de Janeiro: Pallas.
Braga, Julio (1988). *Fuxico de candomblé*. Feira de Santana: Universidade Estadual de Feira de Santana.
Braga, Julio (1995). *Na gamela do feitiço: repressão e resistência nos candomblés da Bahia*. Salvador, Brazil: UFBA.
——— (1998). *A cadeira de Ogã*. Rio de Janeiro: Pallas.
Brandão, Carlos Rodrigues (1980). *Os deuses do povo*. São Paulo: Editora Brasiliense.
——— (1986). *Identidade e etnia: construção da pessoa e resistência cultural*. São Paulo: Editora Brasiliense.
——— (1989). *A cultura na rua*. Campinas, Brazil: Papirus.
Bridgman, Percy W. (1951). *The Way Things Are*. New York: Viking.
Broglie, Louis de (1939). *Matter and Light: The New Physics*, trans. W. H. Johnston. New York: W. W. Norton.
——— (1953). *The Revolution in Physics*. New York: Noonday.
——— (1960). *Physics and Microphysics*. New York: Harper.
Brown, Diana de G. (1986). *Umbanda Religion and Politics in Urban Brazil*. Ann Arbor, Mich.: UMI Research Press.
Brown, Diana de G., and Mario Bick (1987). "Religion, Class and Context: Continuities and Discontinuities in Brazilian Umbanda." *American Ethnologist* 14 (1): 73–93.
Browning, Barbara (1995). *Samba: Resistance in Motion*. Bloomington: Indiana University Press.
Bruhns, Heloisa Turini (2000). *Futebol, Carnaval e Capoeira*. Campinas, Brazil: Papirus.
Buarque de Holanda, Sérgio (1935). *Raízes do Brasil*. Rio de Janeiro: José Olympo.
Butler, Judith (1990). *Gender Trouble: Feminism and the Subversion of Identity*. New York: Routledge.
Butler, Judith, et al. (2000). *Contingency, Hegemony, Universality: Contemporary Dialogues on the Left*. New York: Verso.
Butler, Kim D. (1998). "*Ginga Baiana*—The Politics of Race, Class, Culture and Power in Salvador, Brazil." In *Afro-Brazilian Culture and Politics: Bahia, 1790s to 1990s*, H. Kraay (ed.), 158–175. London: M. E. Sharpe.
Cacciatore, Olga Gudolle (1977). *Dicionário de cultos afro-brasileiros: com a indicação da origem das palavras*. Rio de Janeiro: Forense-Universitaria.
Caillois, Roger (1961). *Man, Play, and Games*, trans. M. Barash. New York: Free Press.
Campbell, Jeremy (2001). *The Liar's Tale: A History of Falsehood*. New York: W. W. Norton.
Cândido, Antonio (1993). *O discurso da cidade*. São Paulo: Duas Cidades.
Canevacci, Massimo (1996). *Syncretismos: uma exploração das hibridações culturais*, trans. R. Barni. São Paulo: Instituto Cultural Italo-Brasileiro.
Capoeira, Néstor (1992). *Capoeira: os fundamentos da malícia*. Rio de Janeiro: Record.
——— (1995). *The Little Capoeira Book*, trans. A. Ladd. Berkeley, Calif.: North Atlantic Books.
——— (1999). *Capoeira: Galo já cantou*. Rio de Janeiro: Record.
——— (2002). *Capoeira: Roots of the Dance-Fight-Game*. Berkeley, Calif.: North Atlantic Books.

Capra, Fritjof (1975). *The Tao of Physics: An Exploration of the Parallels between Modern Physics and Eastern Mysticism.* Berkeley, Calif.: Shambhala.
Carmen, Raff (1996). *Autonomous Development: Humanizing the Landscape.* London: Zed Books.
Carneiro, Edison (1964). *Ladinos e crioulos: estudos sobre o negro no Brasil.* Rio de Janeiro: Civilização Brasileira.
——— (1977). *Capoeira.* Rio Janeiro: FUNARTE.
——— (1978). *Candomblés da Bahia*, 6a ed. Rio de Janeiro: Civilização Brasileira.
——— (1981). *Religões negras e negros anjos.* Rio de Janeiro: Civilização Brasileira.
Carse, James P. (1986). *Finite and Infinite Games.* New York: Free Press.
Cartwright, Nancy (1983). *How the Laws of Physics Lie.* Oxford, U.K.: Clarendon.
——— (1999). *The Dappled World: A Study of the Boundaries of Science.* New York: Cambridge University Press.
Carvalho, José Jorge de (ed.) (1995). *O quilombo do Rio das Rãs: histórias, tradições, lutas.* Salvador, Brazil: UDUFBA.
Carvalho, Murilo (1977). "A capoeira perto do fim?" In *Artistas e festas populares,* M. Carvalho et al. (eds.), 1–21. São Paulo: Brasiliense.
Cataldi, Sue L. (1993). *Emotion, Depth, and Flesh: A Study of Sensitive Space.* Albany: State University of New York Press.
Chaui, Marilena (1986). *Conformismo e resistência: aspectos da cultura popular no Brasil.* São Paulo: Brasiliense.
Chernoff, John Miller (1979). *African Rhythm and African Sensibility.* Chicago: University of Chicago Press.
Chnaiderman, M. (1989). "Contra o jeitinho, a favor do gingando." *Pulsional* 9 (85), 76–78.
Chrisman, L. (1994). "The Imperial Unconscious? Representations of Imperial Discourse." In *Colonial Discourse and Postcolonial Theory: A Reader,* P. Williams and L. Chrisman (eds.), 498–516. New York: Oxford University Press.
Classen, Constance (1993). *Worlds of Sense: Exploring the Senses in History and Across Cultures.* New York: Routledge.
Clifford, James (1986). "Introduction: Partial Truths". In *Writing Culture: The Poetics and Politics of Ethnography,* J. Clifford and G. Marcus (eds.), 1-26. Berkeley: University of California Press.
Comaroff, Jean and John Comaroff (1991). *Of Revelation and Revolution.* Chicago: University of Chicago Press.
Consorte, Josildeth Gomes (1999). "Em Torno de um Manifesto de Ialorixás Baianas contra o Sincretismo." In *Faces da tradição afro-brasileira,* C. Caroso and J. Bacelar (eds.), 71–92. Rio de Janeiro: Pallas.
Corrêa, Norton F. (1992). *O batuque do Rio Grande do Sul.* Porto Alegre, Brazil: Editora da Universidade/UFRGS.
Costa Lima, Vivaldo da (1999). "As dietas africanas no sistema alimentar brasileiro." In *Faces da tradição afro-brasileira,* C. Caroso and J. Bacelar (eds.), 303–318. Rio de Janeiro: Pallas.
Costa Lima, Vivaldo da, et al., eds., (1984). *Encontro de nações-de-candomblé.* Salvador, Brazil: Ianamá.

References

D'Adesky, Jacques (2001). *Pluralismo étnico e multiculturalismo: racismos e anti-racicmos no Brasil.* Rio de Janeiro: Pallas.

DaMatta, Roberto A. (1986). *Explorações: ensaios de sociologia interpretativa.* Rio de Janeiro: Rocco.

——— (1991a). *A casa e a rua.* Rio de Janeiro: Editora Guanabara.

——— (1991b). *Carnivals, Rogues, and Heroes: An Interpretation of the Brazilian Dilemma.* Notre Dame, Ind.: University of Notre Dame Press.

——— (1994). *Conta de Mentiroso.* Rio de Janeiro: Rocco.

——— (1995). "For an Anthropology of the Brazilian Tradition: or "A Virtude está no Meio." In *The Brazilian Puzzle*, D. J. Hess and R. A. DaMatta (eds.), 270–291. New York: Columbia University Press.

Dantas, Beatrice Góis (1982). "Repensando a pureza nagô." *Religião e Sociedade*, No. 8, 15–20.

——— (1987). "Pureza e poder no mundo dos candomblés." In *Candomblés: Desvendando identidades.* C. E. M. Moura (ed), 121–128. São Paulo: EMW.

——— (1988). *Vovó Nagô e Papai Branco. Usos e abusos da África no Brasil.* Rio de Janeiro: Graal.

Davies, Paul (1988). *The Cosmic Blueprint.* New York: Simon and Schuster.

Dealy, Glen Caudill (1992). *The Latin Americans: Spirit and Ethos.* Boulder, Colo.: Westview.

Degler, Carl N. (1971). *Neither Black nor White: Slavery and Race Relations in Brazil and the United States.* Madison: University of Wisconsin Press.

Deleuze, Gilles and Félix Guattari (1983). *Anti-Oedipus: Capitalism and Schizophrenia, I.* Minneapolis: University of Minnesota Press.

——— (1987). *A Thousand Plateaus: Capitalism and Schizophrenia, II*, trans. B. Massumi. Minneapolis: University of Minnesota Press.

DeLong, Howard (1970). *A Profile of Mathematical Logic.* New York: Addison-Wesley.

Derrida, Jacques (1973). *Speech and Phenomena, and Other Essays on Husserl's Theory of Signs*, trans. D. B. Allison. Evanston, Ill.: Northwestern University Press.

——— (1981). *Disseminations*, trans. B. Johnson. London: Athlone.

Desmangles, Leslie G. (1993). *The Faces of the Gods: Voodoo and Roman Catholicism in Haiti.* Chapel Hill: University of North Carolina Press.

Devitt, Michael (1997). *Realism and Truth.* 2nd ed. Princeton, N.J.: Princeton University Press.

Dossar, Kenneth (1992). "Capoeira Angola: Dancing between Two Worlds." *Afro-Hispanic Review* 11 (1–3), 5–10.

Droogers, André (1989). "Syncretism: The Problem of Definition, the Definition of the Problem." In *Dialogue and Syncretism*, J. Gort, H. Vroom, R. Fernhout and A. Wessels (eds.), 7–25. Amsterdam: William B. Eerdmans.

Eduardo, Octávio da Costa (1948). *The Negro in Northern Brazil: A Study in Acculturation.* New York: J. J. Augustin.

Eliade, Mircea (1959). *The Sacred and the Profane*, trans. W. R. Trask. New York: Harper and Row.

Eliot, T. S. (1943). *Four Quartets.* New York: Harcourt Brace Jovanovich.

Epega, Sandra Medeiros (1999). "A volta à África: na contramão do orixá." In *Faces da*

tradição afro-brasileira, C. Caroso and J. Bacelar (eds.), 159–170. Rio de Janeiro: Pallas.
Esteva, Gustavo and Madha Suri Prakash (1998). *Grassroots Post-Modernism*. London: Zed Books.
Farrell, Frank B. (1994). *Subjectivity, Realism and Postmodernism: The Recovery of the World in Recent Philosophy*. New York: Cambridge University Press.
Fernandes, Florestan (1971). *The Negro in Brazilian Society*, trans. J. D. Skiles, A. Brunel, and A. Rothwell. New York: Columbia University Press.
Ferreira, Ricardo Franklin (1998). "A construção da identidade do afro-descendente: a psicologia brasileira e a questão racial." In *Brasil: um país de negros?*, J. Bacelar and C. Caroso (eds.), 71–86. Rio de Janeiro: Pallas.
Ferretti, Mundicarmo Maria Rocha (1985). *Mina, uma religião de origen africana*. São Luis: Sioge.
Ferretti, Sérgio Figuereido (1986). *Querebentan de Zomadonu: etnografia da Casa das Minas*. São Luis: Editora da Universidade Federal do Maranhão.
——— (1995). *Repensando o sincretismo*. São Paulo: Fapema.
——— (1999). "Sincretismo afro-brasileiro e resistência cultural." In *Faces da tradição afro-brasileira*, C. Caroso and J. Bacelar (eds.), 113–130. Rio de Janeiro: Pallas.
Feyerabend, Paul K. (1975). *Against Method*. London: NLB.
——— (1987). *Farewell to Reason*. London: NLB.
——— (1999). *Conquest of Abundance: A Tale of Abstraction Versus the Richness of Being*. Chicago: University of Chicago Press.
Fingarette, Herbert (1969). *Self-Deception*. London: Routledge and Kegan Paul.
Fine, Arthur (1986). *The Shaky Game: Einstein, Realism and the Quantum Theory*. Chicago: University of Chicago Press.
Fonseca, Maria Nazareth Soares (2000). "Visibilidade e ocultação da diferença: imagens de negro na cultura brasileira." In *Brasil brasileiro*, M. N. S. Fonseca (ed.), 67–86. Belo Horizonte, Brazil: Autêntica.
Francisco, Dalmir (2000). "Comunicação, identidade cultural e racismo." In *Brasil brasileiro*, M. N. Soares Fonseca (ed.), 87–115. Belo Horizonte, Brazil: Autêntica.
Freitas, Byron Torres de and Tancredo da Silva Pinto (1956). *Fundamentos de Umbanda*. Rio de Janeiro: Editora Souza.
Freitas, Décio (1982). *Palmares: A guerra dos escravos*. Rio de Janeiro: Graal.
Freyre, Gilberto (1946). *The Masters and the Slaves: A Study in the Development of Brazilian Civilization*, trans. S. Putnam. New York: Alfred A. Knopf.
——— (1959). *New World in the Tropics: The Culture of Modern Brazil*. New York: Alfred A. Knopf.
——— (1963). *The Mansions and the Shanties: The Making of Modern Brazil*. New York: Alfred A. Knopf.
Friedman, Jonathan (1997). "Global Crises, the Struggle for Cultural Identity and Intellectual Porkbarrelling: Cosmopolitans versus Locals, Ethnics and Nationals in an Era of De-Hegemonization." In *Debating Cultural Hybridity: Multi-Cultural Identities and the Politics of Anti-Racism*, P. Werbner and T. Modood (eds.), 70–89. Atlantic Highlands, N. J.: Zed Books.

References

Frigério, Alejandro (1989). "Capoeira: de arte negra a esporte branco." *Revista Brasileira de Ciências Sociais* 4 (10), 85–98.
Fry, Peter (1977). "Mediunidade e Sexualidade." *Religião e Sociedade* 1, 105–125.
——— (1982). *Para Inglês ver*. Rio de Janeiro: Zahar.
——— (1986). "Gallus Africanus Est, ou como Roger Bastide se tornou Africano no Brasil." In *Revisitando a Terra de contrastes: a atualidade da obra de Roger Bastide*, S. von Moraes and O. R. and P. de Queiroz (eds.), 31–45. São Paulo: USP-FFLCH-CERU.
——— (1991). "Politicamente correto num lugar, incorreto noutro? (Relações raciais no Brasil, nos Estados Unidos, em Moçambique e no Zimbábue)." *Caderno de Estudos Afro-Asiáticos* (2), 74–86.
Fryer, Peter (2000). *Rhythms of Resistance: African Musical Heritage in Brazil*. Hanover, Conn.: Wesleyan University Press.
García Canclini, Néstor (1995). *Hybrid Cultures*. Minneapolis: University of Minnesota Press.
——— (2001). *Consumers and Citizens: Globalization and Multicultural Conflicts*, trans. G. Yúdice. Minneapolis: University of Minnesota Press.
Gardner, Howard (1983). *Frames of Mind: The Theory of Multiple Intelligences*. New York: HarperCollins.
Gibson, Charles (1966). *Spain in America*. New York: Harper and Row.
Glass, Newman Robert (1995). *Working Emptiness: Toward a Third Reading of Emptiness in Buddhist and Postmodern Thought*. Atlanta, Ga.: Scholars Press.
Glissant, Edouard (1997). *Poetics of Relation*, trans. B. Wing. Ann Arbor: University of Michigan Press.
Gomes, Laura Graziela, et al. (eds.) (2000). *O Brasil não é para principiantes*. Rio de Janeiro: Editora RGV.
Gomes da Cunha, Olívia Maria (1998). "Black Movement in the 'Politics of Identity' in Brazil." In *Cultures of Politics/Politics of Cultures: Re-Visioning Latin American Social Movements*, S. E. Avarez, E. Dagnino, and A. Escobar (eds.), 220–251. Boulder, Colo.: Westview.
Gonçalves da Silva, Vagner (1999). "Reafricanização e Sincretismo: Interpretações Acadêmicas e Experiências Religiosas." In *Faces da tradição afro-brasileira*, C. Caroso and J. Bacelar (eds.), 149–157. Rio de Janeiro: Pallas.
Goodman, Nelson (1965). *Fact, Fiction and Forecast*. 2nd ed. Indianapolis, Ind.: Bobbs-Merrill.
——— (1978). *Ways of Worldmaking*. Indianapolis, Ind.: Hackett.
Goswami, Amit (1993). *The Self-Aware Universe: How Consciousness Creates the Material World*. New York: G. P. Putnam's Sons.
Goto, Roberto (1988). *Malandragem revistada*. Campinas, Brazil: Pontes.
Goulart, Mauricio (1975). *A escravidão africana no Brasil: das origins à extinção do tráfico*. São Paulo: Alfa Ômega.
Gramsci, Antonio (1971). *Selections from the Prison Notebooks*, trans. Q. Hoare and G. N. Smith. London: Lawrence and Wishart.
Greenfield, Sidney M. and André Droogers, eds. (2001). *Reinventing Religions: Syncretism*

and Transformation in Africa and the Americas. Lanham, Md.: Rowman and Littlefield.
Griffiths, Paul J. (1986). *On Being Mindless: Buddhist Meditation and the Mind-Body Problem.* LaSalle, Ill.: Open Court.
Grigg, Ray (1994). *The Tao of Zen.* Boston: Charles E. Tuttle.
Gruzinski, Serge (2001). *O pensamento mestiço.* São Paulo: Editora Schwarcz.
Guerreiro, Goli (2000). *A trama dos tambores: a música afro-pop de Salvador.* São Paulo: Editora 34.
Guimarães, Antônio Sergio (1995). "Raça, racismo e grupos de cor no Brasil," *Estudos Afro-Asiáticos* 27, 45–63.
——— (1997). "Racismo e restrição dos direitos individuais: a discriminação racial publicizada." *Estudos Afro-Asiáticos* 31, 51–87.
Guimarães, Francisco (1978). *Na roda do samba.* Rio de Janeiro: Funarte.
Gutting, Gary (1999). *Pragmatic Liberalism and the Critique of Modernity.* Cambridge, U.K.: Cambridge University Press.
Haack, Susan (2003). *Defending Science within Reason: Between Scientism and Cynicism.* New York: Prometheus.
Hacking, Ian (1983). *Representing and Intervening: Introductory Topics in the Philosophy of Natural Science.* Cambridge, U.K.: Cambridge University Press.
——— (1985). "Styles of Scientific Reasoning." In *Post-Analytic Philosophy,* J. Rajchman and C. West (eds.), 145–165. New York: Columbia University Press.
——— (1993). "On Kripke's and Goodman's Uses of 'Grue'." *Philosophy* 68, 269–295.
——— (1995). "Entrenchment." In *Grue! The New Riddle of Induction,* D. Stalker (ed.), 193–223. LaSalle, Ill: Open Court.
——— (1999). *The Social Construction of What?* Cambridge., Mass.: Harvard University Press.
Hagen, Steve (1998). *How the World Can Be the Way It Is.* Wheaton: Quest Books.
Hall, Stuart (1992). "Cultural Studies and Its Theoretical Legacies." In *Cultural Studies,* L. Grossberg, C. Nelson and P. Treichler (eds.). London: Routledge.
Halton, Eugene (1995). *Bereft of Reason: On the Decline of Social Thought and Prospects for its Renewal.* Chicago: University of Chicago Press.
Hanchard, Michael (1994). *Orpheus and Power: The Movimento Negro of Rio de Janeiro and São Paulo, Brazil, 1945–1988.* Princeton, N.J.: Princeton University Press.
Hanke, Lewis (1949). *The Spanish Struggle for Justice in the Conquest of America.* Philadelphia: University of Pennsylvania Press.
——— (1959). *Aristotle and the American Indians.* Chicago: University of Chicago Press.
Hanson, Norwood R. (1958). *Patterns of Discovery.* Cambridge, U.K.: Cambridge University Press.
——— (1969). *Perception and Discovery.* San Francisco: Freeman, Cooper.
Harris, Harry (2002). *Things Come to Life: Spontaneous Generation Revisited.* New York: Oxford University Press.
Hasenbalg, Carlos (1994). "Entre o mito e os fatos: racismo e relações raciais no Brasil." *Dados: Revista de Ciencias Sociais* 38 (2), 355–374.

References

Hastrup, Kirsten (1995). *A Passage to Anthropology: Between Experience and Theory.* New York: Routledge.
Hayward, Jeremy W. (1984). *Perceiving Ordinary Magic.* Boulder, Colo.: Shambhala.
——— (1987). *Shifting Worlds, Changing Minds.* Boston: Shambhala.
Heisenberg, Werner (1971). *Physics and Beyond: Encounters and Conversations.* New York: Harper and Row.
Hellwig, David J. (1992). *African-American Reflections on Brazil's Racial Paradise.* Philadelphia: Temple University Press.
Hempel, Carl (1945). "Studies in the Logic of Confirmation." *Mind* 54, 1–26, 97–121.
Henry, Anaiza Vergolino (1987). "A semana santa nos terreiros: um estudo do sincretismo religioso em Belém do Pará." *Religião e Sociedade* 3 (14), 57–71.
Herskovits, Melville (1943). "The Negro in Bahia, Brazil: A Problem of Method." *American Sociological Review* 8 (4), 394–402.
——— (1966). *The New World Negro: Selected Papers in Afroamerican Studies,* F. S. Herskovitz (ed.). Bloomington: Indiana University Press.
Hess, David J. and Roberto A. DaMatta (1995). *The Brazilian Puzzle: Culture on the Borderlands of the Western World.* New York: Columbia University Press.
Hesse, Mary B. (1969). "Ramifications of 'Grue.'" *British Journal of the Philosophy of Science* 20, 13–25.
Hobsbawm, E. and T. Ranger (1983). *The Invention of Tradition.* Cambridge, U.K.: Cambridge University Press.
Hollis, Martin and Steven Lukes, eds. (1983). *Rationality and Relativism.* Cambridge, Mass.: MIT Press.
Hookway, Christopher (1985). *Peirce.* London: Routledge and Kegan Paul.
Horgan, John (1996). *The End of Science: Facing the Limits of Knowledge in the Twilight of the Scientific Age.* New York: Bantam Doubleday Dell.
Howes, David (ed.) (1991). *The Varieties of Sensory Experience.* Toronto: University of Toronto Press.
Hulme, P. (1995). "Including America." *Ariel* 26 (1): 117–123.
Huntington, Samuel P. (1996). *The Clash of Civilizations and the Remaking of World Order.* New York: Simon and Schuster.
Huntington Jr., C. W. (1989). *The Emptiness of Emptiness.* Honolulu: University of Hawaii Press.
Ianni, Octavio (2000). *Enigmas da modernidade-mundo.* Rio de Janeiro: Civilização Brasileira.
Iida, Shotaro (1980). *Reason and Emptiness: A Study of Logic in Mysticism.* Tokyo: Hokuseido.
Inman, Samuel Guy (1942). *Latin America: Its Place in World Life.* New York: Harcourt Brace.
Jacobson, Nolan Pliny (1983). *Buddhism and the Contemporary World: Change and Self-Correction.* Carbondale: Southern Illinois University Press.
JanMohamed, Abdul R. (1985). "The Economy of Manichean Allegory: The Function of Racial Difference in Colonialist Literature." *Critical Inquiry* 12, 59–87.
Jeans, James (1958). *The Mysterious Universe.* Cambridge, U.K.: Cambridge University Press.

Johnson, Paul Christopher (2002). *Secrets, Gossip, and Gods: The Transformation of Brazilian Candomblé*. Oxford, U.K.: Oxford University Press.
Kalupahana, David (1986). *Nagarjuna: The Philosophy of the Middle Way*. Albany: State University of New York Press.
――― (1987). *Principles of Buddhist Psychology*. Albany: State University of New York Press.
Kant, Immanuel (1983). *Perpetual Peace and Other Essays*, trans. T. Humphrey. Indianapolis, Ind.: Hackett.
Kent, R. K. (1965). "Palmares: An African State in Brazil." *Journal of African History* 6 (2), 161–175.
Kline, Morris (1980). *Mathematics: The Loss of Certainty*. Oxford, U.K.: Oxford University Press.
Kloppenburg, Boaventura O. F. M. (1961). *Umbanda: Orientação para católicos*. Petrópolis: Vozes.
――― (1964). *O espiritismo no Brasil: Orientação para católicos*. Petrópolis: Vozes.
――― (1992). "O sincretismo afro-brasileiro como desafio à evangelização." *Teocomunicação* 96, 203–215.
Kraay, Hendrik, ed. (1998). *Afro-Brazilian Culture and Politics: Bahia, 1970s to 1990s*. New York: M. E. Sharpe.
Krausz, Michael, ed. (1989). *Relativism: Interpretation and Confrontation*. Notre Dame: University of Notre Dame Press.
Kubik, Gerhard (1979). "Angolan Traits in Black Music, Games and Dances of Brazil: A Study of African Cultural Extensions Overseas." *Estudos de Antropologia Cultural* 10, 7–55.
Kuhn, Thomas S. (1970). *The Structure of Scientific Revolutions*. Chicago: University of Chicago Press.
Laclau, Ernesto and Chantal Mouffe (1985). *Hegemony and Socialist Strategy: Towards a Radical Democratic Politics*. London: Verso.
Lamego, Alberto (1934). *A planície do solar e da senzala*. Rio de Janeiro: Livraria Católica.
Landes, Ruth (1947). *A cidade das mulheres*. Rio de Janeiro: Civilização Brasileira.
Latouche, Serge (1996). *The Westernization of the World*. Cambridge, Mass.: Polity.
――― (1998). *In the Wake of the Affluent Society*, trans. M. O'Connor and R. Arnouz. London: Zed Books.
Laudan, Larry (1996). *Beyond Positivism and Relativism: Theory, Method, and Evidence*. Boulder: Westview.
Leão Teixeira, Maria Lina (1999). "Candomblé e a [re]Invenção de Tradições." In *Faces da tradição afro-brasileira*, C. Caroso and J. Bacelar (eds.), 131–140. Rio de Janeiro: Pallas.
Leão Texeira, M. L., M. L. Santos and J. F. P. Barros (1985). *O rodar das rodas: dos orixás e dos homens*. Rio de Janeiro: INF/FUNARTE.
Leder, Drew (1990). *The Absent Body*. Chicago: University of Chicago Press.
Leers, O. F. M. Bernardino (1982). *Jeito brasileiro e norma absoluta*. Petrópolis: Vozes.
Leitch, Vincent B. (1996). *Postmodernism: Local Effects, Global Flows*. Albany: State University of New York Press.

References

Lépine, Claude (2000). "Os estereótipos da personalidade no candomblé nagô." In *Candomblé: religião do corpo e da alma*, C. E. M. de Moura (ed.), 139–164. Rio de Janeiro: Pallas.
Lerch, Patricia (1980). "Spirit Mediums in Umbanda Evangelada of Porto Aegre, Brazil: Dimensions of Power and Authority." In *A World of Men*, E. Bourguignon (ed.), 58–76. New York: Praeger.
Levin, David Michael, ed. (1997). *Language beyond Postmodernism*. Evanston, Ill.: Northwestern University Press.
Levine, Robert M. (1997). *Brazilian Legacies*. New York: M. E. Sharpe.
Lévi-Strauss, Claude (1966). *The Savage Mind*. Chicago: University of Chicago Press.
Lewis, J. Lowell (1992). *Ring of Liberation: Deceptive Discourse in Brazilian Capoeira*. Chicago: University of Chicago Press.
Ligiéro e Dandara, Zeca (1998). *Umbanda: paz, liberdade e cura*. Rio de Janeiro: Record.
Lockwood, Michael (1991). *Mind, Brain, and the Quantum: The Compound "I."* London: Blackwell.
Lody, Raul (1995). *O povo do santo*. Rio de Janeiro: Pallas.
Loomba, Ania (1998). *Colonialism/Postcolonialism*. New York: Routledge.
Lopes, André Luiz Lace (1996). "Sinhozinho." *Jornal dos Sports* (February 25): 9–10.
Lowe, Donald M. (1977). *History of Bourgeois Perception*. Chicago: University of Chicago Press.
Loy, David (1989). *Non-Duality*. New Haven, Conn.: Yale University Press.
Lühning, Angela (1999). "Ewê: as plantas brasileiras e seus parentes africanos." In *Faces da tradição afro-brasileira*, C. Caroso and J. Bacelar (eds.), 303–318. Rio de Janeiro: Pallas.
Luz, Marco Aurélio (1995). *Agadá: dinâmica da civilização africano-brasileira*. Salvador: UFBA.
Machado, Vanda (1999). *Ilé Axé: Vivências e invenção pedagógica, as crianças do Opô Afonjá*. Salvador: UFBA.
Malinowski, Bronislaw (1940). "Introducción." In *Contrapunteo cubano del tabaco y el azúcar*, by Fernando Ortiz, xv-xxii. La Habana, Cuba: Jesus Montero.
Mallon, Florencia (1995). *Peasant and Nation: The Making of Postcolonial Mexico and Peru*. Berkeley: University of California Press.
Marcos, Subcomandante (1995). *Shadows of Tender Fury, The Letters and Communiqués of Subcomandante Marcos*. New York: Monthly Review Press.
Margolis, Joseph (1991). *The Truth about Relativism*. London: Basil Blackwell.
Marques, Gabriel (1996). *Da senzala à umbanda: uma nova abordagem da realidade racial no Brasil*. Campinas, Brazil: Editora Planeta.
Martins, Leda Maria (2000). "A oraliteratura da memória." In *Brasil brasileiro*, M. N. S. Fonseca (ed.), 62–86. Belo Horizonte, Brazil: Autêntica.
Matias da Silva, José Gilmário ("Mestre Tigrão") (1994). *Capoeira: herdeiros do cativerio*. Salvador, Brazil: Art-Contemp.
Matta e Silva, W. W. (1969). *Umbanda de todos nós*. 3rd ed. Rio de Janeiro: Livraria Freitas Bastos.
Mattoso, Kátia M. de Queirós (1986). *To Be a Slave in Brazil*, trans. A. Goldhammer. New Brunswick, N.J.: Rutgers University Press.

Mele, Alfred (2001). *Self-Deception Unmasked.* Princeton: Princeton University Press.
Melhuish, George (1967). *The Paradoxical Nature of Reality.* Bristol, U.K.: St. Vincent's Press.
Mendes de Gusmão, Neusa Maria (1998). "Herança quilombola: negros, terras e direitos." In *Brasil: país de negros?*, J. Bacelar and C. Caroso (eds.), 143–162. Rio de Janeiro: Pallas.
Ménendez Pidal, Ramón (1966). *The Spaniards and Their History*, trans. W. Starkle. New York: W. W. Norton.
Merleau-Ponty, Maurice (1962). *Phenomenology of Perception.* London: Routledge and Kegan Paul.
merrell, floyd (1991). *Signs Becoming Signs: Our Perfusive, Pervasive Universe.* Bloomington: Indiana University Press.
────── (1995a). *Semiosis in the Postmodern Age.* West Lafayette, Ind.: Purdue University Press.
────── (1995b). *Peirce's Semiotics Now.* Toronto: Canadian Scholars Press
────── (1997). *Peirce, Signs, and Meaning.* Toronto: University of Toronto Press.
────── (1998). *Simplicity and Complexity: Pondering Science, Painting, and Literature.* Ann Arbor: University of Michigan Press.
────── (2000a). *Signs for Everybody: Or, Chaos, Quandaries, and Communication.* Ottawa: Legas Press.
────── (2000b). *Change through Body, Signs, and Mind.* Chicago: Waveland Press.
────── (2000c). *Signs, Science, and Self-Subsuming Art(ifacts).* Dresden, Germany: Thelem.
────── (2000d). *Tasking Textuality.* Berlin: Peter Lang.
────── (2002). *Learning Living, Living Learning: Signs, Between East and West.* Ottawa, Canada: Legas Press.
────── (2003a). *Sensing Corporeally: Toward a Posthuman Understanding.* Toronto: University of Toronto Press.
────── (2004). *Complementing Latin American Borders.* West Lafayette, Ind.: Purdue University Press.
Mignolo, Walter D. (2000). *Local Histories/Global Designs: Coloniality, Subaltern Knowledges, and Border Thinking.* Princeton, N.J.: Princeton University Press.
Mignolo, Walter D. and Freya Schiwy (2002). "Beyond Dichotomies: Translation/Transculturation and the Colonial Difference." In *Beyond Dichotomies*, E. Mudimbe-Boyi (ed.), 251–286. Albany: State University of New York Press.
Morse, Richard (1993). *A volta de McLuhaíma.* São Paulo: Companhia das Letras.
Mott, Luis R. B. (1999). *Escravidão e homossexualidade.* Salvador: Editora Grupo Gay da Bahia.
Motta, Nélson (1992). "La transe, la nomination et la reconnaissance dans le Xangô de Recife (Brésil)." *Archives de Sciences Sociales des Religions* 37 (79): 47–52.
Moura, Carlos Eugênio Marcondes de (2000). "Reintroduzindo." In *Candomblé: religião do corpo e do alma*, C. E. M. de Moura (ed.), 7–16. Rio de Janeiro: Pallas.
Moura, Clóvis (1981). *Rebeliões da senzala: quilombos, insurreições, guerrilhas.* São Paulo: Ciências Humanas.

References

Moura, Jair (1980). *Arte e malícia*. Salvador, Brazil: Prefeitura Municipal.
Mudimbe-Boyi, Elizabeth (2002). *Beyond Dichotomies*. Albany: State University of New York Press.
Nagel, Ernest and James A. Newman (1958). *Gödel's Proof*. New York: Columbia University Press.
Nandy, Ashis (1998). *Exiled at Home*. New Delhi: Oxford University Press.
Nascimento, Abdias do (1977). "Racial Democracy." In *Brazil: Myth or Reality*, trans. E. L. do Nascimento. Ibadan, Nigeria: Sketch Publishing Co.
——— (1979). *Brazil: Mixture or Massacre?* Dover, U.K.: The Majority Press.
——— 1980). *O quilombismo*. Petrópolis, Brazil: Vozes.
——— (2002). *O Brasil na mira do pan-africanismo*. Salvador: EDUFBA/CEAO.
Nietzsche, Friedrich (1968). *The Will to Power*, trans. W. Kaufman and R. J. Hollingdale. New York: Vintage Books.
Nina Rodrigues, Raimundo (1935). *O animismo fetichista dos negros bahianos*. Rio de Janeiro: Civilização Brasileira.
——— (1977). *Os africanos no brasil*, 5a ed. São Paulo: Editora Nacional.
Nishitani, Keiji (1982). *Religion and Nothingness*, trans. J. van Bragt. Berkeley: University of California Press.
Nishitani, Keiji (1990). *The Self-Overcoming of Nihilism*, trans. G. Parkes. Albany: State University of New York Press.
Nogueira, Oracy (1985). *Tanto preto quanto branco: estudos de relações raciais*. São Paulo: T. A. Queiroz.
Novinger, Tracy (2004). *Communicating with Brazilians: When "Yes" means "No."* Austin: University of Texas Press.
Odin, Steve (1996). *The Social Self in Zen and American Pragmatism*. Albany: State University of New York Press.
Ojo-Ade, Femi (1998). "O Brasil, paraíso ou inferno para o Negro? Subsidios para uma nova negritude." In *Brasil: um país de negros?*, J. Bacelar and C. Caroso (eds.), 35–50. Rio de Janeiro: Pallas.
Oliven, Ruben George (1982). *Violência e cultura no Brasil*. Petrópolis: Vozes.
Oro, Ari Pedro (1993). "As religiões afro-brasileiras: religiões de exportação." In *As religiões afro-brasileiras no Cone Sul*, A. P. Oro (ed.), 57–72. Porto Alegre: UFRGS.
Ortiz, Fernando (1940). *Contrapunteo cubano del tabaco y el azúcar*. La Habana: Jesus Montero.
Ortiz, Renato (1978). *A morte branca do feiticeiro Negro*. Petrópolis, Brazil: Vozes.
——— (1980). *A conciência fragmentada*. Rio de Janeiro: Paz e Terra.
——— (1985). *Cultura brasileira e identidade nacional*. 2nd ed. São Paulo: Editora Brasiliense.
——— (1994). *Mundialização e cultura*. São Paulo: Editora Brasiliense.
Owen, David (1994). *Maturity and Modernity: Nietzsche, Weber, Foucault and the Ambivalence of Reason*. New York: Routledge.
Pagels, Heinz R. (1982). *The Cosmic Code: Quantum Physics as the Language of Nature*. New York: Bantam.
——— (1988). *The Dreams of Reason: The Computer and the Rise of the Sciences of Complexity*. New York: Simon and Schuster.

Parry, Benita. (1994). "Resistance Theory/Theorising Resistance: Two Cheers for Nativism." In *Colonial Discourse/Postcolonial Theory*, F. Barker, P. Hulme, and M. Iverson (eds.), 172–196. Manchester, U.K.: Manchester University Press.

────── (2002). "Signs of Our Times: A Discussion of Homi Babha's *The Location of Culture.*" In *Learning Places: The Afterlives of Area Studies*, M. Miyoshi and D. H. Harootunian (eds.), 119–149. Durham, N.C.: Duke University Press.

Pastinha, Mestre (1969). *Capoeira Angola*. Salvador, Brazil: FUNCER.

Peirce, Charles Sanders. (1931–35). *Collected Papers of Charles Sanders Peirce*, C. Hartshorne and P. Weiss (eds.), vols. 1–6. Cambridge, Mass.: Harvard University Press (references to the *Collected Papers* will be designated *CP*).

────── (1958). *Collected Papers of Charles Sanders Peirce*, A. Burks (ed.), vols. 7–8. Cambridge, Mass.: Harvard University Press (references to the *Collected Papers* will be designated *CP*).

Penrose, Roger (1989). *The New Emperor's Mind: Concerning Computers, Minds, and the Laws of Physics*. Oxford, U.K.: Oxford University Press.

Pierson, Donald (1942). *Negroes in Brazil: A Study of Race Contact in Bahia*. Chicago: University of Chicago Press.

Plotnitsky, Arkady (1994). *Complementarity: Anti-Epistemology after Bohr and Derrida*. Durham, N.C.: Duke University Press.

Polanyi, Michael (1958). *Personal Knowledge*. Chicago: University of Chicago Press.

Pöppel, Ernst (1972). "Oscillators as Possible Basis for Time Perception." In *The Study of Time*, J. T. Fraser, F. C. Haber and G. H. Miller (eds.), 219–241. New York: Springer-Verlag.

────── (1988). *Mindworks: Time and Conscious Experience*. Boston: Harcourt, Brace, Jovanovich.

Póvoas, Ruy do Carmo (1999). "Dentro do quarto." In *Faces da tradição afro-brasileira*, C. Caroso and J. Bacelar (eds.), 213–238. Rio de Janeiro: Pallas.

Prado, Paulo (1962). *Retrato do Brasil: ensaio sobre tristeza brasileira*, 6th ed. Rio de Janeiro: José Olympio.

Prandi, Reginaldo (1991). *Os candomblés de São Paulo: a velha magia na metrópole nova*. São Paulo: Hucitec-Edusp.

────── (1999). "Referências sociais das religiões afro-brasileiras: sincretismo, branqueamento, africanização." In *Faces da tradição afro-brasileira*, C. Caroso and J. Bacelar (eds.), 93–111. Rio de Janeiro: Pallas.

Prigogine, Ilya (1980). *From Being to Becoming: Time and Complexity in the Physical Sciences*. San Francisco: W. H. Freeman.

────── (1997). *The End of Certainty*. New York: The Free Press.

Prigogine, Ilya and Isabelle Stengers (1983). *Order Out of Chaos: Man's New Dialogue with Nature*. New York: Bantam.

Putnam, Hilary (1981). *Reason, Truth and History*. Cambridge, U.K.: Cambridge University Press.

────── (1983). *Realism and Reason*. Cambridge, U.K.: Cambridge University Press.

────── (1990). *Realism with a Human Face*, J. Conant (ed.). Cambridge, Mass.: Harvard University Press.

―――― (1992). *Renewing Philosophy*. Cambridge, Mass.: Harvard University Press.
Querino, Manoel Raimundo (1978). *The African Contribution to Brazilian Civilization*, trans. E. Bradford Burns. Tempe: Center for Latin American Studies, Arizona State University.
Quine, Williard van Orman (1969). *Ontological Relativity and Other Essays*. New York: Columbia University Press.
Rama, Ángel (1982). *Transculturación narrativa en América Latina*. México: Siglo XXI.
Ramos, Arthur (1937). *As culturas negras no novo mundo*. Rio de Janeiro: Casa dos Estudiantes do Brasil.
Ratts, Alessandro J. P. (2000). "(Re)conhecer quilombos no território brasileiro: estudos e mobilizações." In *Brasil brasileiro*, M. N. S. Fonseca (ed.), 306–326. Belo Horizonte, Brazil: Autêntica.
Rego, Waldeloir (1968). *Capoeira Angola: ensaio socio-etnográfico*. Salvador, Brazil: Itapuã.
Reis, João José (1988). "Magia jeje na Bahia: a invasão do calundu no posto de Cachoeira, 1785." *Revista Brasileira de História* 8 (16): 57–81.
―――― (1993). *Slave Rebellion in Brazil: The Muslim Uprising of 1835 in Bahia*, trans. A. Brakel. Baltimore: The Johns Hopkins University Press.
Reis, João José and Flávio dos Santos Gomes (1996) (eds.). *Liberdade por um fio: história dos quilombos no Brasil*. São Paulo: Companhia das Letras.
Reis, João José and Eduardo Silva (1989). *Negociação e conflito: a resistência negra no Brasil escravista*. São Paulo: Companhia das Letras.
Rescher, Nicholas and Robert Brandom (1979). *The Logic of Inconsistency: A Study of the Non-Standard Possible-World Semantics and Ontology*. Totowa: Rowman and Littlefield.
Ribeiro, João Ubaldo (1984). *Viva o povo brasileiro*. Rio de Janeiro: Nova Fronteira.
Ribeiro, Darcy (1997). *Confissões*. São Paulo: Editora Schwarcz.
Ribeiro, René (1969). "Personality and the Psychosexual Adjustment of Afro-Brazilian Cult Members." *Journal de la Société des Américanistes* 58, 109–119.
―――― (1978). *Cultos afro-brasileiros do Recife*. Recife, Brazil: IJNPS.
Ribeiro, Ronilda I. (1998). "Identidade do afro-descendente e sentimento de pertença a networks organizados em torno da temática racial." In *Brasil: país de negros?*, J. Bacelar and C. Caroso (eds.), 235–252. Rio de Janeiro: Pallas.
Risério, Antonio (1981). *Carnaval Ijexá*. Salvador: Corruptio.
―――― (1996). *Oriki Orishá*. São Paulo: Editora Perspectiva.
Ritzer, George (2000). *The Mcdonaldization of Society*. Thousand Oaks, Calif.: Pine Forge Press.
Rivero, Oswaldo de (2001). *The Myth of Development: Non-Viable Economies of the 21st Century*, trans. C. Encinas and J. H. Encinas. New York: Zed Books.
Robert, Jean (1999). "Production." In *The Development Dictionary*, W. Sachs (ed.), 177–191. London: Zed Books.
Rodrigues, Núbia and Carlos Caroso (1999). "Exu na tradição terapêutica religiosa afro-brasileira." In *Faces da tradição afro-brasileira*, C. Carlos and J. Bacelar (eds.), 239–256. Rio de Janeiro: Pallas.
Rosenthal, Sandra B. (1994). *Charles Peirce's Pragmatic Pluralism*. Albany: State University of New York Press.

Sachs, Wolfgang (1999a). *The Development Dictionary*. London: Zed Books.
—— (1999b). *Planet Dialectics: Explorations in Environment and Development*. London: Zed Books.
Sacks, Oliver (1989). *Seeing Voices: A Journey into the World of the Deaf*. New York: HarperCollins.
—— (1990). *The Man Who Mistook His Wife for a Hat, and Other Clinical Tales*. New York: HarperCollins.
—— (1995). *An Anthropologist on Mars*. New York: Vintage.
Said, Edward (1991). *Orientalism: Western Conceptions of the Orient*. London: Penguin.
Sales, Nívio Ramos (2001). *Búzios: a fala dos Orixás*. Rio de Janeiro: Pallas.
Sanchis, Pierre (1999). 'Sincretismo e Pastoral: o caso dos agentes de pastoral negros no seu meio." In *Faces da tradição afro-brasileira*, C. Caroso and J. Bacelar (eds.), 171–210. Rio de Janeiro: Pallas.
Sansone, Lívio (1992). "Cor, classe e modernidade em duas áreas da Bahia (algumas primeiras impressões." *Estudos Afro-Asiáticos* 23, 143–173.
—— (1998). "O olhar forasteiro: seduções e ambigüidades das relações raciais no Brasil." In *Brasil: um país de negros?*, J. Bacelar and C. Caroso (eds.), 15–26. Rio de Janeiro: Pallas.
—— (2003). *Blackness without Ethnicity: Constructing Race in Brazil*. New York: Macmillan.
Santos, Jocélio Teles dos (1995). *O dono da terra: o caboclo nos candomblés da Bahia*. Salvador, Brazil: Sarah Letras.
—— (1998a). "A Mixed-Race Nation: Afro-Brazilians and Cultural Policy in Bahia, 1970–1990." In *Afro-Brazilian Culture and Politics: Bahia, 1970s to 1990s*, H. Kraay (ed.), 117–133. London: M. E. Sharpe.
—— (1998b). "Dilema nada atuais das políticas para os afro-brasileiros: ação afirmativa no Brasil dos anos 60." In *Brasil: país de negros?*, J. Bacelar and C. Caroso (eds.), 221–233. Rio de Janeiro: Pallas.
Santos, Juana Elbein dos (1976). *Os nagôs e a morte*. Petrópolis: Vozes.
Schwarcz, Lilia Moritz (1999). "Ser peça, ser coisa." In *Negras imagens: ensaios sobre cultura e escravidão no Brasil*, L. M. Schwarcz and L. V. de Souza Reis (eds.), 11–29. São Paulo: EDUSP.
Schwarz, Roberto (1977). *Ao vencedor as batatas: forma literária e processo social nos inícios do romance brasileiro*. São Paulo: Duas Cidades.
—— (1987). *Que horas são*. São Paulo: Cia das Letras.
—— (1990). *Um mestre na periferia do capitalismo: Machado de Assis*. São Paulo: Duas Cidades.
—— (1992). *Misplaced Ideas*. London: Verso.
Sebeok, Thomas A. (1991). *A Sign Is Just a Sign*. Bloomington: Indiana University Press.
Segato, Rita Laura (2000). "Inventando a natureza: Família, sexo e género no Xangô do Recife." In *Candomblé: religião do corpo e da alma*, C. E. M. de Moura (ed.), 45–103. Rio de Janeiro: Pallas.
Serra, Ordep (1995). *Águas do rei*. Petrópolis: Vozes.

———— (1999). "A etnobotánica do candomblé Nagô da Bahia: cosmologia e estrutura básica do arranjo taxonómico". In *Faces da tradição afro-brasileira*, C. Caroso and J. Bacelar (eds.), 195–208. Rio de Janeiro: Pallas

Shusterman, Richard (1992). *Pragmatist Aesthetics: Living Beauty, Rethinking Art*. Oxford, U.K.: Blackwell.

———— (1997). *Practicing Philosophy: Pragmatism and the Philosophical Life*. London: Routledge.

Silveira, Renato da (1988). "Pragmatismo e milagres da fé no extremo ocidente." In *Escravidão e invenção da liberdade: estudos sobre o negro no Brasil*, J. J. Reis (ed.), 166–197. São Paulo: Brasiliense.

Skidmore, Thomas (1974). *Black into White: Race and Nationality in Brazilian Thought*. Oxford, U.K.: Oxford University Press.

Smith, Wolfgang (1995). *The Quantum Enigma: Finding the Hidden Key*. Peru, Ill.: Sherwood Sugden.

Soares, Antonio J. (1994). *Futebol, malandragem e identidade*. Vitória: SPDC/UFES.

Sodré, Muniz (1979). *Samba: O dono do corpo*. Rio de Janeiro: Codecri.

———— (1983). *A verdade seduzida: por un conceito de cultura no Brasil*. Rio de Janeiro: Codecri.

———— (1988). *O terreiro e a cidade: a forma social negro-brasileira*. Petrópolis: Vozes.

———— (1991). *O Brasil simulado e real*. Rio de Janeiro: Fundo Editora.

———— (1997). "Corporalidade e liturgia negra." *Revista do Patrimonio Histórico* 25, 21–25.

———— (1999). *Claros e escuros: identidade, povo e mídia no Brasil*. Petrópolis, Brazil: Vozes.

Sousa Reis, Letícia Vidor de (1997). *O mundo de pernas para o ar: a capoeira no Brasil*. São Paulo: Publisher Brasil.

Souza, Mériti de (1999). *A experiência da lei e a lei da experiência: ensaios sobre práticas sociais e subjetividades no Brasil*. Rio de Janeiro: Revan.

Spivak, Gayatri Chakravorty (1988). "Can the Subaltern Speak?" In *Marxism and the Interpretation of Culture*, C. Nelson and L. Grossberg (eds.), 271–313. Urbana: University of Illinois Press.

Spretnak, Charlene (1999). *The Resurgence of the Real: Body, Nature, and Place in a Hypermodern World*. New York: Routledge.

Stalker, D. (1995). *Grue! The New Riddle of Induction*. LaSalle, Ill.: Open Court.

Stearn, Isabel (1952). "Firstness, Secondness, and Thirdness." In *Studies of the Philosophy of Charles S. Peirce*, P. P. Wiener, and F. H. Young (eds.), 195–208. Cambridge, Mass.: Harvard University Press.

Stewart, Ian and Martin Golubitsky (1992). *Fearful Symmetry: Is God a Geometer?* London: Penguin.

Stoller, Paul (1989). *The Taste of Ethnographic Things: The Senses in Anthropology*. Philadelphia: University of Pennsylvania Press.

———— (1997). *Sensuous Scholarship*. Philadelphia: University of Pennsylvania Press.

Stove, O. C. (1982). *Popper and After: Four Modern Irrationalists*. New York: Pergamon.

Synnott, Anthony (1993). *The Body Social: Symbolism, Self and Society*. London: Routledge.

Teixeira, Antonio Alves (1975). *A magia e os encantos da Pomba-Gira*. Rio de Janeiro: Editora Mandarino.

Thompson, Robert Farris (1984). *Flash of the Spirit: African and Afro-American Art and Philosophy*. New York: Random House.
Trinidade, Liana (1985). *Exu: poder e perigo*. São Paulo: Ícone Editora.
Turner, Victor (1974). *Dramas, Fields, and Metaphors: Symbolic Action in Human Society*. Ithaca, N.Y.: Cornell University Press.
Twine, France Winddance (2000). *Racism in a Racial Democracy: The Maintenance of White Supremacy in Brazil*. New York: Routledge.
Valente, Waldomir (1977). *Sincretismo religioso afro-brasileiro*. São Paulo: Ed. Nacional.
Vallado, Armando (1999). "O sacerdote em face da renovação do candomblé." In *Faces da tradição afro-brasileira*. C. Caroso and J. Bacelar (eds.), 141–147. Rio de Janeiro: Pallas.
Varela, Francisco J., Evan Thompson and Eleanor Rosch (1993). *The Embodied Mind: Cognitive Science and Human Experience*. Cambridge, Mass.: MIT Press.
Vasconcelos, Selma (1995). *Zumbi dos palmares*. Recife, Brazil: Fundarpe.
Veja (2002, special edition): *O Brasil que já é Primeiro Mundo* 35 (19).
Verger, Pierre (1964). *Bahia and the West African Trade: 1549–1851*. Ibadan, Nigeria: Ibadan University Press.
——— (1981). *Orixás*. Salvador: Corruptio.
——— (1983). "Syncretisme." In *Recherche pédagogique et culture. Afrique et Brésil*, 41–45. Paris: Audecam.
——— (1987). *Fluxo e refluxo do tráfico de escraos entre o Golfo do Benin e a Bahia de Todos os Santos*. São Paulo: Corruptio.
Viana Filho, Luis (1949). *O negro na Bahia*. Rio de Janeiro: José Olympo.
Vianna, Hermano (1999). *The Mystery of Samba: Popular Music and National Identity in Brazil*, trans. J. C. Chasteen. Chapel Hill: University of North Carolina Press.
Vianna, Oliveira (1934). *Raça e assimilação*. São Paulo: Companhia Editora Nacional.
Vieira, Luiz Renato (1995). *O jogo de capoeira: cultura popular no Brasil*. Rio de Janeiro: Sprint.
Vocks, Robert A. (1997). *Sacred Leaves of Candomblé: African Magic, Medicine, and Religion in Brazil*. Austin: University of Texas Press.
Wade, Peter (2003). "Race in Latin America." In *The Companion to Latin American Studies*, P. Swanson (ed.), 185–199. London: Arnold.
Wafer, Jim (1991). *The Taste of Blood: Spirit Possession in Brazilian Candomblé*. Philadelphia: University of Pennsylvania Press.
Walker, Evan Harris (2000). *The Physics of Consciousness*. Cambridge, Mass.: Perseus.
Walker, Sheila (1990). "Everyday and Esoteric Reality in the Afro-Brazilian Candomblé." *History of Religions* 30, 103–129.
Warren Jr., Donald (1968). "Spiritism in Brazil." *Journal of Inter-American Studies* 10, 393–405.
——— (1970). "Notes on the Historical Origins of Umbanda." *Universitas* 6–7, 155–63.
Weber, Max (1965). *The Protestant Ethic and the Spirit of Capitalism*, trans. T. Parsons. London: Unwin University Books.
Weiss, G. and H. F. Haber, eds. (1999). *Perspectives on Embodiment: The Intersections of Nature and Culture*. New York: Routledge.

References

Werbner, Pnina (1997). "Introduction: The Dialectics of Cultural Hybridity." In *Debating Cultural Hybridity: Multi-Cultural Identities and the Politics of Anti-Racism*, P. Werbner and T. Modood (eds.), 1–25. Atlantic Highlands, N. J.: Zed Books.

West, Morris (1957). *Children of the Shadows*. New York: William Morrow.

Wiarda, Howard, ed. (1974). *Politics and Social Change in Latin America: The Distinct Tradition*. Amherst: University of Massachusetts Press.

Wimberley, Fayette (1998). "The Expansion of Afro-Bahian Religious Practices in Nineteenth-Century Cachoeira." In *Afro-Brazilian Culture and Politics: Bahia, 1790s to 1990s*, H. Kraay (ed.), 74–89. New York: M. E. Sharpe.

Winant, Howard (1992). "Rethinking Race in Brazil." *Journal of Latin American Studies* 24, 173–192.

Wittgenstein, Ludwig (1953). *Philosophical Investigations*, trans. G. E. M. Anscombe. New York: Macmillan.

Wright, Crispin (1992). *Truth and Objectivity*. Cambridge, Mass.: Harvard University Press.

Zajonc, Arthur (1993). *Catching the Light: The Entwined History of Light and Mind*. New York: Bantam.

Zweig, Stephan (1960). *Brasil, país do futuro*. Rio de Janeiro: Civilização Brasileira.

www.ingramcontent.com/pod-product-compliance
Lightning Source LLC
Chambersburg PA
CBHW022104150426
43195CB00008B/255